19th-Century Hungarian Political Thought and Culture

19th-Century Hungarian Political Thought and Culture

Towards Settlement with Austria, 1790–1867

Edited by
Ferenc Hörcher and Kálmán Tóth
Editorial Advisor: Thomas Lorman

BLOOMSBURY ACADEMIC
LONDON • NEW YORK • OXFORD • NEW DELHI • SYDNEY

BLOOMSBURY ACADEMIC
Bloomsbury Publishing Plc
50 Bedford Square, London, WC1B 3DP, UK
1385 Broadway, New York, NY 10018, USA
29 Earlsfort Terrace, Dublin 2, Ireland

BLOOMSBURY, BLOOMSBURY ACADEMIC and the Diana logo are trademarks of
Bloomsbury Publishing Plc

First published in Great Britain 2023
Paperback edition published 2024

Copyright © Ferenc Hörcher and Kálmán Tóth and contributors, 2023

Ferenc Hörcher, Kálmán Tóth and contributors asserted their right under the Copyright,
Designs and Patents Act, 1988, to be identified as Authors of this work.

Cover Images: Coronation of the imperial couple. 1867.© brandstaetter images /
Getty & Election of Kossuth as governor 1849.© Public Domain / Wikicommons

Bloomsbury Publishing Plc does not have any control over, or responsibility for, any third-party websites referred to or in this book. All internet addresses given in this book were correct at the time of going to press. The author and publisher regret any inconvenience caused if addresses have changed or sites have ceased to exist, but can accept no responsibility for any such changes.

Every effort has been made to trace the copyright holders and obtain permission to reproduce the copyright material. Please do get in touch with any enquiries or any information relating to such material or the rights holder. We would be pleased to rectify any omissions in subsequent editions of this publication should they be drawn to our attention.

A catalogue record for this book is available from the British Library.

A catalog record for this book is available from the Library of Congress.

ISBN: HB: 978-1-3502-0291-7
PB: 978-1-3502-0295-5
ePDF: 978-1-3502-0292-4
eBook: 978-1-3502-0293-1

Typeset by Deanta Global Publishing Services, Chennai, India

To find out more about our authors and books visit www.bloomsbury.com and sign up for
our newsletters.

Contents

List of contributors   vi
Preface   ix

Part 1

1   Historical and European context   *Ferenc Hörcher and Kálmán Tóth*   3
2   Ideological debates of the Reform Era (1830–48)   *János Veliky*   13
3   Constitutional and legal thought in the long nineteenth century   *István Stipta*   26
4   Non-Hungarian political thought in the context of ethnic conflicts in nineteenth-century Hungary   *József Demmel*   45

Part 2

5   Hungarian constitutional thought between tradition and innovation in the age of the French Revolution and Napoleonic Wars   *Henrik Hőnich and Ágoston Nagy*   65
6   Ferenc Kazinczy (1759-1831) and his age   *Kálmán Tóth*   87
7   Ferenc Kölcsey (1790-1838)   *Ferenc Kulin*   105
8   Count István Széchenyi (1791-1860)   *László Csorba*   117
9   Baron Miklós Wesselényi (1796-1850)   *Attila István Kárpáti*   133
10   Count Lajos Batthyány (1807-49)   *Gábor Erdődy*   147
11   Lajos Kossuth (1802-94)   *György Miru*   166
12   Baron József Eötvös (1813-71)   *Pál Bődy*   184
13   Baron Zsigmond Kemény (1814-75)   *Ferenc Hörcher*   203
14   Ferenc Deák (1803-76)   *István Schlett*   220

Index of Names   239
Index of Subjects   243

Contributors

Pál Bődy is a retired associate professor at the University of Miskolc, Hungary, and a lecturer at the Genius Savariensis Free University of Szombathely, Hungary. His research interests focus on the history and political thought of nineteenth-century Hungary, including conceptions of reform policies, political ideas of József Eötvös, education and science policies, Austro-Hungarian relations, emigration from Hungary and the nationality question. His most recent book is *Science Policies in Hungary (1867–1910) and the First Generation of Distinguished Scientists* (2017).

László Csorba is Professor of Cultural History at Loránd Eötvös University of Budapest, Hungary. His main research interests are Hungarian cultural history and the history of church politics in the modern period. His most recent book is *Haza és Haladás: Nemzeti ébredés és polgári átalakulás* (2021). He recently published an English-language chapter in *Twin Cities: Urban Communities, Borders and Relationships over Time* (2019).

József Demmel is Senior Researcher of the Institute of Central European Studies at the University of Public Service, Budapest, Hungary, and of the Institute of History of the Slovak Academy of Sciences. His research interests focus on the Slovak-Hungarian relationship in the nineteenth and twentieth centuries. His most recent books are *'Ľudožrút' na Hornom Uhorsku. Príbeh Bélu Grünwalda* (2020) and *Szörnyeteg a Felvidéken: Grünwald Béla és a szlovák–magyar kapcsolatok a dualizmuskori Magyarországon* (2020).

Erdődy Gábor is Emeritus Professor in the Department of Modern and Contemporary Hungarian History at the Loránd Eötvös University of Budapest, Hungary. His research interests focus on social modernization in nineteenth- and twentieth-century Hungary and Europe. His most recent book is *Tradicionális történelmi identitás – modern politikai eszmerendszer: Antall József kereszténydemokrata politikai filozófiája és annak nemzeti történelmi beágyazottsága* (2011).

Henrik Hőnich is a research fellow at Thomas Molnar Institute for Advanced Studies, University of Public Service, Budapest, Hungary. His main fields of interest are the political discourses and the formation of modern national identity in late eighteenth- and early nineteenth-century Hungary, as well as the political culture of the Hungarian nobility in the period. His most recent publication is *Ki az igaz hazafi? Közösségfogalmak és patriotizmus a 18. század végi Magyarországon: Egy politikai értekezés és kontextusai* (2022). He also published an English-language chapter in *Latin at the Crossroads of Identity: The Evolution of Linguistic Nationalism in the Kingdom of Hungary* (2015).

Ferenc Hörcher (Ferenc Horkay Hörcher in Hungarian-language publications) is Research Professor at the Research Institute for Politics and Government at the University of Public Service in Budapest, Hungary, and a senior research fellow at the Institute of Philosophy of the Loránd Eötvös Research Network, Budapest, Hungary. His research interests include the early modern history of political thought, nineteenth-century Hungarian political thought, the political philosophy of conservatism and liberalism, and philosophy of art. He was co-editor with Thomas Lorman and co-author of *The History of the Hungarian Constitution: Law, Government and Political Culture in Central Europe* (2019). His recent books are *The Political Philosophy of the European City: From Polis, through City-State, to Megalopolis?* (2021), *Art and Politics in Roger Scruton's Conservative Philosophy* (2023)

Attila István Kárpáti is Archivist at the Budapest City Archives, Hungary. His research interests focus on nineteenth-century Hungarian cultural history with special emphasis on the life and work of Baron Miklós Wesselényi. He has published several Hungarian articles on this topic. One of his recent publications appeared in the historiographical journal *Századok*, titled *Wesselényi Miklós és az augsburgi Allgemeine Zeitung* (2019).

Ferenc Kulin is a retired associate professor at Loránd Eötvös University and at the Gáspár Károli University of the Reformed Church in Budapest, Hungary. His research interests focus on nineteenth- and twentieth-century Hungarian literature and political thought. His most recent book is *A történetiség elve és a jelen horizontja* (2021).

György Miru is Associate Professor of the Institute of History at the University of Debrecen, Hungary. His research interests focus on the history of politics and of political thought in nineteenth- and twentieth-century Hungary. He published a monograph on the political thought of Lajos Kossuth titled *Szabadság és politikai közösség: Kossuth Lajos politikai alapfogalmai* (2011), and recently published an English-language chapter in *The Creation of the Austro–Hungarian Monarchy: A Hungarian Perspective* (2022).

Ágoston Nagy is a research fellow of Thomas Molnar Institute for Advanced Studies at the University of Public Service, Budapest, Hungary. His field of research interest is eighteenth- and nineteenth-century Hungarian literature and political thought, particularly the political oeuvre of Sándor Kisfaludy, as well as the emergence of patriotic-national tendencies within the noble body politic during the French Revolutionary and Napoleonic Wars. He recently published 'Patriotism, Nation, and Masculinity in the Official Propaganda of the Hungarian *Insurrectio* during the War of the Fifth Coalition (1809)', *Hungarian Historical Review* 11, no. 1 (2022): 3–43.

István Schlett is Emeritus Professor at the Loránd Eötvös University in Budapest, Hungary. His main research interest is the history of political thought in Hungary. His most important publication is a four-volume monograph titled *A politikai gondolkodás története Magyarországon* (2018).

István Stipta is Professor of Legal History, Jurisprudence and Church Law at the Gáspár Károli University of the Reformed Church in Budapest, Hungary. His research interests focus on nineteenth-century Hungarian constitutional history and thought. His most recent book is *A magyar történelmi alkotmány és a hazai közjogi-közigazgatási jogvédelem* (2020). He also published an English-language study titled *The Main Tendencies of Hungarian Legal Historiography in the 20th Century and Its Present Situation* in the *Journal on European History of Law* in 2011.

Kálmán Tóth is a research fellow of the Research Institute for Politics and Government at the University of Public Service, Budapest, Hungary. His research interests focus on eighteenth- and nineteenth-century Hungarian literature, history of ideas and political thought. His most recent publication is a critical edition of the literary and scholarly correspondence of nineteenth-century Hungarian Lutheran superintendent and poet János Kis titled *Kis János (1770–1846) szuperintendens irodalmi és tudományos levelezése* (2021).

János Veliky is a retired professor at the University of Debrecen, Hungary, and the Gáspár Károli University of the Reformed Church in Budapest, Hungary. His main research interest is nineteenth-century Hungarian history. His most important publication is about the changing public roles in the Hungarian Reform Era titled *A változások kora. Polgári szerepkörök és változáskoncepciók a reformkor második évtizedében* (2009).

Preface

About the concept

This book is intended to fill a gap in the existing literature. Until now, no substantial overview of nineteenth-century Hungarian political thought has been available to the English-speaking world. While this critical period in Hungarian history has already been touched upon by other English-language works, their focus was not on political thinking, or they dealt with only specific aspects of it. A good example of the former is László Péter's posthumously published collection of essays,[1] while the latter includes the multi-author volume by Balázs Trencsényi and others, which is more of a transnational synthesis of East-Central-European intellectual history.[2] Individual figures have, of course, been the subject of works in English, including István Széchenyi and József Eötvös, but an overview of a full range of critical figures from this period has not been published recently in English.[3] Yet the period is of crucial importance in Hungarian politics. The long nineteenth century rearranged politics in the country – just as the end of the First World War rearranged the country itself. One can go so far as to claim that this was the Golden Age of Hungarian political thought. It led from the discussions about the impact of the French Revolution after the death of Joseph II in 1790 through the 'lawful' Hungarian Revolution in 1848, and the signing of the Settlement in 1867, which created the Austro-Hungarian Dual Monarchy that endured until the end of the First World War, which resulted in the break-up of the Monarchy and the loss of much of the territory and population of the historical Hungarian Kingdom. Beyond political history, the relevance of the age for the history of Hungarian political thought is that this was when the classical vocabulary of the basic Hungarian political ideologies developed from the early modern vocabularies of politics. Although this volume addresses only the period up to the birth of the Dual Monarchy in 1867, its explicit aim is to provide authentic and factual insights for an international audience interested in the history of nineteenth-century political thought and particularly that of the East-Central-European region. The present authors also believe that this topic is important for those striving for a deeper understanding of the contemporary fault lines in the European political palette.

Methodology

Although the historiography of political thought traditionally develops within a national framework, this volume attaches great importance to placing Hungarian political thought in a wider European framework and shows how European intellectual streams and historical events had an impact on Hungarian politics and political thought. Of course, in order to reconstruct the regional context of this Golden Age of politics it is necessary to take into account rival national narratives. However, the lack of basic studies incorporating multifocal standpoints (which is made even more challenging by the linguistic diversity of the region) reduces the chances of unbiased objectivity and historical authenticity even in overviews like the present one. To reduce the chances of bias and anachronism, the current volume attaches the utmost importance to confronting the political thought of the long nineteenth century on its own terms and aims to avoid, as far as possible, unhistorical interpretations and evaluations based on backward projections of posterior criteria.

The authors of the chapters are pre-eminent researchers in their fields, who approached their topics based on their own methodological concepts, with the editorial principles leaving considerable scope for their individual viewpoints. The only conditions were that they maintain a high level of scholarly competence and that they reflect on the broader European context that shaped each of the political thinkers they chose to write about. Thus, this volume presents not only a range of narrative techniques, rhetorical strategies and methodological convictions that provides an overarching portrayal of the intellectual culture of nineteenth-century Hungary but also the historiographical culture of twenty-first-century Hungary. In fact, taken together, they offer a fresh onlook on a country which has not often been seen clearly and in such an unbiased manner from both global policy and opinion makers.

The structure

The structure of the book requires further explanation. The volume consists of two distinct parts. The first part lays the groundwork for further enquiry by offering longitudinal studies of the period, which provide an overview of the most important factors and circumstances that shaped nineteenth-century Hungarian political thought, such as the historical background, the institutional and intellectual contexts of the political system, the predominant constitutional and legal paradigms, and the nationality question.

Chapter 1, written by the editors, presents an overview of the historical and European contexts of long-nineteenth-century Hungarian political thought, familiarizing readers not very familiar with Hungarian history with the background of the topics discussed in the following chapters of the book.

Chapter 2, by János Veliky, offers an overview of the most important ideological debates in the Hungarian Reform Era (1830–48), presents a large picture of the dynamics of the political life in this period and shows the formulation of modern political orientations which led to the 1848 April Laws.

The third chapter, by István Stipta, presents the main strands of Hungarian constitutionality of the long nineteenth century in both a synchronic and diachronic manner.

In the fourth chapter, József Demmel discusses the problems raised by the multi-ethnic reality of nineteenth-century Hungary, where the rise of clashing national movements threw into question the integrity of the historical Kingdom of Hungary, leading to the emergence of differing concepts of modernization.

The second part of the collection reconstructs the voices of the most outstanding Hungarian political thinkers of the period and traces their impact. This is because, according to the methodological hypothesis of the editors, each and every political community contains major voices that determine, if not the answers, then at least the tone and major questions of the political discussion at a certain moment or even for a certain length of time. We feel that the selection of authors to whom chapters are devoted constitutes a reliable summary of the thought of the major protagonists of the age and what took place in the public exchanges between them. Learning about this pantheon of major players can help orientate the reader as to the nature and major trends of the debate.

The fifth and sixth chapters, which de facto launch our narrative, cover the political thought of the period between 1790 and 1825, and form something of an exception as they address the political thought of multiple political actors, which was made necessary by the unique structure of the public-political sphere of the period. The selection of the political thinkers discussed in the later chapters was essentially based on the consensual canon of Hungarian historiography. Any project of this scope runs the risk of having failed to cover certain political thinkers. Indeed, individual chapters on other influential political thinkers of the period, such as the conservative counts József and Aurél Dessewffy, and the notable radicals Count László Teleki and Mihály Táncsics, would have also had their justification, although they had less impact on political events. Nevertheless, the thinkers who are highlighted by this book represent a broad range of views and all of them had a lengthy and critical influence on the development of Hungarian politics in this period. All of them are unquestionably part of the canon of nineteenth-century Hungarian political thinking.

The fifth chapter, written by Henrik Hőnich and Ágoston Nagy, discusses the constitutional debates between 1790 and 1820. They use the pamphlet literature in the 1790s and early 1800s as an important source of political thinking in the context of contemporary Hungarian Diets, where the political class were able to articulate their political aims.

The sixth chapter was written by one of the editors of the volume, Kálmán Tóth. Its main protagonist is Ferenc Kazinczy (1759–1831), a Hungarian nobleman, writer, linguist and historian, whose far-reaching correspondence is one of the most important sources for research into this era. Kazinczy is widely considered to be the leading figure of the language renewal or neologist movement, which is interpreted in the first part of this chapter in the context of nation-building. The struggle to make Hungarian the official language in the Kingdom of Hungary instead of Latin was one of the most important topics on the agenda in the age.

In Chapter 7, Ferenc Kulin discusses the political thought of the author of the Hungarian national anthem, the poet, writer and delegate to the Diet, Ferenc Kölcsey. Being a well-educated country gentleman, Kölcsey represented a new way of thinking, inspired by both neoclassical and romantic ideas, and the study of ancient Greco-

Roman and classical German philosophy. His role was crucial, both in the first, institution-building phase of modern Hungarian literature and as a leading politician in the context of the county assemblies and the first reform Diets of the 1830s. His textual heritage includes acclaimed speeches made at the Diets as well as more theoretical works, which secured his place as one of the key orators of a classical national liberal programme.

Chapter 8, written by László Csorba, examines Count István Széchenyi, one of the most influential Hungarian political actors in the nineteenth century, who made his name by offering one year's income of his landed property for the purpose of establishing the Hungarian Academy of Sciences. He became the best-known participant in the debates of the Hungarian Reform Era by publishing three consecutive volumes on economic, social, legal and political reforms.

Chapter 9, by Attila István Kárpáti, discusses the political thought of Baron Miklós Wesselényi, one of the leaders of the classical liberal reform movement of the 1830s in both Transylvania and the Kingdom of Hungary. A friend and follower of Széchenyi in his early years, his political thinking shifted towards a programme of national independence and democratic social reforms. Wesselényi was one of the most dedicated advocates of the abolition of serfdom and of a national unification of interests. He was unjustly imprisoned by the Habsburg government. He is also well known for his heroic effort to save lives during the 1838 flood in Pest (the eastern half of what later was renamed Budapest) as 'The Boatman of the Deluge'.

In Chapter 10, which discusses Count Lajos Batthyány, Gábor Erdődy argues that the prime minister of the first responsible government of 1848 should be remembered not only for his martyrdom in 1849 but also as one of the most significant political thinkers of the Hungarian Reform Era. His intellectual contributions to the debates of the age made him one of the key players in those ideological clashes.

Chapter 11, contributed by György Miru, provides an overview of the political thought of probably the best-known Hungarian politician of the nineteenth century, Lajos Kossuth. In Kossuth's political activity, practical politics, political theory and popular journalism were equally important. From the beginning of the 1840s onwards he took over the initiative from Széchenyi and became the decisive voice in this dynamic decade. He became minister of finance in Batthyány's government, and after the Declaration of Independence in 1849, Governor-President of an independent Hungary. After the failure of the War of Independence, he went into exile and remained an ardent opponent of Habsburg rule over Hungary. He opposed the Settlement of 1867 and predicted the fall of the Habsburg Monarchy, which would drag the historical Kingdom of Hungary with it into the abyss. He became the most important popular hero of the people, and alongside Széchenyi, his major antagonist, he remains the greatest icon of classical Hungarian political thinking.

Chapter 12, by Pál Bődy, discusses the political thought of Baron József Eötvös, who represents the intellectual side of the classical liberal political tradition. Also known as a writer of novels, he was the leader of the circle of 'centralists' in the 1840s and became minister of public education and religious affairs in the Batthyány government. In September 1848, he left the country in fear of revolutionary violence, and while in exile in Bavaria he wrote his masterwork, *The Influence of the Ruling Ideas of the*

19th Century on the State, identifying as key ideas equality, liberty and nationality. He took an active part in preparing the Settlement with Austria, and once again held a ministerial position after 1867, during which time he became famous for the tolerant laws he oversaw on primary education and on ethnic minorities, as well as on the emancipation of the Jews.

In Chapter 13, by another of the editors, Ferenc Hörcher, the political thought of Baron Zsigmond Kemény is discussed. A journalist, editor, fiction writer and political adviser, Kemény played an important role in running the leading Hungarian newspaper *Pesti Hirlap* as a member of the centralist circle. He played only a minor role in the first independent government of 1848-9, but after the failure of the revolution, he published a number of theoretically refined essays, in which, besides blaming Kossuth, whom he made the scapegoat, he launched a major critique against those who held a revolutionary political attitude, disregarding political realities. These essays, resembling the writings of Burke half a century earlier, can be regarded as early attempts to formulate a conservative political agenda in Hungarian politics. Kemény remained active in the neo-absolutist period. He wrote works of fiction and essays, and worked as an influential adviser as well as defending Ferenc Deák in his newspaper editorials, and in this way played a major role in the birth of the Settlement with Austria.

The final chapter of the book, written by István Schlett, concerns the most influential political actor of the post-revolutionary period, Ferenc Deák. As an able practising lawyer, he cooperated with the opposition of the reform Diets, defending the rights of the victims of prosecutions by the Court. He was also a member of the first independent government. After the start of the War of Independence, he withdrew to his country house. From the beginning of the 1860s, however, he re-entered public life, moved to Pest-Buda and became the guiding light of the preparation for the 1867 Settlement. His unquestionable authority and his loyalty to the Crown made him an ideal negotiating partner, and most historians regard his negotiations as successful. He did not take a position in the new government that was appointed immediately after the Settlement.

Notes

1 László Péter, *Hungary's Long Nineteenth Century: Constitutional and Democratic Traditions in a European Perspective* (Leiden–Boston: Brill, 2012).
2 Balázs Trencsényi et al., *A History of Modern Political Thought in East Central Europe*, vol. 1, *Negotiating Modernity in the 'Long Nineteenth Century'* (Oxford: Oxford University Press, 2016).
3 See the works of András Oplatka, Pál Bődy and Gábor Gángó.

Part 1

1

Historical and European context

Ferenc Hörcher and Kálmán Tóth

The situation of Hungary within the monarchy of the Habsburgs: A European historical framework

Hungarian political thought in the final decade of the eighteenth century is difficult to understand without a brief historical overview of the relationship between the Habsburg dynasty and the Kingdom of Hungary from the early modern period onwards.

After its crushing defeat by the Ottomans at the battle of Mohács, the medieval Kingdom of Hungary became a buffer zone between two empires. The king of Hungary, Louis II from the House of Jagiello, was killed fleeing from the battle. Half of the surviving political elite supported the claims of Ferdinand of the House of Habsburg, the younger brother of the Holy Roman Emperor Charles V, citing the dynastical treaties of succession that kings Matthias and Vladislav II had entered into with the Habsburg rulers. Ferdinand was crowned the king of Hungary, as the Hungarian political elite were hoping he would be able to defend the country against the Ottoman invaders with the help of the Holy Roman Empire. From the Hungarian nobility's point of view this did not mean the actual loss of the country's sovereignty and its integration into the emerging Central European empire of the Habsburgs but was merely a personal union with Austria where only the person of the ruler was the same, and the Kingdom of Hungary kept its separate statehood and institutional system. (During the medieval period, personal union was a common practice in East Central Europe, and it functioned without undermining the sovereignty of individual states in the Anjou, Luxembourg and Jagiellonian dynasties.)

The other half of the noble elite rejected Habsburg rule and elected the palatine János Szapolyai (Zápolya) as king of Hungary on the basis of the Rákos Decision of 1505, which had declared the right of the nobility to freely choose their king. These rival loyalties to two different candidates for king led to the division of the country into two separate parts. To counteract the military superiority of the Habsburgs, Szapolyai turned to the ruler of the Ottoman Empire, Suleiman I, whose army temporarily left the country in 1526, for support in order to hold onto his throne. After the peace treaty of Várad (today Oradea, Romania) Ferdinand and Szapolyai recognized each other's kingdoms and Szapolyai promised to Ferdinand his part of the country if he died without a male heir. After the death of Szapolyai in 1541, Suleiman once again invaded the country, capturing Buda by a ruse, and claimed Transylvania as a vassal state of the Ottoman Empire under the rule of the widow of Szapolyai and her newborn son, John Sigismond. This resulted in the division of Hungary into three parts, a situation that lasted until the end of the seventeenth century: the western and northern part bordering the Hereditary Provinces came under the rule of the Habsburgs, the middle and southern part became part of the Ottoman Empire and the eastern part, the Principality of Transylvania, enjoyed a fluctuating degree of autonomy depending on the political situation, although the election of its princes was always subject to the permission of the Ottoman Porte. The ethnic Hungarian population of the kingdom experienced a sharp decline due to deportations and massacres during the 150 years of Ottoman rule, as the lowland territories inhabited by ethnic Hungarians were the most exposed to destruction. After the end of Ottoman occupation with the Treaty of Karlowitz (today Sremski Karlovci, Serbia) in 1699, Habsburg kings settled Germans and Slavs in these depopulated territories, and Charles III (Charles VI as Holy Roman Emperor, the father of Maria Theresa) even prohibited Hungarians from settling in the southern territories of the kingdom for decades.[1] The ethnic Hungarian population of the kingdom, which had been around 80-85 per cent before the Ottoman Wars, shrunk to around 45 per cent at the end of the eighteenth century. Thus, the Kingdom of Hungary became a multi-ethnic country.[2]

In Western Europe during this period, modernization, industrialization and colonialization took place, and frameworks of nation-states were created by the centralized power of the national ruling houses. In Hungary, on the contrary, centralization generally served the interests of Habsburg rulers striving for the unification of their 'Gesamt'-Monarchy, and they violated the constitutional sovereignty of the Kingdom of Hungary whose preservation had been the condition set by the Hungarian estates for crowning the Habsburg rulers as kings of Hungary.

After the unsuccessful siege of Vienna in 1683, the Ottoman Empire rapidly started to weaken. As a result of a military campaign led by the Habsburg Holy Roman Emperor, who attracted volunteers from across Europe, Hungary's capital, Buda, was conquered by the Christian army in 1686, and in the space of a decade, with the exception of the most southerly territories, the whole country came under the rule of the Habsburgs. Their subsequent efforts to turn Hungary into a subordinated province sparked significant resistance against Habsburg rule, which culminated in the War of Independence (1703-11) led by the prince of Transylvania Francis Rákóczi II. In spite of the estates' grievances also affecting them, a significant proportion of the nobility did remain loyal to the Habsburgs, especially in the predominantly Catholic west of the kingdom. The War of Independence ended with a settlement between the ruler and the Hungarian estates. Then, in 1723, the Pragmatic Sanction was accepted according to which the Hungarian estates were ready to support the female succession of the House of Habsburg without any resistance, and crowned Maria Theresa queen of Hungary after the death of her father, Charles III, in 1740.

The Empress Maria Theresa, who emerged strengthened from the War of the Austrian Succession largely thanks to the support of the Hungarian nobility, clearly wanted to establish a centralized Gesamt-Monarchy. Her political thinking was a version of absolutism. As a masterful tactician, she considered the sensitivity of the estates but successfully managed to increase the influence of the central power. After 1764, she did not convoke any more Diets (as the Hungarian Parliament was then known, until April 1848, when it became a representative parliament), which was required by the constitutional traditions of the country, and her son and successor, Joseph II, completely disregarded the earlier compromise between Vienna, the imperial capital, and the Hungarian estates. He decided not to have himself crowned (ruling as a 'hatted king') and aimed to end the distinct constitutional status of the Kingdom of Hungary within the Gesamt-Monarchy, as he considered it to be an obstacle to the formation of a unified, centralized empire. His 'enlightened absolutism' was initially supported by many educated Hungarian noblemen and also by intellectuals of non-noble descent under the influence of enlightened ideas (Josephinism). However, among other hostile decisions, in order to establish a unified imperial administration, he issued a language decree which made German the official language of government and schooling, instead of Latin, which had been used since the formation of the Kingdom of Hungary, and as a result, many of his former supporters turned against him. In opposition to this Germanization, critics in the estates demanded that Hungarian be made the official language.

This endeavour was not without precedent, as in the Principality of Transylvania official affairs were conducted in the Hungarian language by the seventeenth century – as opposed to the Latin of the Hungarian Kingdom itself. Moreover, the first Habsburg king of Hungary, Ferdinand I, made a solemn promise to the estates in his own name, and that of his successors, to safeguard the language and the freedoms of the Hungarian nation.[3] Despite being forced to accept some compromises in order to stabilize their reign, the Habsburgs always sought to integrate Hungary into their empire. The framework of the Hungarian estates' political thinking included both loyalty to a lawful king and the collective and individual rights of the nobility provided by the historical constitution. Some members of the estates often referred to the English constitution as its only parallel. In their political system, which has been labelled the dualist structure of the estate system, sovereignty was shared between the ruler and the estates, and that is why the paradigm of absolutism – which aimed to increase the influence of the ruling power – was confronted by the concerted efforts of the estates to defend the nobility's privileges and interests. Under the reign of Maria Theresa, supporters of the absolutist paradigm were already fond of referring to the notion of the common good and to the need to defend the serfs from the burdens placed on them by their landlords. In contrast, the politics of the estates was characterized by the grievance petitions to the ruler (*gravamen*), as in eighteenth-century France, in which the estates articulated their dissatisfaction with the rulers' decisions that they believed to have violated their rights of freedom and interests. The rights of the nobility had been codified by the *Tripartitum*, the work of István Werbőczy, a sixteenth-century jurist and prothonotary, who also served briefly as the country's palatine. The *Tripartitum* never officially became law, but it was considered to be part of the ancient constitution defined as much by custom as codified law. The fundamental rights of the nobility that were laid out in the *Tripartitum* were, thus, largely reaffirmed by most Habsburg rulers and applied to the nobility as a whole. This meant, for example, that there was no legal distinction between aristocrats with large estates and minor nobles with only one or two socages, in terms of their judicial status, and they all benefitted from an exemption from taxation. One of the rulers' longstanding aims was to abolish this exemption. This privilege had originally been underpinned by the nobility's duty to take part in the armed defence of the country. The main argument of the political treatises that were ordered by the rulers in order to underline this aim was that in an era of permanent standing armies the institution of the noble uprising (*insurrectio*) had become outdated, and the maintenance of privileges based upon it would be harmful to the interest of the Gesamt-Monarchy, which they considered to be the common good, because of all the states and provinces of the Habsburg Monarchy, only the Hungarian nobility enjoyed such privileges.

The aspect of nationality also played an important role in the political thought of the final decades of the eighteenth century. The *Natio Hungarica* was a community of the estates based on the rule of law, regardless of ethnicity and language, but this does not mean that ethnic consciousness based on a shared language and origin had not played a significant role in the centuries before the emergence of modern nationalism, although this role was not as decisive as it would be from the nineteenth century onwards.

The impact of the French Revolution and the Napoleonic Wars was also felt in the Kingdom of Hungary. After the liquidation of the Hungarian Jacobin movement of Ignác Martinovics, fears over the ideas of the French Revolution increased among the Hungarian nobility, who rejected radical change, and the political thought of the estates was dominated by a conservative and loyalist standpoint. The Hungarian nobility unanimously supported the Habsburg dynasty during the Napoleonic Wars, and only a narrow circle of intellectuals without any real influence sympathized with Napoleon (such as János Batsányi, Gergely Berzeviczy and József Márton). The vast majority of the political elite did not question the legitimacy of the rule of the Habsburg dynasty over Hungary, and in addition to the preservation of the constitutional autonomy of the country, they also took into account the standpoints of the Gesamt-Monarchy.

The constitutional framework of modernization and the question of language

The traditional county system was one of the most important guarantees of the constitutional autonomy of Hungary within the Habsburg Empire. Its antecedents can be traced back to the early eleventh century and the reign of Hungary's first Christian king, Saint Stephen I. The counties had both administrative and judicial functions – for example, delegates to the Diet were elected by the counties, while members of the nobility with political rights voted at the general congregations of the counties on the programmes that the delegates were expected to follow. The counties were even, to some extent, able to resist royal decrees that violated the ancient constitution, and they therefore played a significant role in the failure of Joseph II's efforts to reorient the country's constitutional development. During the period between 1812 and 1825, when Francis I did not convoke any Diets, the counties were the strongholds of the estates' political activities.

As a result, the counties proved to be a suitable institution to counterbalance the absolutistic measures of the Vienna Court. However, in the first decades of the nineteenth century, the need for significant social and economic reforms increasingly surpassed the grievance-politics of the estates. As a result, from the 1830s onwards, a new discourse was born along European lines: classical liberalism. This ideology was directed towards a reformist agenda, with basic goals such as the abolition of serfdom, equality before the law, the abolition of noble privileges, the extension of political rights, and the modernization of the country within the framework of a nation-state.

The first steps towards social modernization depended, however, on the adoption of a unified official language, which is spoken by a significant number of the country's inhabitants, and which is widespread enough that its other inhabitants, even the less erudite among them, can learn it relatively easily. This necessity had been perceived by Joseph II, who replaced Latin with German as the official language of Hungary in 1784. That, however, triggered widespread social resistance, and he was forced to revoke it on his deathbed in 1790. Instead of Latin, which they also considered outdated, the estates of Hungary then sought to introduce Hungarian as the official language at the Diet of 1790-1. This aim was supported by the estates, but also by the practical fact that Hungarian had by far the largest number of native speakers among all languages spoken in the country. According to the Habsburg ruler, Leopold II, the time had not yet arrived for the introduction of Hungarian as the official language of the country, but Article XVI of the laws of 1790-1 safeguarded the status of the Hungarian language and made the first step towards Hungarian achieving the status of the official language, which it finally did in 1844.

Considering the contemporary European situation, the Hungarian nobility realized that, as in most European countries, modernization could only take place within the framework of a unified nation-state. It is important to stress that the new regulation did not restrict the use of the languages of ethnic minorities, as it only covered language use in official matters that previously had been conducted in Latin, so there was absolutely no forfeiture of legal rights on their part. Besides, since 1791, the official records of the proceedings of the Diet had been written first in Hungarian and then translated into Latin.

While the issue was obviously connected to a programme of national domination by the Hungarian gentry, from a European perspective this was nothing exceptional. In France, for example, where scarcely 50 per cent of all inhabitants spoke French as their mother tongue at the end of the eighteenth century, this had increased to 85 per cent by the middle of the nineteenth century as a result of forced assimilation. In 1851, a law stipulated that the language of education was to be exclusively in French.[4] Great Britain dealt with the nationality question in a similar way, and from the sixteenth century onwards, at the level of legislation, they set comprehensive assimilation as a goal relating to language, and by the middle of the nineteenth century, the use of the languages of ethnic minorities had been largely suppressed.[5] As a twentieth-century Hungarian historian put it: 'Hungarian laws and governmental decrees did not even satisfy the natural and legitimate aims of expansion of the Hungarian language, even less contained any measures injurious or oppressive to the rights of the non-Hungarian languages. The frictions and reluctancy were socially generated, and were mainly manifested in the press and pamphlet-literature.'[6] The Habsburg rulers, fearing for the unity of the Gesamt-Monarchy because of the Hungarians' strivings for self-determination, also played a significant role in intensifying ethnic conflicts, including linguistic controversies, and therefore they used the cause of the non-Hungarian ethnic minorities in order to keep the Kingdom of Hungary under their political subordination.[7]

This situation would only change in the 1860s, when the Austrian elites realized that without the support of the Hungarians, the existence of the Gesamt-Monarchy would be endangered, and the real threat came from the increasingly public aims of the ethnic minorities to secede. This recognition also played a role in the negotiations which led to the Settlement of 1867, and as a result of mutual concessions, the Austro-Hungarian Monarchy was established on a constitutional foundation. On the territory of the Hungarian Kingdom, the law on ethnic minorities (Article XLIV of the Laws of 1868 on the equal rights of nationalities), masterminded by Baron József Eötvös, provided widespread individual rights for the ethnic minorities, who were permitted to freely use their native languages in their administrative, religious and educational affairs. Although this law was based on liberal ideas of regulation, parliamentary delegates from the ethnic minorities (mainly Serbs and Romanians) did not support it, and they demanded that the five largest ethnic minorities should be acknowledged as nations with equal status to the Hungarians and sought collective rights for their national communities. These demands evoked suspicions among the majority of the Hungarian political elite, which led to an escalation of ethnic conflicts that resulted in an increase in measures aimed at the assimilation of the ethnic minorities.

Modernization within a national or an imperial framework?

At the reform Diets between 1832 and 1848, supporters of the classical liberal programme gained a majority in the Lower House of the Diet, but they were not able to achieve a real breakthrough because of the resistance of the conservative majority of the Upper House and, most importantly, the opposition of the Habsburg Emperor. These liberals agreed on the main goals, but their various factions differed on the means, pace and extent of these goals, as the chapters on individual thinkers will show. For the realization of the classical liberal programme, the March Revolution of 1848 marked a turning point, when, as a result of the revolutionary wave which spread over most of Europe, the majority of the Upper House and the ruler accepted reforms to bring in bourgeois modernization. In a process that was both legal and legitimate, the April Laws, sanctioned by King Ferdinand V, laid the foundation for the modernization of the Kingdom of Hungary by abolishing the feudal system. The first independent Hungarian government, which was solely answerable to the Parliament, was formed under the leadership of Count Lajos Batthyány, in which the most prominent political thinkers, public intellectuals and practical politicians of the age (including István

Széchenyi, Lajos Kossuth, Ferenc Deák and József Eötvös) accepted portfolios as ministers. The year 1848 can undoubtedly be considered an outstanding highlight of the historical development of Hungarian constitutionality, as the Hungarian noble elite voluntarily gave up their feudal privileges and helped usher in the abolition of serfdom, declared the equality of all men before the law and established the first Hungarian Parliament based on popular representation on the basis of the unification of interests. The representative parliamentary system provided the right of political participation to a relatively wide section of society even compared to other European states of that period.

Although the creation of a legal framework for social modernization was also acceptable to the elite of the Austrian Empire, they did not accept the Kingdom of Hungary's strivings for self-determination as a nation-state, which would have only remained in the Habsburg Empire on the basis of a personal union. The imperial elite, led by the most influential members of the camarilla, including the Archduchess Sophia, Chancellor Metternich and Prince Felix Schwarzenberg, counter-attacked, persuading the easily influenceable Ferdinand V to take decisions which were contrary to the laws he had previously sanctioned, and provoking an armed conflict by stirring up aggressive nationalist movements among the ethnic minorities. In December 1848, they forced Ferdinand V to resign and made Francis Joseph, the eighteen-year-old son of Archduke Francis Charles and Archduchess Sophia, the new emperor of Austria. The conflict with Hungary was clearly unleashed by an imperial elite striving to uphold the unity of the empire at all costs, and it was this elite which drove the Hungarians to start the War of Independence, even after they had adhered to the achievements of the lawful revolution sanctioned by the ruler. The National Defence Commission headed by Lajos Kossuth escaped from Pest to Debrecen ahead of the attack by the imperial forces, and successfully organized armed resistance. The Hungarian Army of National Defence, set up within a remarkably short period of time and lacking proper training and equipment, achieved significant military successes against the army of the Habsburgs. By that time, most of the earlier government had resigned, and Kossuth was able to pursue his own strategy. In April 1849, he proclaimed the Declaration of Independence that pronounced the dethronement of the House of Habsburg-Lorraine, and declared the independence of Hungary, but left open the question of what form the new state would assume. Francis Joseph was only able to suppress the War of Independence with considerable military help from the Russian tsar Nicholas I. In the following years he attempted to integrate Hungary into the unified New Austrian Empire, governed on the basis of absolutistic principles.

The victorious imperial elite, headed by Prime Minister Schwarzenberg, eradicated the constitutional autonomy of Hungary, made German the sole official language of the whole empire again, and even those parts of the April Laws which remained in force and provided the legal framework for modernization were executed in line with the interests of the imperial elite. Just as in the period after 1795, public discussion of politics was once again largely restricted during this period known as neo-absolutism in Hungarian historiography. This era was dominated by the Minister of Interior Affairs Alexander Bach, who became its iconic political figure. A significant proportion of the political elite of the Reform Era was forced into exile by the threat of retaliatory measures, and a large number of those who could not escape were executed, like former Prime Minister Lajos Batthyány, who was sentenced to death on completely trumped-up charges. (He was accused of triggering the Viennese revolution of 6 October 1848, although he had nothing to do with it in reality.) As no political action was possible, many of the landed nobility chose the path of passive resistance, following the example of Ferenc Deák, but intellectuals and civil servants were largely forced to adapt to the new circumstances.

The road towards the settlement

As a result of the defeats suffered by the Habsburg Monarchy in Northern Italy, Francis Joseph was forced to seek a new settlement with the Hungarian political elite. He relieved the Minister of Interior Affairs Bach of his position and, in 1861, convoked the Hungarian Parliament and issued a rescript asking it to accept the new imperial constitution of February 1861 and to send delegates to the Imperial Council (Reichsrat). At the Parliament that assembled in April 1861, two positions emerged: that of the Resolution Party (*Határozati Párt*), led by Count László Teleki, who did not accept Francis Joseph as the legitimate ruler because of the unlawful way he had come to power, and the Address Party (*Felirati Párt*) headed by Deák, who de facto accepted Francis Joseph as king of Hungary. Both parties, however, rejected the content of the royal rescript and only disagreed on how to respond to it. Teleki committed suicide on the eve of the decisive voting, and the Address Party's position triumphed. The resulting petition, drafted by Deák, insisted on the constitutional autonomy of the Kingdom of Hungary within the Habsburg Empire on the basis of the Pragmatic Sanction and, as a basis for negotiations, the recognition of the April Laws of 1848. The ruler rejected the petition and, in August 1861, he dissolved the Parliament. After a brief intermezzo which was later known as the Schmerling Provision after the new prime minister appointed by Francis Joseph, Anton Ritter von Schmerling, as a result of further international isolation, the ruler once again seemed to be open to a settlement based on mutual compromises, and Ferenc Deák revealed the conditions of the Settlement in his Easter Article published in 1865. He demanded that the ruler and Austrian elites respect the territorial integrity of the country, restore the laws of 1848 and appoint a responsible Hungarian government. If these conditions were met, he declared himself ready to accept the conduct of foreign and military affairs as joint matters with the Austrian part of the empire. At the end of 1865, Francis Joseph convoked a new Parliament and, influenced by the Prussian-Austrian War that broke out during the negotiations, and the defeat at Sadowa (Königgrätz), accepted Deák's concept for the Settlement. In February 1867, he appointed Count Gyula Andrássy as prime minister of Hungary, and the Parliament accepted the Law on the Settlement by a vast majority. On 8 June 1867, Francis Joseph was crowned legitimate king of Hungary. The Habsburg Empire transformed into a dualist state with two centres (and became the Austro-Hungarian Monarchy) with joint policies in foreign and military affairs. The finances related to these two matters were also joint affairs, but there were two separate governments and parliaments.

The period of dualism, which lasted for half a century, undoubtedly brought with it significant economic modernization, although not every part of the society enjoyed an equal share in this material growth. However, tensions evoked by social conflicts and by the unsolved (and within the existing internal and external framework insoluble) nationality question, mostly under the surface, portended that this 'Golden Age' would not be long-lasting. Yet its achievements in both institution building, infrastructural development, economic growth and cultural life were unparalleled, even if the political culture of this Golden Age could not attain the structural clarity and legitimacy that was achieved by the April Laws and the Batthyány government.

Conclusion

The decades from 1790 to 1867 brought unparalleled success in the political life of the country. While in the first half of the period the king was unwilling to fulfil the demands of the Hungarian Diet, and the court did all it could to slow down the pace of change, the majority of the political elite of the kingdom recognized that, in order to keep the ancient constitution, deep-rooted changes had to take place. The best minds of the nation were employed in drawing up plans for possible scenarios which could modernize the country, including Kazinczy, Kölcsey, Széchenyi, Kossuth, Deák and Eötvös. But it required the political genius of Kossuth to make the best of all those plans come true, by seizing the moment, opened up by the waves of European social unrest, which prepared the ground for the April Laws of 1848, the epitome of Hungarian constitutionality in the mid-nineteenth century. Nevertheless, the new ruler and his court eventually emerged victorious in the subsequent War of Independence which led to the revenge of the court and a period of passive resistance in Hungary. The geopolitical realities of the 1860s, however, proved to Austria that a deal with the Hungarians was imperative to salvage some remnants of their international prestige. The win-win agreement of the Settlement of 1867 led to an unparalleled boom in the Hungarian economy and culture by 1900. The following chapters will show how the way was paved for this spectacular development, supported and facilitated by some of the best minds of the country in the long nineteenth century.

Notes

1 Gyémánt Richárd, 'A Bánság újratelepítése, különös tekintettel a 18. századi telepítési folyamatokra' [The Repopulation of the Banat with a Focus on 18th-Century Settlement Processes], *Acta Universitatis Szegediensis Forum Acta Juridica et Politica* 5, no. 1 (2015): 31–48, 41.

2 Hanák Péter, ed., *Egy ezredév: Magyarország rövid története* [A Millennium: A Brief History of Hungary] (Budapest: Gondolat, 1986), 129.

3 Martinus Georgius Kovachich, *Supplementum ad vestigia comitiorum apud hungaros ab exordio regni eorum in Pannonia, usque ad hodiernum diem celebratorum*, vol. 3 (Budae: Typographiae Regiae Universitatis Pestanae, 1801), 101.

4 Nagy Noémi, *A hatalom nyelve–a nyelv hatalma: Nyelvi jog és nyelvpolitika Európa történetében* (Budapest: Dialóg Campus Kiadó, 2019), 85–7.
5 Nagy, *A hatalom nyelve–a nyelv hatalma*, 67–8.
6 Szekfű Gyula, *Iratok a magyar államnyelv kérdésének történetéhez 1790–1848* (Budapest: Magyar Történelmi Társulat, 1926), 205.
7 Szekfű, *Iratok a magyar államnyelv kérdésének történetéhez 1790–1848*, 43–4.

2

Ideological debates of the Reform Era (1830-48)

János Veliky

Modern roles

The social background of modern policy debates should not be conceived of solely in terms of the bourgeoisie who sought modern roles, which took the form of concrete enterprises as well as the theoretical ideas and plans that prepared the way for them. These new roles emerged among individuals and groups of people of varying legal status, including bourgeois intellectuals (and even entrepreneurs), from the early reformers (Gergely Berzeviczy, József Hajnóczy and Ferenc Kazinczy) to István Széchenyi, Lajos Kossuth and József Eötvös.

These new roles embodied civic aspirations, revealed, for example, by István Széchenyi's frequent use of the expression 'heart and reason' when discussing the changes that were occurring in his society, which did not distinguish the opposing individuals and groups according to their privileges, but according to their views on the necessity of transformation.[1] The other driving force of the transformation in the early 1840s, Kossuth, sparked both political and emotional debates in the *Pesti Hírlap* (Pest Gazette) newspaper, which he edited, by reinterpreting the direction of progress in a democratic spirit. Széchenyi reacted vividly to all this. In the dispute between the two, which erupted in 1841, they disagreed on how social modernization would occur, but it was also undoubtedly a semantic struggle that led to a more precise definition of different social and political positions. This dispute then fostered the lively debates that flared up almost every year during the 1840s, in which almost all the players in Hungarian politics adopted a position both publicly and in the various private forums in which they debated.

Such debates revolved around serious social and political tensions, or as Reinhart Koselleck puts it: '*Der Kampf um die "richtigen" Begriffe gewinnt an sozialer und politischer Brisanz*'[2] ('The battle for the "correct" terminology is gaining social and political explosiveness'). In the struggle that raged at the beginning of the decade, Széchenyi sought to develop his own, modern pro-Habsburg programme and to discredit the opposing political school (led by Wesselényi and Kossuth), but this proved an almost insurmountable task as one of the main obstacles was the centralizing imperial government itself, which operated in the spirit of absolutism, but failed to devise a plan for the development of Hungary. In contrast – despite the strong pressure from the imperial government, which was not necessarily to the detriment of those involved, as it increased their popularity – the opposition newspaper *Pesti Hirlap* and its political circle grew increasingly stronger, and Kossuth was able to describe his own political position, which was open to democratization in increasing detail. The political debate that took place between supporters of the imperial government and Széchenyi also meant that Kossuth's reform ideas included, and accorded increasing importance to, the formation of a modern constitutional opposition, which took place first on the pages of the *Pesti Hirlap*, while it was still possible, and then, when the imperial government manipulatively took the newspaper out of Kossuth's hands, in wider society.

The transformation of political ideas into specific programmes was first embodied in the *Kelet Népe* debate. Modernization was initially represented by ideas such as Széchenyi's plan for a bridge over the Danube at Pest, which included modern technical, economic and social elements. Groups were organized behind these projects, as in the case of the elite casino initiated by Széchenyi, and these ad hoc groupings were followed by broader political movements that emerged in the 1840s. As various ideas for reform were proposed, factions emerged backing the various alternatives. The social base of these factions was largely made up of the educated nobility, although non-noble intellectuals were also involved. In the case of one of the most important reforms, the emancipation of the serfs, initially both Széchenyi and Kossuth supported the emancipation of the serfs based on free bargaining, but later their opinions diverged significantly, while Aurél Dessewffy advocated the full compensation of landlords in the *Kelet Népe* debate.[3]

The reformist ideas of this period were framed by modern theoretical models. Széchenyi's worldview was, for example, guided by a liberal utilitarian philosophy, with the concept of profit at the heart of his progressive thought, which he commented on in his first major political work as follows: 'Put aside, therefore, all pompous and bright recommendations, which arouse enthusiasm and have no basis and therefore flare up just as quickly as a straw fire, but last no longer; and go ahead with cold-blooded and sober calculation, because in management and trade it is only the hope of profit or gain that moves things forward.'[4] The theoretical model was underpinned by modern economics, and although without making direct reference to the author, Széchenyi drew on Adam Smith's well-known thesis when describing the concept of 'ideal wealth' or 'capital funds', stating that wealth generation depends on the rate of rotation of capital:

> Money, land and everything else are of the greatest possible use only if I can use either at any moment for what I please. The faster my access to my money or land, and the shorter the time in which I can exchange the first for the second and vice versa, or for other goods of life, the more my one hundred or my one million forints, or my ten or one hundred thousand acres of land are worth to me, and otherwise all their value may be lost, because value is closely tied to the moment.[5]

The desirability of non-noble land ownership influenced the whole of Hungarian thinking on reform, since it affected both the serfs and the landlords, that is, the whole population, which grew to 12-13 million during this period and became one of the most important concepts driving the development of a modern society. At its heart was the emancipation of the serfs. At this time, the land was owned by the nobility (with 600,000 members in the Kingdom of Hungary and 60,000 in Transylvania), which made up almost 5 per cent of society. Their authority was not contested, but the land in the hands of the serfs, who made up three-quarters of society, was envisioned as 'shared ownership' in which the landlord continued to own the land, while the right of use was effectively transferred to the serf.[6] The idea of the emancipation of the serfs was considered so important by the Hungarian reforming elite that Miklós Wesselényi initiated a competition at the Hungarian Academy of Sciences in 1847 to promote and popularize this objective.[7]

Simultaneously, the idea of liberation from serfdom was constantly on the agenda in the various provinces of the Habsburg Empire, and in Hungary it started to become evident in the 1830s, when several market towns launched a process of 'self-redemption'. The nobility's acceptance of self-redemption varied; the majority were small nobles without wealth and a significant proportion of even the higher-ranking nobles did not possess great wealth. Another group of nobles lived in the fifty or so free royal towns, but the majority of the urban population comprised those engaged in industry and commerce. The group that was willing to support social reform included converts from all sections of privileged society, but the multifaceted nature of reform thinking is indicated by the fact that the desire to modernize the economy was not necessarily accompanied by a need to reform society and political participation.

Debates on land reform and serf emancipation

The Diet of 1832-6 displayed a strong desire for change, but there was also a great deal of excitement and nervousness about the reforms, with the secret police stating that the reports 'paint a highly disturbing and gloomy picture of the mood of the nobility in relation to the forthcoming Diet. The misdemeanors, clashes and fights during the election of the parliamentary delegates are beyond imagination.' These reports also indicated that 'the elected delegates who have so far become known are, for the most part, fierce opponents of the rule of the monarchy'.[8] Conservative members of the nobility defended the status quo. The delegate of Esztergom County József Andrássy for example, firmly stated that 'the serf's land belongs to the lord'. Károly De La Motte, the delegate of Gömör County, also criticized the method of reform, considering it 'inadmissible to take the land from the lord free of charge and sell it for money'.[9] However, the reformers, urging change, also focused on the issue of land ownership, such as Ferenc Kölcsey, who was a prolific political activist, and the delegate of Bars County, László Majthényi, who asserted at a meeting of the Lower House of the Diet that 'the serf should not only be able to redeem himself from taxation by the lord, but also to buy his land as property and to be able to bequeath it'. István Bezerédy, of Tolna County, backing the arguments of the liberals, embedded the question of civil property in the idea of the unification of interests, declaring: 'by giving someone the freedom to acquire property, we do not take away anyone's property, but we strengthen property of all kinds, because proprietorship and all its consequences are stronger where it extends to 9 million than where it is limited to a few'.[10]

The idea of equality before the law in the context of property ownership was also debated in the Diet. Ferenc Deák argued, on the basis of general principles of law, that 'the peasant also lives under the protection of the law, his person is inviolable, and he can bring lawsuits and complaints, which means, in other words, that the Hungarian peasant is also a human being'.[11] At the same time, he observed, the concentration of land ownership in a few hands led to the general impoverishment of the landed classes: 'a happy country is that in which the poor are the fewest, not in which the rich are the richest'. Deák also noted that the poor who have lost their plots cannot find work because the country is not industrialized as 'there are no factories, and our commerce is poor'. Generalizing from his experience, he then aptly concluded that the uptake of reforms was influenced by the level of development of the society, since – as he put it – 'it is difficult to transform a peasant nation in one fell swoop'.[12]

Deák's approach demonstrates both the theoretical orientation and the social sensitivity of the liberal reformers. At the same time, Deák's approach to reform was also clearly reflected in his interpretation of the legal status of the land used by serfs. He projected the rights of the serfs back into the past, in an attempt to establish the serfs' right to land ownership. In the debate on the fate of the land that was cleared, he argued that the landlord cannot take back cleared land from the serfs, because 'the unrestricted use of the owner's right would endanger the happiness of our country'. He then went on to state that 'our ancestors were never too late to put a stop to unrestricted use, when the national public happiness, closely interwoven with the fate of the poor taxpayer, made it necessary', so that the main question now was whether 'allowing the redemption of the cleared land will not have dangerous consequences for our country'.[13] After lengthy debates, the issue of serfs' access to land ownership was first resolved at the Diet of 1839-40, when a freely negotiated emancipation from serfdom was formulated, providing for the self-redemption of serfs, and was applied to the plots of the landed estates. Nevertheless, it had little impact; the lack of mobile capital and the resistance of the political forces meant that progress was slow, and only a few per cent of the population were affected, until the truly decisive turning point of 1848, when universal and compulsory serf emancipation with state compensation was granted. A broad sweep of reforms was, therefore, debated at the Diets of 1839-40 and 1843-4, but the process was only completed in 1848-9, when laws were adopted that led to the transformation of the country.

The *Kelet Népe* debate

The thinking of the reform generation progressed slowly. The *Kelet Népe* debate (called so after Széchenyi's book titled *A kelet népe* (People of the East) in which he attacked Kossuth's views), which also possessed modern elements such as widespread publicity, also inspired modern ideological orientations and began the process of party organization. This process can be pinpointed to 1841 with the publication of the *Pesti Hírlap*, edited by Kossuth, which sparked a wide-ranging political debate. Széchenyi was afraid of the emergence of a new, independent political movement, and had already in the 1830s turned down the application of the impoverished nobleman Kossuth to the National Casino, which he intended as the primary political forum of the reformist elite. The institutions which drove reformist thinking were, however, being transformed: from the early 1830s onwards, a reform movement based mainly on the counties gathered pace, where almost all the important issues of civic transformation were discussed, while in the next decade, in the early 1840s, Kossuth operated in a new public sphere, which was more open than either the framework based on the estates or the elite-like formations preferred by Széchenyi. Széchenyi disagreed with this transformation of the public sphere, so in the first round of the debate he responded to the appearance of a newspaper (*Pesti Hírlap*) with a book (*A kelet népe*).

István Széchenyi's position

At the start of the debate, Count Széchenyi approached important figures in Hungarian public life. He spoke with Lajos Batthyány, sent a letter to Deák through Ferenc Pulszky, and even met with conservative figures, including Aurél Dessewffy. At the same time, he discussed the situation with high-ranking imperial officials, meeting with the palatine (Archduke Joseph) and with Chancellor Metternich's confidant, the court advisor Ludwig von Wirkner. Word of his activity spread, and several members of the liberal opposition criticized his actions, including József Eötvös who wrote to him, and Gábor Klauzál who expressed his dissatisfaction verbally.[14] Despite these warnings, Széchenyi completed his book and published it in mid-1841 under the title *A kelet népe*.

In writing his book, Széchenyi was standing firmly in the field of European political romanticism. In this spirit – after his transcendent worldview had finally slipped from under his feet – he became the interpreter of both his private and public life. Ultimately, it was this approach that elevated Széchenyi into the position of a trendsetter and the foremost representative of Hungarian political thought.

At the heart of the principles of reform developed in this work was the concept of reform, linking the nation to liberty. The reforms Széchenyi proposed sought to filter out the incompetence that leads to error, precluding those rival political movements that, he thought, were steeped in emotion: 'The basis of my system of government is that reason has a separate sphere of activity, as does the heart, and that in government, as in medicine, for example, reason alone is allowed to function, while the heart, on the other hand, is not even allowed to flinch, except for the purpose of inspiring the good and the noble.'[15]

After a lengthy discussion of the general principles, Széchenyi highlighted some aspects of modernization that he had previously also favoured, such as the need to develop the capital city, Pest-Buda (it became Budapest in 1873), into a centre of power and capital, the need to create real land ownership by abolishing the *ius aviticum* (i.e. the medieval law that did not allow the selling of noble land), the need for the landowner to have a 'hypothec', that is, credit, and the need for 'free and safe transport'. One reform he discussed in particular detail was the redemption of serfs. He approved of the abolition of serfdom based on free negotiation and self-redemption, as adopted at the 1839-40 Diet. He also believed that the reform was progressing so well that the *ius aviticum* 'is now hanging by a thread and will surely soon be torn down',[16] a position he would not change until 1848.

Kossuth's position

Kossuth also began his discussion in the *Kelet Népe* debate with a description of the ideological orientations. He stated that public life had already been differentiated in the 1830s, when Széchenyi wanted to 'lead to public freedom through public wealth', while Wesselényi wished to 'lead to wealth through public freedom'. In the next decade, however, the debate on change would unfold in a broader, modern perspective, on whether a 'proposal is just and, if just, whether it is modern, according to the rule of logical succession'.[17] When Széchenyi objected to the 'manners' of the *Pesti Hirlap*, Kossuth replied that he should 'found another paper, according to his principles, his own orientation and manners, as in the life of a nation there are many colors and shades, and each one can fit in side by side'.[18]

Thus, Kossuth considers the emergence of distinct ideological programmes to be a 'modern' phenomenon, which 'belongs to the unavoidable stages of national development, and therefore there is absolutely nothing to fear from it'. He demonstrated the modernity of the debates on reform when he circumscribed the concept and differentiated its context: 'It is one thing to oppose authoritarianism, another to struggle on the plane of progressive issues.' He knew that disagreements would inevitably follow, and did not deny that the *Pesti Hirlap* was hastening this division.[19]

A clear dividing line emerged between the two opponents in the debate on the definition of the reformer role. Széchenyi outlines his own position which had not conservative, but liberal-elitist features. He stressed, on the one hand, that they must take the legal road – 'the constitutional road is the road along which we must make the fastest possible progress' – and, on the other hand, made the renunciation of prerogatives and support for the extension of rights conditional, stating, 'no one shall stand in our way with the intention or even the appearance of taking it from us by force'.[20] In contrast, Kossuth's democratic approach defined the positions according to the perspective that there are those who 'were friends of liberalism as long as it could appear in the guise of charity, but the idea has become burdensome for them, and their feelings are offended by an age that needs no charity, that demands justice and right,' and on the other side there is the *Pesti Hirlap*, 'which, with its voice not crying out for mercy but demanding rights, dissuades them of liberalism'.[21]

At the end of his work, Kossuth, like Széchenyi, also elaborated on some of the reforms he considered important, including the issues of the contracts of serfdom redemption, the security of property and related criminal justice issues. In the spirit of the reconciliation of interests, he stressed that those interested in the reform of serfdom were separated by very little, as the contracts of the redemption of serfs were in the interests of both parties. He himself supported the law on the abolition of serfdom in the Diet of 1839-40 and threatened the landlords ('it is in the interest of the landlords to abolish serfdom by free agreement; for if this is not done, sooner or later the compulsory law must come into force, and this will not be as favorable as free agreement.')[22] At the same time, Kossuth also stressed the inviolability of the land remaining in the ownership of the landlords (*allodiatura*), that is, that in expressing his philanthropic views 'no one will be able to take my words as an attack on property and the advocacy of idleness'.[23] He pointed out that acquired land was not free of all feudal ties, indicating that – as he wrote – 'everyone has the right to acquire land as a villein', but also the obligation 'to perform compulsory labor (*robot*) for this land and to give tithes'.[24] In this way, the land that was transferred did not become the secure property of the serf. His plans for the emancipation of the serfs were embodied in the general and compulsory abolition of serfdom, based on agreement and with state compensation, adopted by the Diet in 1847-8, which he helped to develop and pass into law.

His vision was fulfilled when he linked the reform of institutions to the transformation of society. He stressed that the nobility needed help in this area,[25] from a still embryonic middle class. He structured his institutional reform in a web-like manner, in which the embryonic social groups would work in a mutually reinforcing manner, with the intellectuals and the newly liberated market towns being represented in the county assemblies, and the Lower House of the Diet increasing the representation of the free royal towns, thus ensuring the transformation of both institutions into a forum for civil representation.[26]

It should be stressed, however, that Kossuth's political democratism was tempered by a realistic assessment of contemporary society.[27] He started from the premise that the process of reform was unstoppable and stressed that 'neither intrigue, nor suspicion, nor power can prevent progress, or even push it back; for it has become a deeply felt national public necessity'. The 'triumph of the cause of progress is therefore certain', and it is to the benefit of all.[28] This optimistic vision was connected to the intention to expand political rights to a broader base of citizens. Like Széchenyi, Kossuth did not deny the importance of education, but added that 'I will not rack my brains much about the question of primacy [between liberty and education]', because 'liberty is the best educator for liberty', and therefore 'I am not afraid of the idea that rights should precede education.'[29] In this process, his concept of change – as the *Kelet Népe* debate also demonstrated – entailed new, modern forums, the educational function of the press and a strong reliance on the associative spirit to give society greater momentum, in addition to reformed historical institutions. This associative spirit was thus embodied in 'industrial associations [...] for the dissemination of useful knowledge', that is, in its actual application. He believed that 'the ideas of a new age' were having an effect in most of these groups, and 'engineers as the harbingers of modernization' were already active in this territory.[30]

József Eötvös's position

Baron József Eötvös approached the *Kelet Népe* debate as a professional politician, who was excited by the modern phenomenon of a public debate visible to every literate

Hungarian. At the beginning of his contribution, titled *Kelet Népe és Pesti Hirlap*, in which he asked whether Széchenyi was justified in attacking Kossuth's *Pesti Hirlap*, 'which also fights under the banner of progress [. . .] and whether the way in which it did so was such as to promote the cause of progress, legal freedom and free discourse'. He thought that the answer to this question should be decided by public debate, for 'in the field of discussion the truth will be revealed'.[31]

Eötvös described the ways in which reform movements were organized, from the linguistic expression they employed to the content of their programmes, in the framework of an actual conceptual history. 'In our imperfect languages, the number of words does not correspond to the difference of concepts; the meaning of a word often changes from year to year.' He argued that political tendencies are formed by both intellectual and practical reflection, since if

> one who was once a friend and even the initiator of progress does not want to support all progress without exception, when speaking out in favor of some innovations, he opposes others. [. . .] There may be, and even are, cases where those who pursue the same objective become divided, and where the most ardent friends of progress urge moderation; it is only the reason which led them to speak, the time in which they did so, and the manner in which they did so, that makes their actions blameworthy or meritorious; it is only this point around which all sober discourse must revolve.[32]

In Eötvös's opinion, Kossuth's reform plans were guided by the spirit of unification of interests, so the ideas published in the *Pesti Hirlap* did not ultimately create tension between social groups. He sums up the situation by pointing out that, according to Kossuth, the former aristocracy can build its power on new foundations as a result of society's transformation, and can increasingly take on a bourgeois role, as 'today, any aristocracy of birth can only become powerful if it can base its power on property and higher intelligence, in addition to its coats of arms'.[33] Eötvös also makes use of a phrase often used in the *Pesti Hirlap*: 'speaking of that part of our nobility who do not want to fulfil their appointed vocation, he [i.e. Kossuth] clearly states his conviction: [. . .] it is the great cause of progress that the destiny of our nation shall be fulfilled' – 'with you, by you, if it pleases you; without you, against you, if it must be'.[34]

Eötvös's view of the role of state institutions in the transformation of Hungary was linked to the hopes that had been raised in connection to the Diet of 1839-40. That confidence in the importance of the counties, whose representatives had largely pushed for further reforms, is evident when he declared that 'there can be no greater admirer of our municipal liberty, no more zealous defender of it than I', and 'I believe that the survival of our country after so many centuries of struggle is due to our municipal constitution.' He then proceeded to say that 'if our municipalist system' is lost, 'our constitution will lose its value, and the word liberty will become obsolete in our language'.[35] This does not mean that he did not criticize the functioning of this aristocratic institution, although for the time being he was much more sympathetic to it than he would be later.

In this debate Eötvös interpreted with remarkable sensitivity the various reform programmes and, in his view, the idea of progress becomes the central concept of change shared by all of them. The concept of progress in Europe came to the forefront during the Enlightenment. This is also evident in Eötvös's conception, so that for him the natural law aspects that challenged the division of society into distinct estates played an essential role along with the liberal unification of interests that created an effective model of civil progress, and in this spirit the concept of the progressive citizen was born. This citizen is one 'who wants to extend the blessings of our constitution to all citizens of this country, who desires equality before the law for all citizens of Hungary, and renouncing his privileges, wishes to share in the defense of this country and its burdens: a man of progress'.[36]

Aurél Dessewffy's position

The conservative count Aurél Dessewffy, in an essay published at the end of 1841 in the context of the *Kelet Népe* debate, emphasized the historical content of changes in political thought, since, as he explained, change 'is considered to be of the utmost importance mainly in political terms'. He described the essence of the debate as 'preliminary speculations about the orientation', which fundamentally influenced the process of reform, and thus, in his view, the concepts of change were based on a 'political theory' which reshaped public policy.[37]

He described the various orientations in a spirit that was conservative but acknowledged the need for some reform. This is reflected in his description of the concepts lying behind them, when he asserts that 'in Hungary, the political school which can be called the par excellence party of progress is popular in Hungary: unpopular is the one which wishes to moderate this movement, to bind it to legal forms, to respect certain principles, and to preserve our progress from the dangers of improvisation'.[38] He claimed that the 'party of progress', that is, the reformist opposition, is characterized by 'moral terrorism, applause and shushing, flare-ups and noise', while of his own side he claims that it is characterized by 'a careful appreciation of prevailing interests and complex relations'. He goes on to suggest that it is the 'party of progress' which creates tensions, for it is 'not the party of moderation which has systematically encouraged applause and shushing in national meetings, districts, and county assemblies, which has constantly flattered to the self-importance of youth and has introduced harshness in public meetings'.[39]

Dessewffy then proceeded to analyse the programmes of the conservatives and the reformist opposition, explaining that the thinking of the reformist opposition is characterized by 'confusion' caused by 'a group of which each member represents different muddled elements', while the perception of the conservative side's views is characterized by 'versatility'.[40] At the same time, he showed a surprising confidence in political journalism and considered it desirable that the 'many-sidedness' of programmes should be reflected in the public sphere. He noted, for example, that on 'general political issues', dissenters will organize themselves into orientations and express their views in supportive newspapers.[41]

According to Dessewffy, 'Lajos Kossuth's reply is a reprisal and bitter criticism of *A kelet népe*', while Széchenyi 'never wrote more from the depths of his soul than when he wrote *A kelet népe*'.[42] He went on to assert that Kossuth's newspaper is sliding towards 'extremism' when 'it calls the shrieking of the masses public opinion', a tendency which was, according to Dessewffy, also embodied in the content of some reforms, since, for example, 'it advocates the idea of free land in such a way that, if it finds a sympathetic echo, it makes all reasonable provisions impossible in the matter of redemption'. On the other hand, he summarized Széchenyi's position as follows: 'he wanted to exercise his influence mainly through institutions of his own creation' and 'did not sufficiently appreciate county life, forms and influence; he could not insert himself into them'.[43]

Dessewffy also argued that Széchenyi was concerned only with the management of public thought, while Kossuth condemned the role of government 'to that of a benevolent spectator in everything', since his plans 'neglect the necessary rights of the legal supreme power in the direction of the counties'. The central tenet of Dessewffy's conception was conservative progress, that is, 'the progress of good order'. The concept of 'good order', as he interpreted it, was 'to warn the present holders of rights [. . .] of the needs of the times [. . .] and the people of the land of the great things that have happened to them in just a few years'.[44]

Party organization and the reforms of 1848

Soon after the *Kelet Népe* debate, Dessewffy died unexpectedly in 1842. Széchenyi started writing another book, which he did not finish, after realizing that he could only compete with Kossuth's *Pesti Hirlap* by engaging in journalistic polemics. At the end of 1842, in his speech to the new Hungarian Academy of Sciences, which he had founded, he discussed the new political movements, and the following year he agreed with the editors of the *Jelenkor* (*The Present Times*) to publish his writings in this journal – but his attempt swiftly failed. Kossuth, on the other hand, effectively used the *Pesti Hirlap* until the end of June 1844, when the imperial government wrestled the editorship of the newspaper from his hands, which then fell into the hands of the centralizers under the editorship of László Szalay and then Antal Csengery. József Eötvös had a strange journey. After his combative approach in the *Kelet Népe* debate, he followed a similar path to Széchenyi and offered his services to the imperial government in 1843 but chose not to inform the public about it.[45] All this changed later. Eventually, the organization of new parties formally adopting positions that had been sketched out in the earlier debate, was completed by 1846-7. First, the Conservative Party was formed. Its programme set out its political principles and organizational matters, and it stressed that changes should be made constitutionally, 'without subversion', in cooperation with the imperial government.[46] Then, after a long debate, on 5 June 1847, the Opposition Party published its own programme, the *Ellenzéki Nyilatkozat* (Opposition Statement), edited by Ferenc Deák.

After the bloodless revolution that broke out in Pest on 15 March 1848, the Palatine Stephen appointed the Batthyány government on 11 April, which the emperor, under the influence of the Vienna Revolution, subsequently approved. The Batthyány government was a coalition government, but its backbone was formed by the leading figures of the *Kelet Népe* dispute: Széchenyi was placed in charge of transport, Kossuth in charge of finance, Eötvös in charge of religion and public education, and they were joined by Ferenc Deák as minister of justice, while the leader of the liberal opposition, Lajos Batthyány, was the undisputed authority at the head of the Hungarian government.[47] This group's reform efforts were imbued with a strong socially oriented mindset that put them far beyond other political groups.

The April Laws passed by the last Diet of the Estates, thanks to the efforts of the liberal opposition, were the culmination of the social modernization which took place in this period. Article III of the April Laws declared that the monarch exercises executive power in civil, ecclesiastical, treasury and military matters through the responsible ministries. Articles IV–V provided for the annual sitting of the Parliament, elected on the basis of popular representation, in Pest. Articles VI–VII dealt with the reannexation of the Partium and union with Transylvania. Of decisive importance for the abolition of the feudal system were Articles VIII, IX, XIII and XV, which abolished the service obligations of the serfs and the *ius aviticum*. The freedom of the press was provided for in Article XVIII, with equal rights for the established religions covered in Article XX and the establishment of the National Guard in Article XXII.[48]

The most notable of these laws was the one on the emancipation of serfs, which established a general and compulsory abolition of serfdom, based on mutual agreement and supported by state compensation. The ideas of freedom and property, strongly represented by Ferenc Kölcsey, permeated Hungarian liberal public thinking, so understandably it was at the centre of the law of redemption of the serfs. This change certainly affected the nobility, although only a minority of them actually held serfs, and of course the serfs themselves, who made up about 80 per cent of society. The emancipated peasantry, however, was a much more complex group, as it included people who had redeemed themselves after 1840, the militarily dependent social strata of the border regions, the *Jász* and the *Cumans*, as well as numerous craftsmen, tradesmen and miners. These social strata acquired 40 per cent of the cultivated land.[49]

Thus, after a long process of conciliation, and the emancipation of the serfs in 1848, more than 90 per cent of the peasantry became owners of property. At the same time, this did not prevent an increasingly widespread impoverishment, which was compounded by the difficult fate of the nobility, due to delays in receiving the compensation under Habsburg neo-absolutism after the defeat of the 1848-9 Hungarian War of Independence. Historians are right to highlight that the success of the breakthrough was significantly diminished by the fact that a complete social transformation could not be completed by the Hungarian reformist elite who had initiated it.[50]

Notes

1 Koselleck describes the phenomenon, which can be observed in many places in Europe during the modern transition, as follows: '*Auf diese Weise entsteht ein Wettstreit um die wahre politische Interpretation, der Ausschlusstechniken, die den Gegner daran hindern sollen, durch dasselbe Wort anders zu sagen und zu wollen als man selbst.*' Reinhart Koselleck, *Vergangene Zukunft: Zur Semantik geschichtlicher Zeiten* (Frankfurt am Main: Suhrkamp, 1992), 347.

2 Koselleck, *Vergangene Zukunft*, 93-4, 112-13.
3 Dessewffy Aurél, *X. Y. Z. könyv* [X. Y. Z. Book] (Pest: Trattner-Károlyi, 1841), 22-6.
4 Széchenyi István, *Hitel* [Credit] (Pest: Trattner-Károlyi, 1830), 77.
5 Széchenyi, *Hitel*, 42.
6 Varga János, *Jobbágyrendszer a magyarországi feudalizmus kései századaiban 1556-1767* [The Serf System in the Late Centuries of Feudalism in Hungary 1556-1767] (Budapest: Akadémiai Kiadó, 1969); Varga János, *A jobbágyi földbirtoklás típusai és problémái* [Types and Problems of Serf Land Tenure] (Budapest: Akadémiai Kiadó, 1967).
7 Csetri Elek, 'Wesselényi a jobbágyfelszabadítás európai hátteréről ' [Wesselényi on the European Background of Serf Emancipation], *Agrártörténeti Szemle* 40-1, no. 1-4 (1998-99): 26-35.
8 Sándor Pál, 'Deák és a jobbágykérdés az 1832-36. évi országgyűlésen' [Deák and the Serf Question at the Diet of 1832-36], in *Zalai Gyűjtemény* 5, ed. Baranyai György et al. (Zalaegerszeg: Zala Megyei Levéltár, 1976), 123.
9 Sándor, 'Deák és a jobbágykérdés az 1832-36. évi országgyűlésen', etc. 139.
10 Sándor, 'Deák és a jobbágykérdés az 1832-36. évi országgyűlésen', 139-40.
11 Sándor, 'Deák és a jobbágykérdés az 1832-36. évi országgyűlésen', 145.
12 Sándor, 'Deák és a jobbágykérdés az 1832-36. évi országgyűlésen', 155-6.
13 Sándor, 'Deák és a jobbágykérdés az 1832-36. évi országgyűlésen', 159-60.
14 Széchenyi István, *Napló* [Diary], ed. Oltványi Ambrus (Budapest: Gondolat, 1978), 933-5, 943-4.
15 Széchenyi István, *A kelet népe* [People of the East] (Pozsony: Wigand, 1841), 131.
16 Széchenyi, *A kelet népe*, 302, 306-7.
17 Kossuth Lajos, *Felelet gróf Széchenyi Istvánnak Kossuth Lajostól* [Reply to Count István Széchenyi from Lajos Kossuth] (Pest, Landerer és Heckenast, 1841), 22.
18 Kossuth, *Felelet gróf Széchenyi Istvánnak Kossuth Lajostól*, 64, 68.
19 Kossuth, *Felelet gróf Széchenyi Istvánnak Kossuth Lajostól*, 64, 77, 80.
20 Széchenyi, *A kelet népe*, 106-7.
21 Kossuth, *Felelet gróf Széchenyi Istvánnak Kossuth Lajostól*, 80-1.
22 Kossuth, *Felelet gróf Széchenyi Istvánnak Kossuth Lajostól*, 155.
23 Kossuth, *Felelet gróf Széchenyi Istvánnak Kossuth Lajostól*, 178.
24 Kossuth, *Felelet gróf Széchenyi Istvánnak Kossuth Lajostól*, 158.
25 Kulin Ferenc, *Közelítések a reformkorhoz* [Perspectives on the Reform Era], Elvek és utak (Budapest: Magvető Könyvkiadó, 1986), 127-42.
26 Veliky János, *A változások kora* [The Age of Changes] (Budapest: Fok-Ta Bt., 2009), 130-8.
27 Horkay Hörcher Ferenc, 'Az Amerikai demokrácia Magyarországon: A magyar Tocqueville, 1834-43' [Democracy in America in Hungary: The Hungarian Tocqueville, 1834-43], *Holmi* 6, no. 11 (November 1994): 1608-15.
28 Kossuth, *Felelet gróf Széchenyi Istvánnak Kossuth Lajostól*, 221.
29 Kossuth, *Felelet gróf Széchenyi Istvánnak Kossuth Lajostól*, 236, 239.
30 Kossuth, *Felelet gróf Széchenyi Istvánnak Kossuth Lajostól*, 243.
31 Eötvös József, *Kelet Népe és Pesti Hirlap* (Pest: Landerer és Heckenast, 1841), 4-6.
32 Eötvös, *Kelet Népe és Pesti Hirlap*, 4-5.
33 Eötvös, *Kelet Népe és Pesti Hirlap*, 87.
34 Eötvös, *Kelet Népe és Pesti Hirlap*, 89.
35 Eötvös, *Kelet Népe és Pesti Hirlap*, 101-7.
36 Eötvös, *Kelet Népe és Pesti Hirlap*, 119.

37 Dessewffy, *X. Y. Z. könyv*, Preface.
38 Dessewffy, *X. Y. Z. könyv*, 15.
39 Dessewffy, *X. Y. Z. könyv*, 17–18.
40 Dessewffy, *X. Y. Z. könyv*, 3, 7.
41 Dessewffy, *X. Y. Z. könyv*, 17.
42 Dessewffy, *X. Y. Z. könyv*, 41–2.
43 Dessewffy, *X. Y. Z. könyv*, 53–5.
44 Dessewffy, *X. Y. Z. könyv*, 74–8.
45 Horváth Mihály, *Huszonöt év Magyarország történelméből 1823-tól 1848-ig* [Twenty-five Years from the History of Hungary 1823–48] (Pest: Ráth Mór, 1868), 3:12.
46 Dénes Iván Zoltán, *Közüggyé emelt kiváltságőrzés: A magyar konzervatívok szerepe és értékvilága az 1840-es években* [Making the Preservation of Privileges a Common Cause: The Role and Value System of Hungarian Conservatives in the 1840s] (Budapest: Akadémiai Kiadó, 1989), 151–67.
47 Urbán Aladár, *Batthyány Lajos miniszterelnöksége* [Lajos Batthyány as Prime Minister], Nemzet és emlékezet (Budapest: Magvető Könyvkiadó, 1986).
48 Hermann Róbert, 'A törvényes forradalom és az áprilisi törvények' [The Lawful Revolution and the April Laws] in *Millenniumi magyar történet*, ed. Tóth György István (Budapest: Osiris Kiadó, 2001), 378–87.
49 Szabad György, 'A jobbágyfelszabadítás hatása a társadalom szerkezetének alakulására' [The Impact of Serf Emancipation on the Structure of Society], *Agrártörténeti Szemle* 40–41, no. 1–4 (1998–99): 36–41.
50 Szabad, 'A jobbágyfelszabadítás hatása . . .', 39–41.

3

Constitutional and legal thought in the long nineteenth century

István Stipta

Constitutional thought and public law in Hungary

The constitution and the role of law in self-defence

The twists and turns of the long nineteenth-century Hungarian history are difficult to understand without an analysis of the country's constitutional and, in a broader sense, public law position.[1] Taking codified (positive) law as a starting point also offers an appropriate basis for political science and historiography, since from 1790 onwards legal regulation had an increasing influence on actual politics, while the continuing influence of customary law also allows us to trace the traditional social values which were anchored in the law. Parliamentary debates took place within the framework of constitutional customary law and were also an arena for political conflict. During the period of Habsburg absolutism under Joseph II, from 1780 to 1790, members of the Hungarian political elite always assessed their position in legal terms, both when they were defending their customary rights and when they strove to extend their autonomy. These political struggles were fought through legal means, and even the episodes of armed resistance against Habsburg centralization were backed up by legal arguments. Hungary's nobility interpreted their position within the empire in the same way, stressing that Hungary had always elected Habsburg kings since the defeat at Mohács by the Ottoman army, in 1526, eliminated the last Hungarian ruling dynasty and had never agreed to a unified state either then or later. They believed that the same person was the ruler in both countries or in constitutional terminology: there was a personal union. Such a personal union existed, for example, between the Electorate of Hanover and England in the eighteenth century, and no closer state relationship resulted.[2]

The constitutionalist approach is well reflected in Ferenc Deák's address submitted to Francis Joseph, who was like all Habsburg rulers both emperor of Austria and king of Hungary, dated 5 June 1861, which the historian Henrik Marczali (1856-1940) considered to be one of the finest examples of Hungarian constitutional thought:

We do not need a given constitution, we reclaim our ancient constitution, which was not a gift, but developed from the life of the nation. We have law and justice and the sanctity of contracts on our side, and material force against us. The nation is ready to cast a veil over the sufferings of the past, but it must protest against the injustice that is still being inflicted on it. The preconditions for the coronation were: political and territorial unity of the country, the supplementing of the National Assembly (Transylvanian and Croatian representatives had not been included in the new parliament), the full restoration of our fundamental laws, a parliamentary government and a responsible ministry. If this is done, if Hungary is once again a free and independent country, she is prepared to do everything possible, on the basis of fairness, out of political consideration, without prejudice to her independence and constitutional rights, to ensure that under the heavy burdens which the hitherto existing absolute system has brought about, Austria's prosperity and ours will not collapse.[3]

The struggle for self-defence, almost continuous since 1526, had created a number of fundamental constitutional values by the time the 1848 revolution broke out. The idea of human rights emerged, albeit essentially within the limits of a system which divided the population into distinct estates, and – in the eighteenth century, in the works of József Hajnóczy – judicial protection for the constitution began to be required. The idea of constitutionality in the contemporary sense – the idea of limiting the power of the executive – already appeared in Hungary in the Golden Bull (1222), which was proclaimed seven years after the Magna Carta (1215).

The constitutional determination of the legal system, moreover, had eighteenth-century antecedents, since the validity of royal legislation required a consensus based on common law. An important tenet of the doctrine of the Holy Crown of Saint Stephen is precisely the joint right of the legitimately crowned king and the legislature to legislate, that is, to make, repeal and interpret laws (Article XII of 1791 also confirmed this). As for the defence of constitutional governance (*ius resistendi*), Hungarian national consciousness has always insisted on *ius resistendi*, and even Ferenc Rákóczi II himself referred to it in 1701 as a justification for his self-defensive struggle, while Hungarian public law literature between the two world wars considered it an active right.[4]

The historical constitution and its fundamental laws: The definition and scope of legal sources

The concept of the 'fundamental law' is relevant to the relationship between public law and politics, which is a major theme of this chapter. Earlier legislation did not provide a formal definition of a fundamental law, and the major works on the law provided little guidance on this concept.

In 1846, Zsigmond Beöthy (1819–96), the author of one of the earliest works of the fledgling discipline of public law jurisprudence, which was later subjected to extensive criticism, divided the fundamental laws (*leges fundamentales*) into written and customary laws. Among the written fundamental laws, he included, on the one hand, the separate charters and diplomas, and treaties (e.g. the Golden Bull) which were part of the constitution by agreement between the ruler and the estates. According to Beöthy's vague definition, the other group of written fundamental laws includes those laws that are 'woven into the structure of the civil code without any special name or title'. Among the written fundamental laws he included the *partis primae titulus nonus* of the Tripartitum, dealing with the four cardinal privileges of the nobility. Beöthy claimed that a summary of the fundamental laws was also contained in the decrees customarily issued by each king after his coronation (*diploma inaugurale*) and in the coronation oaths of kings ('promising to protect the rights of the country and the people'). After the 1848 revolution, his view that in addition to written laws, Hungary also followed customary fundamental laws, 'which have been left in place by long and continued custom', was severely criticized. Nevertheless, Beöthy's view that the distinguishing feature of these customary fundamental laws is that, unlike the written ones, 'they have never been promulgated, and are known by the Hungarian nation only through the unbroken path of tradition (*traditio*)' was repopularized after 1867.[5]

In 1861, Ferenc Toldy (1805-75) rightly observed that legal scholars are not in complete agreement on the definition of fundamental laws. In the year of the hoped-for restoration of national rights, he also extended the concept of the fundamental law to a wide range of subjects, including all legislation 'dealing with the relations between king and nation, the principles of ruling, governance and legislation'.[6]

It was, however, not possible to precisely define the scope of the Hungarian fundamental laws according to formal characteristics and legal norms. Both Beöthy and Toldy pointed out that the 'solemn' nature of legislative acts could not be a qualifying criterion, since Hungarian rulers issued almost all decrees in a solemn form from the first half of the thirteenth century onwards. It would also be inaccurate to regard as fundamental laws those legal norms of a contractual nature, which were created exclusively by agreement (*tractatus*), since in this case only the Golden Bull, the peace treaties of Vienna and Linz and the coronation charters could be included in the scope of the fundamental laws, which would constitute only a fragment of the norms dealing with the relations between king and nation, and of the principles of ruling, governance and legislation.

Tivadar Pauler (1816-86), an eminent representative of academic jurisprudence, also attempted to establish a set of principles to rank various Hungarian laws. In his scheme, 'fundamental laws are (1) those laws which the legislature has expressly designated as such, or has so designated by its acts; (2) those which, by reason of their content embodying the fundamental principles of the Constitution, are found to be fundamental'.[7] Pauler also pointed out that defining the concrete norms of fundamental laws is a difficult and 'writer-dependent' task. He did not regard the royal charters as fundamental laws but as a 'national guarantee' and, although he regarded customs as 'sources of public law', he did not recognize their force as fundamental laws. It is important to note that Pauler had already taken into account the 1848 enactments, noting that the fundamental laws of the feudal era had been 'substantially changed' by the enactments of Articles III, IV and V of 1848. Of the aforementioned April Laws, two articles (III and V) contained some provisions which fell within the scope of the legal protection of citizens against misuse of power by the public administration.

In the academic literature dealing with the Age of Dualism, the position of Ernő Nagy (1853-1921), an authority on public law who was devoted to legal history, was considered authoritative for a long time in his interpretation of the concept of the fundamental law and the analysis of its contents. In his rather rigid view, the Hungarian state, 'which has never deviated from constitutionality, and on the other hand has remained based on its historical foundations throughout its development, does not have, in the strict sense of the word, any fundamental laws of a separate legal nature'. The author explained this statement, in his later work, by insisting that Hungarian public law understood the fundamental law as an important legal norm that was eternal, and which can thus form the foundation of its statehood. He also noted that the concept of the fundamental law is a vague term, since it is difficult to define the scope of the norms that regulate the cardinal institutions of statehood. The exact identification of these norms was made more difficult by one of the characteristics of Hungarian fundamental laws: they are not formally uniform, their creation has always been linked to a specific historical situation and therefore they are chronologically scattered amidst other legislation.[8]

A question that remains evident in current academic debate is the connection between Hungarian fundamental laws and the social structure, or more precisely, how public thinking in the feudal era (when the population of the kingdom was divided into estates) and in the subsequent 'bourgeois' period (when rights were extended to the middle classes but the majority of the population was excluded from political representation) perceived the stability of laws and the legitimacy of the regulations that made these divisions more rigid. Ernő Nagy pointed out that even in the feudal era there was an attempt to give some laws greater stability and even immutability. For example, Article VIII of 1741, passed at the beginning of Maria Theresa's reign, not only confirmed the freedoms and privileges of the nobility but this law was also exempted from the clause in the *diploma inaugurale* that laws shall only be maintained as long as the ruler and the Diet agreed. The Hungarian revolution of 1848 brought, however, a change in this regard. The politicians of that time believed that immutable laws were contrary to the sovereign nature of the state and the very essence of legislation, which is destined to permanently evolve.

Cardinal acts and constitutional guarantees

In the Hungarian legal terminology of the dualist era, the term 'cornerstone' or cardinal law (*sarkalatos törvény*) did not have a distinct meaning. The term 'cornerstone law' was used by several authors (Tivadar Pauler, Ferenc Toldy, Gyula Schvarcz and János Török) in order to indicate the commonalities between the unofficial fundamental laws in Hungary and the officially promulgated fundamental laws adopted in other states. They called them 'cornerstone laws . . . as these are the corners of our constitution'.[9] Despite the fact that this definition was based on international examples,[10] in Hungarian literature, in both the vernacular and in the actual wording of legislation (notably Article XII of 1867 and Article XXX of 1868), the term 'fundamental law' (*alaptörvény*) remained the standard one.[11] János Suhayda (1818-81) also used the terms 'fundamental law' and 'cornerstone law' as synonyms.[12] Ferenc Toldy did not attribute an independent content to the term but understood them as laws 'which contain the cornerstones of our national constitution, these are the so-called fundamental laws'.[13] The theoretical and journalistic literature on administrative adjudication of this era did not distinguish between the two categories either. The authors who used German legal terminology were most likely to use the term 'fundamental law' (which is a calque of the German Grundgesetz).

In the public debates of the dualist era, and when assessing the constitutional role of the various state institutions, differing interpretations of the constitutional guarantees played a more important role than laws. According to the prevailing views of legal scholarship, in addition to the fundamental laws, there was a need for further measures and regulations to guarantee the survival of the constitution and to prevent its violation or illegal alteration. Most authors included the so-called 'resistance clauses' that had been included in the feudal period in the charters and oaths of monarchs. Ernő Nagy, the author of the *Magyar Jogi Lexikon* (Encyclopedia of Hungarian Law) also considered other institutions and guarantees including

> ministerial responsibility, representation of the people, the right to a budget, the right to refuse taxes and the implementation of conscription, freedom of the press, the right of publicity and free discourse, freedom of association and assembly, the right of petition and complaint, the independence and immovability of judges, the oath of the military to the Constitution, and several autonomous and independent self-governmental organizations.[14]

Most of these criteria were closely linked to the principle of legal protections against administrative abuses. Constraints on the administration (e.g. ministerial responsibility) provided some protection, which was then reinforced by other elements (e.g. the right of petition and the right of complaint). (Ernő Nagy, however, just listed these general guarantees and did not refer to their validity.)

Hungary's specific historical circumstances explain why so many actors in the political sphere regarded a well-developed system of self-government as the most important constitutional guarantee for so long. Many politicians and thinkers in the early nineteenth century demanded the strengthening of the prerogatives of the county system, since a good municipal system 'ensures the influence of the nation in administrative matters'.[15] Even Lajos Kossuth stressed the need for 'the existence of bodies of self-government, regional administrative authorities in public administration between the state government and the individuals [. . .], in which the desire for over-expansion can be broken, and in which the necessary restriction of individual freedom can be achieved with the cooperation of the individuals themselves'.[16] Many leading figures in public life, including Prime Minister Kálmán Tisza (1830-1902), who dominated politics for several decades, considered the self-governance of the counties sufficient to guarantee individual rights and thus considered the protection of other individual freedom to be unnecessary. Over time, this perception changed, as a result of which, by the first third of the twentieth century several observers considered further protections to be necessary.[17]

The changing concept of the historical constitution

The development of the modern Hungarian concept of the constitution is linked to the political events of the 1780s. József Hajnóczy (1750-95) was the first to summarize the principles and the main rules of Hungarian constitutionality, and legal autonomy within the Habsburg Empire, in four anonymous works. Hajnóczy, who was executed for sedition, wrote his works with extraordinary thoroughness, following the dogmatic method. In his first major work, *Dissertatio politico-publica de regiae potestatis in Hungaria limitibus* (A Public Law Treatise on the Limits of Royal Power in Hungary), published in 1791, he argued for the separation of powers. However, Hajnóczy associated this Montesquieuian principle with natural law, the need to guarantee human rights and the Rousseauian ideal of the social contract. His work *De comitiis Regni Hungariae deque organisatione eorundem dissertatio juris publici Hungarici* (A Hungarian Public Law Treatise on the Hungarian Diets and Their Organization), published in the same year, was a novel overview of the history of Hungarian legislation. This included the idea that the Diet does not represent only the noble estate, but the whole nation. He published two works in the following year: *Extractus legum de statu ecclesiastico catholico in Regno Hungariae latarum* (An Extract of the Laws on the Catholic Church in Hungary) and *De diversis subsidiis publicis dissertatio* (A Treatise on the Various Public Taxes), which have been largely overlooked and have not been subjected to thorough comparative analysis. They are basically compendias of scattered public law provisions supplemented by interpretative reflections.[18]

The events of 1848 were extremely important in the evolution of Hungary's historical constitution. It was Ferenc Deák who pointed out that 'we would look in vain for the public law content of some of the changes in our laws in the older times, because they are the result of the greater development of general education and the transformation of public law ideas throughout Europe. Such as the idea of a parliamentary government.'[19] The epoch-changing period of the 1848 April Laws did not break with the concept of the historic constitution, since 'when our legislature came comparatively nearest to such an initiative, the great majority of our parliamentarians wished to have the English Constitution in view, and the other part of them themselves recognized the immense difficulties which they had not had time to overcome in the hasty days of March, to the general benefit and reassurance of the public.'[20] Count Albert Apponyi (1846-1933) considered it the 'most remarkable and most glorious' feature of Hungarian constitutional development that the country was able to move from the constitutionality of the noble estate to the constitutionality of a modern state in 1848 'without the need for, and without the danger of, the absolute sovereign power intervening.'[21]

The legal continuity of Hungary's historical constitution – which minimized the revolutionary changes of 1848 – was most strongly emphasized in a study by Gyula Csillag (1851-1926) published in 1871. Csillag attempted to prove that the Hungarian constitution after the comprehensive reforms of 1848 and 1867 remained a 'historical and legally continuous' constitution and thus had all the advantages of organic development and legitimacy: 'that this constitution is flesh from our flesh, and blood from our blood'.[22]

According to Kornél Emmer (1845-1910), the work is characterized by sharp parallels and new historical approaches, but its main flaw is that 'in many places, it identifies the legal continuity of our institutions with their historical nature, considering the two inseparable. On the one hand, [Csillag] rightly asserts that the revolution is unknown in the development of Hungary's constitutional law, but, on the other hand, as a corollary of this truth, for all our institutions, endeavouring to prove that the idea of it, in our nation's legal perception, had long been present, and that neither 1848 nor 1867 had produced any reform which fell into the category of what we call the reforms of reason.'[23]

The civic achievements of Hungary's historic constitution

After the Settlement of 1867, there was a proliferation of literature which emphasized the criteria of the rule of law in the content of the historical constitution and of the fundamental law, and in outlining the tasks of practical legislation. According to István Egyed (1886-1966), 'the road from tyranny, from the police state to the rule of law is a long one; the most significant stages of this development are the organizational separation of the judiciary, the establishment of constraints on the administration and the establishment of the system of (constitutional) protections'.[24]

The progressive tendencies of the rule of law can be clearly traced in Hungarian law, which developed organically. The establishment of a government independent of the imperial central government, and directly responsible to the elected Parliament, was achieved by Article III of 1848. The basic provisions of Article IV of 1868 served to separate the administration from the judiciary and to ensure judicial independence. The primacy of laws (over royal decrees) was reinforced by Article XII of 1790-1. The separation of public administration and the judiciary took place in principle, but in practice, public administrative bodies judged for a long time.

The philosophical underpinnings of legal education and practice

In reviewing Hungarian legal philosophy in the long nineteenth century, it is worth addressing the frequent accusation[25] that there was a lack of originality in Hungarian legal thought of the time. There is no doubt that at times, Austrian and German intellectual influence was indeed strong, primarily as a consequence of the legislation that was imposed by Vienna and, more broadly, by Hungary's close relationship with Austria and by extension Germany. Thus, for example, Hungarian natural law thinking that emerged at the beginning of the eighteenth century was significantly constrained by the fact that the reforms of Maria Theresa (1777) designated the textbook of Viennese professor Anton Martini (1726-1800) as compulsory material for college lectures. This imperial patent remained in force in Hungary until 1848, and in consequence Hungarian works on natural law reflected the Austrian approach to the law. Nevertheless, even then the Protestant law academies (Eperjes, Debrecen, Sárospatak, Kecskemét) had teachers who taught the Kantian doctrines of the law of reason and expected the same from their students.

The 1830s saw the publication of the natural law works of Antal Virozsil (1792-1868), the first major Hungarian philosopher of law, whose works were at the level of European scholarship and were based on Kantian philosophy. Virozsil's successor and follower, Tivadar Pauler, was also an advocate of the broader Kantian school of philosophy and natural law. Ferenc Deák, who had a great influence on Hungarian public thinking and legislation, also 'nationalized' the concept of natural law, which he had learned so well at the law academy. He invoked natural law when, in 1836, he declared that the right of landlords over their serfs was a usurped power. He did not ask for the personal freedom of the serfs as a 'grace or a gift' but urged it as justice which 'cannot be denied without violating the lawful rights of mankind'. He also saw inheritance as a natural rule based on the 'ideal of love'. Likewise, Deák considered freedom of speech and freedom of thought to be 'natural rights'.[26]

The traditional legal philosophy of the early nineteenth century was also still based on István Werbőczy's *Tripartitum* (1517). The Prologue of the *Tripartitum* does indeed include a remarkable discussion of the relationship between justice, law and jurisprudence and according to his reasoning, justice should be the first among these. Werbőczy was also often quoted as saying that the sole purpose of the law was to achieve justice, and jurisprudence must serve the law and justice. Hungarian legal thinking also traced the doctrine of the Holy Crown back to Werbőczy, and this doctrine was an organic theory of the law and the state, according to which the nation was the source of all private and public law, including the rights of the sovereign. Even as late as the nineteenth century, Werbőczy's attribution of the force of law to customary law, and in a broader sense to the organic tradition, was of great significance in the Hungarian legal system and served as the foundation of its jurisprudence.

Imre Hajnik (1840-1902) is credited with laying the scholarly foundations of the doctrine of the Holy Crown. This doctrine had already been given theoretical form in the *Tripartitum*, but it was Hajnik who first elaborated it as a professional legal historian. He argued that the Holy Crown, as a Hungarian state concept, was a symbol of the public power shared between king and nation, that is, in constitutional law. Hajnik collected the scattered tenets of the doctrine of the Holy Crown and made them into an organic whole. According to this point of view, the territory of the country is the territory of the Holy Crown, because the crown is *radix omnium possessionum*, and all those who have a right to property on this territory become members of the crown (*membra S. regni Coronae*) and constitute the *populus Werbőcziánus*. Hajnik linked to these foundations the legislature (the king wearing the crown and its members making the law together) and the government. In his view, the Holy Crown was the capstone of the law and political life, since each part of the constitution was defined according to its relationship to the Holy Crown.[27]

Until 1848, Hungarian law, and its associated philosophy, regarded Werbőczy's *Tripartitum* as codified law legitimated by the force of tradition. That is why Hungary did not accept Roman law, and why speculations on natural law never gained significant traction in Hungarian jurisprudence. For centuries, Hungarian legal thought was more aligned with Werbőczy than with abstract philosophical speculations.[28] It is noticeable that even pro-reform politicians in Hungary also referred to his rules more frequently than they did to the latest philosophical trends.

Despite all this, Hungarian legal theory in the nineteenth century was not isolated from the world, and in many respects, absorbed French and especially English influences.[29] According to József Szabadfalvi, the process of Hungarian legal philosophy asserting its independence and its originality is as closely related as possible to the development of English law, which was regarded as a role model and exemplar, and that this was the yardstick for the critique of the existing socio-economic and political-legal conditions. The English model of social development and worldview was politically and ideologically dominated by liberalism and by positivism in its philosophical and academic understanding of society, the state and the law. Nevertheless, even those legal scholars and philosophers who advocated the imitation and adaptation of English jurisprudence were also able to critique English law, which is characteristic of the 'realistic', 'historicizing', autochthonous 'Hungarian worldview', which explicitly rejected metaphysics.[30] Hungarian legal philosophy was, undoubtedly, characterized by both a legal conservatism that clung to ancient law and an almost up-to-date absorption of modern European legal theories into Hungarian jurisprudence and legal education. This latter characteristic was certainly evident in the work of the most important Hungarian legal philosophers (Ignác Frank, Gusztáv Wenzel, Tivadar Pauler and Ágost Pulszky).

Trends in legal philosophy and ideological nuances

Natural law

In Hungary, natural law was one of the basic courses of law taught in the universities. Initially, it was taught as part of Roman law at the University of Nagyszombat, but under Maria Theresa it became a separate discipline. The core of the teaching of legal philosophy at this time was the theories of Hugo Grotius, as well as Hobbes, Leibniz, Thomasius, Locke and the rationalist natural law of Samuel Pufendorf and Christian Wolff, who built on the teachings of Ulrich Huber. The main advocate and mediator of these doctrines was Karl Anton Martini, whose works, written in Latin, were compulsory textbooks for Hungarian lawyers until the 1867 Settlement. In this mixed bag of natural law thinking, both the original principles of natural law and toned-down bourgeois aspirations were subordinated to the absolutist state and the will of the monarch. The natural law theories of the time, influenced by the Habsburg court, sought to provide the ruler with a qualified, professional bureaucratic apparatus that understood the needs of state power and served their will.[31]

From the beginning of the nineteenth century, Kant's philosophical insights (the school of reason) had, however, been growing in popularity. Antal Virozsil, the leading legal philosopher of the second third of the nineteenth century, who can be considered the first major Hungarian legal philosopher, was among the earliest to teach legal philosophy in the spirit of Kant's philosophy. Nevertheless, Virozsil's theory remained controversial; he took the Kantian idea of liberty as his starting point, but his conclusions included a number of accessions to the absolutist demands of the court in Vienna. He played a major role in laying the constitutional foundations of the imperial idea (Habsburg centralization) and its legitimation in Hungary. He was a conservative who remained open to reform, an advocate of modern constitutionality and the equality before the law, and a critic of Hungary's ancient constitution. As such, Virozsil was a strict judge of the privileges of the nobility and sympathized with Eötvös's work entitled *Reform*, which he considered the most outstanding work on the reform of the Hungarian constitution. By the middle of the century, Pál Hoffmann (1830-1907), a prominent Roman law jurist and member of the Parliament, had, however, produced works containing critiques of the doctrines of the law of reason in the spirit of the German historical school of law – as represented by Savigny and Puchta – which sought the main source of law in the 'national public spirit'.[32]

Tivadar Pauler, from the 1840s onwards, reflected both the possibility and the difficulty of finding a compromise between contemporary ideas and practical legislative needs. In his theoretical works, he sought to reconcile the foundations of the Kantian law of reason with the approach of the historical school of law, which emphasized historical and national traditions. His later forays into legal positivism also left their mark on the legislature, since as Kálmán Tisza's minister, he was involved in the legal reforms following the Settlement and in the gradual transformation of the judicial and legislative system. Unlike proponents of the historical school of law, he was an advocate of summary collection of laws and codification and played a major role in the creation of the code of substantive criminal law.

According to Gyula Moór (1888-1950), the older school of natural law, including the Aristotelian-Aquinian school, was generally content, with wise moderation, to establish only a few basic principles as requirements of natural law, while the modern school of natural law, known as the classical school, with the arrogance of the Enlightenment, which regarded human reason as the highest authority, produced vast codes of law. Its reign lasted until the beginning of the nineteenth century, 'when it was eclipsed by the onslaught of the school of legal history, which relied on the weapons of developmental, historical and organic understanding, opening the way for the sociological concepts and legal positivism that dominated in the second half of the nineteenth century'.[33]

The legal positivist approach

The Hungarian legal tradition associates the predominance of the positivist conception of law in Hungary with the work of Ágost Pulszky (1846-1901). Pulszky obtained his doctorate in 1872 with a dissertation entitled *Az angol jogbölcselet történetéhez* (The History of English Legal Philosophy), and in 1875 he translated, wrote an introduction to and annotated Henry Maine's famous work entitled *Ancient Law*. Subsequently, in 1888, he published, in English, his major work, *The Theory of Civil Law and Society* (first published in Hungarian in 1885), which was mainly a synthesis of the findings of English scientific positivism. In addition, he did much to promote the achievements of contemporary English philosophy and science in Hungary, for example through his critical exposition of Herbert Spencer's synthetic philosophy.[34]

Pulszky's conception of the state reflected the contradictions of legal thinking in the dualist era when Hungary enjoyed home rule within the Habsburg Empire. He reacted with excellent theoretical sense to the social, economic and political changes that had occurred at the end of the nineteenth century. He also identified the need for state involvement (etatism) in health care, economic development and the alleviation of widespread poverty. Clearly, perceiving the power of capitalist development, he foreshadowed the idea of the early welfare state as a transcendence of classical liberal ideas and drew attention to the nationalist antagonisms that would dismantle historic Hungary at the end of the First World War. His work had a significant impact on the social sciences, especially political science, political theory and sociology. From the 1880s onwards, his intense political involvement diverted his energies from the cultivation of scholarship and his life's work can be considered incomplete.[35]

The positivist approach reached its peak in Hungary at the turn of the century with the work of Gyula Pikler (1864-1937). He approached the workings of the state and the law from the perspective of sociology based on the natural sciences. He considered the philosophy of law to be a natural science and formulated the Hungarian paradigm of sociological positivism in the light of the English model. However, his first major work, *Ricardo. Jelentősége a közgazdaságtörténetében. Érték- és megoszlástana* (Ricardo. His Importance to the History of Economics. The Theory of Value and Distribution, 1885), reveals that Pikler was not simply imitating but critically assessing contemporary theories. In particular, Pikler treated the law as a social fact and developed his own theory of the origin and development of the state and the law. He believed that people do not act instinctively but on the basis of their 'sense of expediency' (the theory of discretion), and in the process created and developed norms and institutions that satisfied their needs ever more perfectly. People thus create a society, institutions and the law that they consider to be rational and expedient. The chief exponents of this sense of expediency, the first ones to recognize it, were the most distinguished members of society, the so-called educated classes. From the early 1910s onwards, Pikler became increasingly interested in the physiological and psychological causes behind social phenomena. As a result, he gradually shifted his focus away from the philosophy of law and the state and began conducting experiments in psychophysics and sensory physiology. He later published his results mainly in German and his influence in Hungary rapidly diminished.[36]

The neo-Kantian movement

The last decade of the long nineteenth century brought a significant change in both wider European and Hungarian approach to the philosophy of law. The rise of the neo-Kantian philosophy of law pushed traditional natural law and legal positivist approaches into the background. The historical approach also lost impetus. Jurisprudence sought new ways of interpreting law by exploring modern ideas and focusing on epistemological and methodological aspects. In Hungarian legal philosophy, this process was primarily expounded by Bódog Somló (1873-1920), whose oeuvre allowed Hungarian scholarship to catch up with developments elsewhere and to establish the pioneering neo-Kantian philosophy of law.

Somló is the best-known representative of Hungarian legal thinking internationally. His relatively short academic career, which lasted a quarter of a century, can be divided into two stages. An essay he wrote in 1910 entitled *A jog értékmérői* (The Yardsticks of Law) is considered to be the seminal work of the period. The first phase of his career was marked by the full acceptance and promotion of Spencer's doctrines, and was also influenced by Gyula Pikler's natural science and psychology-based theory of discretion, as well as partly by the materialist philosophy of history. The problems of naturalistic sociology were the focus of his interest. During this period Somló became the third most prominent representative of Hungarian positivist thinking, alongside Ágost Pulszky and Gyula Pikler. It was in the second period of his academic career that the neo-Kantian movement emerged, creating the most prosperous period of Hungarian thought on philosophy of law, which lasted until the middle of the twentieth century when Marxist legal theory came to dominate. While he had previously equated the philosophy of law with the sociology of law, he now separated the two fields of legal study, in line with the neo-Kantian approach. Somló's later work established his academic reputation as a legal philosopher in Hungary and especially in the German-speaking world. Moreover, Austro-Hungarian jurisprudence produced other neo-Kantians including Rudolf Stammler, Gustav Radbruch, Hans Kelsen and Alfred Verdross.

In Somló's works from around the turn of the century, he criticized the prevailing norms of scholarship of the time on the grounds of scientific positivism and evolutionism. His positivist theoretical stance was complemented by his radical public and academic work. His book *Állami beavatkozás és individualizmus* (State Intervention and Individualism), published in 1903, is one of his major works, while the increase in state involvement, as a concomitant of capitalist development, forced Somló to rethink the function and institutions of law, the state and politics. *Jogbölcseleti előadások* (Lectures on the Philosophy of Law), published in 1906, while retaining his earlier positivist viewpoint, was then developed in his later seminal work entitled *Juristische Grundlehre*. Distinguishing between the pure and the applied (normative) sciences, he focused on two sets of questions: (1) the definition of the preconditions (concept) of law (the basic doctrine of law), and (2) the search for the right law (the value doctrine of law). In fact, the neo-Kantian turning point – under the influence of Rudolf Stammler – had occurred during the debate on the question of the right law, culminating in his voluminous book *Juristische Grundlehre*, published in German in 1917. In his magnum opus, Somló produces an analytical analysis of the conceptual elements of the law, independent of its content, in accordance with the neo-Kantian conception of the time. His theory held that law appears as the imperative of the highest power (the legislature). The enthusiastic reception his work received encouraged him to develop his value doctrine of law with similar thoroughness. As a prerequisite for this, he began to develop an independent philosophical foundation (epistemological approach), which was only able to be published in fragmentary form as a posthumous work after his early death in 1926.[37]

In reviewing the most significant trends and authors of Hungarian philosophy of law, Gusztáv Wenzel's claim that in Hungarian intellectual life, academic controversies have never been as one-sided and sharp as in German literature appears accurate. The theory of natural law and the law of reason did not predominate in Hungary, because they were sufficiently tempered by Werbőczy's organic conception of the law which influenced the development of customary law. The sociological philosophy of law of the nineteenth century dominated Hungarian legal philosophy for barely thirty years, and its greatest representative, Ágost Pulszky, himself represented an idealistic approach.

Finally, even the neo-Kantianism of the twentieth century embodied by Bódog Somló was tempered by his sociological approach.

The legalist approach to the concept of law

Historians agree that the Hungarian political elite was traditionally legal education, and the typical way of speaking about politics was through legalistic argumentation, one of the central elements of which, throughout the long nineteenth century, was to reference the ancient constitutionality. Their admiration for customary law, ancient institutions and the letter – but most of all the spirit – of ancient laws became part of the national self-image. Astute wit and legalistic reasoning all appeared in their pamphlets, literary works and newspaper articles. As early as 1843, Lajos Kossuth wrote in an editorial that the Hungarians were an excessively 'legalistic nation' and not interested in more practical (e.g. economic) matters.[38] This insight did not, of course, prevent him from invoking the principles of ancient constitutionality or the theory of the affinity between English and Hungarian legal development when discussing contemporary political issues.[39] The same stereotype repeatedly appeared in descriptions of Hungarians. In advance of the 1867 Settlement, Francis Joseph I also spoke of the legal approach of Hungarians as a defining feature of their national character, declaring 'the Hungarian nation [. . .] is increasingly a legalistic nation, and Hungarians examine every political question exclusively from a legal point of view, and they also get caught up in subtle legal distinctions which make these issues so significant as would be unimaginable elsewhere'.[40]

István Széchenyi, one of the most influential politicians of the period, also understood the law as something that defined the individual and the entire nation. However, he did not mean codified (positive) law, which might be obsolete, unjust and inexpedient, but a right arising from the dignity of the human person, which led him to call for a reform of obsolete codified law. He was firmly convinced that codified law loses its value as soon as it becomes unjust, which inevitably happened when the circumstances that shaped its enaction had altered. He argued that every positive right is merely a means by which, as a result of historical development, fundamental rights can be realized.[41]

With this (socio-ethical) approach, Széchenyi departed from the traditional view which idealized codified law. In contrast, he argued that the permanent element of law is precisely its most essential content: the pursuit of justice. Accordingly, it is not only a possibility but also a moral duty to reform and improve codified (positive) law if it no longer fulfils its essential purpose of being just. Even the venerable patina of antiquity did not, in Széchenyi's eyes, excuse a legal institution that had become unjust.[42]

Sectoral jurisprudence and specialized legislation

Numerous prominent Hungarian jurists have at various times espoused contradictory approaches when examining the full extent of their writing. The basic methodological dilemma of comprehensive jurisprudential works has long remained unchanged: it is still difficult to choose between the chronological and synchronic approaches, while there are obvious risks in their joint application from a scholarly perspective.

In the two centuries under review, the practitioners of Hungarian sectoral jurisprudence were under a double intellectual pressure. On the one hand, they were influenced by politics as well as professional and social expectations to propose reforms. On the other hand, they faced the challenge of explaining the laws already in force, as well as having to explain foreign models and examining their practical applicability. In the works of the authors who fulfilled such demands, a backward-looking approach became commonplace, and the professional methodological approach was pushed into the background, while a historically authentic interpretation of concepts was often lacking and in many cases they focused on legitimizing existing power relations.

In undertaking a general overview of the state of jurisprudence, it should be borne in mind that this theoretical subfield was also (to a significant extent) characterized by a number of significant works by the greatest legal scholars. In addition, it is necessary to interpret these sources, to examine the circumstances in which they were created and to identify the specific legal intentions behind them. Only after this procedure has been followed can the internal structure of legal institutions be examined. This was the theoretical starting point which defined the method and system of the first histories of the law. The study of legal sources, which naturally preceded the history of legal institutions, invariably led back to Werbőczy.

The broad consensus of scholars of this period is that the development of Hungarian jurisprudence began with István Werbőczy's *Tripartitum*. In fact, Part II, Section 14, of the *Tripartitum* alone lists Hungary's most important laws, and briefly describes their content. This text can also be seen as the first attempt at a history of the sources of Hungarian law. Subsequent histories of the law in Hungary also began with the exploration of regulatory norms and the systematic exposition of legal norms.

There is no consensus in Hungarian jurisprudence as to which of the key works constitute the intellectual heritage of the eighteenth century. This is clear both from historical summaries of the various branches of law and from the few treatises on the history of jurisprudence. There is, of course, no need for a consensus to exist on this issue, if only because of the deep historical roots of Hungarian jurisprudence and the organic development of Hungary's legal system. The dividing lines between the different branches of law were also rather blurred in Hungary in the nineteenth century, with many legal scholars discussing both public and private law, others the contractual foundations of Hungarian public law, while the taxonomic position of criminal law was long debated. One source of this uncertainty was that for a long period of time, the approach used by the humanities and that used by jurisprudence drifted apart from each other and the two disciplines became separated. This is also clear from the way in which the list of early works in the field of jurisprudence was established.

According to Tivadar Pauler, Hungarian legal institutions 'are rooted in history, they originated and developed under the influence of the internal and external conditions of life of the nation, their spirit and nature can only be recognized through the weave of historical truth'.[43] This may explain why, for a long time, Hungarian jurisprudence was not only of academic value, but also played a strong practical role: it was often called upon to help in the drafting of laws and in the interpretation and application of legal norms. In this context, the historical perspective was an indispensable part of legal knowledge, and from the early Reform Era onwards it also became an important tool for the transformation of public law.

This practical bent is connected with the fact that several treatises and summaries were written on the general questions of Hungarian law, and on the origin and development of certain legal institutions.[44] It also explains why for a long time there was no comprehensive scholarly work on Hungarian law as a whole, with the authors of the time instead mainly producing summaries of private law, due to practical needs and the lack of resources. The situation was different in the field of public law: here the authorities had a strong influence, with a marked separation between the Hungarian and imperial approaches in the post-Mohács period, when the contrast between the pro-Habsburg and nationalist attitudes was particularly strong. Collecting historically relevant public law sources was also often difficult, due to their vast quantity, scattered nature and frequent inaccessibility.

The compromise in public law (the theoretical foundations of which were established by Ferenc Deák, Antal Virozsil and János Fogarasi) created by the Settlement also offered a substantial opportunity for the structural transformation of the Hungarian legal system. The significantly enlarged latitude for constitutional (state) law also raised the need for a nationally oriented reform of legal life and fostered the emergence of new theoretical trends. Practical legislation was also faced with tasks that were long overdue, so after 1867, the issue of codification returned to the agenda, which then became the subject of academic debates that reflected various political programmes. The legal historiography of the time was also inspired by the opportunity to evaluate Hungary's legal institutions in a non-political way and to objectively analyse the advantages and disadvantages of the common legal structures of Austro-Hungary.

Conclusion

For an assessment of the state of academic legal historiography in Hungary in the nineteenth century, an overview of the trends in Hungarian public history of the time can provide a good starting point, since the academic achievements of its legal scholars can be measured against this. Unlike the situation in legal studies, Hungarian historiography modernized rapidly in the decades before the First World War. Above all, it saw significant methodological innovation and a broadening of the range of topics of interest to professional historians. This can be explained in large part by the fact that the discipline was influenced by important external impulses, and European historical trends – then considered modern – gained ground in Hungarian historiography too. According to Péter Gunst, however, Hungarian historiography retained its tendency to follow certain patterns.[45] Hungarian historians were still not characterized by a purely theoretical interest in their subjects. A parallel can also be drawn between the contemporary situation of general history and that of the history of law in that the representatives of both fields were motivated by essentially practical considerations, the majority of them being untouched by contemporary European trends. Those authors (and especially the legal historians) who were associated with a particular school of thought invariably changed, or slowly abandoned, their initial orientation in the course of their career.

While the various Hungarian scholars of general history included followers of most of the leading European scientific and ideological trends, the intellectual palette of jurisprudence was much more modest. The Hungarian proponents of the scientific explanation of the law were almost exclusively German-Austrian in orientation, while historiography became more open to the French and English schools of science and ideology. Another important characteristic of the Hungarian jurisprudence of the period was the lack of intellectual schools, academic clusters and distinctive intellectual communities. Almost every European scientific movement of the time had followers in Hungary, but none of them developed into a group of conscious adherents with a firm intellectual basis. During this period, jurisprudence was instead defined by distinctive personalities and outstanding scholars such as Wenzel and Hajnik who changed their views from one creative period to another.

The intellectual trends that emerged in the field of jurisprudence during the Age of Dualism were model-oriented and adaptive. The adherents of the historical school, the proponents of legal positivism, nationalist historians and the Hungarian scholars of the dogmatic school did not go beyond the usual framework of these trends, and by universal standards they hardly produced any works of lasting value. Of course, the traditional Hungarian legal system, the excessive respect for the institutions of the past and the official demand for their authority to be legitimized – especially in the history of public law – which were characteristic of the period of the Settlement, also played a role in this.

Eminent representatives of the history of law stated that the development of the Hungarian constitution in the nineteenth century was organic, and that the country's state and legal life were shaped by continuous reforms. The law-making concept and legislative technique of the post-1848 years was the adoption of norms in a single package. The essence of this was for laws – which were related in content – to be adopted by Parliament together. For a long time, this procedure held back a systematic reform of the constitutional order.

The long nineteenth century lasted in the field of constitutional law and legal life – in the strict sense of the word – until the start of the First World War and the enactment of the Emergency Laws. These laws and lower-level legal norms adopted in the wake of Article LXIII of 1912 on exceptional powers formally interrupted the development of Hungarian laws that had been based until then on the forward-looking traditions of the past.

Notes

1 In this study, I consciously distinguish between constitutional and legal thinking, between historical constitutional law and legal history in the narrower sense. In the present review, I will consider the constitution to be a normative rule for the functioning of the state in the sense developed in the nineteenth century, which took the form of a historical or written source of law. By legal thinking in the narrower

sense, I mean the principles, ideas and practice of legislation and the application of the law.
2 Gergely András, 'Az 1867-es kiegyezés' [The Settlement of 1867], *Rubicon* 6, no. 1-2 (1996): 26-30. According to R. J. W. Evans, this public law relationship was closer and reminiscent of the Polish-Lithuanian union. R. J. W. Evans, *The Making of the Habsburg Monarchy, 1550–1700* (Oxford: Clarendon Press, 1979).
3 Marczali Henrik, *Magyarország története* [The History of Hungary] (Budapest: Athenaeum, 1911), 696.
4 Kulcsár Kálmán, 'Az alkotmányosság és a kontinuitás' [Constitutionality and Continuity], *Valóság* 34, no. 8 (1991): 8; Martyn Rady, 'Law and the Ancient Constitution in Medieval and Early Modern Hungary', in *A History of the Hungarian Constitution: Law, Government and Political Culture in Central Europe*, International Library of Historical Studies 20, ed. Ferenc Hörcher and Thomas Lorman (London–New York: I. B. Tauris, 2018), 29-33.
5 Beöthy Zsigmond, *Elemi magyar közjog* [Elementary Hungarian Public Law] (Pest: Emich Gusztáv, 1846), 7-10; Andrássy Gyula, *A magyar állam fönmaradásának és alkotmányos szabadságának okai* [The Reasons for the Independence and Constitutional Freedom of the Hungarian State] (Budapest: Franklin-Társulat, 1901), 1:155.
6 Toldy Ferenc, ed., *A magyar birodalom alaptörvényei* [The Fundamental Laws of the Hungarian Empire] (Buda: Magyar Királyi Egyetem, 1861), vi.
7 Pauler Tivadar, *Jog és államtudományok encyclopaediája* [Encyclopaedia of Law and Political Sciences] (Pest: Emich Gusztáv, 1862), 105.
8 *Magyar Jogi Lexikon* [Encyclopaedia of Hungarian Law], ed. Márkus Dezső (Budapest: Pallas, 1898), 1:182; Nagy Ernő, *Magyarország közjoga: Államjog* [Public Law of Hungary: State Law] (Budapest: Athenaeum, 1907), 12.
9 Horváth János, 'Az alap-vagy sarkalatos törvények fogalma és helyzete a magyar közjogban' [The Concept and Position of Basic or Cardinal Laws in Hungarian Public Law], *A jog*, 26, no. 40 (1907): 288.
10 Stipta István, 'A 19. századi angol közigazgatási jogvédelem és a magyar közigazgatási bíráskodás' [19th-century English Administrative Legal Protection and Hungarian Administrative Jurisprudence], in *Emlékkönyv Dr. Ruszoly József egyetemi tanár 70. születésnapjára*, ed. Balogh Elemér and Homoki-Nagy Mária (Szeged: Szegedi Tudományegyetem Állam- és Jogtudományi Kar, 2010), 793-810.
11 *Magyar Jogi Lexikon*, 1:182.
12 Suhayda János, *Magyarország közjoga, tekintettel annak történeti kifejlődésére és az 1848-ki törvényekre* [The Public Law of Hungary, in View of Its Historical Development and the Laws of 1848] (Pest: Emich Gusztáv, 1861), 7; Pomogyi László, *Magyar alkotmány- és jogtörténeti kéziszótár* [Dictionary of Hungarian Constitutional and Legal History] (Budapest: M-Érték, 2008), 24-5.
13 Toldy Ferenc, *A magyar birodalom sarkalatos törvényei* [The Cardinal Laws of the Hungarian Empire] (Pest: Emich Gusztáv, 1866)
14 *Magyar Jogi Lexikon*, 1:206.
15 Karvasy Ágost, *Alkotmányi és igazságügyi politika* [Constitutional and Judicial Policy] (Pest: Emich Gusztáv, 1862), 61; Eötvös József, 'Mi teszi megyei rendszerünket az alkotmány' biztositékává?' [What Makes Our County System a Guarantee of the Constitution?], *Pesti Hirlap*, 9 September 1845.
16 Tisza Kálmán, *Parlamenti felelős kormány és megyei rendszer* [Parliamentary Accountable Government and County System] (Pest: Ráth Mór, 1865), 64; Stipta

István, 'Kossuth Lajos 1859-es alkotmánykoncepciója' [The 1859 Constitutional Concept of Lajos Kossuth], *Jogtudományi Közlöny* 50, no. 1 (January 1995): 49–53.

17 Egyed István, 'A közigazgatás, mint alkotmánybiztosíték' [Public Administration as a Constitutional Safeguard], *Jogtudományi Közlöny* 59, no. 4. (1914): 35–36; Csekey István, *Közigazgatási reform és alkotmánybiztosíték* [Administrative Reform and Constitutional Guarantees] (Budapest: Pesti Könyvnyomda, 1914).

18 Stipta István, *A magyar jogtörténet-tudomány kétszáz éve* [Two Hundred Years of Hungarian Legal History], A Pólay Elemér Alapítvány Könyvtára 57 (Szeged: Pólay Elemér Alapítvány, 2015), 54–5.

19 Deák Ferenc, *Adalék a magyar közjoghoz* [Addendum to Hungarian Public Law] (Pest: Pfeifer Ferdinánd, 1865), 88–9.

20 Schvarcz Gyula, 'Alkotmány II' [Constitution II], in *Magyar Jogi Lexikon*, 1:208.

21 Apponyi Albert, *Magyar közjog osztrák megvilágításban* [Hungarian Public Law in Austrian Light] (Budapest: Franklin-Társulat, 1912), 68.

22 Csillag Gyula, *A régi magyar alkotmány és az 1848-ki és 1867-ki évek közjogi alkotásai* [The Old Hungarian Constitution and the Public Law Acts of 1848 and 1867] (Pest: Athenaeum, 1871), 8.

23 Emmer Kornél, 'A régi magyar alkotmány és az 1848.-i és 1867.-i évek közjogi alkotásai'. Irta: Csillagh Gyula, Pest, 1871' ['The Old Hungarian Constitution and the Public Law Acts of 1848 and 1867'. Written by Gyula Csillag, Pest, 1871] *Jogtudományi Közlöny* 6, no. 49 (1871): 378–80.

24 Egyed, 'A közigazgatás, mint alkotmánybiztosíték', 185.

25 Cs. Kiss Lajos, 'Az angol társadalom- és jogelmélet a magyar jogfilozófiai hagyományban' [English Social and Legal Theory in the Hungarian Legal Philosophical Tradition] *Világosság* 43, no. 10–12 (August–December 2002): 108.

26 *Deák Ferencz beszédei* [Speeches by Ferenc Deák], ed. Kónyi Manó (Budapest: Franklin-Társulat, 1903), 1:16, 33.

27 Hajnik Imre, *Magyar alkotmány-és jogtörténelem: Első füzet; Bevezetés a magyar alkotmány- és jogtörténelembe* [Hungarian Constitutional and Legal History: Booklet 1; Introduction to the Hungarian Constitutional and Legal History] (Pest: Heckenast Gusztáv, 1869), 38.

28 Moór Gyula, *A jogbölcselet problémái* [Problems in the Philosophy of Law], Kincsestár 80 (Budapest: Magyar Szemle Társaság, 1945), 42.

29 Concha Győző, 'Egyéni szabadság és parlamentarizmus Angliában' [Individual Freedom and Parliamentarianism in England], in *Értekezések a társadalmi tudományok köréből*, vol. 9, no. 8 (Budapest: MTA, 1888).

30 Cs. Kiss Lajos, 'Bevezető' [Introduction], *Világosság* 43, no. 10–12 (August–December 2002): 82–3.

31 Szabadfalvi József, 'Megújulás és tradíció: A magyar jogbölcseleti tradíció szerepe a jogi gondolkodás megújításában' [Transition and Tradition. Can Hungarian Traditions of Legal Philosophy Contribute to Legal Transition?] *Világosság* 40, no. 5 (January–June 1999): 56.

32 Szabadfalvi József, *Jogbölcseleti hagyományok* [Traditions in Legal Philosophy] (Debrecen: Multiplex Media–Debrecen University Press, 1999), 244.

33 Moór Gyula, 'A természetjog problémája' [The Problem of Natural Law], in *Értekezések a Filozófiai és Társadalmi Tudományok Köréből*, vol. 4, no. 10 (Budapest: MTA, 1934), 4.

34 Cs. Kiss, 'Bevezető', 82–3; Szabadfalvi József, 'Angolszász hatások a magyar jogbölcseleti gondolkodásban' [Anglo-Saxon Influences in Hungarian Legal

Philosophical Thinking], *Collectio Iuridica Universitatis Debreceniensis,* vol. 2 (Debrecen: Multiplex Media–Debrecen U. P., 2002), 123–55, 133.

35 Szabadfalvi József, 'Transition and Tradition: Can Hungarian Traditions of Legal Philosophy Contribute to Legal Transition?' *Rechtstheorie,* Beiheft 20 (1999): 1–19; Nagy Endre, 'Pulszky Ágost társadalom- és államtana' [The Social and Political Theory of Ágost Pulszky], *Szociológia,* no. 2 (1977): 209–10.
36 Szabadfalvi, 'Transition and Tradition. . .', 1–19; Cs. Kiss, 'Bevezető', 82–3.
37 Szabadfalvi, *Jogbölcseleti hagyományok,* 244.
38 Kossuth Lajos, 'Magyarország és Erdély' [Hungary and Transylvania], *Pesti Hirlap,* 16 March 1843.
39 Regarding the discourse of ancient constitutionality present in Hungarian political life since the eighteenth century, see Takáts József, *Ismerős idegen terep* [Familiar Foreign Terrain] (Budapest: Kijárat, 2007), 171–201, 175–83.
40 Letter from Robert Morier, Secretary of the British Embassy in Vienna, to Lord Bloomfield, about his conversation with Francis Joseph, 4 February 1866.
41 Pauler Ákos, 'Széchenyi társadalmi erkölcstana' [Széchenyi's Social Ethics], in *Széchenyi eszmevilága,* Kultura és tudomány, ed. Gaal Jenő et al. (Budapest: Franklin-Társulat, 1914), 2:75.
42 Horkay Hörcher Ferenc, 'Ahol a politikai és a gazdasági eszmetörténet metszi az irodalomtörténetet: A *Hitel* tudományközi kontextusai' [Where Political and Economic History of Ideas Intersect the History of Literature: The Interdisciplinary Contexts of *Hitel*], in *Jólét és erény: Tanulmányok Széchenyi István Hitel című művéről,* Hagyományfrissítés 2, ed. Fórizs Gergely (Budapest: Reciti, 2014), 14.
43 Pauler Tivadar, 'Bartal György jogtörténeti commentárjai: Első cikk' [Legal Historical Commentaries by György Bartal: First Article], *Új Magyar Muzeum* 8, no. 2 (February 1858): 65.
44 István Stipta, 'The Main Tendencies of Hungarian Legal Historiography in the 20th Century and Its Present Situation', *Journal on European History of Law* 2, no. 1 (2011): 72–9.
45 Gunst Péter, *A magyar történetírás története* [The History of Hungarian Historiography] (Debrecen: Csokonai Kiadó, 2000), 241.

4

Non-Hungarian political thought in the context of ethnic conflicts in nineteenth-century Hungary

József Demmel

One of the most important characteristics of Hungary in the eighteenth and nineteenth centuries, and one which also led to the dismantling of the country in the twentieth century, was its multi-ethnicity and multilingualism, as in addition to the Hungarians there were dozens of other nationalities living in the country. Ethnic relations were largely shaped by the Turkish occupation in the sixteenth and seventeenth centuries, which resulted in the depopulation of significant areas in the south of the country, and by the resettlement of these regions after the expulsion of the Turks by a significant German and Slavic population.[1] Thus, by the eighteenth century, the multi-ethnic nature of Hungary had been formed that would endure until 1918.[2]

In addition to the majority of Hungarians living in the interior of the country, the northern, mountainous areas were predominantly inhabited by Slovaks, while in the east, in Transylvania and its peripheral areas, the majority was Romanian. Between these two large ethnic groups, in the northeast, were the Rusyns (Ruthenes). In the south there were mainly Serbs, in the south-west in Croatia and in the bordering Hungarian counties Croats, and north of them Slovenes. The urban population was also enriched by Germans and a growing Jewish population, while there were also significant Romani, Armenian and Greek minorities in the country.

In terms of political thought in the nineteenth century, the most important question in relation to these ethnic groups was linked to the modern idea of nationalism. The critical question was whether there was an elite group among the speakers of a given language that envisioned its mother tongue community as an independent nation and whether this group had ambitions that in the eyes of the Hungarian elite threatened the integrity of the country (its recognition as an independent nation, collective rights, autonomy, the creation of an independent state or a union with one of Hungary's neighbouring states). In consequence, I have divided Hungary's non-Hungarian nationalities according to their aspiration to achieve collective rights (the existence/non-existence of statehood, the idea of creating an independent state or joining an existing state, or the lack thereof). I will first look at the nationality which already had an autonomous statehood (Croats), then at the nationalities without nation-state traditions but which gravitated towards an existing nation-state (Serbs, Romanians), then at the nationalities which did not enjoy the support of an external nation-state but which relied on certain (ecclesiastical or county) autonomy traditions, perhaps aspiring to cultural or territorial autonomy or seeking external support (Slovaks, Rusyns, Slovenes), and then at the nationalities which emphasized cultural ties with the communities of the same mother tongue beyond the borders to a greater or lesser extent but which did not pursue political goals as a nation in their own right within Hungary (Germans, Gypsies, Armenians, Greeks and Jews). Before examining these ethnic groups individually, however, it is worth considering the broader intellectual context that influenced the political activity of non-Hungarian nationalities in the nineteenth century.

The framework

Hungarus patriotism

Up until the first decades of the nineteenth century, the non-Hungarian-speaking inhabitants of Hungary were characterized by an early form of civic nationalism, known as *Hungarus* patriotism: a cultural identity that was loyal to the kingdom, not to the mother tongue, while on the local level speaking the same language was the basic determining factor in their sense of community and belonging. In the eighteenth century, the majority of non-Hungarians (with the exception of the Croats, who had independent statehood) had not yet formed separate national societies, delimited on the basis of language and in sharp contrast to speakers of other languages. Religious affiliation or the estate one belonged to were more dominant dividing lines than linguistic difference – and within these groups, rivalry between representatives of different linguistic groups was rare. [3]

Plural identity constructs

Other important factors were multilingualism and multiple ethnic identities, which were certainly part of everyday life for the masses until the middle of the nineteenth century. The language one spoke often depended as much on the context, the situation, the medium and the network in which it was expressed, as on the identity or linguistic characteristics of the speaker. For example, for a Lutheran citizen of a town in Upper Hungary in the early 1840s, it was still normal for him to go out into the street and speak German and Slovak to his friends, with whom he would listen to a Czech language service in church, but at the church assembly he would speak Latin, and then when he met the same people at the county assembly, he would naturally speak Hungarian, the increasingly widespread language of politics. Another telling example is Lajos Kossuth, whose Hungarian identity is beyond doubt, but whose close relatives, notably his uncles and cousins who remained in Turóc County, still spoke mainly Slovak during family meetings, and the minutes of these meetings, held in connection with the settlement of common estates, were kept in Latin to a small extent, but mostly in Slovakized Czech.⁴ This also meant that the national community to which one belonged was not a self-evident *gift*, clearly linked to the mother tongue, but rather an individual *decision*, dependent on a number of factors, changing over time and heavily influenced by the social context, and not necessarily dependent only on the language (i.e. the mother tongue) that one learned for the first time in one's life.

The persons taking part in politics and political thinking

The fact that, in a practical sense, the nobility had a virtual monopoly in politics until 1848 had a serious impact on the political thinking and actions of the non-Hungarian nationalities. Although there were German-, Slovak- and Romanian-speaking members of the nobility and German-, Serbian-, Rusyn- or Slovene-speaking intellectuals, in fact, there was often a lack of political actors in the national minority movements who were familiar with and experienced in county and national politics and the everyday practice of public life.⁵ In many cases, this lack of practice was reflected in both their political thinking and political action. For a long time, those who contributed to the political thought of the nationalist movements were mainly drawn from the ranks of clergymen who tended towards abstract thinking, and although they gradually began to include people with greater everyday experience such as lawyers, engineers and doctors, these people also had serious difficulty translating their aspirations into the language of political action, that is, from the world of symbolic gestures to the world of actually achievable results.

Religions, ethnic groups, nations

In addition to the lack of practical experience in politics, the political thinking of the various nationalities was also determined by religion. It can be clearly observed that within the individual nationalities, one's denominational affiliation also influenced a person's attitude towards Hungarians, the state and the nationality question. Typically, a Slovenian Catholic and a Slovenian Lutheran, or a Slovak Catholic and a Slovak Lutheran, or a Romanian Greek Catholic and a Romanian Orthodox had different thoughts on these issues. The picture is further complicated by the fact that the different nationalities within the same religion did not share the same views – for example, among the Slovenes, the Catholics held a self-conscious national idea while Lutherans were for reconciliation with the Hungarians, while among the Slovaks, Catholics tended to search for compromise, whereas Lutherans strived for radical national goals. However, the fact is that in almost all cases (in terms of personnel, organization, infrastructure, networks and political representation) church society was an important source of support for national movements, and it was typical that both types of identity (religious and national) mutually reinforced each other and the internal cohesion of these fractured ethnic identities.

Political alternatives

The political actors of most of the national and ethnic groups ranged across a relatively broad spectrum in terms of their political visions, from those who advocated the acceleration of assimilation to those who called for complete separation from the Hungarians and independence from Hungary. However, there were many individual paths between these two extremes: many people drifted to one side or the other more than once in their lives, while there were also those who actively and generously supported a particular national movement in the cultural sphere, but who in an official or political capacity demonstratively persecuted the very same people. Typically, however, three types can be distinguished for almost all the nationalities: those who were loyal and committed to the economic, social and political reforms initiated by the Hungarian political elite and thus also to Hungarianization; the intellectuals who accepted the laws, the constitutional order and the Hungarian political system as a framework, but who also stood up for their own linguistic and cultural rights; and finally the zealots who rejected the existing order and sought to change it (mostly with the help of external powers). This threefold division was typical only until the mid-1870s, as after the spectacular success of Hungarian politics in securing the 1867 Settlement it became clear that the group seeking an intermediate solution could no longer operate, while the zealot nationalists had considerably less room for manoeuvre.

Croats

At the beginning of the nineteenth century, the number of Croats in Hungary was estimated at 900,000, who not only lived in a geographically distinct society but also had their own political institutions and were integrated into the state-political structure of Hungary as a legally recognized nation. For example, the representatives of the provincial assembly, the Sabor, also participated in the sessions of the Diet in Pozsony (today Bratislava, Slovakia).

An important factor in the awakening of Croatian national consciousness was Napoleon's unification of the conquered Croatian and Slovenian territories as French provinces in 1809, under the name of the Illyrian provinces, which established religious and civil equality, as well as making Serbo-Croat a medium of instruction in primary and secondary schools. The Croatian national movement began to emerge in the 1830s, led by politically active nobles and the intelligentsia of noble origin, as well as the Catholic clergy and the growing merchant class including the urban bourgeoisie. A key figure of this period was Count Janko Drašković, who called for the development of the Croatian language and culture and founded several national institutions (the National Museum, the Matica Hrvatska) in his palace in Zagreb. Drašković's work was continued by the bourgeois intellectual Ljudevit Gaj, who argued for the creation of a Croatian literary language, using the dialect closest to Serbian and Bosnian as its basis. The theory of Illyrianism is also associated with him, according to which the South Slavs, descended from the ancient Illyrian people, form a single nation, which must be reunited through first cultural, and eventually political, unification of the Croatian, Serbian, Slovenian and Bulgarian nations.

In the 1840s, Gaj's Illyrian movement organized itself into a political party, which put forward moderate liberal demands for reform (e.g. the emancipation of serfs), and called for the introduction of Croatian as an official language. Representatives of the movement spoke in Latin instead of Hungarian at the sessions of the Hungarian Parliament and adopted a more confrontational attitude towards their fellow deputies from Hungary as well as the Hungarian-friendly Croatian party, which had the support of some of the largest landowners as well as the 'noble peasant community' of Túrmező (today Turopolje, Croatia).[6]

In the spring of 1848, the unification of Dalmatia, Croatia and Slavonia as the new Triune Kingdom and the right to communicate with the Hungarian authorities in the Croatian language were the two most important Croatian national goals. In 1848, the imperial military officer Josip Jellačić, who had been appointed Ban of Croatia, occupied Fiume (today Rijeka, Croatia) and Muraköz (today Međimurje, Croatia), and clashed militarily with the revolutionary Hungarian government. From 1849, the so-called 'left wing' of the Croatian national movement sought a reconciliation with the Hungarians, but no real cooperation took place.[7] From the 1860s onwards, the People's Liberal Party, led by Bishop Josip Juraj Strossmayer, became the leading political force among Croatian intellectuals, who sought to create an autonomous South Slav state within the framework of the Habsburg Monarchy, which they felt should be reorganized on a federal basis. The other main force opposing them was the Party of Rights, led by Ante Starčević and Eugen Kvaternik, whose main objective was to break away from the Habsburgs and to link Croatia to Hungary only by a personal union, which would make it fully independent in all other respects. The third movement was the Unionist Party, which sought to maintain the traditional constitutional relationship with Hungary. In the spring of 1867, as the negotiations that would result in the Austro-Hungarian Settlement progressed, the emperor ordered the Sabor to reconcile with the Hungarians. When it refused to do so, he dissolved it and appointed the Hungarophile Baron Levin Rauch as the acting Ban. Baron Rauch achieved a landslide victory for the Unionists in the elections by administratively changing the relations with the press and expanding the franchises (so that the peasantry who supported the Unionist Party could also vote).[8] On 25 June 1868, the newly constituted Sabor accepted the Croatian-Hungarian Settlement, according to which Croatia-Slavonia became a member state of the Lands of the Crown of Saint Stephen, and within it a political nation with its own territory, with its own government headed by the Ban, who was formally appointed by the monarch but in reality nominated by the government of Budapest. Croatian became the official language of the internal administration and Hungarian and Croatian flags were given equal prominence outside official buildings.

Romanians

In the 1830s, Romanians were the second most populous ethnic group in the kingdom after the Hungarians. According to official statistics, some 2.2 million Romanians lived within the country's borders. This nationality constituted the majority of the population in Transylvania, in the eastern part of Banat, in the Partium on the edge of the Hungarian Great Plain and in the counties of Temes, Krassó and Arad. The majority were desperately poor peasants, but there was also a significant strata of prosperous landowners.[9] Moreover, in the Transylvanian Saxon towns, there was a steadily increasing Romanian presence, as well as thousands of Romanian-speaking nobles who could be considered part of the *Natio Hungarica*, the Hungarian noble nation, only some of whom chose the path of Hungarianization in order to preserve or even raise their social status. Some of the wealthier boyar noble families also remained receptive to Romanian national aspirations.[10]

In contrast to the Romanian principalities, Moldavia and Wallachia, that had been liberated from Turkish rule, and the United Principalities, where the processes of state- and nation-building overlapped, in Hungary the Romanian national project was pursued by a non-dominant ethnic group, and thus the primary framework of Romanian political thought in Hungary was for a long time exclusively situated on the local level, in Transylvania. The most important intellectual innovation of the eighteenth century was the establishment, legitimization and dissemination of the Daco-Roman theory. The central claim of the Daco-Roman theory was that the Romanians were the original inhabitants of Transylvania as they were, prior to the Hungarian conquest, the descendents of Roman soldiers who had driven out the Dacians.

The creation of this origin myth of the Romanians is closely linked to the establishment of the Greek Catholic Church. After the expulsion of the Turks, the Habsburgs attempted to strengthen Catholicism in Transylvania, which was ruled at the time by Protestants. As a violent campaign of re-Catholicization had proved ineffective, Leopold I resorted to other means. This resulted in a plan to found the Greek Catholic Church in Transylvania. By granting exemption from serfdom for the Orthodox clergy, the monarch gave them not only financial benefits but also a new status. Along with this sudden social mobilization, however, a new, tense relationship emerged between the new Greek Catholic intellectual elite and the broader populace. In such circumstances, a common ancient ancestry, traced back to the glorious Roman legionaries, proved to be a reference point that was able to re-establish a community embracing both the wider population and the new clerical elite.[11] It is no coincidence, then, that the most important proponents of the Daco-Roman theory were mostly Greek Catholic priests and monks such as Samuil Micu-Klein, Petru Maior and Gheorghe Șincai.[12]

The most important political action related to the Daco-Roman theory was the petition known as the *Supplex Libellus Valachorum*, which was presented to the monarch in 1791. Invoking, among other things, the presumed Roman-Romanian continuity, they demanded that the Romanians be recognized as politically equal to the three governing Transylvanian estates, the Hungarians, the Szeklers – a branch of the Hungarians – and the Saxons. Among their requests were that the Romanian majority in Transylvania should be able to hold office in proportion to its numbers, that it should be able to participate in the work of the Diet and that the Romanian language should be allowed to be used in Romanian-majority areas. The monarch forwarded the requests to the Transylvanian Diet, which promptly rejected them.[13]

Two of the emblematic figures of the Transylvanian Romanian movement in the first half of the nineteenth century, George Bariț and Timotei Cipariu, who also came from the new Greek Catholic ecclesiastical elite, broadened the scope of the nationalist movement. Bariț was primarily a journalist, having founded the first Romanian newspaper in Transylvania, the *Gazeta de Transilvania*, but he also spread his ideas as a teacher at the Lyceum in Balázsfalva (today Blaj, Romania). Cipariu elaborated the first comprehensive grammar of the Latinist school, published the first Romanian church book in Latin letters in 1835 and persuaded the Transylvanian Greek Catholic Church to convert to the new writing system. The spread and initial standardization of the Latin alphabet, and the popular press based on it, became decisive factors in the national mobilization of the Romanians by the mid-nineteenth century.[14]

In March 1848, under the influence of the Hungarian revolution, the Romanian intelligentsia in Transylvania also voiced their nationalist demands. The appeals made by Simion Bărnuțiu in Nagyszeben (today Sibiu, Romania) and by Ioan Buteanu, Florian Micaș and Ioan Suciu in Kolozsvár (today Cluj Napoca, Romania) broadly reiterated the demands of the *Supplex*: invoking the ancient Roman origins of the Romanians as a basis for legitimacy, they called for the recognition of the Romanian nation as the fourth political nation, and for the use of the Romanian language in public administration and schools.[15] In mid-May, at a demonstration in Balázsfalva, these national demands received popular endorsement, and were supplemented by the demand for the immediate emancipation of the serfs without compensation for the nobility, a more radical measure than the April Laws.[16] The keynote speaker, Bărnuțiu, explained that if their demands were rejected, there would be no point in joining forces with the Hungarians.[17] By the beginning of autumn, events had escalated into a regional civil war in which thousands of people lost their lives.[18]

The re-establishment of parliamentarism in Hungary in the 1860s created a new situation. On the one hand, thanks to the electoral laws of 1848, many constituencies in Transylvania sent Romanian representatives to the National Assembly on behalf of the 'National Party of Romanians in Hungary'. (In contrast, the other Romanian party, the 'National Party of Romanians in Transylvania', chose a strategy of passivity and did not participate in the parliamentary elections.[19]) On the other hand, the political movement of the Romanians in Transylvania was also influenced by events across the border when the unification of the two Romanian principalities occurred in 1859, which created an autonomous Romanian nation-state within the Ottoman Empire, that became fully independent only in 1877. In the wake of these changes, three competing concepts of homeland emerged among the Romanians in dualist Hungary. One position, the most open to cooperation with the Hungarians, considered Transylvania to be the dominant political and administrative framework. The other saw the future of Romania within the framework of a reformed, federalized Habsburg Empire. The third concept, which appeared the furthest from reality up until 1918, but which was the one which was finally realized, envisaged the unification of the Romanian-inhabited territories of Hungary with the Kingdom of Romania.[20]

Serbs

The majority of the approximately 1.25 million Serbs in Hungary by the 1830s were uniformly Eastern Orthodox, made up largely of free 'soldier-settlers' and, in some towns, a significant number of Serbian merchants. This social structure was an important factor in the awakening of national consciousness, since border guards often played a role in leading the Serbian national movement, while the masses of peasants living on the so-called Military Frontier (which formed the south-eastern borderlands of the Habsburg Monarchy) gave extra weight to their demands.

The leading Serbian cultural figures came from the ranks of the wealthier landowners and the ecclesiastical intelligentsia, since the Greek Orthodox Church enjoyed considerable wealth, privileges and autonomy. At their congress in Temesvár (today Timişoara, Romania) in 1791, they demanded territorial autonomy and a central government body, as well as the right to retain their civil liberties and not to be serfs in the territories under Hungarian rule. Most of these demands were met (except for territorial autonomy) and the Orthodox Church became an established religion, with Serbian bishops invited to the Upper House of the Hungarian Diet.

These privileges meant, for example, that the majority of Serbs were not subject to Hungarian-language laws, and thus the spiral of public conflict with the Hungarian political elite, that Croats and Slovaks fell into, was avoided. Nevertheless, Josip Rajačić, who was elected metropolitan at the Karlóca (today Sremski Karlovci, Serbia) National Congress in 1842, energetically represented Serbian national interests at the Pozsony Diet, while in the 1840s, the idea of uniting the South Slavic peoples was also raised – under Serbian leadership, of course, with Belgrade as the centre.

Since in the eighteenth century the Serbian intelligentsia had used an Old Slavonic ecclesiastical language that was barely understood by the common people, the Serbian language reform was of great significance. In the process, Vuk Štefanović Karadžić elevated the Shtokavian dialect of Serbian into a literary language, which by the 1840s had become widespread. The Serbian student societies in Pozsony, Pest and Szeged played a major role in this. Pest-Buda was the most important Serbian cultural centre in Hungary, as almost all the important Serbian books of the time were printed there (300 titles in four decades). The first Serbian scientific and literary journal and the first political newspaper were also published there, and the *Matica Srpska* was founded in Pest-Buda.[21]

In 1848, the Serbs of Pest-Buda and Újvidék (today Novi Sad, Serbia) also prepared a petition: in addition to the recognition of Hungarian nationality and the official Hungarian language, they demanded the recognition and free use of the mother tongue of the Serbs, the holding of a national assembly and autonomy, albeit this final demand was not precisely formulated. Although these petitions sought to obtain the confidence of the Hungarian side, political negotiations in Pozsony failed, and by mid-April the demand for the creation of an independent Serbian Vojvodina was announced. In mid-May, at the Serbian National Assembly in Karlóca, the delegates called on the Serbian population to take up arms, and soon afterwards they also formed an alliance with the anti-Hungarian Croatian Ban, Josip Jellašić. By June, the situation had escalated into a military conflict. The army, estimated at 30,000 soldiers, made up of peasants and thousands of volunteers from Serbia, constituted a considerable force, and it took months to suppress the uprising. As in Transylvania, the civilian population suffered atrocities during the fighting.[22]

After 1849, the region was known as Serbian Vojvodina and the Banat of Temes, which functioned as an Austrian province until 1860. After 1867, it was re-incorporated into the Hungarian state, and shortly afterwards the Military Frontier ceased to be a separate regional entity. By 1867, Serbia had gained independence from the Ottoman Empire and was officially recognized as an independent country in 1878, providing additional support for the Serbian nationalist movement in Hungary.

Slovaks

Apart from the Hungarians, the only other nationality whose population lived exclusively within the borders of Hungary was the Slovaks. They constituted the majority of the population in the northern counties and in addition to the peasantry, the vast majority of the nobles in these counties were also Slovak-speaking.

The basic elements of Slovak community identity were already in place by the end of the eighteenth century. A Slovak literary language existed, with its own grammar and dictionary,[23] but it was only used by a part of the Slovak-speaking Catholic clergy.[24] Among the Lutheran Slovaks, who made up about a fifth of the Slovak-speaking population, the so-called Bibličtina, or (Slovakized) Czech language of the Kralice Bible, was the predominant language among the intelligentsia.

Catholic clergymen and monks first formulated ideas about the common history of the Slovak-speaking people.[25] The aim of these amateur historians was not to create a modern national identity, but rather to improve and protect the position of Slovak native speakers within Hungary that also fully embodied *Hungarus* patriotism.[26]

In the 1820s, Lutheran scholars crossed these boundaries. The gap between the history of the medieval Moravians and that of the nineteenth-century Slovaks was filled with a clever rhetorical device ('one thousand years of slavery'). According to the theory associated with Pavel Jozef Šafárik, after the Hungarian conquest of the Carpathian Basin and the fall of the Great Moravian Empire, the Slavic people of the Carpathian Basin fell into 'Hungarian captivity' and entered 'a thousand-year sleep' from which they had to be awakened.[27] Thanks to Ján Kollár's literary work, the basic elements of symbolic Slovak nationalism were also created at this time: the Tatras became the 'most Slovak' landscape (with a topographical interpretation and a serious emotional meaning) and Slavic history, 'Slavic heaven' and 'Slavic hell' were also 'populated'.[28] He also defined the Slovak national characteristics (religiousness, industriousness, innocent cheerfulness, gentleness, love of the mother tongue).[29] Through the idea of Slavic reciprocity, Kollár also created a political concept in a literary guise, according to which the Slavs form a single tribe with four dialects – Russian, Polish, Illyrian and Czech – and the smaller Slavic peoples must use the dialect closest to them.[30]

In the 1830s, Kollár's vision was reinforced by even more overtly political texts. Samuel Hoič, a Lutheran chaplain in Zólyom County, in a pamphlet entitled *Sollen wir Magyaren werden* (Should we become Hungarians), criticized the 1830 law which made Hungarian-language skills a condition for holding public office. The text, published under a pseudonym, had huge resonance, and it was even suggested in the Diet that the author should go on trial for high treason.[31]

The new generation that emerged in the late 1830s and early 1840s, particularly the movement led by Ľudovít Štúr which was initially composed primarily of Lutheran youth, also took Kollár's theory of reciprocity (i.e. small nations should unite with their larger relatives) as its starting point, but in the early 1840s, they realized that they could only integrate the masses of Slovak native speakers by raising their own language to the level of a literary language. By taking this step, raising the Central Slovak dialect spoken in Liptó and Turóc counties to a literary and public language, they took a giant stride towards a modern Slovak national community. The publication of the first Slovak-language political newspaper in 1845 provided the language and the Slovak national idea with a suitable platform, one which successfully transcended the earlier confessional and class differences. Štúr's movement was now backed not only by the young Lutheran elite of the region, but also by the Catholic intelligentsia, and for a time even managed to win over the nobility, led by Juraj Kossuth, the uncle of Lajos Kossuth.[32]

In 1848, Štúr's movement, overestimating their real political weight and the extent of Slovak nationalism's popular appeal, demanded strong national-regional autonomy at a meeting in Liptószentmiklós (today Liptovský Mikuláš, Slovakia). An investigation was launched by the authorities, but by then the leaders had left the country. When they returned in September 1848, they took part in the fighting on the side of the Austrian Empire, but they were unable to organize a serious popular uprising, and their political aims remained immature. In January 1849, a third campaign achieved some success, insofar as the pro-emperor Slovak leaders were indeed received positively by the majority of the territory of Turóc County. It was this impulse that gave birth to the idea of Slovak statehood for the first time in history: Štúr, with about a dozen Slovak intellectuals by his side, presented a petition to Francis Joseph, asking for the establishment of an independent Slovak crown province. The monarch gave some thought to the idea, but as it could not be proved that there was public support for the proposed state, the issue was dropped from the agenda.[33] The movement's lack of a real political power base was shown by Štúr's later move: in 1851, he argued that the fate of the Slovaks could only change for the better within the framework of the Russian Empire. As fate would have it, this was to be his political testament – he was fatally wounded in a hunting accident when he was barely forty.[34]

With the loss of its most charismatic leader and the appearance of a political detente between Hungarians and Slovaks, the Slovak national movement split into two factions. One argued in favour of respecting the existing constitutional framework, and that the Slovak emancipation struggle should be carried out within the constitutional framework of post-1867 Hungary, in cooperation with the Hungarian political elite. The other group, on the other hand, clinging to the traditions of Štúr, insisted on the creation of an autonomous Slovak territory, which no member of the ruling Hungarian political elite considered worthy of support.[35]

It is also true, however, that in the early years of dualism, when the mainstream of the Hungarian political elite was still defined by the liberal principles of Deák and Eötvös, the Slovak movement had a lot of room for manoeuvre. They gained a number of regional political positions and even seats in Parliament, and continued to build up the Slovak national institutions (a national press, national bank, Slovak-language school network, Slovak printing house, Slovak cultural associations) that had begun in the 1860s. However, after a paradigm shift in the Hungarian political elite in the first half of the 1870s, and after the escalation of personal conflicts, the Hungarian government dismantled a large part of the Slovak institutional system within a year and a half, forcing the national movement into embittered passivity.[36]

Rusyns

The Rusyn ethnic group was one of the smaller ethnic groups in nineteenth-century Hungary, with a population of less than half a million. The majority of Rusyn society was made up of shepherds and peasants, and their national awakening was seriously hampered by the lack of a native nobility or sizeable bourgeoisie. It is revealing, for example, that in 1840, in the Hungarian Diet, the delegate of Máramaros County, representing the Rusyn regions, disagreed with the delegate of Turóc County, who wanted to slow down the introduction of the bill requiring the use of the Hungarian language in all areas of administration.[37] Even the Hungarianized Rusyn intellectuals living in Budapest at the turn of the century themselves expressed opinions such as that 'the Rusyn people, because of its small number and its poverty and lack of intelligence, has no claim to an independent national existence'.[38]

The history of Rusyn political thought and action would probably have been limited to a mere acknowledgement of its eventual assimilation without the work of Adolf Dobriansky. Born to one of the elite families, Dobriansky, the son of a Greek Catholic priest and the Lőcse (today Levoča, Slovakia) mayor's daughter, studied at the Forestry Academy in Selmecbánya (today Banská Štiavnica, Slovakia) and worked as a mine engineer from 1840, by which time he had developed close links with the Czech and Slovak nationalist movements. In the spring of 1848, Lajos Kossuth drew on his expertise in mine engineering, and in the early summer Dobriansky even tried to win a mandate in Hungary's first parliamentary elections, but by the turn of 1848–9, he was trying to persuade Francis Joseph to annex the Rusyn areas of Hungary to Galicia, aiming to create an independent Rusyn province. The language of administration was to be Russian, and he wanted it to be the language of education as well. His goals included the establishment of a higher education institution and a newspaper.[39] Although the autonomous Rusyn province administered from Vienna did not materialize, Dobriansky was appointed in October 1849 as the representative of the Ungvár (today Uzhhorod, Ukraine) civil district, which included the counties of Ung, Bereg, Ugocsa and Máramaros. Dobriansky held this position until the Ungvár district was abolished, i.e. until the end of March 1850, and he regarded this administrative unit, overseen by the military district of Kassa (today Košice, Slovakia) as a basis for the creation of an autonomous Rusyn province. Although the Rusyn church hierarchy did not agree with the marginalization of the Rusyn language in favour of Russian, no serious national activity was evident within the church structures,[40] and Dobriansky was the only one who later formulated the most far-reaching Rusyn demands. At the beginning of the 1860s, in the context of the renewed parliamentary election campaigns, he again raised the demand for an independent Russian administrative unit, this time within Hungary, where an autonomous Russian national assembly would be held annually, which would handle national, religious and school affairs independently, while a Russian department would also be created in every central governmental body.⁴¹ In 1865, Dobriansky himself became a member of parliament, but his influence soon began to wane, and in the early 1880s he emigrated to Vienna. His oeuvre was appreciated by the Rusyn generation that followed him, as evinced by the following words: 'But fate had a different reckoning with the Ruthenians: it gave them a man who, basing his happiness and that of his people on illusions, set himself and his people on the road to destruction.'⁴²

Slovenes

The Slovenes were one of the smallest ethnic groups in Hungary, numbering around 40,000 in the first half of the nineteenth century and 90,000 by the time of the First World War. For a long time, they had no contact with Slovenes living beyond Hungary's borders. In fact, the ethnonym itself evolved over a long period of time, and it was József Kossics, the parish priest from Alsószölnök, who first used the ethnonym 'Slovene' for the Slavs of the Muravidék (today Prekmurje, Slovenia) region in the 1820s.⁴³

Religion was also a major dividing line: two-thirds of the Slovenes were Catholic and one-third Lutheran, and it was among the latter that sympathy for the Hungarian political elite was strongest. This was also reflected in 1848, when the Catholic Slovenes initially chose the Austrian side, while the Lutherans supported the Hungarian side. Assimilation among Slovenes also accelerated under dualism.⁴⁴

Germans

Germans had lived in Hungary since the Middle Ages, but unlike a significant proportion of other ethnic groups, they did not have a contiguous settlement area, and different groups of Germans were separated from each other by significant legal, lifestyle and cultural differences. While some of them had formed the urban population of Upper Hungary and Transylvania for centuries, larger masses of German speakers arrived after the end of the Turkish wars in the eighteenth century to settle and cultivate the abandoned areas of the south of the country and also to Transdanubia. Although a national political movement did not develop among the Germans in the first half of the nineteenth century, they too were faced with the challenge of choosing between assimilation and building their own national movement. The German bourgeoisie of the towns of the Great Hungarian Plain clearly chose the first option, while the peasants who remained in their isolated villages ignored the question and preserved their local identity.

The Transylvanian and Upper Hungarian bourgeoisie, however, were less enthusiastic about the challenge of assimilation. Younger generations studying at universities in Germany, inspired by the idea of 'young Germany', stressed the importance of cultivating the German language and resisting assimilation into Hungarian culture, but these aspirations did not become political goals before 1848.

The aftermath of the March Revolution of 1848 left the German-speaking population in Hungary more sharply divided: the ethnic Germans of the southern regions and of the Great Hungarian Plain suffered greatly from the consequences of the attacks of the Croatian and Serbian armies, and therefore clearly supported the Hungarian side, while throughout the war, the region of Szepes County, which had a high proportion of German speakers, was a regional base for the Hungarian military industry. The Transylvanian Saxon towns, on the other hand, were the most important Transylvanian base of the imperial armies from October 1848, and during the war they fought against the Hungarian revolutionaries on behalf of the Habsburgs.[45]

The year 1849 was a turning point for the Germans in that the programme of Germanization of the country put them in a position of advantage over all other nationalities. However, it is also true that German groups previously loyal to the Hungarians protested against being included among the supporters of the imperial ideal of neo-absolutism by their insistence on using the Hungarian language.[46]

During the Dualist period, this kind of demonstrative embrace of Hungarian identity became even more pronounced, although, at around the turn of the century, political initiatives defending the use of the German language, such as the *Ungarlandische Deutsche Volkspartei* or the *Deutsch-Ungarischer Landes Bauerbund*, also appeared.[47]

Armenians

Most of the Armenians in the Hungarian lands arrived in Transylvania in the seventeenth century, where they were granted settlement permits and privileges by the Transylvanian prince Michael Apafi I. These Armenians were mainly craftsmen and traders. Two of their most important towns, Szamosújvár (today Gherla, Romania) and Erzsébetváros (today Dumbrăveni, Romania), were granted the status of free royal cities in 1786, and the Transylvanian Diet of 1791 elevated the Armenian citizens of these two towns to the ranks of the Hungarian estates.[48] From the eighteenth century onwards, the Armenians continued to move from Transylvania to other parts of Hungary. Becoming involved in the traditional Transylvanian cattle trade, many families amassed great wealth, and during the reign of Maria Theresa they had the opportunity to buy Hungarian nobility.[49]

These Armenians actively supported the Hungarian culture and language. In 1769, for example, the town of Szamosújvár offered a substantial sum of money for the future foundation of the Hungarian Learned Society, which was paid to the treasury the following year.[50] At the Transylvanian Diet of 1841–3, the Armenian delegates stressed their love for the common homeland and made it clear that their main aspiration was to live in harmony with the Hungarians.[51] During the Hungarian War of Independence of 1848–9 more than seventy officers of Armenian origin served in the army.[52] As retaliation for their supporting the Hungarian cause, Szamosújvár was forced to pay a forty thousand forint ransom to the Habsburg commander Colonel Karl von Urban,[53] while in Erzsébetváros, the imperial forces were twice given permission to pillage the town.[54]

During the Dualism era, many politicians, economists and artists of Armenian origin made substantial careers for themselves. However, assimilation did not mean the denial of their roots; they continued to maintain their dual Hungarian-Armenian cultural identity. [55]

Jews, Romani, Greeks

In addition to those described above, Hungary was also home to considerable populations of other nationalities – some of which had centuries-old traditions or had acquired key positions in economic and social life – such as the Jews, the Romani or the merchants of Balkan origin, who were of Greek Orthodox religion and were collectively called 'Greeks' by their Hungarian contemporaries. However, as these groups were not tied to a particular territory, they also did not have any aspirations for independence or autonomy. In fact, most of them were interested in speeding up the process of assimilation, of 'becoming Hungarian', or at least in emphasizing the external elements of Hungarianness. Only the emancipation aspirations of the Jews displayed signs of common political action within the territory of Hungary.

Conclusion

After the rise of modern nationalism in the nineteenth century, the narratives of ethnic distinctiveness that had functioned within the same interpretative, and essentially loyal, framework were now formulated as separate national discourses, often in opposition to each other. By the last decades of the century, members of elite groups with political rights or who were in any way active in public life were personally forced to choose between assimilation and national activism. After all, just like the Hungarian political elite, the representatives of the nationalities were unable to resolve the great dilemma of nineteenth-century Hungary, which was the tension between extending civil rights to an ever-wider range of citizens, including the elites of the nationalities, and preserving the integrity of the Hungarian state.

Notes

1 Gyémánt Richárd, 'A Bánság újratelepítése, különös tekintettel a 18. századi telepítési folyamatokra' [The Resettlement of Banat, with Special Attention to the Settlement Processes of the Eighteenth Century], *Acta Universitatis Szegediensis Forum Acta Juridica et Politica* 5, no. 1 (2015): 31–48, 41.
2 Hanák Péter, ed., *Egy ezredév: Magyarország rövid története* [A Millennium: A Short History of Hungary] (Budapest: Gondolat, 1986), 129.
3 H. Németh István and Soós István, 'A magyarországi hungarus-tudat' [The Hungarus Consciousness in Hungary], in *Az együttélés történelme: Nemzetiségi kérdés Magyarországon* [A History of Coexistence: Ethnicity in Hungary] (Budapest: Magyar

Nemzeti Levéltár, 2020), 59–76; cf. Tarnai Andor, *Extra Hungariam non est vita . . .: Egy szállóige történetéhez* [Extra Hungariam Non Est Vita . . .: History of a Proverb], Modern filozófiai füzetek 6 (Budapest: Akadémiai Kiadó, 1969).
4 József Demmel, *Ľudovít Štúr: Zrod moderného slovenského národa v 19. storočí* (Bratislava: Kalligram, 2015).
5 Tibor Pichler, 'Uhorská politická kultúra a slovenské národovecké myslenie', in *Kapitoly z histórie stredoeurópskeho priestoru v 19. a 20. Storočí: Pocta k 70-ročnému jubileu Dušana Kováča*, ed. Edita Ivančiková (Bratislava: Historický ústav SAV, 2011), 200; Tibor Pichler, *Národovci a občania: o slovenskom politickom myslení v 19. storočí* (Bratislava: VEDA, 1998); Tibor Pichler, *Etnos a polis. Zo slovenského a uhorského politického myslenia* (Bratislava: Kalligram, 2011); Tibor Pichler, 'Fundačný akt dualistického Uhorska a kritickí národovci', in *Kľúčové problémy moderných slovenských dejín* (Bratislava: VEDA, 2012).
6 Molnár András, 'Etnikumok és nemzetiségi mozgalmak a reformkori Magyarországon' [Ethnicities and Nationality Movements in Reform-Era Hungary], in *Az együttélés történelme. Nemzetiségi kérdés Magyarországon* (Budapest: Magyar Nemzeti Levéltár, 2020), 91–89.
7 Nagy Mariann and Katus László, 'A magyar korona országainak nemzetiségei a 18–19. Században' [The Nationalities of the Countries of the Hungarian Crown in the 18th-19th Centuries], Árkádia Szakmódszertani Portál, accessed 22 January 2022, http://arkadiafolyoirat.hu/index.php/1-nemzetisegek-es-nemzetisegi-mozgalmak/49-a-magyar-korona-orszagainak-nemzetisegei-a-18-19-szazadban.
8 Heka László, 'Az 1868. évi horvát–magyar kiegyezés a sajtó tükrében' [The 1868 Croatian-Hungarian Settlement in the Press], *Acta Universitatis Szegediensis de Attila József Nominatae Acta Juridica et Politica* 54, no. 9 (1998): 17–18.
9 Molnár, 'Etnikumok és nemzetiségi mozgalmak a reformkori Magyarországon', 80.
10 Ioan Drăgan, 'Az erdélyi román nemesség a 16–18. Században I' [The Romanian Nobility in Transylvania in the 16th–18th centuries, Part 1], trans. Rigán Lóránd, *Korunk* 3rd ser. 22, no. 7 (2011): 82–8. Ioan Drăgan, 'Az erdélyi román nemesség a 16–18. Században II' [The Romanian Nobility in Transylvania in the 16th–18th Centuries, Part 2], trans. Rigán Lóránd, *Korunk*, 3rd ser. 22, no. 8 (2011): 81–90.
11 Bakk Miklós, 'Két nemzetépítés, egy állam: Románia száz éve' [Two Concepts of Nation-Building, One State: Hundred Years of Romania], *Kisebbségi Szemle* 3, no. 3 (2018): 35–53.
12 Bakk, 'Két nemzetépítés, egy állam', 37.
13 Molnár, 'Etnikumok és nemzetiségi mozgalmak a reformkori Magyarországon', 80.
14 Bakk, 'Két nemzetépítés, egy állam', 37–40.
15 Spira György, 'A nemzetiségi kérdés a negyvennyolcas forradalom Magyarországán' [The Nationality Question in Hungary During the 1848 Revolution] (Budapest: Kossuth, 1980), 141–3, 150–1.
16 Hermann Róbert, 'Nemzetiségek az 1848–49-es forradalomban és szabadságharcban' [Nationalities in the 1848–49 Revolution and War of Independence] in *Az együttélés történelme: Nemzetiségi kérdés Magyarországon*, ed. L. Balogh Béni et al. (Budapest: Magyar Nemzeti Levéltár, 2020), 103; Spira, 'A nemzetiségi kérdés a negyvennyolcas forradalom Magyarországán', 170–2.
17 Hermann, 'Nemzetiségek az 1848–49-es forradalomban és szabadságharcban', 104.
18 Hermann, 'Nemzetiségek az 1848–49-es forradalomban és szabadságharcban', 108–11.
19 Bakk, 'Két nemzetépítés, egy állam', 40.

20 Miskolczy Ambrus, 'Románok a történeti Magyarországon' [Romanians in Historical Hungary] (Budapest: Lucidus Kiadó, 2005); Ábrahám Barna, 'Az erdélyi románság polgárosodása a 19. század második felében' [Embourgeoisement of Transylvanian Romanians in the Second Half of the 19th Century] (Csíkszereda: Pro-Print Könyvkiadó, 2004); Lucian Boia, 'Vesztesek és győztesek: Az első világháború újraértelmezése' [Losers and Winners: Rethinking the First World War] (Budapest: Cser Kiadó, 2015), 79.
21 Molnár, 'Etnikumok és nemzetiségi mozgalmak a reformkori Magyarországon' 87–9.
22 Hermann, 'Nemzetiségek az 1848–49-es forradalomban és szabadságharcban', 101–6.
23 Anton Bernolák, *Grammatica slavica* [Slavic Grammar] (Pressburg: Landerer, 1790); Anton Bernolák, *Slowár Slowenski, cesko, latinsko, nemecko, uherski seu: Lexicon slavicum bohemico–latino–germanico–ungaricum* (Budae: Reg. Univers. Hungaricae, 1825).
24 Ján Hučko, 'K charakteristike vlasteneckej inteligencie v prvej fáze slovenského národného obrodenia so zreteľom na jej sociálne zloženie a pôvod', in *K počiatkom slovenského národného obrodenia. Sborník štúdií Historického ústavu SAV pri príležitosti 200. ročného jubilea narodenia Antona Bernoláka* (Bratislava: Vydavateľstvo Slovenskej Akadémie Vied, 1964).
25 Georgius Papánek, *Historia gentis Slavae: De Regno regibusque* (Pécs: Jeliner, 1793). Georgius Papánek, Georgius Fándly and Georgius Sklenár, *Compendiata historia gentis Slavae* (Tyrnaviae: Jelinek, 1793); Georgius Sklenár, *Vetustissimus magnae Moraviae situs et primus in eam Hungarorum ingressus et incursus* (Pozsony: Landerer, 1778).
26 Ján Tibenský, Juraj Papánek and Juraj Sklenár, *Obrancovia slovenskej národnosti v XVIII. Storočí* (Martin: Osveta, 1958), 66.
27 Andrej Findor, 'Tisícročná poroba?', in *Mýty naše slovenské*, ed. Eduard Krekovič, Elena Mannová and Eva Krekovičová (Bratislava: AEP, 2005), 71–6.
28 Róbert Kiss Szemán, *Az emblematikus nemzetrajz: földrajz néprajz, növény- és állatrajz Ján Kollár művében* [Emblematic ethnography: geography, ethnography, flora and fauna in the work of Ján Kollár]. In same author: Magyarország panaszától Szlávia panaszáig. Irodalmi tanulmányok. [From Hungary's lament to Slavia's lament. Literary studies]. (Budapest: ELTE BTK Szláv Filológiai Tanszék, 2007), 62–81.
29 Kiss Szemán Róbert, '. . .garázda emberek az Etymologusok' ['. . .Etymologists are Riotous People'] (Budapest: ELTE BTK Szláv Filológiai Tanszék, 2008), 48–68.
30 Ján Kollár, *Über die literarische Wechselseitigkeit zwischen den verschiedenen Stämmen und Mundarten der slavischen Nation* (Pest: Trattner–Károlyi, 1837).
31 József Demmel, *'Ľudožrút' na Hornom Uhorsku: Príbeh Bélu Grünwalda* (Bratislava: HÚ SAV–VEDA, 2020), 32–42.
32 József Demmel, *'Ľudožrút' na Hornom Uhorsku*,154–8.
33 József Demmel, *Panslávi v kaštieli. Životná dráha Jozefa Justha a neznámy príbeh slovenského národného hnutia* (Bratislava: Kalligram, 2016).
34 Ľudovít Štúr, *A szlávok és a jövő világa: Válogatott írások* [Slavs and the Future World: Selected Writings], ed. Demmel József (Pozsony: Kalligram, 2012).
35 Tibor Pichler, *Národovci a občania*; Pichler, *Etnos a polis*.
36 Demmel, *'Ľudožrút' na Hornom Uhorsku*, 157–239.
37 *Felséges első Ferdinánd Ausztriai császár, Magyar és Csehországoknak e néven ötödik apost. királyától szabad királyi Pozsony városába 1839-dik esztendei szent Iván havának 2-ik napjára rendeltetett Magyarország közgyűlésének jegyzőkönyve: I. Darab* [The Minutes of the Assembly of Hungary Scheduled for the 2nd Day of the Month

of St. Ivan in the Year 1839, in the City of Pozsony, a Royal Free City by Virtue of Ferdinand I, Emperor of Austria, and Fifth Apostolic King of Hungary and Bohemia: Part 1] (Pozsony: Belnay, Wéber and Wigand, 1840), 163–5.

38 Ábrahám Barna and Demmel József, 'Gyökerek és választások: Anyanyelv és identitás a dualizmuskori Magyarországon' [Roots and Choices: Mother Tongue and Identity in the Dualist Era in Hungary], in *Az együttélés történelme: Nemzetiségi kérdés Magyarországon* (Budapest: Magyar Nemzeti Levéltár, 2020), 154.

39 *Mészáros Károly önéletrajza* [Curriculum Vitae of Károly Mészáros], A Hajdú-Bihar Megyei Múzeumok Közleményei 22, ed. Csorba Csaba (Debrecen: no publisher, 1974), 62.

40 Molnár Ferenc, 'A kiegyezés és a ruszin mozgalom' [The Austro-Hungarian Settlement and the Rusyn Movement], in *'Indivisibiliter ac Inseparabiliter:' 'Feloszthatatlanul és elválaszthatatlanul;' A kiegyezés 150. évfordulója alkalmából rendezett tudományos konferencia előadásai*, ed. Szakál Imre (Beregszász–Ungvár: RIK-U Kft., 2018), 22–34.

41 Ruszoly József, 'Mészáros Károly és a rutén nemzetiségi törekvések 1861-ben' [Károly Mészáros and the Rusyn Nationalist Aspirations in 1861] in *Hajdúsági Múzeum Évkönyve 5*, ed. Nyakas Miklós (Hajdúböszörmény: Alföldi Nyomda, 1983), 129–54, 140–1.

42 Udvari István, 'Adalékok Sztripszky Hiador pályakezdéséhez: Nagyszombati levéltári források alapján' [Additions to Hiador Sztripszky's Early Career: Based on Sources from the Nagyszombat Archives], in *Szabolcs-Szatmár-Beregi levéltári évkönyv 15* (Nyíregyháza: Szabolcs–Szatmár–Bereg Megyei Önkormányzat Levéltára, 2001), 312.

43 Molnár, 'Etnikumok és nemzetiségi mozgalmak a reformkori Magyarországon', 95.

44 Mayer László and Molnár András, ed., *Források a Muravidék történetéhez: Szöveggyűjtemény* [Resources for the History of the Prekmurje: A Chrestomathy] (Szombathely–Zalaegerszeg: Vas Megyei Levéltár–Zala Megyei Levéltár, 2008), 2:117–243.

45 Hermann, 'Nemzetiségek az 1848–49-es forradalomban és szabadságharcban', 111–12.

46 Deák Ágnes, 'Nemzetiségi együttélés rivalizálás, együttműködés és konfliktusok erőterében: 1849–67' [Ethnic Coexistence in a Period of Rivalry, Cooperation and Conflicts: 1849–67], in *Az együttélés történelme: Nemzetiségi kérdés Magyarországon* (Budapest: Magyar Nemzeti Levéltár, 2020), 126–7.

47 Ábrahám and Demmel, 'Gyökerek és választások', 149–51.

48 *Az erdélyi három nemes nemzetekből álló tekintetes rendeknek 1790-dik esztendőben Karátson havának 12-dik napjára szabad királyi városba Kolosvárra hirdettetett, és több következett napokon tartatott közönséges gyüléseikben lett végzéseknek és foglalatosságoknak jegyző könyve* [Minutes of the Decisions and Discussions of the General Assemblies of the Respectable Orders of the Three Noble Estates of Transylvania, Held in the Year 1790, on the 12th Day of the Month of Christmas, and on Several Subsequent Days, in the Free Royal City of Kolozsvár] (Kolozsvár: Ref. Kolégyom, 1791), 610–12.

49 Tarján G. Gábor, 'Ahogy magukat nevezik–magyar örmények' [As They Call Themselves–Hungarian Armenians], *Acta Universitatis Szegediensis: Acta Historica*, Tom. 141 (2017): 108–9.

50 Szongott Kristóf, *Szamosújvár szab. kir. város monográfiája: 1700–1900* [Monograph of Szamosújvár Free Royal City: 1700–1900] (Szamosújvár: Aurora, 1901), 1:134.

51 Auguste de Gerando, *La Transylvanie et ses habitants* (Paris: Imprimeurs-Unis, 1845), 2:195.

52 Bona Gábor, *Az 1848/49-es szabadságharc örmény hősei* [Armenian Heroes of the Hungarian War of Independence of 1848/49] (Budapest: Országos Örmény Önkormányzat, 1995), 6.
53 Szongott, *Szamosújvár szab. kir. város monográfiája*, 2:451.
54 Bona, *Az 1848/49-es szabadságharc örmény hősei*, 4.
55 Pál Judit, 'Az örmények integrálódása és az örménységkép változásai Erdélyben a 18-19. században' [The Integration of Armenians and Changes in the Image of Armenians in Transylvania in the 18th–19th Centuries] in *Örmény diaszpóra a Kárpát-medencében*, Művelődéstörténeti Műhely: Felekezet és Identitás 2, ed. Őze Sándor and Kovács Bálint (Piliscsaba: Pázmány Péter Katolikus Egyetem Bölcsészettudományi Kar, 2007), 2:77–94.

Part 2

5

Hungarian constitutional thought between tradition and innovation in the age of the French Revolution and Napoleonic Wars

Henrik Hőnich and Ágoston Nagy

The Hungarian estates polity at the turn of the nineteenth century: The challenges of absolutism, revolutions and wars

On 26 January 1790, Joseph II withdrew most of his decrees relating to the Kingdom of Hungary, where, from around the end of 1789 until the summer of 1790, the 'noble-national' movement had gained ground against the Viennese government, led by the prosperous landowning (*bene possessionatus*) gentry.[1] This movement gave voice to the grievances (*gravamina*) the nobility harboured under the reign of Joseph II and began to re-establish the old system of liberties and, in particular, greater autonomy for the local county administrations. By doing this, the nobility could demonstrate its political significance in the eyes of not only the ruler (after the death of Joseph II on 20 February 1790, his brother, Leopold II, became his successor) but also the burghers of the royal free cities and the 'miserable' taxpaying commoners (*misera plebs contribuens*). Due to the revolutionary events in France and in the Austrian Netherlands, the government, however, believed the discontented Hungarian nobility was threatening the unity of the empire.

The main political forums of the opposition were the county assemblies, and after the summoning of the Diet in June 1790, the district sessions – unofficial meetings of the representatives of the four districts of the country.[2] The heated political atmosphere also manifested itself in a torrent of political pamphlets and occasional verses, whose main topics were linked to the collective identity of the nobility and the defence of their ancient liberties and privileges.[3] Many treatises dealt with the symbolic dimensions of the corporate-national identity of the nobility, praising the rebirth of ancient Hungarian virtues, national character and military valour. In addition to such traditional topics, the theme of awakening of the Hungarian language from its 'centuries-long slumbers' also became important.[4]

Several crucial aspects of the political system of the Kingdom of Hungary in the second half of the eighteenth century played an essential role in these processes. The political dualism of the crown (or the king) and the 'country' (*regnum*, or *ország*) defined the polity. The two poles were linked politically by the process of negotiation during the sittings of the Diet (*tractatus diaetalis*), which formed an institutional sine qua non of the system. Thanks to the shift from confessional to constitutional questions throughout the eighteenth century, the defence of noble privileges came to the foreground in politics and the estates were able to take a strong line against the crown in the Diet on several political topics: the size of the annual tax paid by the commoners for military expenses (*contributio*), the noble levy that provided an additional militia for the crown (*insurrectio*) and the voluntary aid for military purposes (*subsidium*) paid by the privileged (who enjoyed an immunity from the *contributio*), as well as (from the end of the eighteenth century) the precise number of Hungarian recruits to the regular Habsburg army. Simultaneously, the estates adopted a new pattern for interpreting these issues, conceptualizing them increasingly as constitutional questions. This process mitigated the polarization within the estates and set them up against the crown, narrowing the possibility of compromise between king and estates.[5]

This change took place at the political level but was also connected to socio-economical transformations. In the first half of the eighteenth century, the prosperous landowning gentry emancipated themselves from the wardship of magnates (*familiaritas*) and swiftly took the leading role in county-level politics. The dissolution of the old relationship between the magnates and the junior nobles resulted in a higher degree of independence for the *bene possessionatus* nobility. Since the counties functioned as the strongholds of local self-government, their historically developed 'local administrative authority' formed the basis for their resistance against the crown and its most ardent supporters, the predominately Catholic magnates. This transformation was also of the utmost importance at the national level, since the prosperous landowning gentry was able to dominate the proceedings of the Diet. The noble-national movement in 1790 was part of this process, as it was an attempt by the *bene possessionati* to reshape the political system according to its own interests and values.[6]

From 1780 onwards, the polarization within the political system intensified these long-term social and institutional processes as Joseph II's arbitrary rule incited the nobility's anger. Examples of this included his refusal to undergo a separate coronation as king of Hungary; his refusal to summon the Diet for the duration of his reign; his removal of the Holy Crown, the most important political symbol of the country from Pozsony (today Bratislava, Slovakia) to Vienna in 1784; the language decree, which made German the official language; the national census and land survey, which terminated the tax immunity of the nobility; and the replacement of the county system with ten districts. Consequently, the estates, and above all, the prosperous landowning gentry regarded the regime of Joseph II, and even his successor Leopold II, as an unconstitutional menace and some even plotted to align with Prussia to overthrow Habsburg rule.

After his arrival in Vienna, Leopold took immediate action against the gathering opposition to his own reign. He organized a network of secret agents whose main task was to gather information about the political mood and monitor the leaders of the opposition. Hack writers were also deployed against the noble-national movement, who produced pamphlets, which lampooned their opposition to the crown. Secret operations were prepared, and even partially launched, to incite the peasantry and the burghers against the nobility, at the same time Leopold II returned the Holy Crown to Hungary, underwent a coronation in Pozsony and convened the Diet for the first time in ten years. These actions were all aimed at weakening the noble opposition, which gathered at the Diet convened in June 1790, where the political programme of the nobility predominated. Largely based on the idea of the Tennis Court Oath of the French Revolution, the county delegates of the Lower House were obliged to take a 'patriotic oath', to swear not to act against the rights of the country and the estates' liberties. During the summer, a proposal for a new coronation charter (*diploma inaugurale*) was formulated, based on a radical oppositional programme. Nevertheless, Leopold insisted on the text of the old *diploma* of his predecessors. His refusal indicated the weakening of the estates' position and the strengthening of the ruler's. The Treaty of Reichenbach (27 July 1790) between the Habsburg Monarchy and Prussia precluded the possibility of an armed conflict between them. Leopold also deployed six cuirassier regiments to Hungary, shaking the self-confidence of the estates, and their scope of action decreased drastically.[7]

The Diet was moved from Buda to Pozsony in November 1790, where the son of Leopold, Archduke Alexander Leopold, was elected palatine and the coronation ceremony took place. The seventy-four articles passed by the Diet of 1790-1 represented a compromise between the king and the estates. One of the most important accomplishments of the opposition was Article X of 1791, which described Hungary as a free and independent kingdom, to be governed by its own laws and customs. Nevertheless, the *decretum* in general fell a long way short of the initial aims of the noble-national movement. Further reforms were, however, discussed by the nine 'national' committees (*deputatio regnicolaris*), established by Article LXVII. These were charged with the task of elaborating systematic reform works (*operata systematica*) regarding the constitutional, judicial, economical, educational establishment of the kingdom, which were to be negotiated at the next Diet.[8]

Between 1792 and 1815, the Habsburg Monarchy was in a state of almost constant military and ideological struggle with the French Republic, and later with the Napoleonic Empire.[9] The fear in the Habsburg lands intensified after the French military efforts turned to exporting revolutionary ideas and the news of the proclamation of the Republic, the executions of Louis XVI and Marie Antoinette (the penultimate daughter of Maria Theresa) and the beginning of the Terror. The court also tried to leverage the trial and execution of the Hungarian Jacobins (1794–5) as a means of developing anti-revolutionary public sentiment. Mainstream public opinion in Hungary regarded the advance of the French Army, as well as the infusion of the war with radical ideological content, as a menace to the traditional constitutional system and social hierarchies of the Hungarian Kingdom. This constituted a solid basis for temporary compromises between the Hungarian nobility and the Vienna Court. A modus vivendi took shape between them, united against the Revolution and later Napoleon, although neither the nobility gave up seeking remedies for their grievances, nor did the court stop attempting to expand its authority.

In terms of actual policy-making, the new era after the death of Leopold II is best characterized as 'Cabinet Absolutism'. Francis I relied upon a narrow circle of confidential advisers and most affairs were decided in the study (*Kabinett*) of the ruler. In Hungary, the palatine, the highest-ranking officer of the country, was responsible for executing the will of the government. Between 1790 and 1795, this position was filled by one of the younger brothers of Francis, Alexander Leopold, who submitted a proposal to his elder brother right after the execution of the Hungarian Jacobins to stop the flow of revolutionary and rebellious ideas.

The escalation of mistrust under the conservative-minded rule of Francis I, and the increase of governmental control and repression by means of the secret police and censorship, soon resulted in the invigoration of the oppositional attitude among the Hungarian political elite. Many of them opted to resign from state offices while continuing to actively participate in county-level politics, as well as at the occasional Diets that were summoned in this period. Nevertheless, both the pressing needs of the anti-French Wars and the repression of the press, particularly of politically radical voices, narrowed the field for open political thought and practice.

After the death of Alexander Leopold, Archduke Joseph was chosen as palatine by the Diet in 1796. Although he was chiefly concerned with the interests of the empire, he lived in Buda and, in the course of time, won over the nobility and forged a balancing role for himself between them and the Vienna Court. Political life at this time followed the routine of the *diaetalis tractatus*. The Diet was summoned seven times in the period, although thoroughgoing reforms were avoided. The Hungarian nobility urged to touch upon the systematic reform works several times, but further discussion on them was repeatedly postponed. Issues concerning 'taxes and soldiers' instead dominated the sessions,[10] while questions of cultural nation-building (e.g. the establishment of the National Library and a new Hungarian-language Military Academy) were also raised but in terms of politics, these were of lesser importance.

Since *ius ad bellum* (the right to start a war) was reserved as a royal prerogative, the nobility could influence the crown only when a Diet was summoned as, according to custom, this was required to approve additional recruits for the army, as well as any changes to the *contributio*, *subsidium* and the *insurrectio*. Approval for an *insurrectio* in particular was jealously guarded by the nobility. In their view, it was perceived not only as a substitute for a Hungarian national army, which did not exist, but also as a duty, a 'blood-tax', which justified their liberties and privileges, particularly their tax immunity. Although this levy was employed four times between 1789 and 1815, the noble soldiers were only deployed once, in 1809. As a temporary militia, which lacked permanent organization, its military strength proved to be limited. Nevertheless, as it was largely arranged and paid for by the nobility, who constituted the bulk of the political community, that is, the noble nation, the *insurrectio* was extremely significant in terms of their political positions, constitutional thought and collective identity.

The constitution during this period, composed as it was of various laws and customs, could therefore be harnessed to serve multiple competing programmes, and the flexibility of this legal framework allowed extensive, fierce and even obstructive debates, as well as temporary compromises between the country and its king-emperor.

The revival of noble constitutionality: Key concepts, symbols and political discourse

In early modern Hungary, the political and legal system of the various noble estates was based on custom (*consuetudo*). This meant that custom was considered legally stronger than statutory law, that is, the laws (*decreta*) consisting of articles (*articuli*). The notion of the superiority of customary over statutory law was decisive in relation to noble liberties, which were conceived as rights primarily rooted in custom and occasionally also in written law. (This was partly because the most important and best-known legal manual in early modern times in Hungary, which in fact functioned as the bible of customary law, the *Tripartitum*, written by the sixteenth-century jurist and politician István Werbőczy, was never codified.) At the end of the eighteenth century, a conceptual innovation took place: the term *constitutio* and its Hungarian counterpart *alkotmány* became synonymous with the entire socio-political system, with special regard to the liberties of the noble estate. This change turned out to be pivotal for the fundamental patterns and trajectories of Hungarian constitutional thought in the next decades, and became the conceptual foundation for nineteenth-century developments in political discourse and the politics of grievance in particular.[11]

Joseph II's arbitrary reform policies, which challenged the existing socio-political order and the liberties of the estates as a whole, proved to be crucial in this regard. The impact of Montesquieu's *De l'esprit des lois* was also important. Adopting his constitutional ideas, the Hungarian political class came to reconceptualize the dualistic political system of Hungary and the set of rights and duties of the country in relation to the country as a *constitutio*. Thus, the Hungarian nobility became aware that they had a constitution, not only separate laws, liberties, rights and privileges. Moreover, the process of *tractatus diaetalis* was increasingly considered to be legislative power, exercised jointly by the monarch and the estates, and distinct from the prerogatives of executive power which were exercised by their Habsburg rulers.[12]

In fact, this new terminology was based upon the traditional distinction between *reservata* (sphere of rights reserved exclusively for the ruler) and *communicata* (matters to be handled only on the Diets in tandem with the noble estates). Defining the boundaries between these two spheres was the essence of the dispute between the two political poles, as was the question of which of the laws in the legal collection of the *Corpus Juris Hungarici* were fundamental (or cardinal), and how they should be properly interpreted. Nevertheless, this did not mean that there was support for the systematic collection and revision of the sources of the 'ancient constitution' (*avita constitutio*) to correct and elucidate its obscure elements. The vagueness of the old laws permitted considerable flexibility of interpretation, which was utilized politically by both sides. This was one of the main reasons why the legal historian Márton György Kovachich was unable to revise, complement and amend the *Corpus Juris Hungarici* in the first decades of the nineteenth century.[13] The noble-national movement of 1790 strove to gain general acceptance that the Kingdom of Hungary was a constitutional monarchy, although, in fact, the nobility attempted not only to counterbalance royal authority, but also to ensure its position vis-à-vis the magnates. The political programme of the

Lutheran nobleman Péter Balogh of Ócsa became the basis of numerous instructions given to the county delegates to the Diet. In his proposal, he formulated the principle of *filum successionis interruptum*, according to which the 'thread' of succession of the Habsburgs had been 'interrupted' in Hungary, chiefly because Joseph II had not allowed himself to be crowned as the king of Hungary and consequently his rule was unlawful. In a contractualist manner, Balogh argued that the political community had then regained its sovereignty from the ruler and a new contract had to be concluded between them. He claimed that the appropriate constitutional form of that would have been a new coronation charter as one of the traditional prerequisites of coronation.

The proposed measures of the draft aimed to provide intellectual ammunition for the nobility, which was attempting to assert itself as the main political force of the country. Balogh also recommended the establishment of a senate alongside the king, with the intention of restricting the monarch's executive power. At the same time, he would have given more leeway to the nobility in legislation by removing the ruler's right to veto legislation. This oppositional, noble-national view of the constitution was widely accepted by the nobility in the period. These vigorous claims were based on the idea of the nobility's traditional right to resist its monarch (*ius resistendi*), which retained its significance in the political thinking of the nobility, despite the fact that they had been forced by Leopold I to renounce it at the Diet of 1687.[14]

The defence of the ancient constitution was closely intertwined with the tenets of natural law and the social contract theory. Alongside 'contract', popular sovereignty and the concept of the 'people' (*populus*) played a crucial role in contemporary arguments. The nobility interpreted the *populus* in an exclusive sense: even the burghers of free royal cities and mining towns, and the taxpaying commoners were excluded. As was the case in Balogh's draft, the term was often understood in an even narrower sense, excluding also the aristocracy, denoting primarily the nobility as the body politic. The semantic flexibility of *populus* fitted well into the nobility's ideology, which emphasized the importance of equality towards the magnates, while tightening the boundaries downwards, distancing itself from the vast majority of the politically excluded, unprivileged population.[15]

The prosperous landowning gentry took the lead within the oppositional movement that emerged in 1790. The attraction of the movement proved to be strong enough that not only the masses of the nobility joined it, but also some reform-minded magnates and even a few radical reformers took part in this broad-based coalition against Habsburg absolutism. In the turbulent early months of 1790, the return of the Holy Crown from the Imperial Treasury to Hungary generated widespread enthusiasm. The solemn procession from Vienna to Buda was greeted in the counties by welcoming ceremonies, and the relic arrived on 21 February 1790 at the castle of Buda. The county nobility quickly sent volunteers to guard the crown (*banderia*), who took turns guarding the crown until the coronation of Leopold II on 15 November, exhibiting through this not only symbolic but also real military power.[16]

The term 'nation' was also in wide use in the early 1790s, but it was mainly understood to mean only the *Natio Hungarica*, that is, the nobility of the kingdom. The expansion of the term took place at the expense of the traditional use of 'country' and gradually reinterpreted the noble nation as a pre-eminently ethnic Hungarian community. Such an awareness of ethnic and linguistic boundaries was not unprecedented in early modern Hungary. The concept of *natio* or *gens* had periodically borne ethnolinguistic connotations, which could also expand the limits of the political community. The inclusion of non-nobles was a consequence of military mobilization during the Ottoman Wars (involving the non-noble border guards of the 'valiant order'), as well as during the anti-Habsburg Bocskai uprising (1604–6) and Rákóczi's War of Independence (1703–11). However, in most of the eighteenth century, the *natio* was synonymous with the nobility as a corporation of the privileged, or, using the terms coined by Anthony D. Smith, a 'lateral' or 'aristocratic' ethnic community, irrespective of language criterion.[17]

Around 1790, a new idea appeared, which held that the mother tongue was one of the pivotal, distinctive features of the nation. This laid the foundations of an ethnolinguistically based concept of the national community.[18] The thesis about the significance of the mother tongue was also picked up by the noble estates in the debates about the official language in the Lower House of the Diet resulting in the enactment of Article XVI of 1791, the first statute in the history of Hungary dealing with the Hungarian language.[19]

Preserving, reforming or abolishing the estates system? Mapping the political landscape

The political landscape of the period can be divided into three basic attitudes with regard to the so-called estates system in which the nobility predominated: conservative constitutionality, moderate reformism and radical reformism. Only the latter went beyond the bounds of the existing political and social structures and proposed something radically different. The effort to limit the rights and freedoms of the Hungarian nobility, also known as the aulic tendency, was a fourth tendency whose representatives primarily sought to tilt the power relations as much as possible in favour of the court, in order to be able to govern Hungary in an absolutistic manner, in some cases even including the intention of incorporating the country into the Hereditary Lands.

Conservative constitutionality: The noble mainstream

The mainstream of the *bene possessionati* followed Péter Balogh's draft, which aimed to cement the political power of the noble body politic by proposing some innovative institutional measures while remaining socially quite conservative. The lower ranks of the nobility probably thought in a more traditionalist manner, striving simply to restore and preserve their good old liberties. In the mainstream of public-political thought of the period, the protection of the ancient constitution against the absolutist designs of the court took centre stage. This struggle was fought between the aulic party and the nobility at the Diets, but both sides were supported in an indirect way by erudite officials, jurists and scholars. The offensives initiated by the court led the estates to take up a rather defensive stance, although their rejoinders helped them to articulate the very foundations of their political standpoint. The conflict was tempered from time to time, however, by the common interest of the court and the estates to combat revolutionary France.

The reception of the French Revolution was rather positive in its immediate aftermath within oppositional circles.[20] At the outset, it was perceived as a constitutional change, promising the foundation of a mixed monarchy, with a balancing power of the estates. Later, due to the radicalization of the Revolution, the nobility began to view the changes in France as a threat. The anti-revolutionary current of political literature before the Diet of 1796 was represented above all by traditionalist writers and clergymen. Count József Gvadányi, a retired officer, loyal magnate and well-known poet of his time, made the protagonist of his 1796 pamphlet a village notary, who personified the traditionalist, and at the same time bitingly satirical viewpoint of the author.[21] The notary represented the values of conventional Christian morality against theological and philosophical fashions, particularly atheism, deism and naturalism, which were associated with the French. 'Evil books', written by philosophers like Voltaire, Lessing and Rousseau were blamed as the main causes of such delusions. This view was in line with the government's position, which imposed stricter censorship to 'protect' the common people from 'dangerous' writings.

The Catholic clergy reacted especially vehemently to the anticlericalism of the Revolution. Anti-Revolutionary and even anti-Enlightenment topics appeared frequently in Catholic sermons and in the political poetry produced by clergymen.[22] Priests and military chaplains warned their audience to be loyal to God and the king, as well as to accept their position in the social order. At the Diet of 1796, the Hungarian estates offered recruits, extraordinary aid and an extra levy for the king. The governmental watchwords to win the benevolence of the estates were the defence of the throne, of the rights and privileges of the nobility, as well as to protect religion against the French Republic and the Revolution. Occasional poems also praised the military and civic virtues of classical republican patriotism. During the Diet, the Primate of the Catholic Church in Hungary, Count József Batthyány, emphasized that the war had to be fought also against the furious enemies of Christianity, to tame the Revolution and re-Christianize the people. The war became not only officially ideologized but obtained sacral legitimation as a 'religious war'.

The propaganda supported the mobilization of the nobility for wars, seeking to strengthen their loyalty to the king and their love of the country. The defence of the ancient constitution and the liberty of the country were common themes during the period. Primarily, the hatred was directed against the republican political system, its leaders and its fundamental ideas, and later against the person of Napoleon. He was evaluated ambivalently by the Hungarian elites, varying from glorification to hate and disdain.[23] A part of the cultivated public regarded the French emperor through a Romantic lens as a great man, who could shape history, but even they kept a distance from him.

From the Austrian side, the War of the Fifth Coalition was an experiment in popular mobilization and the extensive use of official propaganda, derived from the idea of a 'national' or 'people's war'. From 1808 onwards, the government built up an institutional network of official propaganda with the collaboration of prominent anti-French and pro-German intellectuals. In Hungary, the propaganda in support of the (last) noble levy of 1809 was also outstanding.[24] At the Diet of 1808, thanks to Palatine Joseph, the idea of a national war was implemented involving the mass mobilization of the privileged within the framework of the traditional defence of the country.

Official propaganda in Hungary was concentrated in the hands of the palatine. He charged Sándor Kisfaludy, a retired officer and highly esteemed writer of the time, with making an appeal to the Hungarian nobility. Kisfaludy was expected to remind the noblemen of the 'value of their obsolete privileges', which they enjoyed at the expense of their military duties, without awakening a generalized animosity against the French. The work grew into a lengthier text and, after some of its paragraphs had been crossed out by the palatine, was published in the spring of 1809 under the title of *Hazafiúi Szózat a' Magyar Nemességhez* (Patriotic Appeal to the Hungarian Nobility). The pamphlet represented the mainstream constitutional viewpoint of the estates with a strong historical awareness, combined with a political romanticism, which was also employed to legitimize the cause and bolster noble patriotism.[25]

The appeal claimed that the Hungarian nobility enjoyed an unparalleled position because of their 'Golden Liberty', which was made possible by the ancient constitution. In exchange for this privilege, due to their constitution, they owed personal military service to their King and Country, since the 'Country, the King and the Constitution is inseparably one', and the first two had to 'preserve, embrace, protect' each other so that the latter, the constitution, could persist as the 'spirit of both'. Kisfaludy proposed a sort of patriotism for the nobility, which mixed emotional and rational elements, as well as classical republican civic and military virtues, with a commitment to the core values of ancient constitutionality. Although Kisfaludy deemed, with a 'nativist' argument, that anyone could be capable of loving the country in a rudimentary form, he stressed that the Hungarian nobility was able to (and had to) possess this emotion at a superior level, because of their noble liberty. He suggested a remedy to the moral and military crisis of the noble nation through fortifying its constitutional awareness and asserting its collective identity.

Both the mainstream of the Hungarian political elite and the masses of the privileged classes enthusiastically supported the war against the French. Austria struck first, invading Bavaria, but the offensive rapidly turned into a defensive war when French and allied troops advanced into the core Austrian territories. The French quickly reached the Kingdom of Hungary, where they gained a decisive victory near Győr over the army of Archduke John, which incorporated a considerable proportion of the noble irregulars. Several counties in West-Transdanubia were occupied by the French Army for some months, but the short cohabitation of the local authorities, the civil population and the foreign military proved to be basically non-violent. Consequently, the originally pre-emptive character of war – as Kisfaludy also emphasized – was redefined as a kind of self-defence from the standpoint of the Hungarian noble elites.

Moderate reformism

Reformist thinking was not unprecedented in late eighteenth-century Hungary, and Hungarians proved to be open to new ideas. This manifested itself in various forms and represented a wide spectrum of political values and loyalties, which were shaped largely by Western cultural transfers, primarily the adoption of enlightened French political thought (e.g. Montesquieu, Voltaire, Rousseau) and of German natural jurisprudence, cameralism and the state sciences (*Staatswissenschaften*).

As regards the perception of the French Revolution, the reformers interpreted the events as a symptom of the need for social and political change. János Batsányi, a poet of non-noble birth, in his famous poem, which he wrote in 1789, *A frantziaországi változásokra* (On the Changes in France), called upon the nations suffering under the yoke of servitude, as well as their 'hangmen', to cast their eyes on Paris. The radicalization of the revolution, however, was abhorrent to most of the Hungarian political class, including the majority of the enlightened nobility. The unfolding war with France profoundly changed the political climate and made it temporarily impossible to contemplate reforms.

However, before this change took place, in the heated and at the same time optimistic atmosphere around 1790, some reform-minded plans were worked out by the leaders of the enlightened nobility, mainly magnates, most of whose worldviews were formed by their activity in the masonic lodges, where they were imbued with the ideas of the Enlightenment.[26] In the set of texts they produced (manuscripts and printed works alike), an evolutionist perspective prevailed where the possibility of a revolution – not least on the grounds of notions arising from the contemporary events in France – was perceived as an alarming possibility, a scenario that seemed to be avoidable only through a sequence of modest reforms of existing political and social conditions.

In their political programmes, drafts and proposals, these thinkers sought to reconcile their dedication to enlightened ideals (and indeed, to some of the achievements of Joseph II's reign) and their commitment to pre-existing patterns of social-political order, including their insistence on institutional guarantees of liberty based on the nobilities' privileges. Most of them idealized the political system of England and, in the vein of Montesquieu, preferred the model of a constitutional monarchy. The moderate reformers gave preference to the separation of powers, where the power of the monarch would have been restricted by the nobility's constitutional prerogatives, involving both the passing of legislation and even influencing the executive. Simultaneously, they were keen to tackle problems relating to social questions, most importantly the issue of serfdom, and improve the general condition of the peasants, and were ready to entertain the possibility of a partial emancipation from feudal bonds, while never promoting the abolishment of the estate system as a whole, persisting with the division of society into corporate entities and the system of specific rights and duties each member was endowed with.[27]

Count Alajos Batthyány, a reform-minded magnate, argued in his *Ad amicam aurem*, published anonymously in four volumes in 1790–1, that the threat of a revolution could only be avoided by relieving social tensions. Batthyány's commitment to enlightened thought manifested itself most spectacularly in his quite radical propositions on religious emancipation, where he favoured the equality of denominations and claimed that freedom of conscience has to be guaranteed by the state. On social and political questions, however, his treatise was much more moderate. Batthyány proposed to give certain rights to commoners, such as the right to hold offices and to possess landed property. However, investing the masses with political rights seemed to be inconceivable to him, since he viewed the peasants as ill-suited to political participation, being ignorant and lacking the ability to take decisions autonomously. For these reasons, representation of their interests had to be assigned to the nobility. This paternalistic attitude towards the serfs was quite a typical feature of moderate reformism, which in turn also supported the continuing tax immunity of the nobility. Batthyány himself only proposed that the nobility should contribute a share of taxation voluntarily.[28]

Count Ferenc Széchényi, another illustrious representative of moderate reformism,[29] attempted to sum up the main tasks of the estates in a memorandum entitled *Unpartheische Gedanken* (Impartial Thoughts), which he wrote in 1790. Széchényi held important offices in the early 1780s but later turned against Joseph II and became an important figure of the noble opposition around 1790.[30] In his manuscript, he argued that moderate reforms were necessary to remedy the shortcomings of the constitution, most importantly on the issues of religion and the condition of the peasantry. At the very heart of his memorandum was the idea of a reconciliation of interests: he argued that in order to be able to avoid dissent and discord, which threatened to ruin the constitution and the common good, the politically dominant factors should make concessions to the weaker groups of the country. Most importantly, the Catholic clergy should guarantee some rights and liberties for the Protestant minority and the nobility should (at least partially) shoulder the burden of the annual war-tax, the *contributio*, paid hitherto by the commoners.

Except for a short period from 1790 to 1791, the moderate reform drafts remained confidential and were written exclusively for the decision-making political elites. Some of them dealt not only with the political and economic system, but also with military issues. Several high-ranking officers and military leaders also reflected on the obsolete and ineffective defence system of the kingdom, which was grounded in the levy, and proposed improvements. After the War of 1809, which ended with Austrian defeat, Palatine Joseph produced a draft on possible ways to modernize both Hungary and the empire as a whole (*Freimüthige Gedanken über die Regenerirung des österreichischen Kaiserstaates, mit Beziehung auf das Königreich Ungarn* – Sincere Thoughts on the Regeneration of the Austrian Empire in connection with the Kingdom of Hungary). He pointed out that in the Habsburg Monarchy two governing principles existed: the constitutional doctrine, fitted to the spirit of the age in Hungary and Transylvania, and the absolutistic approach which prevailed in the rest of the empire. The plan weighed up the chances of alternative ways of reform, including the 'Hungarianization' of the Monarchy, that is to extend the benefits of Hungarian constitutionality and its representative political system to the rest of the empire at the expense of a loss of princely power.[31]

'Hungarianization' as a possible means of reform also appeared in the late political writings of Count Ferenc Széchényi. The heart of his prudent reform plans was the idea of a unified constitutional monarchy, where the monarch still wielded considerable power. In his constitutional draft from 1809, entitled *Flüchtige Gedanken über die künftige Sicherheit der Oesterreichischen Monarchie* (Passing Thoughts on the Security of the Austrian Monarchy), the Count proposed radical changes to unify the Monarchy under the aegis of the expanded and improved Hungarian constitution. It relied on the leading statesmen having become cautious due to the spread of the ideas of liberty and equality as an irreversible result of the French Revolution while seeking to channel the excitement of the people within proper boundaries. According to his draft, unlike 'delusive Napoleonic efforts', the House of Habsburg had to guarantee 'moderate', that is, 'real liberty based on religion and laws' for its subjects, modelled after the Hungarian and English systems. It proposed a new representative political system, based on the establishment of national assemblies for every province, as well as a common imperial assembly (*Reichs-Landtag*), where Hungary would have been represented by the most delegates due to the size of its population. On social issues, it was worded cautiously, stating that it did not aim to abolish the nobility, but 'only' to impose the same amount of taxes on them as in the Hereditary Lands.[32]

Radical reformism

Around 1790, the commitment to social and political reform was not inevitably connected to noble constitutionality: more radical attitudes were also present. On the ideological spectrum they ranged from readiness to cooperate with the noble-national movement to secret plans to transform the entire polity.

An important proponent of radical reformism was Károly Koppi, a Piarist monk, freemason and professor of world history at the University of Pest, whose early works displayed his commitment to cameralism and the Josephinist reforms of the Catholic Church. Nevertheless, in a treatise written in 1790, he apparently gravitated to the noble opposition when he argued that the Hungarian nobility was entitled to elect their kings freely. In his reasoning, he applied the theory of the social contract in the vein of Rousseau, stressing that monarchs obtained their power from the people, which automatically reverts to the latter if the ruler infringes the contract. While this echoed the principle of *filum successionis interruptum*, his social and political allegiances profoundly differed from that of the mainstream of the noble opposition. Koppi dealt with the well-being of the peasantry exhaustively in his works and insisted that the peasants were entitled to freedom and safety. He also emphasized that their full emancipation was necessary to incorporate them into the nation.[33]

The most systematic theoretician of the radical reformist camp was József Hajnóczy, a Lutheran intellectual of non-noble birth, a freemason and a Deist, as well as an erudite expert in Hungarian common law, who was deeply influenced by the English and French Enlightenment. He served as Ferenc Széchényi's personal secretary in the 1780s and held office as vice lord-lieutenant (*vicecomes*; *alispán*) of Szerém County during the reign of Joseph II. The most significant characteristic of his thought was an ardent promotion of social reforms and empathy with the peasantry. He depicted the miserable condition of the taxpaying commoners and condemned the oppressive and harsh treatment of them. Already, in 1778, he had proposed to Maria Theresa the liberation of the serfs.[34]

Hajnóczy was cautious when discussing noble privileges, since his hope was that reforms could be realized in the future with the support of the nobility. In 1790–1, he wrote several treatises in this vein, with the aim of demonstrating that the restoration of the ancient constitution was not in the interest of the privileged. He outlined the framework of a new constitution, using the traditional legal language of politics, deducing his premises largely from the laws of the country. In contrast to the mainstream opposition to Habsburg centralization, he did so not to underpin the nobles' privileges but to relativize them and hence to diminish or even abolish them.[35] As such, he emphasized that the socio-political incorporation of vast masses of non-nobles was urgently needed, to give them a stake in the new social-political order. Yet, Hajnóczy and his radical reformist comrades became resigned to the fact that the chief aim of the noble opposition was simply to regain and preserve their old privileges. The radicals were forced to concede that winning over the nobility to fundamental reforms was an illusion.

The rapid radicalization of the French Revolution and the death of the reform-minded Leopold II in March 1792 necessarily entailed the revaluation of the programme which aimed to reconcile the interests of the nobility and their non-noble compatriots. The moderate enlightened nobility gravitated towards the court, while a small group of radicals became more antagonistic to the existing system. The latter group spawned a secret organization, usually referred to as 'Hungarian Jacobins' in historiography. This clandestine movement comprised two separate societies, with divergent programmes: the Society of Reformers and the Society of Liberty and Equality. This arrangement of a rather spontaneous conglomeration of radical reformists into an organized political movement was the achievement of Ignác Martinovics, a former Franciscan friar, university lecturer in the natural sciences and disaffected supporter of Enlightened Absolutism, who served the Habsburg Court as a secret agent until the rule of Francis I.[36]

Martinovics composed two catechisms for each of the societies. With his *Catechismus occultae societatis reformatorum in Hungaria* (Catechism of the Secret Reform Society in Hungary), he attempted to target noblemen who were disaffected with the burdens of the French War and the strengthening absolutistic tendencies under the reign of Francis I. For them, Martinovics outlined a plan to establish a noble republic and depicted the burdensome situation of the nobility under the Habsburg rule, employing all the typical themes of the noble opposition. By contrast, the main aim of the *Catéchisme de l'Homme et du Citoyen* (Catechism of Man and Citizen), which was published under the pseudonym *Democrite la Montagne*, was to provide a programme for democratic radicalism, laying emphasis more on social problems and the condition of the peasantry. Martinovics echoed the egalitarian vision of the French Revolution by arguing that 'the rights of man can never in any way be annulled. So long as man lives, he has the right to preserve and protect his life, freedom, property, and individuality.'[37] Attempting to harmonize the radically divergent points of these programmes would have posed severe difficulties. However, Martinovics and his confederates never had to face this problem. In 1794, the conspiracy was uncovered, its leaders, including Martinovics and Hajnóczy, were executed and the alliance between the king and the nobility was restored (if dubiously and reluctantly on both sides) to defend against the armed expansion of the French Revolution.

The issue of reform was still kept on the agenda, however, primarily by the two main representatives of radical reformism in the period, Gergely Berzeviczy and János Batsányi. Berzeviczy, a wealthy, well-travelled and educated Lutheran nobleman and former freemason from Upper Hungary, can be considered an early forerunner of Reform-Era Liberalism, mostly due to his ideas on market and taxation policy, as well as his support for equality before the law for the peasants. Nevertheless, his rejection of language- and ethnicity-based cultural nationalism and his insistence on keeping Latin as the official language of the country attached him to the intellectual tradition and collective identity model of the 'colour-blind' *Hungarus* patriotism of the eighteenth century. Constitutional radicalism was a constant characteristic trait of Berzeviczy's thought, in which, in the course of time, criticism of both the existing conditions and democratic tendencies became increasingly decisive factors. Berzeviczy developed an anti-Habsburg, anti-absolutistic stance early on. In 1790, he attached his hopes in a short Latin treatise to the dethronement of the Habsburgs and the coronation of a king of English origin to secure the 'free constitution' of the kingdom. Although Berzeviczy remained an adherent of the independence of Hungary, the Jacobin trial made him more cautious, and he openly stressed only the importance of bettering the relationship between Austria and Hungary. In his book *De commercio et industria Hungariae* (On the Commerce and Industry of Hungary, 1797), he harshly criticized the economic policy of the court in Hungary and stated that the discriminative customs forced the kingdom into being a 'colonial state'. The treatise, influenced by physiocracy, proposed that the creation of free markets and industry could solve the problem of economic development.

Berzeviczy was also concerned about social problems, characterizing the condition of the *misera plebs contribuens* of Hungary as among the worst in Europe. In his pamphlet on the Diet of 1802, published abroad, he criticized the anachronistic and chaotic nature of the constitution. He pointed out that while the rather weak aulic party tried to appeal to the 'common good', the bulk of the nobility, portraying the promotion of their own interests as 'patriotism', refused the initiative based on aristocratic principles. Consequently, nothing happened to improve the condition of the peasantry. In a later treatise, which was published illegally in 1806, Berzeviczy proposed the abolition of serfdom, although in the 1802 work this idea was prudently not stressed. He emphasized the common benefits of a limited refinement of the peasants and called on the nobility to better the constitutional and legal grounds of their serfs. Berzeviczy became increasingly mistrustful of the mainstream of the nobility, which cleaved desperately to its privileges, and considered that the aulic party and the government were too weak to implement reforms. He looked forward to a 'military government', which would be powerful enough to carry out fundamental reforms from above. His thinking became more and more pessimistic, and his position became increasingly isolated within the rigid two-pole political system.

With the outbreak of the war, both of these tenacious radicals, Batsányi and Berzeviczy, pinned their hopes on Napoleon. The 'Hungarian Bonapartists' gazed wishfully on the Napoleonic model, cherishing the hope that through the assistance of the French emperor, Hungary would be able to secede from the Austrian Empire and immediate reforms could be put into force with external support from above.[38] On the eve of war, Berzeviczy elaborated a hopeful French-language constitutional draft for Napoleon, which the emperor never received.[39] It gave a general outline of social, political, economic and religious tensions within the country and its relations with Austria, and presented some guidelines for future constitutional reform. He suggested introducing a general tax on the nobility to boost public revenues and ensure equality before the law, while also granting ownership rights to the peasants and abolishing feudal taxes and other payments in kind, and proposing a considerable expansion of the rights to hold office for non-nobles including the right to send delegates to the Diets, as well as introducing the *Code Napoléon* in Hungary with the necessary modifications.

Shortly after the occupation of Vienna (15 May 1809), Napoleon issued a proclamation to the Hungarians. It was published in a three-column broadsheet form in two versions with the same content, but in different languages (in French–Latin–Hungarian and French–German–Hungarian versions). János Batsányi, who stayed in Vienna, in all probability contributed to the translation and correction of the Hungarian text.[40] Napoleon addressed the Hungarian noble nation, offered it a separate peace and used familiar constitutional rhetoric to convince them to restore the independence of the country by abolishing Habsburg rule. The proclamation quickly came to the attention of governmental circles and the palatine commissioned Sándor Kisfaludy to formulate a suitable response.

After the war, Batsányi was forced to leave Vienna because of his collaboration, and followed the French troops to Paris. In 1810, his German-language pro-Napoleonic political work, *Der Kampf* (The Struggle), a lyrical poem with an *Anhang über das Feudalwesen und das neue europäische Staatensystem oder die republikanisch-konstitutionelle Monarchie* (Appendix on Feudalism and the New System of European States or the Republican-Constitutional Monarchy) was published anonymously in Tübingen. Batsányi emphasized the freedom, capabilities and potential of humanity, taking Napoleon as an example, although without openly mentioning his name: 'See him on his trajectory, you mortal! And what a man can do, learn from him.' The *Appendix*, finished independently of the first poetic part of the work in August 1809 in occupied Vienna, was an erudite treatise of political and social philosophy, which dealt with the struggle against feudalism and promoted the Napoleonic concept of Europe.[41]

At that time, Batsányi's ideal was the republican-constitutional monarchy, which he treated in the Kantian sense as a republican form of government (*forma regiminis*), based on representation, recognition of the rights of the citizen and separation of legislative from executive power. He deemed the form of sovereignty (*forma imperii*) secondary, as the 'pure democracy' or 'popular government' which existed in the cantons of Switzerland was not realistic in large states. In a constitutional monarchy, the monarch needed to be the 'first representative, head and leader of state power', whose 'rights and claims are based on the rights of the entirety of the citizens'. The work condemned the 'systematic subjugation of the people' and 'barbaric Feudalism' and put its hopes in Napoleon, who struggled for the 'Freedom of Europe' and for 'human dignity'.

All this demonstrates that while Berzeviczy and Batsányi can be classified, in a sense, as radical thinkers who were open to the future democratization of the Hungarian constitution, they were not advocates of democracy or of the republican system in its revolutionary sense. They were strongly committed to constitutional monarchies and believed in an evolutionary path of reform, which could even have accepted the temporary preservation of noble privileges to some extent. Nevertheless, both became more and more pessimistic and disillusioned with the iron law of political dualism and the attitude of the nobility, and thus turned into adherents of Napoleon in the hope that he would impose modernization on Hungary.

Anti-noble aulic writers

The nobles' understanding of the Hungarian constitution was essentially contested by the court. During the reign of Maria Theresa and Joseph II, some scholars attempted to legitimize the practice of Habsburg enlightened absolutism through theoretical arguments. Karl Anton Martini, a government adviser and professor of law at the University of Vienna between 1754 and 1782, and an adherent of Samuel von Pufendorf and Christian Wolff, claimed that individuals transferred their sovereignty to the ruler in a 'pact of subjection' (*pactum subiectionis*). In Vienna, a chair of *Polizey- und Kameralwissenschaften* was established in 1763 under the leadership of Martini's disciple, Joseph von Sonnenfels. Their works became prescribed texts in higher education in the Hereditary Lands (1769) and in Hungary (1777), thus spreading the new ideas across the Monarchy through educational cultural transfers, particularly in the field of jurisprudence.

The Vienna Court exploited scientific notions in the service of governance. Based on the idea of the pact of subjection, the monarch claimed that he was obliged only to consult with his subjects, not to share in the legislation with them. The idea of 'good governance' (*gute Polizey*) comprised various aspects of theoretical and empirical knowledge in public administration, education, health, the economy and security. The pivotal notion of enlightened monarchism was the 'common good'. It legitimized the efforts of the central authorities to intervene in the lives of their subjects. This perspective identified itself with rationality and usefulness, disregarding historical rights: the abolition or reduction of legal divisions within the estate polity seemed to be a necessary means to achieve its aims.[42]

Critiques of the nobilities' 'ancient constitutionalism' were elaborated by several aulic jurists and scholars, for example, Zsigmond György Lakits, Michael Piringer and Anton Wilhelm Gustermann. All of them were followers of the intellectual tradition of the historian Ferenc Ádám (or Adam František) Kollár, a *Hungarus* of Slavic origin, well connected with the State Council (*Staatsrat*), who, as an advocate of enlightened absolutism, was a notorious critic of noble nationalism and legal thought.[43] At the core of their writings lay the assumption that the struggle against the Hungarian nobility could be fought more successfully with their own intellectual weapons. Instead of a mere flat denial of the validity of noble constitutionality, these efforts were carried out by authors of great erudition, disguised as thoroughgoing historical-academic projects on constitutional issues. However, they served the purposes of the court by undermining the nobles' view of the constitution and bolstering the efforts of the government to expand royal power. They used legal-historical methods to pick apart legal sources and subvert their accepted interpretation, by redefining some of the key concepts of ancient constitutionality.

György Lakits contested the mixed character (i.e. the power is divided between the ruler and the nobility) of the Hungarian constitution, claiming that it had become deformed over time, and that it originally had an absolutistic spirit.[44] Consequently, the task was to go back to its first principles. Within the original, pure monarchical constitution, the superior power was practised by the king alone, who may opt to consult notable persons, but was not obliged by laws to do so. Royal power was limited by blurred 'basic treaties' and 'laws', although the ruler had permission to ignore them in exceptional circumstances. The power of the nobles became stronger only in the troubled times, thus the power of the Diets was a usurpation of former royal prerogatives. Lakits's view of the nobility was extremely hostile. Contradicting Montesquieu, he questioned the necessity of the nobility in monarchies at all, pointing out that the nobles performed their military duties less and less frequently, while increasingly tying the monarch's hands by an unconstitutional expansion of their own power.

The aulic attacks on the Hungarian constitution grew more intense in the 1810s. While Lakits's writings remained in manuscript form and influenced only higher governmental circles, printed books by Michael Piringer and Anton Wilhelm Gustermann triggered a general outrage among the Hungarian nobility. Gustermann's treatise explicitly dealt with 'the development of the constitution', while Piringer who seemingly dealt with the Hungarian military establishment also had as his main goal to deny the rights of the nobility to limit royal power. Both Piringer and Gustermann claimed that before Stephen I, the Hungarians had been savage barbarian nomads, and only the first king created a new constitution by copying the Western (German) feudal model, based on fiefdom, where the ruler had unlimited power. By means of legal history, their aim was to set up a normative, absolutistic ideal of the 'original' Hungarian constitution, which could be utilized in the service of the aulic party against the estates.

Arguing for the nobility, the prolific legal scholar Márton György Kovachich refuted Piringer's reasoning. He criticized the postulate of total subjugation of the nobility to the king, claiming that the 'native' Hungarian constitution bore a federative character before Stephen I, which he deduced indirectly from the Blood-oath. This determined the duties of the nobility and others, who lived under bilateral treaties, based on negotiations between two equal sides, the king and the country. Kovachich also defended the nobility against the aulic accusation that they did not perform their military duties.[45] Nevertheless, censorship did not allow this refutation of Piringer's claims to be published.

Conclusion

Concerning the long-term political agenda, the principal tendency of mid- to late eighteenth-century Hungarian politics was the transition from confessionalism to constitutionality. That is, the Diets abandoned religious issues and the noble political elite focused principally on defending their privileges. This led on the one hand to the decrease of polarization within the estates, on the other hand it gave rise to a new form of antagonism vis-à-vis the Habsburg rulers, which considerably reduced the possibility of compromises.

Nevertheless, in the narrower period from 1789 to 1815, the relations between the crown and the country were not always hostile. After the open political resistance of the estates in 1789–90, the tension was released, although the dissatisfaction within the Hungarian political and intellectual elites did not cease entirely. The Jacobin trial and executions, as well as the removal of reform-minded local politicians, marked a traditionalist turn in the principles and methods of governance. However, the immediate needs of the French Wars led to a modus vivendi between the nobility and the king, which provided limited opportunities to implement moderate reforms at the Diets. This fragile compromise, which persisted due to the shared perception of threatening danger, lasted until the Diet of 1811–12, which was followed again by an era of rule by decree, as well as the increasing opposition of the nobility, particularly in their strongholds of the county assemblies.

Regarding the transformation of the language of politics, the following main tendencies have to be stressed. In the first half of the 1790s, and especially around 1790–1, a double trend appeared in the political discourse. In addition to the consolidation of ancient constitutionalism (including the increasing significance of the Hungarian language in noble political thinking), an unprecedented opening of political discourse and thought can be observed, both in terms of quantity and quality. Broadly speaking, cultural transfers of Enlightenment had the greatest significance in this latter regard, both within and outside of noble thinking. However, the more radical trends did not survive the retaliation of the Hungarian Jacobin organization and the general conservative turn of politics in the country. Nevertheless, among the political innovations of the first half of the 1790s, two main currents proved to be durable in the longer term. First, the predominant rhetoric of ancient constitutionalism became more consistent and complex. Second, within the invigorating 'nationalization' of the estates' polity and the noble political community, efforts at cultural nation-building and ethnocultural identity also emerged and became increasingly significant in the first half of the nineteenth century.

Notes

1 In the following we distinguish nobles (*nobiles*) and magnates (*magnates*) within the entire Hungarian nobility, irrespective of its inner stratification, based on wealth, that is, the size of landed possession. For the sake of simplicity, we refer to the former plainly as 'nobility' on its own. Concerning the latter, we speak about 'aristocracy', 'aristocrats' or 'magnates', that is, about those people who owned a hereditary title of a baron, count or prince. Despite the legal fiction of István Werbőczy's *Tripartitum*, the 'one and the same liberty' (*una eademque libertas*) of the nobility, between the status of nobles and magnates were legal differences, for example, as for their political rights.

2   As István Szijártó points out, 'the unofficial sessions of the *sessio circularis* developed into the main decision-making foci by 1790'. István M. Szijártó, 'The Birth of the Constitution in Eighteenth-Century Hungarian Political Thought', in *A History of the Hungarian Constitution Law, Government and Political Culture in Central Europe*, ed. Ferenc Hörcher and Thomas Lorman (London–New York: I. B. Tauris, 2019), 52.
3   Márton Zászkaliczky, 'The Language of Liberty in Early Modern Hungarian Political Debate', in *Freedom and the Construction of Europe*, ed. Martin van Gelderen and Quentin Skinner (Cambridge: Cambridge University Press, 2020), 1:274–95.
4   Concha Győző, *A kilenczvenes évek reformeszméi és előzményei: Irodalomtörténeti vázlat* [Reform Ideas of the Nineties and Their Antecedents: A Sketch of Literary References] (Budapest: Franklin-Társulat, 1885); Ballagi Géza, *A politikai irodalom Magyarországon 1825-ig* [Political Literature in Hungary until 1825] (Budapest: Franklin-Társulat, 1888).
5   László Péter, *Hungary's Long Nineteenth Century. Constitutional and Democratic Traditions in a European Perspective. Collected Studies*, ed. Miklós Lojkó (Leiden–Boston: Brill, 2012), 4–5; István M. Szijártó, *Estates and Constitution: The Parliament in Eighteenth-Century Hungary* (Oxford: Berghahn Books, 2020), 9–115. Szijártó, 'The Birth of the Constitution in Eighteenth-Century Hungarian Political Thought', 46–62.
6   Szijártó, *Estates and Constitution*, 275–99.
7   Denis Silagi, *Ungarn und der geheime Mitarbeiterkreis Kaiser Leopolds II.* (München: Oldenbourg, 1961); Benda Kálmán, 'A magyar nemesi mozgalom (1790–92)' [The Hungarian Noble Movement (1790–92)], in *Magyarország története 1790–1848*, ed. Vörös Károly (Budapest: Akadémiai, 1980), 29–69; Szijártó, *Estates and Constitution*, 217–19.
8   Benda Kálmán, 'A magyar nemesi mozgalom (1790–92)', 86–102; Pajkossy Gábor, 'Az abszolutizmus és a rendiség utolsó küzdelmei: Az első reformtörekvések' [The Final Struggles Between Absolutism and the Estates: First Reform Efforts], in *Magyarország története a 19. században*, ed. Gergely András (Budapest: Osiris, 2005), 134–6; László Kontler, *Millennium in Central Europe: A History of Hungary* (Budapest: Atlantisz Publishing House, 1999), 220.
9   Eduard Wertheimer, *Geschichte Österreichs und Ungarns im ersten Jahrzehnt des 19. Jahrhunderts*, 2 vols. (Leipzig: Duncker & Humblot, 1884); Poór János, *Kényszerpályák nemzedéke: 1795–1815* [Generation of Forced Directions] (Budapest: Gondolat Kiadó, 1988); Dobszay Tamás, *A rendi országgyűlés utolsó évtizedei (1790–1848)* [The Last Decades of the Diet (1790–1848)] (Budapest: Országház Könyvkiadó, 2019); Poór János, *Adók, katonák, országgyűlések 1796–1811/12* [Taxes, Soldiers, Diets 1796–1811/12] (Budapest: Universitas, 2003).
10 János Poór, *Adók, katonák, országgyűlések 1796–1811/12*, 7–16.
11 László Péter, 'Die Verfassungsentwicklung in Ungarn vor 1848', in *Die Habsburgermonarchie 1848–1918*, vol. VII/1, *Verfassung und Parlamentarismus*, ed. Helmut Rumpler and Peter Urbanitsch (Wien: Verlag der Österreichischen Akademie der Wissenschaften, 2000), 239–61.
12 Péter, *Hungary's Long Nineteenth Century*, 155–61; Philip Barker, 'Resurrecting the Past, Reshaping the Future: The Rise of the "Ancient Constitution" at the Diet of 1790/1', in Hörcher and Lorman, eds., *A History of the Hungarian Constitution*, 63–4.
13 V. Windisch Éva, *Kovachich Márton György, a forráskutató* [Márton György Kovachich, the Source Researcher] (Budapest: MTA Történettudományi Intézet, 1998), 181–203.

14 Mónika Baár, 'Echoes of the Social Contract in Central and Eastern Europe, 1770–1825', in *Engaging with Rousseau: Reaction and Interpretation from the Eighteenth Century to the Present*, ed. Avi Lifschitz (Oxford: Oxford University Press, 2016), 95–113; Péter, *Hungary's Long Nineteenth Century*, 111–33.
15 Barker, 'Resurrecting the Past, Reshaping the Future', 69.
16 On the movement and its ideology: Mályusz Elemér, ed., *Sándor Lipót főherceg nádor iratai 1790–95* [Documents of Palatine Archduke Alexander Leopold 1790–95] (Budapest: Magyar Történelmi Társulat, 1926), 3–231, 3–37; Henrik Hőnich and Ágoston Nagy, 'The Crown Guarding Banderium-Movement of 1790 in the Kingdom of Hungary: Organizational Issues and Political Discourses', in *Pamphlets and Patriots*, ed. Henrik Hőnich, Ágoston Nagy and Frank Judo (Bruxelles: Standen en Landen, 2023). In press.
17 Jenő Szűcs, *Nation und Geschichte: Studien*. (Budapest: Corvina, 1981).
18 Almási Gábor and Lav Šubarić, 'A magyar nacionalizmus gyökerei: nemzeti diskurzusok a 18. század végén' [Roots of Hungarian Nationalism: National Discourses at the End of the 18th Century] *Aetas* 35, no. 2 (2020): 66–103. Henrik Hőnich, 'Which Language and Which Nation? Mother Tongue and Political Languages: Insights from a Pamphlet Published in 1790', in *Latin at the Crossroads of Identity. The Evolution of Linguistic Nationalism in the Kingdom of Hungary*, ed. Gábor Almási and Lav Šubarić (Leiden–Boston: Brill, 2015), 35–63.
19 Hőnich Henrik, 'Latin, vagy magyar? A nyelvkérdés a diéta előtt 1790–91-ben' [Latin or Hungarian? The Question of Language at the 1790–91 Diet], in *Rendi országgyűlés, polgári parlament: Érdekképviselet és törvényhozás Magyarországon a 15. századtól 1918-ig*, ed. H. Németh István et al. (Budapest: Magyar Nemzeti Levéltár, 2020), 273–93.
20 Borbála Gesmey, *Les débuts des études françaises en Hongrie (1789—1830): Essai de bibliographie*, Études françaises 18 (Szeged: Institut Français de l'Université de Szeged, 1938); Eckhardt Sándor, *A francia forradalom eszméi Magyarországon* (Budapest: Lucidus, 2001).
21 Bíró Ferenc, *A felvilágosodás korának magyar irodalma* [Hungarian Literature in the Era of Enlightenment] (Budapest: Balassi, 1994), 308–18.
22 Nagy Ágoston, 'Kreskay Imre inszurrekciós költészete és az egyházi értelmiség szereplehetőségei a háborús mozgósításban' [Insurrectional Poetry of Imre Kreskay and the Role of Clerical Intellectuals in War Propaganda], *Sic itur ad Astra*, no. 68 (2019): 173–244.
23 Orsolya Szakály, 'Opportunity or Threat? Napoleon and the Hungarian Estates', in *Collaboration and Resistance in Napoleonic Europe. State-formation in an Age of Upheaval, c. 1800–15*, ed. Michael Rowe (Basingstoke–New York: Palgrave Macmillan, 2003), 153–68.
24 Nagy Ágoston, 'Az 1809-es ötödik koalíciós háború hivatalos propagandájának keretei a Habsburg Monarchiában' [Frameworks of the Official War Propaganda of the Fifth Coalition War of 1809 in the Habsburg Monarchy], *Századvég*, no. 2 (2021): 43–76.
25 Ágoston Nagy, 'The Uses of Republicanism and De l'Esprit des lois in a Hungarian War Pamphlet from 1809', in *Lumières et républiques: Entre crises et renouvellement*, ed. Jean Mondot and Christophe Miqueu (Bordeaux: Presses Universitaires de Bordeaux, 2018), 205–22.
26 Ludwig Abafi, *Geschichte der Freimaurerei in Österreich-Ungarn*, 5 vols. (Budapest: Aigner, 1890–99); Domokos Kosáry, *Culture and Society in Eighteenth-Century Hungary* (Budapest: Corvina, 1987), 47–51; Éva H. Balázs, *Hungary and the*

Habsburgs, 1765–1800: An Experiment in Enlightened Absolutism (Budapest: CEU Press, 1997), 270–9.
27 Pajkossy Gábor, 'Törekvések a magyar rendi alkotmány korszerűsítésére az 1790-es évek első felében' [Efforts at Modernizing the Hungarian Ancient Constitution in the First Half of the 1790s] in *A felvilágosodás jegyében. Tanulmányok H. Balázs Éva 70. születésnapjára*, ed. Klaniczay Gábor et al. (Budapest: ELTE, 1985): 163–74.
28 Pruzsinszky Sándor, *Természetjog és politika a XVIII. századi Magyarországon: Batthyány Alajostól Martinovicsig* [Natural Law and Politics in 18th-Century Hungary: From Alajos Batthyány to Martinovics] (Budapest: Napvilág, 2001).
29 Miskolczy Ambrus, *Széchényi Ferenc a szabadkőművesség erénykultuszától a katolikus megújulásig* [Ferenc Széchényi from the Masonic Cult of Virtue to Catholic Renewal] (Budapest: Universitas, 2019).
30 H. Balázs, *Hungary and the Habsburgs, 1765–1800*, 304–7.
31 Wertheimer Ede, 'József nádor eszméi Magyarország és Ausztria regenerálásáról' [Palatine Joseph's Thoughts on the Regeneration of Hungary and Austria], *Budapesti Szemle* 26, no. 52 (1881): 102–12.
32 Miskolczy, *Széchényi Ferenc a szabadkőművesség erénykultuszától a katolikus megújulásig*, 45–57, for Széchényi's draft, see 109–50.
33 Benda, 'A magyar nemesi mozgalom (1790–92)', 79–80; Forgó András, 'Koppi Károly szerepe a 18. század végi nemesi-értelmiségi reformmozgalomban' [The Role of Károly Koppi in Late 18th-Century Noble-Intellectual Reform Movement] in *A piarista rend Magyarországon*, ed. Forgó András, Művelődéstörténeti műhely 6 (Budapest: Szent István Társulat, 2010), 132–7, 143.
34 Benda, 'A magyar nemesi mozgalom (1790–92)', 81.
35 V. Windisch, *Kovachich Márton György, a forráskutató*, 29.
36 On Martinovics and the history of the 'Hungarian Jacobins', see Benda Kálmán, *A magyar jakobinus mozgalom iratai* [Documents of the Hungarian Jacobine Movement], vol. 1 (Budapest: Akadémiai Kiadó, 1957), lxiii–xc; Denis Silagi, *Jakobiner in der Habsburger-Monarchie: Ein Beitrag zur Geschichte des aufgeklärten Absolutismus in Oesterreich* (München: Herold, 1962).
37 Balázs Trencsényi et al., *A History of Modern Political Thought in East Central Europe*, vol. 1, *Negotiating Modernity in the 'Long Nineteenth Century'* (Oxford: Oxford University Press, 2016), 119.
38 Éva H. Balázs, 'Notes sur l'historie du bonapartisme en Hongrie', in *Nouvelles Études Hongroises: Volume 4–5, 1969–70*, ed. Béla Köpeczi (Budapest: Corvina, 1970), 186–207.
39 Éva H. Balázs, 'Notes sur les relations franco-hongroises: Berzeviczy et Napoléon', *Annales Historiques de la Révolution Française* 45, no. 212 (1973): 245–63.
40 The question of the translator and corrector has been discussed for a long time in the Hungarian historiography, see Kosáry Domokos, *Napóleon és Magyarország* [Napoleon and Hungary] (Budapest: Magvető, 1977).
41 *Batsányi János Összes művei IV. Der Kampf (A viaskodás)* [Collected Works of János Batsányi IV. The Struggle], ed. Keresztury Dezső, Tarnai Andor and Zsindely Endre, trans. Hill Erzsébet (Budapest: Akadémiai, 1967).
42 Teodora Shek Brnardić, 'Modalities of Enlightened Monarchical Patriotism in the Mid-Eighteenth-Century Habsburg Monarchy', in *Whose Love of Which Country? Composite States, National Histories and Patriotic Discourses in Early Modern East Central Europe*, ed. Balázs Trencsényi and Márton Zászkaliczky (Leiden–Boston: Brill, 2010), 631–61.

43 Andor Csizmadia, *Adam Franz Kollár und die ungarische rechtshistorische Forschung* (Wien: Verlag der Österreichischen Akademie der Wissenschaften, 1982).
44 Poór János, 'Király és rendiség Lakits György Zsigmond magyar államjogában' [Crown and Estates in György Zsigmond Lakits' Hungarian Constitutional Law], *Levéltári Közlemények* 71, no. 1–2 (2000): 53–77.
45 Poór János, 'Egy recenzió és recenziója: Kovachich Márton György a magyar alkotmányról és hadszervezetről' [A Review and its Review: Márton György Kovachich on the Hungarian Constitution and Military System], *Levéltári Közlemények* 74, no. 1–2 (2003): 105–33.

6

Ferenc Kazinczy (1759-1831) and his age

Kálmán Tóth

The appreciation of the Hungarian language and culture from the middle of the eighteenth century onwards

The appreciation of the Hungarian language and culture in the final decades of the eighteenth century was integrally connected to the ideological influence of the European Enlightenment and its political impact. For well-educated Hungarian noblemen well acquainted with contemporary European culture and thinking, and especially the Protestant ecclesiastical intelligentsia, it became increasingly obvious that among the educated nations of Western Europe, the use of the Latin language had not only disappeared from the domains of politics and administration but also lost its significance in the cultivation of the sciences and the arts. In the Protestant countries, Latin had completely lost its position by the end of the eighteenth century with the exception of classical philology, while in the Catholic countries it remained in ecclesiastical use but was no longer the primary language of intellectual debate. In Western Europe, besides the largely overlapping geographical position of dynastic states and linguistic-ethnic blocks, the appreciation of the vernacular was made possible by the practical decisions of absolutistic rulers. It is also worth noting, however, that even in France, the country considered to be the most homogenous in Europe from a linguistic and ethnic perspective, there have always been several native ethnic minorities, some of them still existing today (e.g. Basques, Bretons, Occitans). This fact indicates that even the violent enforcement of absolutist unifying intentions did not lead to complete linguistic and cultural homogeneity. In the Kingdom of Hungary, the application of Western models of the nation-state and linguistically unified nation faced two major obstacles. The first was the country's multi-lingual and multi-ethnic character, which was mainly the result of one-and-a-half centuries of Ottoman conquest, during which period the Hungarian-inhabited parts of the country suffered the greatest demographic losses. These territories were partly repopulated through spontaneous migration (the gradual expansion of Romanians in Transylvania) and partly due to the organized resettlement policies of the Habsburg rulers who invited Germans and Slavs to settle in the depopulated territories. Among them were a number of Catholic Swabian settlers who also received significant privileges. The other major obstacle against affording the Hungarian language a dominant position was the person of the foreign, Habsburg ruler, who, although forced by the balance of power to respect the rights and privileges of the Hungarian nobility based on the ancient constitution, more or less continuously aimed at furthering the unification of the Gesamt-Monarchy, as German had already become the official language in the administration of the Hereditary Provinces in the early modern period. Unlike in the independent Western European states, there was no royal will to make the language of the country's most populous and also historically dominant ethnic group the official language.

One of the first to raise the issue of the necessity to make Hungarian the official language was János Ribiny, who was of Slavic and non-noble origin, and as such, cannot be accused of ethnic or social bias towards the Hungarian ethnic group or the Hungarian nobility. He was rector of the Lutheran lycée of Sopron when he published his *Oratio*[1] in 1751. In this Latin speech, Ribiny referred to the example of the Western European states and to the favourable characteristics of Hungarian as the 'domestic language', making its improvement and the fight for its official status a duty of his noble students in their later careers. Among the students mentioned by name in the dedication of the *Oratio*, Baron László Prónay – who later became lord-lieutenant (*supremus comes, főispán*; leading official in county administration) of Csanád County and one of the district commissioners under Joseph II – was among the most dedicated of the magnates who supported the Hungarian language's introduction as the state's official language in the Upper House of the 1790-1 Diet.

The year 1772 is often regarded in Hungarian literary history as the beginning of the Hungarian Enlightenment, although the exact date has only symbolic significance. Nevertheless, György Bessenyei, the first outstanding personality of the Hungarian Enlightenment, had three of his works published that year. Bessenyei, who came from a noble family which owned medium-sized lands (*bene possessionatus*), went to Vienna to join the Royal Hungarian Life Guards that had been founded by the Empress Maria Theresa, where he was influenced by the works of European (mainly French) enlightened thinkers. The influential enlightened programme that he subsequently elaborated held that the ultimate goal for human society is the improvement of the common good (*közboldogság*), and the most important instrument for achieving this is the broadest possible dissemination of sciences, arts and knowledge. The wider use of his native tongue was not the ultimate goal for Bessenyei, but rather it was the most effective instrument for the dissemination of the arts and sciences to improve the common good. He believed that ordinary people cannot be expected to learn foreign languages, and the example of educated Western European nations would appear to validate what is probably his most famous quote: 'Every nation became learned in their own language, but never in a foreign one' (*Magyarság*, 1778). The adherence of the nobility to their ancient freedoms and rights in the face of the absolutist and empire-building Vienna Court was transformed by intellectuals such as Bessenyei into a national ideology of freedom, that is, the nation no longer embraced only the nobility, it included every Hungarian-speaking inhabitant of the country.

As vernacular literature was gaining ground in the final decades of the eighteenth century, contemporaneously with Bessenyei's instrumental concept of language, the idea of the artistic formation of language by writers also emerged. It aimed at transplanting sophisticated linguistic-stylistic forms of expression into the Hungarian language, from ancient Greek and Roman and from modern Western European authors they considered exemplary, predominantly through translations. The long-term vision was to create original Hungarian works that compared to the most outstanding products of Western literature. However, the writers aiming for this goal realized that they would first need to enrich the language through translations. The first outstanding representative of this movement was Sándor Báróczy, an author of Transylvanian noble descent, who, similarly to Bessenyei, came to Vienna as a member of the Royal Hungarian Life Guards. From the viewpoint of the history of political thought, his most important work is *A védelmeztetett magyar nyelv* (The Defended Hungarian Language), published in 1790 in Vienna. In this work, Báróczy argues that Hungarian is suitable to be the country's official language.

The appreciation of the public importance of the Hungarian language is reflected by the appearance of Hungarian-language newspapers starting from the 1780s. This new medium also gave space and publicity on a never-before-reached scale to new political ideas, helped by the relatively light censorship in force during the reign of Joseph II.

Ferenc Kazinczy and the question of language

As a result of the Habsburg rulers' refusal to permit the establishment of a Hungarian academy, and especially as a result of the retaliation following the exposure of a conspiracy led by Ignác Martinovics, the public sphere was more restrictive after 1795. As a result, the improvement of the Hungarian language could mostly only be pursued through informal means, in the arts and sciences, using soft power while avoiding direct political action. The work of Ferenc Kazinczy (1759–1831), who is regarded as the dominant voice of the period discussed in this chapter, was of crucial importance in these endeavours.

Early years

Coming from a noble family with medium-sized lands, Kazinczy was interested in literature and arts from an early age and studied at the prestigious Calvinist college of Sárospatak. His first work, a short book on the geography of Hungary, appeared in 1775, when he was sixteen. His love for his fatherland was already apparent early in his life, inspired by his ancestors who were supporters of Rákóczi's War of Independence against Habsburg rule that had broken out at the beginning of the eighteenth century.

Enlightened ideas also had a great influence on Kazinczy. In 1776, he translated *Der Amerikaner* (The American), Bessenyei's philosophical short story, from German into Hungarian. He sent a copy to the author, who responded with a letter of appreciation and encouragement. As a legal trainee, he realized under the influence of French and German enlightened writers that 'poetry and the novel can become new forms of the fight for social change'.[2] In 1784, Kazinczy took up public service, first as a deputy-notary, then as a judge of the county court (*táblabíró*) in Abaúj County. In 1786, alongside Count Lajos Török, director general of the Kassa (today Košice, Slovakia) school-district, he became inspector of the schools of the ten northeastern counties. He held this office until 1791.

During this time he also became acquainted with the ideas of freemasonry under the influence of Count Lajos Török, who later became his father-in-law. On the recommendation of Török, he was admitted to the Lodge of the Virtuous Cosmopolitans in Miskolc (*Tugendhafte Kosmopoliten zum brennenden Busche gegen Orient*) and took the pseudonym Orpheus at his initiation.

The secret society of the freemasons was one of the primary conduits of the enlightenment in Hungary. Their lodges were composed mainly of noblemen sympathizing with the ideas of Enlightenment. Most of their members, like Kazinczy, were also supporters of the enlightened absolutist rule of Joseph II, whose decrees, however, increasingly alienated them from the ruler who tried to bring the lodges under central control with the Patent of Freemasonry he issued in 1785.

Kazinczy remained an active freemason even after the dissolution of the Miskolc lodge. For him, the masonic movement was a carrier of both national and cosmopolitan ideas. He suggested the creation of new lodges, especially in his letters to his Transylvanian friend, György Aranka, the most active organizer of literary life there. He also proposed establishing a Hungarian-language lodge in Pest.

He translated an excerpt from Rousseau's *Considérations sur le gouvernement de Pologne* (Considerations on the Government of Poland) into Hungarian, which he published in his journal *Orpheus*, entitled *A törvényszabásról* (About lawmaking). This text outlined a diverse concept of freedom encompassing the freedom of thinking, religious tolerance and the opportunity for cultural betterment for all. He also considered the realization of all three of these as a criterium of enlightened patriotism. The philosophical and political reflection manifested in his journal were an instrument to foster the formation of a national awareness that went beyond the nobles' claim to be the exclusive '*Natio Hungarica*'.

The Jacobin conspiracy

In 1790, the Hungarian nobility's resistance to Joseph II's centralizing policies prevailed and on his deathbed Joseph rescinded his reforms with the exception of the Patent of Toleration and the Decree on Serfs. His younger brother and successor, Leopold II, was forced to accept a compromise with the Hungarian estates and convened a new Diet. The promotion of enlightened thinking, human freedom and equality, the literary, cultural and intellectual rise of the Hungarians and the renewal of the vernacular remained Kazinczy's major goals after this Diet. In order to achieve these aims, he sought political outlets alongside his literary activity, as he started to demand the freedom of the press and equality before the law. The reading circle (*Lesekabinet*) of Pest was founded in 1792 under the leadership of József Hajnóczy and Márton György Kovachich. This group subscribed to the *Moniteur*, the journal of the French Revolution, and discussed contemporary political events. Similar circles were founded in many places throughout the country, some of which functioned as Jacobin clubs.[3]

Kazinczy was a member of the Kassa circle and had good relations with the main club in Pest. He had already become acquainted with the Hungarian Jacobins in 1791, among whom he especially admired Hajnóczy. The ever-increasing dissatisfaction among those Hungarians who sympathized with revolutionary France spawned the republican movement, organized under the leadership of Ignác Martinovics (although this may have been no more than a provocation by the court, as Martinovics had earlier been an agent of Leopold II.)[4] Martinovics founded two societies, the Society of Reformers of the Hungarian Kingdom (*Magyarországi Reformátorok Társasága*) and the Society for Freedom and Equality (*Szabadság és Egyenlőség Társasága*). The former represented the endeavours of the dissatisfied middle-ranking nobility for independence and constitutionality, while the latter pursued the revolutionary goals of a small group of radical intellectuals, who considered themselves Jacobins and wanted to establish a bourgeois republic. According to their plans, when a republic was declared they would abolish noble privileges. They even considered granting autonomy to Hungary's ethnic minorities.[5] However, these goals were entirely unrealistic politically at that time.

Kazinczy came into contact with the Society of Reformers and he copied and disseminated their catechism as well as helped them organize in northeastern Hungary. The leaders of the movement were arrested in the summer of 1794, and Archduke Alexander Leopold, palatine of Hungary, who had grown alarmed at the self-highlighting confession of Martinovics, advised his older brother, the ruler, to take strict measures. On 20 October 1794, Francis I ordered the start of the judicial proceedings. In December 1794, on the evidence of the captured leaders' confessions, fifty-three members were arrested, including Kazinczy. Gergely Berzeviczy, the outstanding economist, who was also involved in the conspiracy but who avoided prosecution thanks to family ties, wrote later about those on trial in his anonymous work *Der Majestätsprozess in Ungarn 1795* (The Trial for High Treason in Hungary 1795), published in 1800:

> Most of them were excellent, talented and strong men, respected scholars, well-known writers, so one could have believed that a war had been declared on talent and sciences. Such learned and enlightened heads, such witty and fine company were nowhere to be found as in the Franciscan monastery [the building expropriated under Joseph II was used as a prison during that time] where they were held captive. [. . .] No Hungarian could think of this monastery without crying.[6]

Of the fifty-three men arrested, eighteen were sentenced to death at first instance. Kazinczy was one of them. In the end, only seven death sentences were carried out. On 20 May 1795, Martinovics and the four leaders of his movement, Hajnóczy, János Laczkovics, Ferenc Szentmarjay and Count Jakab Zsigray, were decapitated in Buda. Then, on 1 June, Pál Őz and Sándor Szolártsik, who were considered to be incorrigible, were executed. The sentences of the others were commuted to indefinite imprisonment. Kazinczy was released from Munkács (today Mukachevo, Ukraine) on 28 June 1801 after 2,387 days of captivity.

Language and culture as soft power

Shortly after regaining his freedom, Kazinczy was asked by his literary friends to resume his earlier activities. He was confronted by many changes that had happened in the country during his imprisonment. His former friends and supporters of aristocratic rank considered him a 'marked man' (*bélyeges ember*) and rejected his attempts to get in touch with them again. The absolutistic rule of Francis I made any kind of direct political action aimed at Hungarian nation-building impossible, so for Kazinczy and his fellow writers the improvement of the Hungarian language through literary works, predominantly translations, proved to be the only possible route. Kazinczy strived to perfect the Hungarian language by the application of the aesthetic ideas of classicism, and this aim represented both aesthetic striving for artistic perfection as well as a hidden political aim (soft power) of improving national culture. The former aimed at reaching immortality like the ancient Greek and Roman authors, while the latter would pave the way for future political independence through the cultural rise of the nation. In a political sense, the greatest fear of the era was the dread of the French Revolution and of any social change. It determined the thinking not only of the ruler and the circles of the Vienna government, but also that of the vast majority of the Hungarian nobility, or as László Z. Szabó puts it: 'The changes in European politics that took place during the opening years of the nineteenth century, and Napoleon's rise to power meant the establishment of the most radical reaction in the countries under the rule of the Vienna Court.'[7] Kazinczy was at risk of complete isolation as his opinion on the standard of the Hungarian language and on the aesthetic values of contemporary literature also brought him into conflict with both the ecclesiastical and the secular leadership of the Calvinist community in Debrecen. Kazinczy was totally convinced of the rightness of his classical aims and the need for modernization.[8] He also favoured centralized leadership instead of the particularism of the decentralized intellectual and artistic life that characterized Hungary until that time. He wanted his own manor, Széphalom, to become the centre of this cultural activity, and he managed to form an alternative informal public sphere through his extensive correspondence, even though this was obstructed by the authorities, for, as Z. Szabó explains, 'he wanted to make his opponents realize that the linguistic movement served the intellectual rise of the Hungarians'.[9]

With his correspondents from across Hungary he also elaborated his views on contemporary world politics. He judged the value of individuals and their actions from an enlightened perspective, focusing on their contribution to the progress of humanity and considered Napoleon to be an extraordinary historical personality.

Kazinczy was fully aware of what was at stake in the struggle: with the advent of the modern age, shared language and culture had become the most important factors shaping the transformation of the nation, so gaining control over these domains was crucially important from the perspective of the entire nation's future. One of the key issues of nation-building endeavours was the creation of a unified linguistic standard, which lay behind the orthography debate[10] between 'jottists' and 'ypsilonists', which also had an indirect political dimension. Ferenc Verseghy, who was imprisoned for his participation in the Martinovics movement for even longer than Kazinczy, was a supporter of an 'ypsilonist' orthography that was based on current language use irrespective of its inconsistencies. Kazinczy, in contrast, was a dedicated supporter of the 'jottist' viewpoint represented by Miklós Révai that advocated a reformed language based on the consistent application of historical etymology. Kazinczy played a decisive role in ensuring the victory of the latter. More and more young writers joined Kazinczy, who considered the creation of a modern language suitable for literature and sciences to be the prerequisite for national independence and social modernization and made every effort to promote it.

The issue of making Hungarian the official language in the territory of the Kingdom of Hungary was again put on the agenda by the opposition estates at the Diet of 1807. After the Diet was disbanded without enacting any significant reforms, the court in Vienna attempted to gauge the real extent of the Hungarian national movement, at the recommendation of Court Secretary Johann Michael Armbruster (1761–1814), by offering a prize for the best essay on this controversial topic.[11] In 1808, under the auspices of the publishing book store Cotta of Tübingen, the competition was launched and candidates were asked to submit an essay discussing the possibility of making Hungarian the official language in the Kingdom of Hungary, with the winner's prize supposedly donated by a 'Hungarian patriot'. Its real goal was probably to identify writers fighting to make Hungarian the official language as Kazinczy suspected. The nearly seven years he had spent in prison made him cautious, yet he still considered it his duty to be a patriot and stand up for the Hungarian language. In the essay he submitted, he spoke in the name of his whole nation and attempted to prove the legitimacy of the community's demand for the right of language.[12]

In the end, twenty-one prize essays were submitted, and among these, only five supported introducing Hungarian as the official language in the Kingdom of Hungary. A further four would have introduced it conditionally, but the other prize essays were in favour of German or Latin. The authors of most of the prize essays belonged to the non-Hungarian-speaking ethnic minorities of Hungary. Of the well-known Hungarian writers, only Kazinczy and Gábor Döbrentei took part in the competition, which soon became irrelevant for the Vienna Court's purposes, and so in the end no results were declared, and no prizes were given. Kazinczy's prize-essay remained unpublished during his lifetime, although it is one of the most important documents of his political thinking. In it, he argued with crystal-clear logic for the necessity of making Hungarian the official language and proved its equal worth with other European languages. His focus was 'the good of the nation and its glory'[13] together with the nation's political, commercial and scholarly interests and the level of intellectual value it had already achieved. The most important value stressed in the essay was patriotism based on the love for the fatherland, which is free of the nationalism that depreciates other nations. This does not stand in contrast with the cosmopolitan ideas of Enlightenment. In fact, it can be interpreted as its purest manifestation, as one can only do something for the whole of humanity through helping one's own nation to rise. Kazinczy's goal was to enable Hungarians to take their rightful place within the larger family of learned European nations, a place to which it was clearly entitled by the historical and constitutional rights of the Hungarian nation. Kazinczy also makes it obvious in his arguments that the Hungarian national idea was not invented (or 'imagined') by a small group of intellectuals as was the case for that of most ethnic minorities living in the Kingdom of Hungary, but can be traced back to an ethnic consciousness similar to that of Western nation-states. However, due to the lack of a national ruler, the wars with the Ottomans and the empire-building designs of the Habsburgs, it was not able to blossom to the same extent as national identity in the West during the early modern period.

Kazinczy believed that the only possible way of closing this gap with Western Europe was to make Hungarian the official language. He insisted that the means to achieve this was the improvement of the language to make it suitable for public affairs and the sciences. Even if this meant confrontation with the government, he had the courage to speak up for the national language, social modernization and enlightened ideas. In his view of history, the development of national characteristics is manifested within an international framework. He also outlined the history of Hungarian literature, portraying it as embedded in the history of human culture. With this, he only partly exceeded the concept of *historia litteraria* but incorporated it nonetheless into an independent framework based upon his own point of view.

Kazinczy was a supporter of an idea of progress that had its roots in the reality of Hungarian life and that was feasible under the actual circumstances. His perception of reality and his political sense outlined for him what he had to do. The aesthetic criticism he levelled at his contemporaries derived from differences in worldview and approach. For him, being a patriot and being a cosmopolitan coexisted in harmonious unity in his fight for social modernization. His standpoint was shaped by the interests of national progress where the nation was not only the nobility but a linguistic and cultural community.

This progressive approach constituted the main dividing line in his debate with Gergely Berzeviczy. The two thinkers respected each other and both had been part of the Jacobin movement, but Kazinczy considered it his duty to make his critical remarks known to Berzeviczy as regards the latter's views about the peasantry in the Kingdom of Hungary. As opposed to the cosmopolitan Berzeviczy, the patriot Kazinczy articulated his concern for his nation. According to Berzeviczy's views, the right way for the inhabitants of the Kingdom of Hungary to progress would be not only to abolish the privileged status of the nobility, but also to give up the linguistic and cultural distinctiveness of the nation to facilitate economic rationality and greater prosperity. The adoption of German language and culture would bring economic improvement and material progress, and thus the strengthening of the Gesamt-Monarchy. For Kazinczy, progress was also important, but it could only be made within a national framework. He regarded the elimination of the distinct linguistic identity of a nation as political murder. For him, the existence of his nation was undoubtedly more important than economic progress and material wealth. Bringing the domestic language to utmost perfection was the most important factor in the furtherance of the common good, and the road towards achieving it led through aesthetics.

The role of politics in the struggle for the renewal of the language

Nation-building and neology

As explained above, the idea that a shared native tongue played a key role in forming the nation also appeared in the territory of the Kingdom of Hungary in the closing decades of the eighteenth century and rapidly gained more adherents. This idea, first espoused by enlightened writers, also influenced the defenders of the nobility's constitutional autonomy against the paradigm of absolutism and its attempt at a technocratic unification of the Habsburg Empire. For these proponents of the noble nation,[14] based on the shared noble freedoms which could be traced back to Werbőczy, the national language was becoming increasingly important.

The major political divide in Hungary in this period was between the proponents of reform and progress and those who defended the traditional exclusive conception of the nobility. Their debates, and their struggle for language renewal, served as a substitute for the political debates that were not permitted by the Vienna Court. The question of national existence was at stake: whether unavoidable social and economic modernization would be accomplished in the Hungarian language, and within the existing constitutional framework, or whether modernization would be an imperial project driven by the court, in which case the Hungarian language and culture, failing to keep up with modernity, would disappear, together with the ancient privileges of the nobility that were unsustainable in the long term. This was the struggle that mobilized a significant number of Hungarian writers, which emerged in the second decade of the nineteenth century, when the Vienna Court rejected all kinds of social and political change out of fear of the consequences of the French Revolution and the Napoleonic Wars, and thus narrowed down the possibility of political action to linguistic-cultural endeavours pursued primarily through informal channels. However, as the Habsburgs needed the military aid of the Hungarian nobility, further centralizing measures were temporarily suspended. This period of relative calm allowed time for the literary processes to unfold, which would prepare the way for Hungarian political reform aspirations in the subsequent decades.

The struggle for the formation of a national language consciousness and the recognition of the native tongue had been a political tool since the times of Bessenyei. Kazinczy had been a participant in this movement since the start of his literary career. He was instrumental in promoting the pioneering role of the Royal Hungarian Life Guards who became writers, notably Bessenyei, Ábrahám Barcsay and Sándor Báróczi. Báróczi's translations had a particularly great influence in popularizing Kazinczy's aesthetics-based neologisms. Kazinczy's awareness of the necessity of cultivating the language made him the leading figure of the language renewal that sought to prepare the way for social modernization and set him against the opponents of linguistic standardization. His previous conflicts with the Calvinist intellectual elite of Debrecen can be traced back to this. Kazinczy's battle for language reform, as a conduit for modernization within a national framework, involved battles on multiple fronts:

against all kinds of provincialism, noble narrow-mindedness and 'orientalism', that is, backwardness (*napkeletiség*).[15] He fought for the continued existence and progress of the Hungarian nation with the instruments of science and arts, that is, with a masterful application of 'soft power'. Those who subscribed to the nobility's view of the nation, idealizing the feudal past, declared Kazinczy's reforms unpatriotic and turned against them, clinging onto older principles and purism. The so-called 'making of words' which his opponents criticized the most was, in reality, only one element of a comprehensive literary and scholarly programme that was aimed at improving the expressiveness of the language in order to bring it up to the level of the cultivated Western languages. His neologisms were both linguistic and aesthetic at the same time. He placed the ideal of *beauty* at the centre of his classicist aesthetics, which was complemented by the notion of the *good*, that is, 'a thoughtful, intelligent and aesthetical service of human action'.[16]

On the issue of linguistic affinity, which also had political ramifications, Kazinczy had a unique perspective: although he accepted the 'oriental' origin of the Hungarian language, he unambiguously stressed its connections with Western languages. The debates on the Scythian-Hunnic, Turkic and Finno-Ugric origin of Hungarians were of no interest to him. In the tradition of Miklós Révai, he considered only written linguistic records important, and advocated the freedom of writers to shape the language. Speech habit, considered to be of central importance to his opponents, only mattered to him as a means of subsequent approval. To substantiate his endeavours to modernize by emulation, he held up German literature as an example, which started to prosper as a result of the language battles in the German states in the middle of the eighteenth century. As Germany was in a state of political disunity, the creation of a unified linguistic standard had played a very important nation-building political role there, too.

Kazinczy's circle and the Hungarian Diet of 1811–12

Besides the essay he wrote for the prize-essay competition of Tübingen, Kazinczy also sought other ways to underline the rightfulness and necessity of making Hungarian the official language. In particular, as Dezső Dümmerth put it, '[t]he literary movement, which was awakening national self-consciousness, met with political reality' at the Hungarian Diet of 1811-12. This was the first time that 'literature and scholarship appeared as leading forces in the forum of political life, in order to lead the way towards further progress'.[17]

Even after several years had passed, no response had come in connection with the prize essays that were sent in for the Tübingen competition. Furthermore, the publishing of essays promoting the Hungarian language was hindered by official censorship, while works arguing in favour of Latin and German could be published without difficulties. Count József Dessewffy, a scholarly aristocrat, friend and correspondent of Kazinczy, brought this issue to the attention of the estates in a speech at the Diet.[18] He referred to Kazinczy's prize-essay, which he knew well, in which Kazinczy referred to the promises Ferdinand I (the dynasty's ancestor and founder of the continuous Habsburg rule over Hungary) had made to the Hungarian nobility in 1527, the year after his election, to safeguard and support the Hungarian language. Kazinczy cited this promise, which he found in Márton György Kovachich's collection of historical documents, without naming the exact source. Kovachich was a learned historian of Croatian origin who, as a result of his research into the history of the law, pledged his support for Hungarian national freedom.

As the drafter of the petition of grievances (*gravamen*) which included a request to introduce Hungarian as the state's official language, Dessewffy included the relevant letters of Ferdinand I as historical evidence supporting the constitutional status of the Hungarian language. At the Diet, during the debate over this petition, it was István Horvát (a historian and close friend and correspondent of Kazinczy, who later became a professor at the University of Pest) who provided 'an authentic historiographical basis for the oppositional nobility not familiar with historical data'.[19] Horvát was present at the Diet as the secretary of the judge royal (*iudex curiae regiae, királyi országbíró*) József Ürményi who invoked the antiquity of native Hungarian written culture, whereas most of the leading nobles were highly ignorant about the country's past.[20] The vast majority of the Lower House supported making Hungarian the official language, and they demanded it based on the promises made at the 1790-1 Diet by Leopold II. At the debate on the *gravamen* at the session of the Diet held on 4 December 1811, citing Horvát's historical evidence, Imre Péchy, the delegate of Pest County, convincingly defended the tradition of the official usage of the Hungarian language against the arguments of the chief justice (*personalis praesentiae regiae in judiciis locumtenens, királyi személynök*) György Majláth, evoking the 'frenzied cheering' of the Lower House's oppositional majority. The historical sources cited were from Kovachich's collection of sources *Supplementum ad vestigia Comitiorum apud Hungaros celebratorum Tom. 3-tius* and concerned the promises Ferdinand I had made about the preservation of the freedom and language of the Hungarian nation. This uncomfortable confrontation of the Vienna Court with the broken promises made by the ancestor of all subsequent Habsburg kings occurred at a time when the government was devoting all its efforts to obscuring the free and independent past of the Hungarians and disseminating the idea of eternal servitude.[21] These aims had been served, inter alia, by the books of Michael Piringer[22] (royal court secretary and councillor, also an agent of the Vienna state police[23]) and Anton Wilhelm Gustermann[24] (professor of the Theresian Academy in Vienna) that attacked the Hungarian constitution, denied the nation's free past and strived to abolish not just noble privileges but the nation's entire independence, and which also employed 'historical arguments'. At the Diet, the Hungarian nobility failed to ban these works. No decision was made on the issue of the Hungarian official language, either, because of the resistance of the ruler and the majority of the Upper House. The scholarly refutation of Gustermann's work was accomplished by Kovachich in one of his German-language writings, which he finished on 10 May 1812, during the final days of the Diet. His work[25] is the first example of domestic historical scholarship taking action against anti-national propaganda.[26] The censors did not allow the printing of this work despite the fact that it was free from any nationalistic sentiment and prejudice. It was a factual rendition of Kovachich's scholarly views on Hungarian state law and a refutation of the false claims that had appeared in numerous pamphlets published since the 1790s.

Uncovering the truth in a rational manner became a defensive political tool in the service of the writers' nation-building efforts to resist the centralist policies of the Vienna Court. The circle of Kazinczy and his friends aimed to reveal the nation's free and independent past with the help of historical scholarship and their reform of the vernacular.²⁷

Neology versus orthology

Among the contributors to language renewal who struggled for control over the literary language (whom Kazinczy termed 'glottomachs', i.e. language-fighters), Sándor Kisfaludy became the leading figure among Transdanubian orthologists who were in opposition to Kazinczy. His personal relation to Kazinczy was largely influenced by Kazinczy's *Himfy* review and *Himfy* epigram (*Himfy* was the poetic pseudonym of Kisfaludy, under which name he published two cycles of poems). Kisfaludy regarded these texts as essentially offensive to his noble self-esteem. The conflict between neologists (proponents of language reform) and their orthologist critics revealed not just different views about linguistics and aesthetics but also different concepts of the nation. Proponents of orthology considered any kind of renewal to be a crime against the nation, and they had an aversion to enlightened thinking. For Kisfaludy, patriotism came first, while poetic and aesthetic values were only of secondary importance. In turn, for Kazinczy and his neologist followers, the idea of the autonomy of the *belles-lettres* diverged from the patriotism espoused by the estates. For them, literary performance was determined by aesthetic value.

In the beginning, blinded by the praise of his corresponding partners, Kazinczy could not perceive the anger he evoked with his satirical poems criticizing backward tastes. These only became evident to him after he came across the *Mondolat*, a tasteless pamphlet compiled in 1813 by Gedeon Somogyi, a juror in Veszprém County, which attacked him personally and blamed him for every excess of language-renewing endeavours. It was not the attack itself which was most annoying for Kazinczy, but the blazing ignorance and boorishness that put him in the same category as the tasteless language reformers who he himself had criticized. In lieu of Kazinczy, who became irresolute as the battle degenerated into vulgar comments and personal attacks, his young followers, including Ferenc Kölcsey, who later became one of the pre-eminent political thinkers of the 1830s, and Pál Szemere, authored a response to the *Mondolat* in 1814, but because of the censorship in those years, it was not published as a book (*Felelet a Mondolatra*, A reply to the *Mondolat*) until 1815. In their book, Kölcsey and Szemere not only took issue with Gedeon Somogyi, but also attacked the entire orthology movement with sarcastic mockery. However, the intensity of the fight decreased in the following years, as the aesthetic-linguistic ideology, known as neology, initiated by Kazinczy significantly broadened the range of artistic expression possible in the Hungarian literary language. As a result of his discussions with young writers while staying in Pest, Kazinczy realized that the differences between the orthologist and neologist viewpoints were not as great as he had thought. On his way home after visiting Vienna, he asked for personal meetings with some of the Transdanubian writers belonging to the circle of

Sándor Kisfaludy, seeking reconciliation, through the mediation of Abbot József Ruszek. Kisfaludy, however, rejected the olive branch Kazinczy extended to him, and by voicing his personal grievance, revealed his own aristocratic prejudices. He completely distanced himself from the literary endeavours that aimed at modernization and continued to proclaim the superiority of noble patriotism. Kazinczy, on the other hand, was able to soften his previously rigid views in the interest of cooperation for the good of the nation. He made an effort to live in peace with those who realized the inevitable necessity of the improvement of the language, while also making concessions on the question of language usage. His fight for language renewal can be considered victorious in spite of some minor differences that still existed. The new generation of writers, who entered the stage in the 1810s, were following in Kazinczy's footsteps, but at the same time they already surpassed his views. Kölcsey also drifted away from his former master, when by the year 1817 it became clear to him that the proponents of neology had triumphed, and that in the changed European political situation the struggle for language renewal could not be continued in its current form. For him, the necessity of creating unity was the main goal in order to preserve the nation's existence and its sovereignty against the absolutist efforts of the Habsburgs. As room for political action remained restricted, Kölcsey also had to remain in the field of literature and sciences. However, instead of Kazinczy's eternal, cosmopolitan classicistic ideal of beauty, his guiding principle became the Herderian idea of the preservation of the traditions that organically establish a nation.

Kazinczy himself demonstrated his desire for reconciliation in his great treatise *Orthológus és neológus nálunk és más nemzeteknél*[28] (Orthologists and neologists in our midst and in other nations), in which he revised his previous principles in the interest of creating a new national consensus. He took as his starting point the theses of universal language development that was valid for all languages and conceived the development of the national characteristics within this framework. In his view, both language reformers and their opponents were driven by their love for their mother tongue, with the former striving for its development while the latter were concerned about the deterioration which changes could bring. Thus, the right balance needed to be found between these two endeavours, in the spirit of organic language development.

Kazinczy's treatise ended an important period in the struggle for the language, although the different viewpoints did not completely disappear subsequently. The orthologists' aversion to Kazinczy's aesthetic principles can be explained by their adherence to their noble way of life. In their view, literary ability and personal rank were inseparable, which is why they took aesthetics-based literary criticism as a personal insult. The new generation further developed Kazinczy's ideas and introduced new romantic ideals in the fight for the nation's continued existence. Aesthetic guidelines were brought into harmony with national characteristics, and an appreciation of originality took precedence over language development and classicistic imitations.

Kazinczy's final years

Kazinczy's position as a leader ended in the 1820s, although he remained an active participant in Hungarian arts and sciences and continued to be relevant politically. In his work titled *Fogságom naplója* (Diary of my captivity), which was not intended for publication, he discussed the years of his imprisonment. Although he did not write about his political ideas and only referred to his role within the Jacobin movement in general terms, nevertheless, a man of character emerges from the text, who remained faithful to his ideas and was guided by the highest moral standards of stoicism during his time of vulnerability and suffering. The text can also be interpreted as a political confession, and it is an important source of historiography, although one should not use it without reservation, since the imprisoned Kazinczy could only obtain much of his information (e.g. on the executions of Martinovics and other leading Jacobins) through hearsay.

Kazinczy formulated his Hungarian nation-building ideas within an enlightened cosmopolitan framework. He also respected the cultures of ethnic minorities. He was interested in Slovak and Romanian folksongs, and was a close friend of Mihály Vitkovits, a Serbian and Hungarian bilingual writer and poet. He also corresponded with the Serbian poet Lukijan Mušicki on the development of Serbian literature.[29]

Furthermore, Kazinczy took part in the institutionalizing of cultural life in the 1820s. He was one of the first elected members of the newly established Hungarian Learned Society, the predecessor of the Hungarian Academy of Sciences (Magyar Tudományos Akadémia). Mostly in order to address his financial difficulties, he also applied for the position of secretary, but Gábor Döbrentei, his former follower turned personal enemy, snatched it away from him.

Kazinczy followed political developments with vivid interest and could see the continuation of his own linguistic and cultural pursuits in the political activities of the next generation of reformers who first gained publicity in the 1820s and 1830s. In 1831, in an unfinished epistle addressed to Count István Széchenyi, he expressed this in a poetic way. He agreed with the Count's reform ideas and counted them among his own. Besides Széchenyi and his father, Count Ferenc Széchényi, both of whom he personally knew and highly respected, the young Lajos Kossuth also attracted Kazinczy's attention with one of the speeches he delivered at a county convention.[30]

Conclusion: 'Széchenyi's predecessor was Kazinczy'[31]

The options for political action broadened again when the Diet was once again called together in 1825. Alongside the wielding of soft power through the advancement of national culture, and the noble patriotic direction defending the ancient constitution against centralization, a new way of political thinking appeared that reflected a new paradigm: Liberalism. Its advocates clearly coupled the defence of constitutionality with a programme aimed at the economic and social modernization of the country. These endeavours can be traced back to the enlightened reform efforts of the first half of the 1790s.[32]

Hajnóczy had already called for the abolition of noble privileges and the need for radical social reform. Ever since the counties' resistance against Josephinism (especially against the 1784 language decree forcing the official use of German), the narrow noble interpretation of the concept of the nation had begun to shift towards a new linguistic and cultural nationalism. For the majority of the nobility this only involved the appreciation of the role of the Hungarian language but they insisted on their constitutional privileges. They even tried to justify their claim to make Hungarian the official language of the kingdom by reference to the ancient constitution.

The enlightened linguistic programme started by Bessenyei had already brought significant results in the 1780s with the creation of a public sphere for cultivating the Hungarian language, together with an appreciation of the role of enlightened intellectuals. The modernizing currents, which followed the example of Western European nation-states, first started to emerge in the field of national language culture and scholarship, but they were clearly linked to the political aim of attaining national independence within a constitutional framework. The efforts to make Hungarian the official language were helped by the literary and cultural cultivation of the language.

After the dissolution of the Martinovics movement, the absolutism of Francis I viewed any kind of modernizing initiatives with alarm, afraid that it would emulate revolutionary France. The ruler enjoyed the support of the Hungarian nobility who were likewise afraid of radical political change, although they still tried to keep the issue of the national language on the agenda.

The issue of the cultivation of the language gained even greater political significance as the public sphere was restricted and there were no opportunities for direct political action to build a modern nation-state. The court secretary Armbruster, who initiated the prize-essay competition of Tübingen, was well aware of the community spirit of Hungarian writers and the close connection between literature and politics within their circle. However, at the time of the Napoleonic Wars, the financial and military support provided by the Hungarian nobility was indispensable for the Vienna Court, and they most likely did not fully realize the political dimension of these linguistic activities. The debates between the supporters of different linguistic and literary-aesthetic ideas undoubtedly contributed to the development of the Hungarian language and culture, as it began to reach the level of Western cultures. The language had become suitable for its new status as an official language, as well as for the cultivation of all kinds of sciences. The establishment of the journal *Tudományos Gyűjtemény* (Scientific Collection) in 1817 can be seen as an immediate antecedent to the formation of the Hungarian Academy of Sciences.[33]

The Diet that was called together again in 1825, after more than a decade, brought forth new efforts to restore the constitutionality of the Kingdom of Hungary. Based on the achievements of the linguistic and cultural programme of modernization, these aims were slowly but surely complemented by elements of a new national-liberal programme, striving to create the conditions for social and economic modernization. A symbolic act of this process was the offer of Count István Széchenyi to found the Academy, after which the Hungarian Learned Society (from 1840 the Hungarian Academy of Sciences) whose creation had been suggested by Bessenyei half a century before, could finally be established. Just like the national unification of interests and the social basis for the political acts of the Reform Era, none of this could have been achieved without the influence of the linguistic and cultural modernization which became synonymous with the name of Kazinczy, which had already begun with Bessenyei and other writers in the final decades of the eighteenth century. At a time when opportunities for direct political action were strongly restricted, this movement created, using the instruments of soft power,[34] the linguistic and cultural prerequisites of Liberal reform efforts aiming to replace the constitutionality of the estates with the constitutional framework of modern national development.

Zsigmond Kemény[35] succinctly summarized this process: 'Without any doubt, language reformers prepared the way for political reformers. They fertilized the spirit, made it flexible for change, and suitable for the reception of new ideas. Triumphant neologism brought with itself the necessity and victory of state and social reforms. Széchenyi's predecessor was Kazinczy.'[36]

Notes

1. Ioannis Ribiny, *Oratio de Cultura Linguae Hungaricae*. Sopronii Calend. Jan. M. DCC. LI. [1751.] Typis Joannis Josephi Siess.
2. Z. Szabó László, *Kazinczy Ferenc* (Budapest: Gondolat Kiadó, 1984), 41.
3. Z. Szabó, *Kazinczy Ferenc*, 125.
4. More about his German reports to secret police: Benda Kálmán, ed., *A magyar jakobinus mozgalom iratai* [Documents of the Hungarian Jacobin Movement], vol. 1 (Budapest: Akadémiai Kiadó, 1957), 440–507.
5. Z. Szabó, *Kazinczy Ferenc*, 127.
6. Benda Kálmán, ed., *A magyar jakobinusok iratai* [Documents of the Hungarian Jacobin Movement], vol. 3 (Budapest: Akadémiai Kiadó, 1952), 330.
7. Z. Szabó, *Kazinczy Ferenc*, 169.
8. On the aesthetical dimensions of Kazinczy's relation to the discourse of politeness, see Bodrogi Ferenc Máté, *Kazinczy arca és a csiszoltság nyelve. Egy önreprezentáció diszkurzív háttere* [The Face of Kazinczy and the Language of Politeness. The Discursive Background of a Self-Representation] (Debrecen: Debrecen University Press, 2012) (Csokonai könyvtár 51.), 175–316.
9. Z. Szabó, *Kazinczy Ferenc*, 185.
10. More on the debate: Bíró Ferenc, *A legnagyobb pennaháború. Kazinczy Ferenc és a nyelvkérdés* [The Greatest War of Pens. Ferenc Kazinczy and the Question of Language] (Budapest: Argumentum Kiadó, 2010), 321–4.
11. Armbruster wrote in his proposal to Joseph Thaddäus Freiherr von Sumerau (1749–1817), vice-president of the Polizeyhofstelle on 26 October 1807: 'Whoever knows the state of literature, knows well that national writers with some fame nowhere have such great influence on the thinking of cultivated and half-cultivated classes of the people, as in Hungary. And there is no such esprit de corps between writers of any nation as among Hungarian writers. As in other provinces, men who worship on the altar of literature, persecute, bring down, wrongly accuse each other, Hungarian writers form a kind of unvisible church, the members of which, no matter whether they live at home or abroad, take care of the glory of the parts and of the whole as their common good, win over the common sense and keep it up in the interest of the good of the fatherland. They always correspond with each other, and literature goes hand in hand with politics among them'. Quoted by Wertheimer Ede, 'Az 1807-ik évi magyar országgyűlés' [The Hungarian Diet of 1807], *Századok* 30, no. 4 (1896): 305.
12. More on Kazinczy's prize-essay: Bíró, *A legnagyobb pennaháború*, 428–39.

13 Kazinczy Ferencz, *Tübingai pályaműve a magyar nyelvről 1808* [Ferenc Kazinczy's Tübingen Prize-Essay on the Hungarian Language from 1808], Régi Magyar Könyvtár 37, ed. Heinrich Gusztáv (Budapest: Magyar Tudományos Akadémia, 1916), 138.
14 However, this does not mean that ethnic consciousness did not exist before. Anti-Habsburg movements of the early modern period led by nobles always tried to integrate the dissatisfaction of the commoners against the foreign occupiers. In fact, serfs led by Tamás Esze turned to Ferenc Rákóczi II and asked him to lead their movement against Habsburg oppression.
15 Z. Szabó, *Kazinczy Ferenc*, 245.
16 Z. Szabó, *Kazinczy Ferenc*, 254.
17 Dümmerth Dezső, *Írástudók küzdelmei: Magyar művelődéstörténeti tanulmányok* [Struggles of Scribes: Studies on Hungarian Cultural History] (Budapest: Panoráma, 1987), 283.
18 Cf. *Felséges Első Ferentz Austriai Tsászár, Magyar, és Cseh Ország Koronás Királyától Pozsony Szabad Királyi Városába 1811-dik Esztendőben, Kis-Aszszony Havának 25-dik Napjára Rendeltetett Magyar Ország' Gyűlésének Jegyző Könyve, melly Eredet-képpen Magyar Nyelven Íratott, És Az Ország Gyűlésének Fő Vigyázása Alatt Hitelesen Deák Nyelvre Fordítatott* [Minutes of the Hungarian Diet Ordered by His Majesty Francis I, Austrian Emperor, Crowned King of Hungary and Bohemia to be Held in the Royal Free City of Pozsony on August 25, 1811, Originally Written in Hungarian and Authentically Translated into Latin under the Supervision of the Diet] (Pozsony: Wéber, 1811–12), 340–1. Kazinczy is not mentioned by name in the official record of parliamentary proceedings, but Dessewffy told Kazinczy about it in a letter. (*KazLev* 9:185.)
19 Dümmerth, *Írástudók küzdelmei*, 286.
20 Dümmerth, *Írástudók küzdelmei*, 287.
21 Dümmerth, *Írástudók küzdelmei*, 291.
22 Michael von Piringer, *Ungarns Banderien, und desselben gesetzmäßige Kriegsverfassung überhaupt*. Erster Theil (Wien, 1810).
23 Dümmerth, *Írástudók küzdelmei*, 292.
24 Anton Wilhelm Gustermann, *Die Ausbildung der Verfassung des Königreiches Ungern* (Wien, 1811).
25 Kovachich Márton György, *Die Ausbildung der Verfassung des Königreichs Ungarn dargestellt von Ant. Wilh. Gustermann* [. . .], Fol. Germ. 219, OSZK Kézirattár, Budapest, Hungary.
26 Dümmerth, *Írástudók küzdelmei*, 296.
27 Dümmerth, *Írástudók küzdelmei*, 299.
28 *Tudományos Gyűjtemény* 3, no. 11 (1819): 3–27.
29 Váczy János, ed., *Kazinczy Ferencz összes művei. Harmadik osztály. Levelezés* [Ferenc Kazinczy's Collected Works. Third Class. Correspondence], 21 vols. (Budapest: MTA, 1890–1911), 9:275–7 (hereafter cited as *KazLev*).
30 Kazinczy to László Bártfay, 25 January 1831 (*KazLev* 21:457).
31 Kemény Zsigmond, *Tanulmányai* [Studies of Zsigmond Kemény], ed. Gyulai Pál (Pest: Ráth Mór, 1870), 1:326.
32 On the historiographical debate on the issue of this continuity, see Ferenc Hörcher, 'Enlightened Reform or National Reform? The Continuity Debate about the Hungarian Reform Era and the Example of the Two Széchenyis (1790–1848)', *Hungarian Historical Review* 5, no. 1 (2016): 22–45.

33 cf. Kollár Zsuzsanna, 'Mintaadó szervezeti formák a Magyar Tudós Társaság működési rendjében' [Example-Giving Forms of Organization in the Functioning Order of the Hungarian Learned Society], in *Aranka György és a tudomány megújuló alakzatai*, ed. Biró Annamária és Egyed Emese (Kolozsvár: Erdélyi Múzeum Egyesület, 2018), 279–297.
34 On the use of this term in an early nineteenth-century Hungarian context, see Hörcher Ferenc, '"Soft power" a reformkorban? A Széchenyiek tudománypolitikai céljai' ['Soft power' in the Reform Era? The Goals of the Széchenyis' Scientific Policy], *Korall*, no. 62 (2016): 5–28.
35 See Chapter 13.
36 Kemény, *Tanulmányai*, 326.

7

Ferenc Kölcsey (1790-1838)

Ferenc Kulin

This chapter, which examines the political thought of Kölcsey – a thinker who was well versed both in Greek philosophy and in the historical, theological and ethical literature of his own time – will not merely browse the table of contents of the philosophical studies of its protagonist but will also pay close attention to the trends in Kölcsey's philosophical orientation that shaped his entire life's work. We must take seriously the assessment of József Szauder, the most formative and influential cultivator of Kölcsey philology to date, who declared that 'Ferenc Kölcsey, the classic of Hungarian literature, the greatest ideologist and aesthete of Hungarian Romanticism, was also an original, profound researcher of the modern philosophy of his time. He did not create a system, but an original philosophy of morality and history that served the development of Hungarian society with great impetus on the practical political plane.'[1] The reason why Szauder himself emphasizes and includes Greek philosophy in the title of one of his most influential studies – alongside Kant's name – is precisely because it was in examining this part of Kölcsey's education that Szauder discovered the foundations of the worldview and thinking of the mature politician, which advocated harmony between epistemology, aesthetics, religion and the moral motives of political action. As Kölcsey himself put it, 'the subject of philosophy is the human soul. [. . .] Accordingly, philosophy extends into two branches: because it is concerned either with human knowledge or with human action, that is, it seeks to determine what it is that man can know and what it is that man must do.'[2] In short, Kölcsey was not only the author of the Hungarian national anthem but also a philosopher wrestling with the emotional, moral and philosophical problems of action, and a politician exploiting his historical potential.

Family background and early years

Ferenc Kölcsey was born in Sződemeter (today Săuca, Romania) to a Protestant noble family. Each of these dry biographical facts would become decisive factors in the course of his life. His native village is located in Central Szolnok (later Szilágy) County, in the Partium – on the territory of post-1918 Romania – a part of the country that throughout its history has belonged either to Transylvania or to the Kingdom of

Hungary, or formed a separate administrative area with the other borderland counties known as the Partium. The idea of the unity of national culture, of the union of the 'two homelands' (Transylvania and Hungary) – the guiding ideas of Kölcsey's career – were naturally first formulated in this region. The self-consciousness and worldview of the contemplative young man were determined to no lesser extent by the fact that even in the nineteenth century the Kölcsey family lived on what was called 'ancient property', that is, land inherited from the ancient Hungarian ancestors when they conquered the Carpathian Basin. As Ernő Taxner-Tóth argued, 'the consequence of this remained of great importance in Kölcsey's thinking. In his opinion formulated as a mature politician, the Hungarian constitution [. . .] was originally not feudal in nature, i.e., not a feudal gift [. . .] but derived from the agreement of the free Hungarian ancestors conquering the Carpathian Basin.'[3]

His relationship with the literary leader of his time, Ferenc Kazinczy, the organizer of the language renewal movement, can be considered of equal importance to these geographical and ancestral factors. It was thanks to the 'master of Széphalom' (who suffered almost eight years in prison for his enlightened views and dedicated patriotism) that Kölcsey was able to embark on a career as a poet and critic, and to keep himself informed about contemporary European literature and philosophy. All this cultural material, flowing in from outside, is almost imperceptibly superimposed on the basic substratum of the ideological heritage of the Protestant Hungarian nobility of the eighteenth century. This intellectual heritage included the class and national consciousness of the feudal nobility and the religious ethos of Hungarian Calvinism with its '*kuruc*'[4] oppositional spirit that drew inspiration from Rákóczi's War of Independence (1703-11) against Habsburg rule. All these different – and in many respects even contradictory – intellectual influences could easily have cancelled each other out, but these personal gifts, in the fortunate coincidence of the historical-political circumstances, arranged themselves into a harmonious worldview that inspired creative activity.

For Kölcsey, his family background and Kazinczy's patronage offered him the opportunity to establish contacts with the intellectual and political elite of the time. But this network – and this is true of most members of his social stratum – did not help him to create a secure existence for himself. He suffered some of the most common and dramatic scenes of the life of the lower-income nobility. He had the humiliating experience of helplessness as a young boy (he lost his father at the age of six and his mother at the age of eleven, and the 'financial support' of the family, Sámuel Kölcsey, died a year earlier): his schooling was paid for by a charitable foundation, and his relation with his relatives was overshadowed by dramatic scenes of conflict over the division of the inherited family land (after the death of his brother, he took responsibility for the upbringing of his nephew, Kálmán Kölcsey, the future hero of the War of Independence, knowing that he would also be forced to take on the burden of the household of the widow, abandoned by the grandparents), and one of his relatives, Mihály Kölcsey, practically made a pauper of him.

One of the most important lessons of his biography is that he was unable to live purely as either an intellectual or as a landowner, and that it was owing to this constant existential crisis that, in addition to his legal and sociological study of land tenure relations, he also became interested in the study of agriculture, animal husbandry and trade, that is, he also delved into the disciplines that were relevant to achieving the modern, material conditions for social modernization. He was, therefore, not a poet but an 'amateur' economist who took up politics.

The unfolding of the political career

Not only did he know about, but he also deeply felt the dilemma posed by the uncertainty of the preservation of independent existence – which threatened the majority of the Hungarian middle and small landowners of the eighteenth and nineteenth centuries – to which there were only two obvious solutions. One solution was to obtain a public office, the other way was through the economic modernization of one's own land. Most of his fellow nobles in a similar situation chose the former option, and he himself also tried to provide for his family as an office-holder. In 1828, he took up the post of vice-notary of Szatmár County, and later he flirted with the idea of becoming secretary general of the Hungarian Learned Society (later the Hungarian Academy of Sciences). Eventually, the failure of these experiments convinced him that the need for sovereignty in creative intellectual work is difficult to reconcile with the material security of holding a public office, and it was this recognition that prompted him, at least theoretically, to reconcile the ethical, legal, economic and political demands of freedom and property.

Bearing in mind how the *operata systematica* (i.e. systematic reform works) of 1791 have been reviewed and revised by new national committees appointed under Article VIII of 1827, and because Ferenc Kölcsey, then chief notary – who participated in the 1832 Diet as a delegate – played a key role in forming an opinion regarding these reforms in Szatmár County, it is worth paying particular attention to how this document raises a fundamental question that would again become unavoidable during the debate on Széchenyi's *Hitel* (Credit). This concerned the freedom of trade and its place in the system created by the reform works. Kölcsey agreed with the 1807 resolution of the Diet stating that 'the Kingdom of Hungary, as a country independent of the other half of the Empire, has the right, as regards trade, to seek to ensure that its interests are not subordinated to any other foreign interest', and that explains why, as an opposition envoy, he would later oppose the emperor's proposals which 'would have put trade and public law works only fifth or sixth on the agenda of the Diet'.[5]

This does not mean that a Reform Era liberal programme of social and economic modernization could have been elaborated years before Széchenyi's *Hitel* was published, which is still regarded as a fundamental work of economic philosophy of the period. Still, in the first third of the nineteenth century, a scenario of modernization began to mature in the minds of the middling nobility, who attempted to abolish the system of serfdom without the 'vaccine'[6] proposed by Széchenyi, that is, before he suggested the use of international/supranational capital. A proposal for the emancipation of the serfs was commissioned by the General Assembly of Szatmár County and written with Kölcsey's participation between 1829 and 1831. Kölcsey wrote its introduction before the outbreak of the 1831 cholera rebellion. This extremely important document has been analysed by István Barta,[7] who summarized its essence thus:

> Commercial work (Commerciale Operatum) came first. To properly appreciate the importance of this work, we need to know that it included, far beyond its name, all the problems that were related to the field of the national economy. It dealt with external and internal trade and customs, the development of industry, the problems of agricultural development, new settlements, land and water transport, the establishment of a public fund (fundus publicus) for large investments, etc. [. . .] And, most importantly, the most ardent hopes of the Hungarian landed classes in crisis were linked to this work: the abolition of the exploitative Austrian economic policy, the introduction of free trade or at least of reciprocity, and the removal of certain obstacles to internal industrial development and circulation would have been the panacea for them which would have made the landowner rich, the peasant well-off and contented, and would have eliminated or at least postponed the need for radical social reform [. . .]. Kölcsey's introduction was drafted before the peasant uprising of the summer of 1831; according to its date, it was discussed by the committee already on June 3. In this way, the progressive elements of the 1790-91 operata were carried over into the new work, which cannot be said of the other works.[8]

The increasing interest of a jurist and poet in the legal and political conditions of the serfs would not deserve special attention if it were only a sign of the moral sensitivity of a man of letters who is merely being true to his principles. In fact, it was a result of his involvement that the question of serfdom became an explosive point of conflict between the various proponents of reform. In fact, this was the critical point where the political paths of Ferenc Kölcsey and István Széchenyi (whom Lajos Kossuth called the 'greatest Hungarian') intersected and the latent conflict between these two political giants, which existed from the very beginning. This was not simply the 'traditional' opposition between the Protestants and Catholics, or the 'aulic' supporters of the court and the rebellious anti-Habsburg Hungarian nobility, but also a tension caused by the lack of a clear Hungarian political hierarchy.

Before taking a closer look at this, it is important to note that it was not in Széchenyi's famous work that Kölcsey first encountered the concept of 'credit' and the economic and national policy issues related to it. Even as a young man, Kölcsey showed as much interest in modern social and economic sciences as he did in the humanities as a writer, poet and critic. These two strands of his intellectual orientation were therefore not the result of his public-political experience. On the contrary, his political interests would be shaped by the fact that he encountered works on social and economic sciences in his reading as a student. His unpublished writings,[9] discovered in the 1960s, show that he intensively continued the statistical studies he had begun in 1811 with the book by Süssmilch[10] and other, mainly French, works. From 1822, several notes survive, ranging over several pages, on the population of South America, the population statistics of England, the relation of English imports and exports and so on. And he had long since completed his notes on the causes of the French Revolution, the situation of the French peasantry and bourgeoisie at that time and the course of the Revolution and its heroes, which he had prepared, together with his friend Ferenc Kállay, in the wake of Girtanner's voluminous historical work.[11] Besides, as his correspondence and his own economic diary testify, 'he had his own experience of the immediate problems of the serfs'.[12]

Returning to the Diet of 1832-6, it is worth noting that the convening of this Diet was, of course, not forced by domestic political processes. In fact, tectonic rumblings had alerted the monarch that without a deal with the reformers, the empire itself could collapse. The French Revolution of 1830 (the July Revolution) had brought an end to the reign of King Charles X in France, precipitating the fall of the House of Bourbon. An uprising had broken out in Warsaw against the Russian Empire, and Vienna had been forced to call in the military to suppress a cholera uprising in Upper Hungary. Neither event posed an immediate security threat to the Habsburgs, but they had reason to fear that the infiltration of French revolutionary ideas on the one hand, and the destabilization of the Eastern European region on the other, might weaken their position. At the same time, the impact of the bloody events abroad sharpened the opposing trends of Hungarian reform policy, and Kölcsey's political activities, which were intended to reconcile and pacify but which nevertheless prepared the way for the 1848 revolution through the influence of his works, fits into this process.

Although the overwhelming majority of the Lower House also considered him to be their leader, there were increasing signs that the Hungarian opposition and Vienna would not be able to reach an agreement on the most important social and economic policy issues, neither then nor later. Not only the majority of the parliamentary opposition but Kölcsey himself were suspicious of any 'reform' of the power structure that strengthened the relationship between the Hungarian aristocracy and Vienna, and his own historical knowledge made him doubt whether Austria could still impose conditions on the other European financial powers.[13]

Kölcsey versus Széchenyi

Although Kölcsey did not take a public stand in the debate between Count József Dessewffy – who in his *Taglalat* (Treatise) criticized *Hitel* in public – and Széchenyi's camp, he was not ignorant of the sensitive economic, ethical and value-philosophical problems connected with the triumph of money and capital in the modern era. He was well aware – as Széchenyi himself informed his readers[14] – that it was not Széchenyi who had been seeking the sources of financial capital, but it was an 'English financier' who had approached Széchenyi. The investors were not looking for distinguished merchants and industrialists but wanted to ally themselves with a large landowner who had a personal interest in taking out a loan and who would also serve as a political guarantor for the stability of Hungary's status within the empire. He also knew from the same source that Széchenyi had rejected the financier's proposal, citing the lack of 'our monetary laws' entitling him to borrow money. Kölcsey was therefore convinced that the author of *Hitel* was motivated to enter the political arena by his belief in the legal and political 'world-changing' power of capital, and therefore by the lack of clarity about the verifiability of capital. This conviction, however, did not prevent him from criticizing both the economic views and political position of the Count.

Széchenyi was drawing on the well-known theorem of Adam Smith to describe the circulation of 'ideal wealth' or 'capital' when he stated that wealth depends on the rate of circulation of capital:

> Money, land, and everything else are of the greatest possible use only if I can use one and the other at any moment for whatever I please. The sooner I can get my money or land, and the sooner I can exchange the first for the second, or the one or the other for other goods, the more my hundred or one million forints are worth to me, or ten or a hundred thousand acres of land, and at the same time all my earnings may be lost, for 'value is closely tied to the moment.'[15]

It is not only the ruthless logic of economics that is expressed by this 'utilitarian philosophy', but also a political worldview where there is no place for the (in Széchenyi's words) 'enthusiasm-generating' way of thinking popular among educated Hungarian landowners, whose economic principles were represented by János Balásházy,[16] and whose moral philosophy was formulated by Kölcsey the following way: 'the economy and the science of status' is related to 'poetry and oratory' in that 'it also lives and moves in the extensive range of expression and progress of human society, and it either turns directly into action, or is calculated to express and bring forth future actions.'[17]

Although in the light of Széchenyi's works as a whole, there is no reason to doubt either his commitment to 'spiritual values' or that, as the author of *Hitel*,

> drawing on his experiences in England, he sincerely believed that the 'leap in the speed of the circulation of money' could lead to 'public freedom' in the national interest through 'public wealth,' it should also be apparent that this belief was not based on the same historical knowledge and cultural ideals as that represented by the majority of the opposition in the Lower House or by Kölcsey, who, at that time was already openly opposing Széchenyi, representing a political stance in accord with Baron Wesselényi's strategy. In the spirit of Wesselényi, who, in practice, on an independent path, on a much broader base of the nobility, focusing on the questions of the abolition of absolutism, trod the only possible path to a political breakthrough.[18]

While Széchenyi, who emphasized the beneficial effects of capital, was transfixed by the example of England, the world's leading trading power, and saw in the institutionalization of credit an unlimited opportunity to expand the political scope and latitude of his own class, the Hungarian aristocracy,[19] Kölcsey's perception of material goods was dominated by the values of another type of cultural heritage, and by his readings warning of the serious dangers of intertwining the power of money and politics. Széchenyi argued reasonably and convincingly against those who 'in their dreams of independence are always teaching the theory of poverty, according to which, it is true, a poor nation can be free from foreign powers, but it will be all the more a slave to its own ignorance – which is the greatest and most dreadful slavery',[20] but he was not familiar with the works that formed Kölcsey's view of history, nor with the Hungarian harsh reality that shaped the historical consciousness of the author of the sorrowful national anthem. How could he have known that Kölcsey, even before he was twenty years old, had become acquainted with Girtanner's work analysing the history of the French Revolution[21], which – especially with its chapter on the History of the Deficit of the French Country[22] – would convince the young scholar-candidate that 'power' and 'money' are inseparably intertwined, as he himself wrote:

> He who has money rules, whatever place he takes in the body politic. So long as the obedient part of society has no more money than the commanders, the kingdom may be at rest, but if it has more money, revolution cannot be avoided. This seems to be the real theory of the revolution of the state and the foundation of all politics.[23]

There is no doubt that Kölcsey's ethical, religious, theoretical and historical-anthropological views were also strongly influenced by classical authors propagating the 'theory of poverty', although, it is important to note, his practical proposals for modernizing the landowning system and for further social reforms are devoid of that particular idea.

Kölcsey, the political philosopher

The 'theory of poverty' from the works of the Greek Cynics and Stoics influenced Kölcsey as much as his knowledge of the ascetic morality of ancient and medieval Christianity and the puritan tendencies of Hungarian Protestantism. He was greatly influenced by his master, Ferenc Kazinczy, who considered independence at the cost of deprivation more important than prosperity at the cost of political dependence.[24] Kölcsey himself – on behalf of his communities: as a family provider and as a local and national politician – tirelessly sought opportunities to increase material prosperity, but never at the cost of principled behaviour. He professed the principle of ancient Greek *parrhesia* (i.e. free speech) when he told his friend: 'I, for my part, have steadfastly devoted myself to the straightforward expression of my own feelings and thoughts at all times.'[25] This was the principle he applied to the debates on censorship arguing that 'each writer has an independent status; he is free to associate himself with others or to isolate himself from others; he is free to wander for good or ill; he is free to speak well or ill of his fellow writers; he is free to squander or establish his peace and glory'.[26]

While Kölcsey, as one of the most prestigious advocates of the linguistic-cultural movement, argued that the intelligentsia can protect the institutions of politics and culture from the uncontrolled role of capital, as a politician he proclaimed that material wealth does not automatically violate moral laws.

The task of organizing political resistance against the unrestricted penetration of foreign capital would ultimately fall to Kossuth in the 1840s, who, as early as 1844 declared that 'political independence without industrial independence is nothing but a pipe dream, and a self-deception that cannot be maintained for long'. He would also play a decisive role in the Batthyány government's refusal to participate in the repayment of Austria's public debt in April 1848,[27] as well as preventing Hungary from renouncing the national currency in return for a large, one-off sum of foreign capital.[28] The importance which was attached to the need for the country's financial independence in the legislative work of the 1832-6 Diet of Pozsony (today Bratislava, Slovakia), which Kölcsey was involved in, was also demonstrated by the fact that the adoption of the bill was intended not only to guarantee that noble estates could be pledged. In addition, this law 'would have put an end to [...] the untenable practice of the Lower Austrian Commercial Court judging Hungarian citizens in cases of claims arising from commercial transactions'.[29]

In attempting to mark Kölcsey's place on the intellectual map of contemporary Europe as a political thinker who also oriented himself towards the disciplines of history and philosophy, we can draw – with some reservations – on András Gerő's claim that 'Four main directions (or rather emphases) can be distinguished, the prevalence of which varied in proportion and internal dynamics, but which nevertheless existed in a tangible, constant way. One is the French Enlightenment and the liberal considerations that followed closely from it.' The second was 'dominated by the utilitarian nature of English liberalism'. The third emphasis, 'which – out of the European liberalisms of the time – was most characteristic in the German liberalism [...] is none other than the element that gives liberalism its meaning and purpose: the nation'. Finally, the fourth one is 'transforming Christian morality into liberal ethics'.[30]

Nevertheless, Gerő overlooks the fact that the French Enlightenment and the liberal influences that followed from it were more deeply and intricately intertwined with the then contemporary currents of conservatism in Kölcsey than anywhere else in Western Europe.[31] Moreover, Gerő overstates the influence of German-style liberal nationalism on Kölcsey's political thinking. While there is no doubt that the expanding/conquering dynamics of French and German nationalism, which ascribes a prominent place to their own achievements in world culture (on the cultural-theoretical foundations laid by Winckelmann), were also desired by Hungarian nationalists, it is equally indisputable that Kölcsey not only remained outside this current of ideological and political history but also resolutely opposed it. It should be noted that when – in his parliamentary speeches – he called for including the serfs behind the 'nation's ramparts', he was extending the political concept of nation to the non-Hungarian-speaking population, too.

Nation and tradition

It was a source of regret for Kölcsey that Hungarians could not point to written records and memories of their heroic age, the time before they had conquered the Carpathian Basin in 895-6. This did not, however, change his conviction that 'Christianity, politics and science have in many ways brought our Hungarians closer to our European neighbors; however, their own status, language, customs and mutual alienation have in many ways withdrawn them from them. This is why many European colors were taken on by them, and at the same time many non-European ones were retained.'[32]

Thus, he interpreted the interaction between Hungarianism and Europeanism primarily as a cultural, spiritual phenomenon, although, according to his conception, the spirit is neither a self-contained essentiality nor a subjective counter-pole to the objective world, but – through the relationship of successive generations – it is itself a historical phenomenon and as such it is the chief principle, the core and the essence of the destiny of national communities. For Kölcsey, however, this national community was not the bearer of some kind of folk spirit (Hegel's *Volksgeist*), nor was it merely a political community of citizens and legal subjects, to which the individual is subordinated (as in Kant), but a socio-psychic medium which was created through the concrete relationship between concrete individuals of successive generations, and whose content and quality depended exclusively on the conduct and moral and intellectual quality of the individuals who cultivate this relationship.

Ferenc Kölcsey's views on the past, on tradition and on the nature of the national community form a solid basis for his political thinking. Even though we can find rhetorical clichés adapted to the prevailing rhetorical fashions in his speeches to the county assemblies and in the Diet of 1832-6, he never allowed himself to subordinate either domestic or world historical examples to the 'current political' aims of his speech. This may be explained by his conviction – which was echoed by Odo Marquard's paper entitled *Universalgeschichte und Multiversalgeschichte*: 'That which we call the university of history is but a tapestry of fragments; and even in these fragments only a part of the globe appears. Our historical science is based on the histories of only a few peoples, but there is not one among these few that we can trace from its origin to late times.'[33]

Kölcsey was also wary of reconciling the heterogeneous elements of his personal experiences – that is, the dissonances of his historical consciousness, partly inherited and partly acquired through self-cultivation – through the lens of various theories. He was not influenced – as we have seen – by Hegel's notion of the 'folk spirit', nor by Schiller's vision of 'universal history'. On the subject of those who have 'created hypotheses out of their own heads', he remarks:

> The hypothesis-maker gradually becomes accustomed to believe as a certainty what he at first thought to be a suspicion; and to seek no longer the truth, but the establishment of the hypothesis itself. He lends connections, analogies, clarity, not from fragments of memory to hypothesis, but from hypothesis to fragments of memory; and, deceiving himself unperceived and unwittingly, begins to see everything in a false light; and instead of investigation he goes astray into blind faith.[34]

John Lukacs's insights are applicable to Kölcsey when he wrote that

> the recognition of the historical dimension not merely of our existence but of our consciousness opens the way to a new philosophical unity (indeed, to a new monistic view of the universe) through a historical philosophy, which is the very

opposite of a philosophy of history. The latter tried to achieve the knowledgeability of history, but a historical philosophy attempts something else, more modest but also more profound: the recognition of the historicity of human knowledge, with its inevitable limitations.[35]

Political thinking and 'politicians' thinking' have never been independent of the thinking that seeks to understand history. A fuller awareness of Kölcsey's way of thinking can also help us to grasp the problems of the nineteenth-century Hungarian Reform Era, which endure down to the present day.

Notes

1 Szauder József, *A romantika útján: Tanulmányok* [On the Road of Romanticism: Studies] (Budapest: Szépirodalmi, 1961), 163.
2 *Kölcsey Ferenc Összes Művei* [Collected Works of Ferenc Kölcsey] (Budapest: Szépirodalmi Könyvkiadó, 1960), 1:997.
3 Taxner-Tóth Ernő, *Kölcsey és a magyar világ* [Kölcsey and the Hungarian World] (Budapest: Akadémiai Kiadó, 1992), 17.
4 Followers of Rákóczi's anti-Habsburg movement during the 1703–11 War of Independence.–Ed.
5 Völgyesi Orsolya, 'Alkotmányos függetlenség és gazdasági szabadság: A szuverenitás kérdése Kölcsey és a magyarországi reformellenzék politikai diskurzusában, 1832-33' [Constitutional Independence and Economic Freedom: The Question of Sovereignty in the Political Discourse of Kölcsey and the Hungarian Reform Opposition] *Magyar Tudomány* 174, no. 4 (2013): 432–7.
6 Széchenyi István, *Hitel* [Credit] (Pest: Trattner–Károlyi, 1830), 260.
7 Barta István, 'Kölcsey politikai pályakezdete' [The Beginning of Kölcsey's Political Career], *Századok* 93, no. 2–4 (1959): 252–302.
8 Barta, 'Kölcsey politikai pályakezdete', 287.
9 *Kölcsey Ferenc kiadatlan írásai: 1809-11* [Unpublished Writings of Ferenc Kölcsey: 1809–11], ed. Szauder József (Budapest: Akadémiai Kiadó, 1968), 25.
10 Johann Peter Süssmilch, *Die göttliche Ordnung* [. . .], (Berlin: Daniel August Gohl, 1742).
11 Christoph Girtanner, *Historische Nachrichten und politische Betrachtungen über die französische Revolution*, 17 vols. (Berlin: Johann Friedrich Unger, 1793–1803); *Kölcsey kiadatlan írásai*, 237–87, 275.
12 Szauder, *A romantika útján*, 274.
13 Kölcsey did not live to see the historical moment when the empire's vulnerability to the banking world was exposed before the Diet, but he came to such conclusions on the basis of his studies of world history; see Urbán Aladár, *Batthyány Lajos miniszterelnöksége* [Lajos Batthyány as Prime Minister], Nemzet és emlékezet (Budapest: Magvető, 1986), 303–11.
14 In his book *Világ* (Light), Széchenyi describes a 'conversation' with an 'English financier'. According to this account, the Count was brought together at a lord's place in Paris 'several years ago' (i.e. before the writing of *Hitel* and *Világ*) 'by chance with several English agents, who, delegated by more notable English companies, wished to lend the capital which they had accumulated excessively with interest,

on the Continent. This was just before the period which, because of the numerous failures which had occurred in Britain at that time, was known to almost everyone [. . .]. There was at that time, for certain reasons, a great flood of money in England, but also a great frivolity about money–so that there was hardly a thing for which the most considerable capital could not be obtained. It was at that time that the Colombian, Greek, Spanish, and other such money-lending contracts were being made'. *A mai Széchenyi* [Today's Széchenyi], ed. Szekfű Gyula (Budapest: Révai, 1935), 223–6.
15 Széchenyi, *Hitel*, 42.
16 The here referred work is: Balásházy János, *Tanátsolatok a' magyarországi mezei gazdák számára* [Advice to Farmers in Hungary] (Sárospatak: Nádaskay András, 1829). It is also noteworthy that in the case of Balásházy, we are talking about an author in whose intellectual sphere the young Lajos Kossuth, who in the 1840s became Széchenyi's most influential debating partner and later his political opponent, started his public career.
17 Kölcsey Ferenc, *Erkölcsi beszédek és írások* [Moral Speeches and Writings], ed. Onder Csaba, unnumbered vol. 8 of *Kölcsey Ferenc Minden Munkái*, ed. Szabó G. Zoltán (Budapest: Universitas Kiadó, 2008), 85.
18 Gergely András, *Egy nemzetet az emberiségnek* [A Nation for Mankind] (Budapest: Magvető Könyvkiadó, 1987), 187–8.
19 Széchenyi wrote to Wesselényi on November 8, 1831: 'our most sacred duty–and I am fully convinced that it is our most sacred duty–is to bring about a quiet reformation in our country, and this can only come from the Upper House'. *Gróf Széchenyi István Levelei* [Count István Széchenyi's Letters], vol. 3 of *Gróf Széchenyi István Munkái*, ed. Majláth Béla (Budapest: Athenaeum, 1889), 1:204.
20 *Gróf Széchenyi István válogatott munkái* [Selected Works of Count István Széchenyi], ed. Beöthy Zsolt (Budapest: Franklin-Társulat, n.d.), 2:35.
21 *Kölcsey Ferenc kiadatlan írásai*, 237–87.
22 *Kölcsey Ferenc kiadatlan írásai*, 247.
23 *Kölcsey Ferenc kiadatlan írásai*, 252.
24 Ferenc Kazinczy's letter to Gergely Berzeviczy, July 23, 1810. *Kazinczy Ferencz összes művei. Harmadik osztály. Levelezés* [Ferenc Kazinczy's Collected Works. Third Class. Correspondence], vol. 22, ed. Harsányi István (Budapest: MTA, 1927), 254–9.
25 Ferenc Kölcsey to Pál Szemere, February 25, 1823. *Kölcsey Ferenc Összes Művei*, 3:281.
26 *Kölcsey Ferenc Összes Művei*, 1:673.
27 Szabad György, *Kossuth irányadása* [Kossuth's guidance] (Budapest: Válasz Könyvkiadó, 2002), 76.
28 This was in relation to the proposal of 14 June 1848, in which the Austrian Minister of Finance offered 12.5 million interest-free loans in Austrian banknotes on the condition that the Hungarian government would recognize the monopoly of the Bank of Vienna on the issue of banknotes, that is, that it would forego its planned banknote issue. See Urbán, *Batthyány Lajos miniszterelnöksége*, 303–5.
29 Barta, 'Kölcsey politikai pályakezdete', 289.
30 Gerő András, *Magyar polgárosodás* [Hungarian Embourgeoisement] (Budapest: Atlantisz Könyvkiadó, 1993), 96–100. Quoted in Ferenc Kulin, *Küldetéstudat és szerepkeresés* [A sense of mission and role-seeking] (Budapest: Argumentum, 2012), 53.
31 Kulin, *Küldetéstudat és szerepkeresés*, 28–56.
32 *Kölcsey Ferenc Összes Művei*, 1:514.

33 *Kölcsey Ferenc Összes Művei*, 1:1271.
34 *Kölcsey Ferenc Összes Művei*, 1:1265.
35 John Lukacs, *Historical Consciousness: The Remembered Past* (New Brunswick, NJ: Transaction Publishers, 2009), xxxvii.

8

Count István Széchenyi (1791-1860)

László Csorba

Family and early years

In Vienna, on the banks of the Danube, the seat of the Holy Roman Emperor, later the centre of the Austrian Empire, in a stately baroque palace in the Herrengasse that winds behind the Hofburg, István, the son of Count Ferenc Széchényi[1] and Countess Julianna Festetics, was born on 21 September 1791. He would go on to become one of the most important figures of nineteenth-century Hungarian history and political thought.[2]

His father, Count Ferenc Széchényi (1754-1820), had inherited a huge, landed estate in the economically more developed western part of Hungary. As a believer in the Enlightenment and the Masonic movement, Count Ferenc was initially a sincere supporter of the enlightened reform programme of Emperor Joseph II (reigned 1780-90). In time, however, his faith in this project was shaken by the absolutist determination with which the monarch – who, as a devout Catholic, considered the service of the common good to be a divinely inspired mission – sought to abolish Hungary's relative self-government within the empire, that is, to do away with the governmental institutions that gave the estates (the nobility, the clergy and the burghers of the royal free cities) a say in the running of the country. In 1802, Ferenc Széchényi provided an outstanding example of sacrifice in support of the country's development when he donated his particularly valuable collection of books, medals and maps to the nation, thus laying the foundations of the Hungarian National Museum, which continues to expand to this day.

In the past, many people joked about whether Count István – who was later given the honorary title of the 'greatest Hungarian' – was actually a native Hungarian speaker. The question, rather, is whether, in the context of the polyglot upbringing of aristocratic children of his time, it is possible to speak of a mother tongue at all, since nursemaids were much more involved with these children than their mothers. Széchenyi's mother did not speak Hungarian well, but one of his nannies was Hungarian, and among the first written records of his childhood, several are in Hungarian. According to other recollections, Hungarian was also the language most used in the family's everyday life. The little boy probably learned German and Hungarian at the same time, although the latter language remained at a lower intellectual level, since his regular education with tutors was exclusively in Latin and German. It was inevitable, then, that when he started writing his diary in 1814, at the age of twenty-three, the adult Széchenyi chose German because he was better able to express himself in this language. As he developed a life programme that tied him to the Hungarians, however, he made up for his linguistic disadvantage with intensive reading and the help of his friends, and developed his Hungarian-language skills to the highest cultural standards.[3]

Military career and intellectual evolution

In 1809, several events shaped the life of the young István Széchenyi. In May, the French emperor Napoleon Bonaparte (1769-1820) conquered Vienna, the capital of the Habsburg Empire. At their king's bidding, the Hungarian nobles went to war against him, but on 14 June they suffered a severe defeat near Győr. Serving as a young officer, Széchenyi stood his ground amidst a hail of bullets, and this inspired him to become a soldier: he continued his service first in an Uhlan and then in a Hussar regiment, now as a professional. In October 1813, he carried out an important courier mission in the 'Battle of the Nations' in Leipzig and later took part in the campaign that ended with the capture of Paris. He stayed in the army as a captain after the end of the French wars, but for the next ten years he hoped in vain for promotion – and never found out that an unfavourable informer's report had stalled his military career. In the meantime, a very important transformation took place: through intense romantic infatuations and failures, exciting and inspiring journeys full of physical and mental trials, wide reading and inspiring friendships, his personality gradually changed and he developed the self-awareness that led him to choose a new calling in life.

His political views were, of course, part of the broader framework of his worldview, and his travels to the Eastern Mediterranean in 1818-19 can be seen as a particularly important period for his intellectual maturation. He wandered around Greece, then part of the Ottoman Empire, along the Anatolian coast of the Aegean Sea, finally visiting Sicily, taking stock in his diary of many classic problems of culture, history, philosophy and religious thought, which then became personal dilemmas for him.

From the end of the war-years onwards, Széchenyi made up for his earlier lack of education with great vigour. Until 1820, he mainly read fiction (Lord Byron, Vittorio Alfieri, Friedrich de la Motte Fouqué, Adolf Müllner, Torquato Tasso, Johann Wolfgang Goethe, Voltaire, Jean-Jacques Rousseau, Friedrich Schiller, Samuel Richardson, E. T. A. Hoffmann, Mme de Staël, Walter Scott), but then, around 1823, the philosophical works of Rousseau and Voltaire, as well as the books and studies of Montaigne, Benjamin Franklin, David Hume, Montesquieu, Johann Gottfried Herder, John Locke, Jean-Louis de Lolme and later Adam Smith, David Ricardo, Jeremy Bentham, Thomas Malthus and John Stuart Mill came to the fore.[4]

He travelled to England twice, in 1815 and 1817, where he studied that country's institutions, economy, technical achievements, political institutions and everyday civil life. His diary shows that he found three things particularly remarkable in the island nation: its unwritten constitution, its technological advances and its horse breeding. Subsequently, he rejoined his military unit and was stationed in Hungary, where he was confronted with the everyday life of a decaying feudal world and the stark contrasts between a nation he admired and the country's alarming underdevelopment. Today, most historians believe that his friendship with Miklós Wesselényi, in 1821, was the catalyst for the reorganization of all these experiences into a new harmony.[5] A baron from Transylvania, Wesselényi was five years younger than Széchenyi, but his sense of vocation, his family traditions, his enthusiasm for Hungarian, his determination and, not least, his personality, which asserted all this with a special charm, provided a model for Széchenyi: that of the – emphatically Hungarian – aristocrat, who possessed a family even more ancient than his own, political traditions, an old and famous stud farm, political popularity and, above all, true personal independence, and who, having benefitted from a thorough European education, clearly recognized that the application of the ideas and good practices that had proved themselves in the modernization of countries further west would provide the remedy for the ills of the Hungarian homeland. The discussions the two had, and the plans they hatched, as well as their joint trip to England (1822), brought Széchenyi to his final decision about his own vocation in life: he would leave the army and become Hungary's 'awakener' and 'saviour', that is, he would undertake the task of raising the 'poor Hungarian nation' and its 'backward country' to the level of civilization of the most advanced state of the time, England.[6]

The initiator of the Reform Era

The implementation of this programme required political thought and action in the broadest sense of the word, while, in terms of 'what' and 'how', the very terrain of the formulation – and even in part the implementation – of what was to be done was itself subject to the same process of transformation. The need for public discussion of the reforms, and hence public scrutiny of those acting for and on behalf of the community, was at the forefront of Széchenyi's concerns, but it is more of a historical accident that he had a particular talent for choosing the right kind of gestures when participating in public forums. This explains his highly publicized appearance at the Diet of Pozsony (today Bratislava, Slovakia) in 1825. When the idea of founding a Hungarian scientific society was repeatedly raised during the deliberations, Széchenyi unexpectedly asked to speak up at the meeting of the county representatives on 3 November and offered one year's income from his estates as capital for the foundation of a learned society (soon to be renamed the Hungarian Academy of Sciences).[7]

This act, which was greeted with great enthusiasm and soon became a powerful national symbol,[8] was obviously born of a momentary inspiration, but from the outset it was in line with a perspective he had cultivated. The importance of the link between language and nation was recognized by many theorists of the Enlightenment and later Romanticism, and thus became one of the driving forces behind the literary and musical interest in folk culture, which was soon hailed as a source of national tradition. The establishment of a scholarly society initiated in this intellectual milieu, however, was also linked to an idea that Széchenyi had held from the very beginning, to create a national centre where the political, economic and intellectual elite whose task it was to lead the country, could discuss reforms and decide what needed to be done. This was also one of his main motives for the introduction of horse racing, beyond the obvious economic and military benefits of horse breeding. The starting pistols were first fired in Pozsony in the spring of 1826, and in Pest in the summer of the following year, and the ambitious enterprise set off on its uninterrupted conquest of the country. Likewise, Széchenyi's other creation, the National Casino – essentially a political club for the elite – began in Pozsony and moved to Pest at the end of the session of the Diet, providing a prestigious meeting place for all those he wished to win over to his reform programme.[9]

As an increasingly conscious promoter of the restructuring of social and political public opinion, Széchenyi initiated – as a result of discussions with his friends, especially Wesselényi, in the second half of the 1820s – an increasingly vigorous campaign of patriotic propaganda promoting reform in the forums of the burgeoning press (in both books and newspapers). From that time onwards, for two decades, he was also active as a public writer and his work was regarded by his contemporaries as being not only political but also of a distinctly literary nature and quality.[10] The development of the political thinker's ideas can be traced through his books and articles, but it is always worth bearing in mind András Gergely's warning: 'It is impossible to understand Széchenyi's entire activity from his system of ideas, for he was not always consistent.'[11] This is particularly true in relation to the topic of Széchenyi's political thought:

> The system of ideas in political action, as in Széchenyi's case, is integrally related to, but not identical with, a system of political thought, which unifies the ends and means of concrete political action. This organic relationship is not necessarily consciously understood, and the individual often thinks of the political concept as being deduced from his system of ideas, but the actual relationship is often reversed.[12]

The theorist of modernization

There is no doubt that Széchenyi's first book, *Lovakrul* (On Horses), published in 1828, aimed to be more than just a hippological treatise. He combined the presentation of the importance of horse breeding for the national economy with an explanation of the country's underdevelopment in this area and the reasons for it.[13] The success Széchenyi expected did not materialize, but he found himself compelled to write and sought the literary form, structure, language and manner of speaking with which he could address his compatriots most effectively. Then, on 19 November of the same year, he received a letter from Baron Nathan Arnstein, one of the heads of the Arnstein and Eskeles banking house in Vienna. The businessman had refused his request for a loan of ten thousand forints, citing a lack of funds. A few days later the bank sent the money, but Széchenyi had already begun to realize that Hungary's backward constitution and feudal laws made it impossible for his estate to be creditworthy on the modern financial market. Thus, after arriving at many dead ends, credit was to be the thread that would lead him out of the labyrinth: in his new book he based his entire reform agenda on it. Over the course of three months of writing, he travelled around the most varied virtual 'landscapes' of contemporary Hungarian life, and where he encountered problems, it was not difficult to show that a lack of credit was the cause of the problem (at least in part). In January 1830, *Hitel* (Credit) appeared – the most influential book published by the Hungarian press up to that point.

By giving two different meanings to the term 'credit' at the beginning of his book, the author also established the dual character of his work. In its dedication to 'the noble-minded women of our land', he said: 'I speak of the Credit, and what flows from it, of honor, of the holiness of the given word, of the uprightness of deeds.' However, three pages later, under a separate heading 'Information', he stated: 'I take this term, Credit, in the sense which in public life is signified by Creditum, which is nothing else than the confidence and security obtained by certain obligations concerning our movable or immovable assets in the hands of others.'[14] The moral and economic meanings of the concept were not, of course, independent of each other, but this duality also makes clear the extent to which the linguistic and intellectual world of Széchenyi's book was familiar to his contemporaries, and what it was that astonished, inspired or shocked them. From the point of view of the concept of moral credibility, Széchenyi produced a moralizing polemic which fitted in well with the Enlightenment's public literature of social improvement and moralizing, inspired mainly by British authors, which was still popular reading in Hungary in the first half of the nineteenth century. However, in his focus on credit, he employed the rational discourse of English economics with which he could question the long-term effects of economic actions or their limits with theoretical validity and apply it to subjects and topics that were often unknown to the majority of Hungarian readers. On this basis, Széchenyi's work was characterized by a specific combination of the ideas he used and the particular language that conveyed them, which scholars of the modern political history of ideas today try to describe not primarily in the schemata of classical ideological history, but through the more language- and discourse-centred methods of analysis popularized by J. G. A. Pocock and his followers.[15]

In this context, Ferenc Horkay Hörcher points out that, within the intellectual world of the British Enlightenment, Széchenyi's contribution can be linked to 'the eighteenth-century context of Adam Smith, including the *rich country–poor country* debate', in respect of which

> [István] Hont, who has worked on this research topic, pointed out, among other things, that if we reconstruct his views with the appropriate intellectual-historical thoroughness, Smith himself is not the ideologue of classical capitalist economics, as the Ricardo school and its nineteenth-century followers understood it, but belongs to the early modern context marked by the names of Grotius, Hobbes or Samuel Pufendorf.[16]

Horkay Hörcher then asserts that this parallel, which may at first glance seem surprising, does not, however, contradict the positive personal experience of economic industriousness imbued with the Protestant work ethic, because Széchenyi's

Anglomania was such a strong mediating element that it 'allowed the transition from the values of the Central European aristocracy to those of the urbanized British aristocracy'. An important demonstration of this transition was the use of the language of politeness – in the words of József Takáts, 'refinement' (*csinosodás*) and 'politeness' (*csiszoltság*) – in Széchenyi's writings, including *Hitel*.[17] By analysing the set of metaphors and the vocabulary used in *Hitel*, Takáts shows how the imagery of the author's main message was served and supported by the power of the imagery itself. For example, as Takáts puts it, 'countries and nations that have reached the highest shelf of refinement or are at the forefront of the common path can serve as models for other countries and nations. This is one of the most powerful political messages of the *Hitel*, and one that can be read in many different formulations.'[18] In the same way, Széchenyi's opposition to the unthinking reference to old laws (and thus to old customs) serves the purposes of the book, because he professes his faith 'in a law adapted to the "needs of the time", against the idea of an immutable law'. As József Takáts stresses: 'These ten pages[19] [...] are a frontal attack against the feudal constitution based on the national approach (i.e., that of the nobility).'[20] Finally, Takáts highlights the new relationship between 'republican' and 'cultural nationalist' modes of discourse, since, he argues, 'the passages on the nation and national feelings in the *Hitel* [,...] "speak" the multi-layered, mixed republican-organicist basic language used in the nationalist argumentation of Hungarian political texts of the first half of the nineteenth century'.[21]

As regards the linguistic and intellectual context of contemporary economics, Sándor Hites also finds that *Hitel* was largely in line with the British moral philosophical tradition, but in a way that 'systematically (or even incidentally, but characteristically even in its rampant and non-systematic use of metaphor) captures and describes non-economic phenomena and images with the concepts of economics'.[22] In Hites's words, it is an astonishing attempt to convince readers that the competitive free market

> stimulates virtues as well as economic growth, because the former provide the material rewards that justify the practice of the latter. From this point of view, the spread of trade and the creation of new forms of credit, such as the promissory note (*váltó*), which allow the free movement of capital, do not lead to the decline of society, but by generating credit, they endow citizens with the capacity for mutual trust. Széchenyi also envisaged the creation of such a community.[23]

Mutual trust can also create a more modern way of financing the state, which manages the common affairs of its citizens. As Hites also points out, this logic is connected with the contemporary changes in the concept of public debt in the money market, since if 'debt becomes the financial basis of the modern state, its relationship with its citizens changes: by buying (and selling to each other) securities issued at the expense of the Treasury, its own citizens now lend to the State, and the collateral for their loans represents their confidence in the future existence and prosperity of the State'.[24]

In a letter written seven years after its publication, József Eötvös, one of the most prominent thinkers of the Reform Era liberal generation by European standards, summed up the significance of Széchenyi's work most succinctly: '*Hitel* is not just a book, *Hitel* is something more, something nobler; *Hitel* is a patriotic act.'[25] The decisive meeting of gesture and moment is also emphasized by Ferenc Horkay Hörcher:

> Széchenyi throws a stone into the waters of domestic public opinion to gauge reactions. Confronting the question of credit is therefore not an act of intellectual gymnastics for its own sake, but a gesture that also prompts political actors to make a confession: it asks where you, the reader, stand on these issues. The significance of *Hitel* is therefore greater than its meaning – it represents political action which itself encourages similar actions. [26]

Count József Dessewffy (1771-1843) questioned the desirability and necessity of comprehensively transforming Hungary and the need for personal participation of individual citizens in his work *Taglalat* (Treatise). While this is not the place to go into the details of the debate, it is worth noting that recent analyses have found that the critic did not want to reject, but rather to complement Széchenyi's message, among other things, by emphasizing the values of the past, praising classical antiquity and stressing the role of landed property in preserving the nobility. The author of *Hitel*, however, took the criticism as a personal insult and wrote a vitriolic response entitled *Világ* (Light), taking the opportunity not only to 'throw light' on the perceived or actual errors of his critic but to expound more broadly on several important details of his previous book.[27] It was also at this time that he put down on paper what would later become his motto – which can also be seen as a personal *ars poetica* – about how actions are the most important in judging the writer and the speaker: 'deeds first, words second'.[28]

Széchenyi's first comprehensive programme of transformation, however, was set out in his third book, which he titled *Stadium*, in which he argued that the necessary transformation of the country was in its first stage, or 'stadium', of a long process of development. The contribution this book made to the growing, if indirect, criticism of the status quo was by now too much for Metternich's censors, so it could only be published in Leipzig in 1833 and smuggled illegally into the countries of the Habsburg Empire.

The debate with Kossuth

By the second half of the 1830s, Széchenyi found himself in a delicate political situation. He was deeply convinced that Hungary had to preserve its right to self-determination and carry out its civil transformation within the Habsburg state, because in the sea of Germanic and Slavic peoples the small Hungarian nation could not do without the protective umbrella of the great power of the empire. He believed that a programme for the enrichment of the Hungarian nation would be more of an advantage than a disadvantage for the Austrian and Czech hereditary provinces, because the future lay in the parallel development of the constituent parts of the empire, not in their subordination and subservience to one another. During the Reform Era, he held a deep belief that the Austrian chancellor Klemens Metternich would see the light and support the implementation of his ideas. He therefore considered it a serious mistake when the Vienna Court tried to prevent the strengthening of the Hungarian reformers in the second half of the 1830s by oppressive measures. From the 1840s, he welcomed the more conciliatory approach by Vienna and wanted to believe that the government was also striving for reform, albeit clearly in a different way from the mainstream of the Hungarian reformers.[29]

However, the new decade saw another change in the political landscape, thanks in part to the earlier achievements of Széchenyi and others. A new generation emerged, led by Lajos Kossuth, who had gained great prestige and national fame for his advocacy of freedom of speech. The young lawyer was released from prison in May 1840 and in January 1841 became editor of the political newspaper *Pesti Hirlap* (Pest Gazette). In the decaying feudal world, the misery of the serfs, the cruelties of exploitation, the maladministration, the corruption, the abuse of power and the backwardness of the economy and infrastructure were among dozens of topics Kossuth dealt with in the pages of this newspaper, while at the same time offering criticism and suggestions that encouraged modernization. Széchenyi soon began to see Kossuth not as the continuer of his reforms but as his main political opponent and launched a public debate against him, which, with varying intensity, lasted until the revolutionary period of the spring of 1848. It was during this debate that he further developed the most important ideas of his political ideology.

In the spring of 1841, Széchenyi published a pamphlet entitled *A kelet népe* (People of the East), in which he outlined the basis for his attack on the *Pesti Hirlap*, describing the kind of community which he feared might arise from the propaganda of this new gazette. In doing so, he also detailed an area of his thought that he had left largely unexplored in his previous three books. As András Gergely emphasizes, Széchenyi now warned that

> one should focus not so much on the age of nations [. . .], but on national characteristics. [. . .] And the Genius (i.e., vocation) of the Hungarian people is not science, not commerce, not even art, but the development of constitutionality and nationality, which must be done taking into account the fact that the Hungarians are people of the East, the only Asian offspring settled in Europe, so they must save and preserve these Eastern characteristics.[30]

The Eastern origin of Hungarians, which was also alluded to in the title of the book, is certainly an ancient, centuries-old tenet of Hungarian consciousness. However, it is a community which 'needs work', as some of its ancient traditions have become obsolete. It needs to be changed, reformed, adapted to modern times, but in such a way that its original and valuable 'Eastern' characteristics are not lost. András Gergely rightly emphasizes that this turn of events gave Széchenyi a 'fine literary toolkit' which enabled him to 'judge his own policy as being measured and correct, and his opponent's as excessive, or on the contrary, over-cautious'.[31] It is not known, of course, what he himself thought about these 'peculiarities' beyond an undoubted emotional identification with them, because, on the one hand, he did not explain the exact content of this 'oriental' element and, on the other hand, his reflections on it are contradictory.[32] It is likely that he had little patience for fully elaborating the theoretical background, perhaps because he was too busy concentrating on presenting the ideas and activities of his opponent, Kossuth, as the most dangerous.

To do this, he drew on a particular narrative: his idiosyncratic concept of divine providence overseeing nations and his direct, personal experiences of this. He claimed that in the previous year,

> in Pozsony, on the threshold of the end of the Diet, [...] I felt it clearly in every drop of my blood and the innermost depths of my soul, without in the least wishing to diminish the merits of others, that invisible powers are guiding me, and even the greatest among us is little more than an obedient instrument in higher hands.[33]

The joy and surprise he experienced at the fortunate resolution of the conflict that had so dangerously intersected with his political plans (Vienna's policy of terror of the previous years) inspired in him a 'religious' way of speaking, in which he 'translated' this outcome as an almost mystical intervention of the 'God of the Hungarians'. At the same time he insisted that it was no coincidence that the nation experienced this at this point in its life: 'And the more invisible creatures are involved in the destiny of a people, the younger that people is, and there is no greater symptom of youth than this for nations; for the Gods have given the human race two guides, Genius and Reason, and the less Reason is developed and still in childhood, the more often the Genius provides assistance.'[34] Thus, when a nation grows up, it is no longer assisted by direct divine providence (the Genius), but must manage for itself with the help of the gift of Reason.

An unexpected intellectual twist was that, while the starting point of the broader concept of the 'God of the Hungarians' is clearly Christian, Széchenyi used polytheistic language linked to ancient civilization ('invisible beings', 'Gods') to project it onto the nation. He must have been, of course, well aware that his 'two guides' theory was in fact outside the linguistic and spiritual world of Christian anthropology and sociology. The mechanism he depicted, by which Providence leaves adult nations to fend for themselves, now to manage on their own with (albeit Creator-given) Reason, is purely Széchenyi's personal – '(quasi-)theological' – invention but the subjective validity of it (i.e. that he himself believed in it in some sense) should not be doubted. The circular logic of this reasoning was completed by the argument that, in this respect, too, 'a completely new era has dawned for our country since the last Diet. [...] I see the nation-family, of which I am but a small but faithful member, coming of age.'[35] The argumentation, which becomes deistic at this point, thus prepares his main political charge against the opponent: since only Reason can guide the nation as it grows up, Kossuth's propaganda, based on emotions instead of Reason, in fact leads the Hungarian nation to its doom. Széchenyi thus warned, in a dramatic tone, those who had hoped in vain for direct help from Providence: 'It all hangs by a thread, my dear Compatriots: one misstep – and all is irreparably lost. – This is the diagnosis of our state.'[36]

Széchenyi also stressed that the debate was not about principles, but about means, and specifically about style.[37] What was wrong with Kossuth's style? According to Széchenyi, Kossuth speaks to the Heart that guides the child and not to the Reason that guides the adult man, sadly missing the sole necessary means of action to avert disaster. Széchenyi's advice was to retain the 'manly dignity' of the Hungarians, which is 'peculiar to the peoples of the East', and not to substitute for it the 'immature itches and frivolous changeability of the superficial Gaul'. On the contrary,

> the editor's [i.e. Kossuth's] lines and sophisms reveal the red thread that leads astray [. . .], the emotional [i.e., revolutionary] style [. . .], a style [. . .] that works in the realm of emotion, and is no different from that followed by Camille Desmoulins, Danton, St-Just, Marat, Robespierre, from Mirabeau to the heroes of contemporary French propaganda, from the heartfelt Lamennais to Père Enfantin, etc.[38]

Was Széchenyi right to put the Phrygian cap on Kossuth's head? The reception of *A kelet népe* clearly favoured the object of his criticism, mainly because Széchenyi's fears were based on the tensions of his own inner world, and had no basis in the reality of the time. Kossuth was only a moderate liberal, but he understood the deeper political message of the book: the scourging of the 'uninitiated' and the 'ignorant', who are 'driven by the itch for leadership', sent the message that, in Széchenyi's view, only a small group of reformers from the magnate elite were capable of leading the transformation. Although Széchenyi himself acknowledged in *Világ* that public opinion alone could be the arbiter of public debate, he believed that he was in such an elevated moral position – having once awakened the nation from its medieval slumber and being the all-knowing physician to the sick national body – that he could determine who should be allowed to play a role in public policy-making. But the age of uncontested traditional authority was over, and a new force was now shaping public opinion: the voice of the hitherto disenfranchised, who had become equal participants in the process of transformation as a result of the democratic broadening of the reform base, was the one to decide who to follow and what to accept.

In line with the modern view of history, Kossuth's reply, the *Felelet* (Answer), stated that great transformations cannot be the result of the efforts of individuals, however great, and that the perspective from which Széchenyi judged his own role was therefore flawed. The 'great awakener of the nation' and the 'wise physician' were not realistic self-images, but just pretty metaphors. The *Pesti Hírlap* was a creature of the reality which it occupied, and its impact was because it expressed the needs of its time – obviously with many errors and imperfectly – but for this very reason Széchenyi 'should rather deem the one, whose path he now seeks to stand in the way of, worthy of his advice and corrective guidance'.[39] To set Reason against the Heart was a false dichotomy, Kossuth stressed,

> and the mastery of the doctrine of government is perhaps precisely to reconcile the two, not to separate them; from which I think it naturally follows that he who wishes to influence public opinion must draw from both sources: he must put into words the suggestions of Reason with a pen dipped in the ink of human love; in other words, [. . .] he must lead his thoughts through the heart.[40]

He also addressed Széchenyi's 'grounding' of his thought in quasi-mystical personal experience, stating: 'I don't usually give much credence to miracles, direct intervention of Gods, Genii and the like in the life of nations', because it would violate the idea of 'divine providence governing the universe according to wise eternal laws' to presuppose that any 'ant-hill' would be lifted out of 'the chain of cause and effect'.[41] 'As a wise Englishman once put it: "God acts but by general laws."'[42] Finally, Kossuth summarized the elements of his critique by refuting his opponent's self-mythologizing claims, while at the same time setting out a realistic framework for his (i.e. Széchenyi's) true historical greatness:

> He that comes early, stands isolated, and the steps of the one who is solitary shall have no lasting effect. [...] He who comes late, lights the lamp in broad daylight, and one may yet give thanks if his work be but useless. [...] Count Széchenyi was seized at an opportune moment by the power of the needs of the age. His language became the language of his age; he gave words to the thoughts of the better men of the nation; and it is here that the secret of his influence lies. [...] He put his fingers on the artery of the times and understood its pulsations; and that is precisely why I consider him the greatest Hungarian.[43]

Through the 1840s, the debate rolled on. There were, however, two important points which further complicate the picture of Széchenyi's political views. In the speech he made to the Academy on 27 November 1842, Széchenyi – in a partial critique of the 'cultural nationalist' discourse of the time – criticized the attempts at Hungarianization of other nationalities living in Hungary (Croats, Serbs, Romanians, Slovaks). While he had every right to criticize the proponents of excessive ethnic nationalism, it was a political sleight of hand on his part to condemn only the opposition for what was one of the most serious problems of Hungarian political life as a whole. It is true that most of the reformers were not free from dreams of national greatness and displayed narrow-mindedness towards the national minorities, but the *Pesti Hirlap* condemned this chauvinistic Magyarization just as much as Széchenyi. It was particularly offensive for him to present his fellow reformers as the sole cause of the clashing nationalist movements, ignoring both the objective factors of national development and the divisive, manipulative activities of Habsburg power politics. Moreover, Széchenyi's need for rational tolerance did not always prevent him from sharing the political intolerance of his contemporaries. When, in June 1842, Kossuth proposed at the county assembly in Pest that the entire administration and legislature of Croatia should be separated from that of Hungary, Széchenyi wrote in a contemporary note that there are 'quacks [...] who, wherever the national body is hurting, even if it were a whole country, such as Croatia [...], without any hesitation propose amputation.'[44]

Likewise, it was also uncertain how Széchenyi's theoretical liberalism was to further development in a democratic direction. József Takáts notes that Széchenyi had already stated in *Hitel* what he believed the ideal form of government to be:

> In the constitution, in the way of government, the majority prefers to see power in the hands either of one or of the people alone – and so only plan for the short term – because the first is the simplest, and the second is a form of government in which they themselves may participate. They fail to take into account that men

like Marcus Aurelius, Antoninus Pius and Traianus were few and far between, not even suspecting the unshakeable truth that the many cannot soberly lead the few, but only the few the many.[45]

The 'few' who lead the 'many' were, of course, the group of young aristocrats in a virtuous alliance, called upon and obliged by their wealth, education and abilities to lead the transformation and to occupy the positions of power as required. It was from this point of view that he perceived it as a serious danger when the reformist opposition replaced the 'people's advocacy' – on the initiative of Kölcsey, Wesselényi and, of course, Kossuth – with the demand that they 'fight together'.

In one of his articles criticizing Kossuth, Széchenyi referred to a biblical example. According to him, the reason why it is dangerous to involve the immature masses in politics is that 'the people have always erred in their judgment, and even left our Lord Christ in the minority in the face of Barabbas'.[46] Kossuth, of course, did not deny in his reply that a serious danger was posed by the illiteracy of the masses: 'I know that the judgment of the people may often be mistaken, and that it left even our Lord Christ in a minority against Barabbas; and therefore I consider a man who denies himself in order to flatter the judgment of the people a miserable coward' – which is why one of the most serious political sins is the demagogic exploitation of the illiteracy of the masses. He recognized, however, that the political rights of the people were still an inevitable commandment of the times, a hard reality, and so he continued his answer:

> but I also know that the people, though they be mistaken in their judgment, do judge; and our Lord Christ had to die, because the people left him in the minority against Barabbas; and therefore I would think it the greatest error of pride for any man to feign indifference to the judgment of the people; on the contrary, I think it wise to endeavor to win the approval of the people for what the individual man of sense, with honest intentions, has found to be good for the community; for, in a constitutional country, without the will of the constituent people, one may not even attempt to make the people happy.[47]

The belief in the positive influence of public opinion was imbued with an enlightened view of man's eternal perfectibility, confident in the 'omnipotence' of pedagogy, which counterbalances the real risk posed by the extension of rights if the 'judgment' of the people were to prevail in politics before its representatives had acquired the minimum of knowledge and judgment necessary to influence it.

However, Széchenyi did not see it this way, because he was not a democrat. He did not believe that the right to life naturally implied the right to have a say in the collective management of one's own destiny. He fought for the right to property but expected the majority to voluntarily place political leadership in the hands of an intellectual and propertied elite within the formal framework of a constitutional monarchy. On the question of the emancipation of serfs, he maintained that, since it also affected the property relations of the nobility, the state could not oblige landowners to allow their serfs to purchase charters of redemption (i.e. to permanently emancipate their serfs for a fair sum). He did not realize that time was running out, and that his younger comrades were rushing through reforms in order to prevent the social explosion that was about to happen, taking into account the warnings of the French Revolution's Reign of Terror. For this reason, and also because of the escalation of other antagonisms, Széchenyi became politically isolated in the second half of the 1840s. His attack on Kossuth and his constant struggles against him were not supported by other influential reformers (Ferenc Deák, Lajos Batthyány, József Eötvös, László Teleki, Zsigmond Kemény, etc.) because they saw the opponent he demonized not as a radical agitator but as a moderate reformer like themselves, whose outstanding talents would serve the cause of transformation.[48]

1848 and after

All these differences were not so serious as to call into question Széchenyi's epoch-making role in the previous decades, so it was unsurprising that Lajos Batthyány, the head of the first independent, responsible Hungarian government, called the Ministry (*minisztérium*), established during the revolutionary events of March 1848, entrusted him with the leadership of the Ministry of Transport and Public Works. As Kossuth had also been appointed to the cabinet as Minister of Finance, their open dispute ended. In public, they shared the government's position on various current political issues, even though Széchenyi continued to criticize his fellow minister on many issues in his diary. In the summer of 1848, he was struck down by a nervous breakdown, and by the time of the War of Independence (the failed war of self-defence against the court's invasion of the country) he was already being treated in the Döbling psychiatric asylum near Vienna, and it would be years before his condition improved.[49]

Many believed that he had been cured, so much so that he may never have been ill at all – but the accounts of his treating physicians and the 'ego documents' of his time convince today's medical experts that, from 1857 onwards, he merely had an asymptomatic period in what was a cyclical illness.[50] Since the underlying disease did not affect his logic or memory, but rather distorted his emotions and motives, this enabled him in time to produce secret political pamphlets, as he slowly regained the will to work, criticizing with merciless sarcasm the Austrian despotism that had crushed the Hungarian War of Independence in 1849 and which had already been in power for ten years at that time. His political views had changed on the essential point that he was now much more sympathetic towards Kossuth and believed that Viennese absolutism had forced him to become the leader of the War of Independence and to declare the dethronement of the Habsburg dynasty in the spring of 1849.

In the spring of 1860, the Austrian State Police exposed Széchenyi and his colleagues' pamphleteering activities and, following a search of his house – which uncovered compromising manuscripts – threatened to transfer him from the private asylum to a state institution. His condition then suddenly deteriorated again, his depression worsened and on the night of 8 April he took his own life.[51]

His honorary sobriquet, which he owed to Kossuth, still lives on: Széchenyi remains 'the Greatest Hungarian'. János Arany, one of the greatest poets of Hungarian literature, said his farewell to him in a beautiful poem titled *Széchenyi emlékezete* (The Memory of Széchenyi, 1860), predicting the future of his cult, that has been unbroken for more than a century and a half: 'His clear light is ever growing, / As in time and space he departs.'[52]

Notes

1 The two Széchenyis, father Ferenc Széchényi and son István Széchenyi used different ways of spelling their names.–Ed.
2 The best English-language summary of Széchenyi's life and work to date is still George Barany, *Stephen Széchenyi and the Awakening of Hungarian Nationalism: 1791–1841* (Princeton, NJ: Princeton University Press, 1968).
3 Gergely András, *Széchenyi István (1791–1860)* (Pozsony: Kalligram, 2006), 9–14.
4 Gergely András, *Széchenyi eszmerendszerének kialakulása* [The Development of Széchenyi's System of Ideas], Értekezések a történeti tudományok köréből–Új sorozat 62 (Budapest: Akadémiai Kiadó, 1972), 56.
5 Cf. Trócsányi Zsolt, *Wesselényi Miklós* (Budapest: Akadémiai Kiadó, 1965), 61–74.
6 Csorba László, *Széchenyi István* (Budapest: M-érték Kiadó, 2010), 59–95.
7 Csorba, *Széchenyi István*, 98–102.
8 Széchenyi's arrival made such a strong impression that for a long time, scholars counted 1825 as the beginning of the 'Reform Era' in Hungarian history, that is, the founding phase of Hungarian modernization. Only in recent decades has the date of the beginning been moved to 1830, the beginning of the real reform debates; see Pajkossy Gábor, 'A reformkor' [The Reform Era], in *Magyarország története a 19. században*, Osiris Tankönyvek, ed. Gergely András (Budapest: Osiris Kiadó, 2003), 191–2.
9 Csorba, *Széchenyi István*, 107–20.
10 Széchenyi's most successful book, *Hitel*, was in fact awarded the Academy Prize as a literary work.
11 Gergely, *Széchenyi eszmerendszerének kialakulása*, 8.
12 Gergely, *Széchenyi eszmerendszerének kialakulása*, 174.
13 Gergely, *Széchenyi eszmerendszerének kialakulása*, 35–41.
14 Széchenyi István, *Hitel* [Credit] (Pest: Trattner–Károlyi, 1830), V, VIII.
15 Cf. István Hont, 'The Language of Sociability and Commerce', in *The Languages of Political Theory in Early Modern Europe*, ed. Anthony Pagden (Cambridge: Cambridge University Press, 1987), 253–76.
16 Horkay Hörcher Ferenc, 'Ahol a politikai és a gazdasági eszmetörténet metszi az irodalomtörténetet: A *Hitel* tudományközi kontextusai' [Where the History of Political and Economic Ideas Intersects with the History of Literature: The Interdisciplinary Contexts of the *Hitel*], in *Jólét és erény: Tanulmányok Széchenyi István Hitel című művéről*, ed. Hites Sándor (Budapest: Reciti, 2014), 9–27, 14–15, 18. He adds that 'Széchenyi must have been aware of the importance of Hume and Smith. Nothing proves this better than the fact that already his father, Ferenc Széchényi, reports in his diary of his travels in England that he met Smith and visited Hume's tomb. [. . .] Széchenyi could thus have received as a direct inheritance from the Anglophilia/ Anglomania that included the Scots'.
17 Horkay Hörcher, 'Ahol a politikai és a gazdasági eszmetörténet metszi az irodalomtörténetet', 12.

18 Takáts József, 'Metaforák, elbeszéléssémák és politikai nyelvek a *Hitelben*' [Metaphors, Narrative Schemas and Political Languages in the *Hitel*], in *Jólét és erény*, 45–50.
19 The referenced section is on pages 190–9 of the *Hitel*.
20 Takáts, 'Metaforák, elbeszéléssémák és politikai nyelvek a *Hitelben*', 53–4.
21 Takáts, 'Metaforák, elbeszéléssémák és politikai nyelvek a *Hitelben*', 59.
22 Hites Sándor, 'Hypotheka vagy hypothesis: A valóságos és a képzeletbeli a *Hitel* gazdaságtanában' [Hypothec or Hypothesis: The Real and the Imaginary in the Economics of the *Hitel*], in *Jólét és erény. . .*, 104.
23 Hites, 'Hypotheka vagy hypothesis', 109.
24 Hites, 'Hypotheka vagy hypothesis', 120.
25 Csorba, *Széchenyi István*, 126.
26 Horkay Hörcher, 'Ahol a politikai és a gazdasági eszmetörténet metszi az irodalomtörténetet', 20.
27 Vaderna Gábor, *Élet és irodalom: Az irodalom társadalmi használata gróf Dessewffy József életművében* [Life and Literature: The Social Use of Literature in the Oeuvre of Count József Dessewffy] (Budapest: Ráció Kiadó, 2013), 253–94.
28 Széchenyi István, *Világ vagy is felvilágosító töredékek némi hiba's előítélet eligazítására* [Light, or Enlightening Fragments to Correct Some Errors and Prejudices] (Pest: Landerer, 1831), 244.
29 Csorba, *Széchenyi István*, 216–18.
30 Gergely, *Széchenyi eszmerendszerének kialakulása*, 95–6.
31 Gergely, *Széchenyi eszmerendszerének kialakulása*, 97.
32 In one passage he says that 'melancholy is in the Eastern blood of Hungarians', in another he speaks of 'hot Oriental blood', and in yet another he condemns 'Oriental indolence'. Likewise, the remarks about 'our quicker Eastern blood', 'Eastern laziness' and 'Eastern dignity' are inconsistent. See Gergely, *Széchenyi eszmerendszerének kialakulása*, 97–8.
33 Széchenyi István, *A kelet népe* [People of the East] (Pozsony: Wigand, 1841), 36.
34 Széchenyi, *A kelet népe*, 37.
35 Széchenyi, *A kelet népe*, 40–1.
36 Széchenyi, *A kelet népe*, 170.
37 'Let me reiterate that I do not doubt in the slightest the intentions of the *Pesti Hirlap*'s editor, and I largely share his principles; [. . .] so the only thing I can and do object to are the manners according to which, as he believes, he uplifts the country, but as I believe, he buries the nation'; see Széchenyi, *A kelet népe*, 99.
38 Széchenyi, *A kelet népe*, 143, 172.
39 Kossuth Lajos, *Felelet gróf Széchenyi Istvánnak Kossuth Lajostól* [Reply to Count István Széchenyi from Lajos Kossuth] (Pest, Landerer és Heckenast, 1841), 13.
40 Kossuth, *Felelet gróf Széchenyi Istvánnak Kossuth Lajostól*, 134.
41 Kossuth, *Felelet gróf Széchenyi Istvánnak Kossuth Lajostól*, 9–10.
42 Kossuth, *Felelet gróf Széchenyi Istvánnak Kossuth Lajostól*, 10. Kossuth was probably thinking of the following lines by Alexander Pope: 'No, ('tis replied) the first Almighty Cause / Acts not by partial, but by gen'ral laws'; see Alexander Pope, *An Essay on Man* (London: Knapton, 1745), 35. (Epistle I, lines 145–6.)
43 Kossuth, *Felelet gróf Széchenyi Istvánnak Kossuth Lajostól*, 17–18.
44 Csorba, *Széchenyi István*, 242.
45 Széchenyi, *Hitel*, 86.
46 Széchenyi István, 'Német szinházi botrány's ahhoz még egy kis advány' [A German Theater Scandal, with a Little Addendum], *Jelenkor* 12, no. 2 (January 8, 1843): 7.

47 Kossuth Lajos, 'Vezérczikk: Közvélemény' [Editorial: Public Opinion], *Pesti Hirlap*, February 2, 1843.
48 Csorba, *Széchenyi István*, 224–69.
49 Csorba László, *Széchenyi Döblingben* [Széchenyi in Döbling], A magyar történelem rejtélyei (Budapest: Kossuth Kiadó, 2016), 6–11.
50 Csorba, *Széchenyi Döblingben*, 14–23.
51 Csorba, *Széchenyi Döblingben*, 24–45.
52 *Arany János költeményei* [The poems of János Arany], ed. Szalai Anna (Budapest: Helikon, 1983), 313.

9

Baron Miklós Wesselényi (1796-1850)

Attila István Kárpáti

Despite his outstanding political activity, Baron Miklós Wesselényi was for a long time not a major focus of historical research and was best known for his rescue work during the 1838 flood in Pest.[1] Zsolt Trócsányi's monograph, published in 1965, was the first work to provide an insight into Wesselényi's political ideas and played a major role in establishing Wesselényi's place alongside István Széchenyi, Lajos Kossuth and Ferenc Deák among the major politicians of the Reform Era.

The leader of the reformist liberal opposition

Early years and gaining experience in Transylvanian politics

Miklós Wesselényi's upbringing prepared him for politics. His father, Baron Miklós Wesselényi senior (1750-1809), was a prominent representative of the Transylvanian opposition of the late eighteenth and early nineteenth centuries, and he consciously prepared his son for a political career. It was as a result of this parenting programme that as a nine-year-old boy he made a speech to the estates of Közép-Szolnok County on 26 January 1806, in which he committed himself to the happiness of his homeland and to working for the common good: 'Count on me, fathers! Remember that I committed myself today as a patriot.'[2] This conscious political preparation was primarily based on the pedagogical principles of philanthropism. The surviving writings of the young Wesselényi reveal his educational principles, notably the ideal of universal philanthropy, the reconciliation of communal and private interests, and the defence of law, liberty and justice.[3] The success of this educational programme was confirmed by his acquaintances: Ferenc Kazinczy, who maintained a friendly relationship with Wesselényi's father, bestowed the permanent title of 'Princeps Juventitus Hungaricae', the 'first among Hungarian youth', on the young Wesselényi. After Miklós Wesselényi senior's death in 1809, he was imbued by his contemporaries with expectations and hopes, and they held up his father as a role model to follow. His social sensitivity was noticed from an early age and spurred him to action even in his youth, as well as playing a role in his political agenda, which prioritized the social and economic betterment of the serfs.[4]

Wesselényi's political career started in 1819 in the debate on the Transylvanian serf services and the regulation of the relationship between landlords and serfs. This problem would occupy Wesselényi for his whole public career and was one of the most important issues in Transylvania, and in Hungary, in the Reform Era.[5] Plans for the elaboration and introduction of an *urbarium* to regulate serf services to the landlord in Transylvania were also discussed in the second half of the eighteenth century during the reigns of Maria Theresa and Joseph II, but no substantial results were achieved. The Transylvanian Diet of 1790-1 entrusted a committee with elaborating a detailed proposal to address this problem, and one was duly prepared, but it was not even put on the agenda at the Transylvanian Diet of 1810-11. Between 1813 and 1817, famine struck Transylvania due to the appalling weather conditions, and serfs fled Transylvania in droves to escape starvation. During his trip to Transylvania in 1817, Francis I received thousands of complaints, which confronted him with the urgent need to regulate the issue of serf services in Transylvania. Finally, a draft reform was ready by May 1819, and the Vienna Court decided that the county assemblies should approve it instead of convening a Transylvanian Diet. The court sent three royal commissioners to Transylvania, who were empowered – contrary to the ancient constitution – to conduct the sessions on the draft in place of the lord-lieutenant (*supremus comes*; *főispán*; leading official in county administration) and the vice lord-lieutenant (*vicecomes*; *alispán*). However, in the sessions of the legislative assemblies, the government met with fierce opposition and protests, both because of the illegality of the procedure and because there was opposition to limiting the privileges and incomes of the landlords. Among the members of the opposition was Wesselényi, who was guided by his father's political heritage, that of the constitutionalist opposition. In several counties, he made public statements emphasizing the violations of the law: on the one hand, he demanded the convocation of the Diet, and on the other hand, he spoke out against the illegal actions of the royal commissioners.[6]

Friendship with István Széchenyi

Transylvanian politics in the 1820s forced Wesselényi to become a member of the constitutionalist opposition. However, his initial meeting with István Széchenyi, and the subsequent close friendship between the two, opened up new horizons for him. During their joint trip to Western Europe in 1821, Wesselényi gained an insight into German, French and English political life, and paid close attention to agricultural and industrial achievements. After his return home, he used his experience abroad to modernize his own estates. In the second half of the 1820s, he served as an important organizer for Széchenyi's social initiatives. Their exchange of ideas resulted in a political programme which shared many principles until it broke up at the end of 1831. Although they both aimed at the abolition of feudal conditions, they did not agree on the means to achieve it. While Széchenyi looked to the wealthiest aristocrats to implement reforms and would have even cooperated with the Viennese government, Wesselényi refused to cooperate with Vienna and considered the lower nobility his base.[7]

Wesselényi's organizational skills and success in uniting all of the liberal-minded reformers were among his major contributions as the leader of the opposition at the height of his active political career, in the 1832-6 Pozsony (today Bratislava, Slovakia) Diet. As he explained in his diary:

> Most people think that they have fulfilled all their duties by appearing and speaking in the sessions, and that they can use their time outside the sessions as they please, when it is outside the sessions that the real scope of the work of an eager parliamentarian lies. *Out of doors.* Here it is necessary to prepare and arrange things by the not easy art of knowing and handling people [...] Sessions are rather places of spectacle and show, but if the objects are not brought there ready, the outcome is mostly left to blind luck.[8]

Even during the Transylvanian dispute over court proposals to reform the obligations and services of serfs in 1819-20, Wesselényi had worked hard to unite the opposition. Through his correspondence with the representatives of the Transylvanian opposition, as well as through regular in-person meetings, he aimed to develop and implement unified political tactics. He was unable to speak at the Diet of Pozsony in 1825-7 as he did not own landed property in Hungary but nevertheless tried to influence the Diet from behind the scenes. (In 1825, Wesselényi owned land only in Transylvania, but to take part with the right to speak in the Upper House at the Diet in Pozsony, one had to own land in Hungary. However, between 1827 and 1830, he got a small land from a friend in Hungary, so he could take part in the Diet with full rights.) He maintained lively contacts with the opposition members of both the Upper and Lower Houses of the Diet, and his diary contains daily records of discussions before or after its sessions, and the participants he met, especially the representatives of the Lower House who were active participants in the 1830 and 1832-6 Diets. He paid close attention to the public mood, and – in specific debates – to persuading, influencing and creating a united position within the opposition, to concentrate their efforts. As early as 1825, in letters he sent reporting on the Diet, there is evidence that he was not only an observer of the Diet, but also took part in elaborating the strategy of the opposition in the Upper House and saw the opposition as a group capable of being united. An interesting source of his community-organizing efforts was Wesselényi's concept of a 'virtue alliance', which he established with his friends István Széchenyi and Károly Eszterházy at the end of 1825. While Széchenyi defined the goal primarily in terms of moral development, Wesselényi's plan – which was ultimately not implemented – outlined a framework for a concrete political organization. Under the leadership of the three of them, he wanted to create a community whose members would actively participate in public life to achieve their goals by exerting influence both in private and in public, through rational argument or through praise and scorn.[9]

On false prejudices

Wesselényi's diary suggests that he may have been working on his first major work entitled *Balítéletekről* (On False Prejudices) as early as 1828. The version was intended to be published by the autumn of 1830, but partly due to delays with editing and correction work, and primarily because it was scrutinized by the censors, the book was eventually published in 1833 in Otto Wiegand's Leipzig edition, and was not distributed in Hungary and Transylvania before 1834. This delay also affected the reception of the work. Wesselényi would have timed the appearance of his book to coincide with the 1832-6 Diet of Pozsony, which at the time of its publication was already in the midst of discussing proposals for improving the situation of the serfs, which are also a central element of Wesselényi's work. In addition, Széchenyi was also ahead of his friend with the publication of his works entitled *Hitel*, *Világ* and *Stadium*, which Wesselényi himself acknowledged bore a high degree of similarity to his own book. The traces of years of joint thinking in the works by Wesselényi and Széchenyi can be seen in the image of the nobility and the aristocracy, the exploration of economic problems, their assessment of the need for change and social transformation, and the solutions they both proposed.[10]

Wesselényi's seminal work concluded that the problems Hungary and Translyvania confronted, and the causes of their underdevelopment, were all rooted in prejudices. It is from mentality, individual motivations and the resulting behaviour that he traced the faults of social life, the conflicts between the various groups in society, the antagonisms between the aristocracy, the nobility, the burghers and the peasantry. In particular, he focused on the conflict between the nobility and the peasantry as well as the tensions between the various religious denominations and ethnicities in the country as well as the critical economic problems. By revealing and eliminating false prejudices, Wesselényi aimed to perfect the individual and ultimately the nation. This idea also appears in Széchenyi's writings, but in Wesselényi's case its roots can be traced back to his upbringing, as he had already formulated it in 1814 in a letter to Ferenc Kazinczy, declaring that the goal of human existence was perfection in physical, spiritual and moral terms.[11] Self-perfection was no longer presented in the pages of Wesselényi's *Balítéletekről* only as a goal, but also as an individual duty, whereby the individual should also be of use to others, and should aim at the intellectual and moral advancement of the community. This desire for perfection is the driving force of development and progress, which, according to the laws of nature, must be continuous, and therefore require constant innovation in order to build on the positive aspects of the present and resolve its problems.[12]

Wesselényi interpreted Hungarian history in accordance with the liberal view of history popular in the Reform Era.[13] Both in his speeches and in the pages of *Balítéletekről* and his later work *Szózat a magyar és szláv nemzetiség ügyében* (Speech on the Hungarian and Slavic Nationalities, 1843), he saw the reigns of prominent medieval rulers such as Louis I (the Great) and Matthias Corvinus as harsh and pervaded by despotism, and discerned a moral decadence evident in the history of the previous centuries. At the same time, he projected the social and political problems and tasks of his own time – the need for a civil constitution and the nineteenth-century concept of the nation – back into the past and blamed the rulers and political elites of bygone eras for these failings.[14] This view of history also provided an opportunity for him to bolster his programme of social modernization and illustrate the negative aspects of feudalism. Wesselényi did not consider the institution of serfdom to be an indigenous phase of Hungarian historical development, and traced the loss of the personal freedom of the serfs back to the sixteenth century, to the laws passed after Dózsa's peasant-revolt of 1514, which he interpreted as having created an inhuman and despotic situation on the one hand, and played a significant role in the defeat at Mohács in 1526 on the other. The following centuries did not bring any substantial change and the underlying social problems persisted and even threatened to explode, which is why reform was so pressing for himself and his contemporaries.[15]

The view presented in Wesselényi's seminal work, which argued that the problems of Hungarian social, economic and political conditions were all rooted in false prejudices, fits in with the Reform Era's liberal view on modernization. Wesselényi devoted extensive sections of *Balítéletekről* to changing the thinking, lifestyle, social behaviour and mentality of Hungary to fall in line with Western European models, although he also warned against reckless imitation. For example, he promoted 'politeness', which he described as the abandonment of wild, coarse instincts and the attainment of erudition, refinement and moral development for which parts of Western Europe, notably enlightenment France, were famous.[16] For Wesselényi, the transformation of the mindset of society was an important step towards perfection in itself, but it also prepared the way for the new legal conditions, writing:

> And spiritual and moral education draws good laws without delay and immediately. Laws are successful and lasting when they are written from the heart of the nation onto the tablets of the law.[17]

Wesselényi's educational programme was linked to this belief in the individuals' responsibility to participate in broader social modernization. 'A patriot and a citizen, and that is all that every man should be educated to be', he declared in *Balítéletekről*.[18] For Wesselényi, the role of education and upbringing was primarily to deepen one's patriotism and emotional attachment to the nation, and the ultimate goal was to educate people to strive for the happiness of their fellow human beings and their homeland. Through this educational programme, children would learn about their homeland, its history, its legal and geographical characteristics and their civic duties. As for the method of teaching, Wesselényi relied on philanthropic pedagogy, and instead of teaching based on memorization, which was central to the educational system, he proposed a method that stimulated critical thinking as well as the emotions of the students.[19]

All these elements of his political programme to create a modern civic nation were not new. Széchenyi's book, *Stadium*, which reached readers a few months earlier than *Balítéletekről*, contains almost all of Wesselényi's proposals, such as equality before the law, the right of non-nobles to acquire property and to be represented in county assemblies, the equal distribution of public burdens and the removal of restrictions on trade and industry. However, Wesselényi went further on a few points. On the one hand, to quickly improve the situation of the serfs, he proposed the idea of emancipation from serfdom under the conditions laid down by law (while Széchenyi preferred the 'voluntary' way, when the serf and the landlord agreed with each other about the financial conditions). On the other hand, it is clear from Wesselényi's proposal for equal distribution of public burdens that his aim was not only the abolition of feudal subordination of the serfs, but also the abolition of absolutism and the free disposal of the nation over its public property, which also implied the idea of national independence and ministerial responsibility. Alongside all this was the formulation of the representation of the people as one of the most important aspects of Wesselényi's concept of freedom. Thus, the real importance of Wesselényi's political programme lies in the fact that he was the first to reconcile these demands.[20]

In addition to his programme, Wesselényi was also innovative in the political tactics he employed to achieve reforms. As regards the larger question of progress and development, he advocated a slow transition and organic development. His political base was predominantly the nobility who enjoyed representation in the county assemblies and were the foremost representatives of the dissatisfied opposition to the Vienna Court, and he used arguments in his speeches and in *Balítéletekről* to persuade them to support his proposed reforms. In the fight against absolutism, he considered the existing institutions, primarily the county assemblies, indispensable, and he wanted to base the newly created modern civil institutions on them. Thus, he also believed that Hungary's ancient constitution provided all the guarantees needed to prevent the advance of absolutism and contained certain features necessary to enact reforms on a liberal basis: limitations on royal power, the rights of the Diet, protection of persons and property, the right to take part in public affairs and freedom of speech in the national and county assemblies. He felt that the importance of the counties lay in their ability to refuse to implement illegal measures under the leadership of their freely elected officials. He basically divided the constitution into two parts: the crucial, "original" elements, the fundamental parts, for example, sections guaranteeing the freedom of the individual or covering the operation of the Diet, the county assemblies and the judiciaries, which are in line with the spirit of the age and therefore did not need to be changed as they would be the basis for future reforms. In contrast, he considered other elements of the constitution, for example, the tax exemption of the nobility, to be secondary, not original parts of the constitution and therefore subject to change. Since these were not original, changing or correcting them would not result in any structural change.[21] It was in this spirit that Wesselényi pioneered the use of the ancient constitution to achieve the goals of the reformers. From the 1790s onwards, the representatives of the opposition had become fond of referring to the ancient constitution, but Wesselényi and the liberal reformist opposition used this argumentation in a reinterpreted way to prove that the measures they proposed were not contrary to the feudal constitution but enabled, for example, the equal distribution of the tax burden and improvements in the lives of the peasantry.[22]

An important element of Wesselényi's political programme was the restoration of the unity of Hungary and Transylvania. In 1541, the independent Principality of Transylvania was established, which until then had been part of the Kingdom of Hungary. In the course of the sixteenth century, a peculiar Transylvanian system with its own of separation of powers developed, according to which the three leading nations of Transylvania – the Hungarians, the Szeklers and the Saxons – exercised political rights in the Transylvanian Diet. Despite the fact that in the sixteenth and seventeenth centuries the restoration of the territorial integrity of the medieval Kingdom of Hungary was a constant goal of the political elite, when the Principality of Transylvania became part of the Habsburg Empire at the end of the seventeenth century, it did so as an independent province. The *Diploma Leopoldinum*, issued in 1690, maintained the separate government of the Principality of Transylvania and the dominance of the three nations, as well as ensuring the free exercise of religion for Catholics, Calvinists, Lutherans and Unitarians that had been declared in 1568. In Transylvanian public thought, until the eighteenth century, this separation from Hungary ensured both political and religious freedom. The policies which the Habsburg government enforced in Transylvania in the eighteenth century changed this position. The Habsburg-backed administration's violations of the constitution, its preference for Catholics and Saxons in political office, and the development of a Romanian nationalist movement demanding equal political rights with the Hungarians, Szeklers and Saxons led the Transylvanian political elite to move closer to Hungary. The Transylvanian Diet of 1790-1 put the question of the union of Hungary and Transylvania on the agenda, although opinions were divided on the matter. The Hungarians believed that unification with Hungary would ensure greater protection for their constitutional rights whereas the Saxons and Szeklers feared the loss of their privileges and the Protestants and Unitarians feared the restriction of the freedom of religion they enjoyed. As a result, the unification effort failed. After this, the question of the union of Hungary and Transylvania did not appear on the agenda of the Diets until the 1830s.[23]

Wesselényi raised the issue of the union at the 1832-6 Diet of Pozsony, as well as making an appeal to the Transylvanian legal authorities. Wesselényi was aware that the political programme of the Liberals could not be implemented in Transylvania because of its underdeveloped conditions. (There was no *urbarium* in Transylvania; the absolutist regime had greater influence there than in Hungary, and there was no liberal opposition, so the basic points of the liberal political programme could not or could hardly be achieved under these circumstances.) Moreover, it was only in 1834 that the Habsburg ruler convened a new Transylvanian Diet after 1811. The difference between Hungary and Transylvania was clearly demonstrated by the 1832-6 Diet of Pozsony, which discussed the complete emancipation from serfdom, where in Transylvania not even an *urbarium* regulating the relationship between landlord and serf was issued. As a result, Wesselényi's political aspirations for Transylvania narrowly focused on improving public law and resolving religious grievances. The union offered Wesselényi a solution for the implementation of a liberal reform policy in Transylvania, as the reforms authorized by the Pozsony Diets would also be automatically enacted in Transylvania. In the Transylvanian Diet of 1834-5, however, his efforts to achieve this were in vain since he was unable to put the issue of the union of Hungary and Transylvania on the agenda, and the emperor then dissolved the Transylvanian Diet in February 1835.[24]

The 'dead citizen' and the nationality question

Wesselényi's political career was interrupted in the mid-1830s. After the failure of the Transylvanian Diet to enact meaningful changes, he was attacked from two sides in

1835. On the one hand, a lawsuit was filed against him in Transylvania for publishing a diary of the events of the Diet despite this being banned. On the other hand, he was prosecuted for high treason in Hungary for a speech he made on the emancipation of serfs on 9 December 1834 at the Szatmár County Assembly, in which he criticized the government. It is important to stress, however, that he criticized the government, and not the monarch, which was the key of his defence. The trial, which lasted four years, ended in February 1839 with Wesselényi being sentenced to three years' imprisonment. Because of his deteriorating eyesight, he was allowed to serve part of his sentence at the Gräfenberg Spa in Upper Silesia. The cure was not successful, however, and in the summer of 1844 Wesselényi lost his sight permanently. In 1840, Vienna granted amnesty to political prisoners, and in 1843 he returned to his estate in Zsibó (today Jibou, Romania), but he never regained his role in political life. In Gräfenberg, and after his return to Zsibó, he was kept informed about public events through the newspapers and his correspondence with his former political allies, but his ill-health prevented him from taking part in person in the political struggles of those years. As a result of this state of affairs, he created a new political self-definition for himself, as one of the 'dead citizens', who, excluded from political action, can only serve as a memory for his own country.[25] In addition, in his writings, a new, characteristic image of the homeland appeared, portrayed as a sick entity, with the most important problems portrayed as symptoms, notably the nationality question:

> we must either remedy our wounds and our illnesses, or the wound and the worsening illness, which spreads day by day, will end the national and civil existence of our homeland after a long period of lying in bed.[26]

The nationality issue, which became a central topic of political discourse in the 1840s, highlighted the tensions erupting within the liberal nationalist movement in the Reform Era. These internal conflicts stemmed from the coexistence of the notion of the nation in the political sense and the notion of the nation in the ethnic and cultural sense. On the one hand, the liberals wanted to give civil liberties by abolishing feudal social and economic relations, thus creating a community of citizens with equal rights. On the other hand, they regarded culture and the emotional identification resulting from it as key factors in a community identity and necessary for the cohesiveness of the nation. In a multi-ethnic country, however, the creation of a culturally homogeneous nation inevitably encountered obstacles. The liberals saw the solution to the problem in the hope that the civil liberties guaranteed to all by the constitution would be such an attraction for non-Hungarian ethnic groups that ethnic divisions would disappear, the non-Hungarian ethnic groups would be merged into the Hungarian nation, and the Hungarian nation would become both a civic and a cultural nation.

Nevertheless, there was a potential contradiction because the reformers' goal of disseminating the Hungarian language and culture could clash with their desire to extend political rights more widely. This contradiction was also evident in Wesselényi's thought in the 1830s. In *Balítéletekről*, he supported the dissemination of the Hungarian language without coercion and agreed with the idea that the extension of political rights to the ethnic minorities, who were mostly serfs, would make assimilation into the Hungarian nation more attractive. Although in his work he called for exercising discretion and condemned mocking other nationalities, in his programme for the emancipation of the serfs he also made the right to own land conditional on the serf's Hungarian-language skills or Hungarian identity.[27]

Speech on the Hungarian and Slavic Nationalities

It was during his medical treatment in Gräfenberg that Wesselényi formulated the ideas of his second great work, entitled *Szózat a magyar és szláv nemzetiség ügyében*. He began this book in 1841, collecting statistical and historical data with the help of his circle of acquaintances. It was then published in 1843 and was later translated into German. His contact with Germans, Czechs, Poles and Romanians while recovering in the Czech spa town clinic not only raised his awareness of the nationality issue but also broadened his political horizons.[28] The emergence of various nationalist movements in Hungary intensified the Hungarian liberals' sense of danger and their concern for the future of the Hungarian nation. This was also influenced by external factors, especially the German press and pamphlets, which often quoted the late eighteenth-century German philosopher Johann Gottfried Herder's idea that the Hungarian language and culture would eventually disappear, swallowed up by the sea of Slavs around them. Moreover, after the Russian suppression of the Polish uprising in November 1830, Hungarian liberals, including Wesselényi, saw the Russian Empire as a potential source of danger, as the embodiment of absolutist authoritarianism. The Russians were also believed to be the external factor behind the development of the pan-Slav nationalist movements in Hungary, which aimed at uniting the Slavs led by Russia.[29]

Wesselényi also examined the nationality question from a comparative European perspective, which makes it stand out among contemporary Hungarian works dealing with the nationality issue. The Hungarian liberals did not want to come into conflict with the government by criticizing the absolutist conditions in the other provinces of the empire – in order to protect the feudal institutions – so the reform proposals they formulated dealt only with Hungary. Since Wesselényi was convinced that Russian influence and pan-Slavism were behind the nationalist movements, he was convinced that Russian ambitions had to be countered across Europe. His expectation was that a defence of constitutionality by a Franco-English-German alliance would counter both the revolutionary aspirations of the Slavic nationalist movements and the absolutism of Russia. Wesselényi also believed that constitutional reform was the only way for the Habsburg Empire to maintain its great power status. Wesselényi maintained that Vienna should put the Habsburg Empire on a new footing by showing more trust in the Germans, Hungarians, Italians and Poles, and by carrying out a constitutional reform in each of its provinces. His scheme was for a new imperial structure comprising a confederation of five provinces – the Austrian Hereditary Lands, Lombardy, Bohemia-Moravia, Hungary and Galicia – but he did not go into detail, instead concentrating on the constitutional reorganization of the provinces of the empire. In the wider European arena, Wesselényi – reviving the rhetorical element of the sixteenth-century anti-

Ottoman struggles – intended his country to play the role of the bastion of Europe, and saw the interests of the Hungarians in an alliance with the Germans against Russia.[30]

In response to Széchenyi's accusation, Wesselényi saw the reason for the emergence of nationalist movements not as a response to the 'aggressive' spread of the Hungarian language, but as part of the spirit of the age, and regarded it as a natural process. While recognizing the importance of national feeling as a cohesive force, he considered civil liberties, extended equally to all, to be paramount. Wesselényi therefore assessed the nationalist movements on the basis of their attitude towards the constitution, and his verdict was that, while the Hungarians were in favour of the unity guaranteed by the constitution, Slav and Romanian nationalists were undermining the constitution by threatening the unity of the state. He made a similar distinction when deciding whether to meet the demands of the various nationalist movements. While he would have given the Croats – who had their own institutional system – permission to use Croatian or Latin as an official language, for other nationalities he would have restricted the use of their mother tongue to private life. Nevertheless, he called for the legal protection of the private use of the mother tongue of the nationalities, and for the prohibition of the harassment and mockery of nationalities, and was against the dissemination of the Hungarian language by force. He saw the dissemination of the Hungarian-language and gradual assimilation as the right solution to eliminate the differences resulting from ethnic divisions. As the combined Hungarian-speaking population of Hungary and Transylvania exceeded, the Slavic nationalities did not represent a significant majority over the Hungarians, and as he felt that the Hungarians had an advantage in the field of education, he did not regard the linguistic claims of the Slavic nationalities as justified. Thus, he urged that Hungarian language should be declared by law to be the official language of legislation, public administration and education. A novel aspect of his Magyarization policy was to assign an important role to kindergartens, and while he would have only included Hungarian as one of the subjects in elementary public education, in the kindergartens he envisaged Hungarian would be the compulsory language of instruction.[31] However, liberalism and nationalism sometimes came into conflict with each other in his political programme. Although in theory Wesselényi put individual civil liberties and constitutionality before nationality, in his practical proposals for the extension of the rights, he sought to give an advantage to those who chose the Hungarian nationality. While in *Balítéletekről*, education and erudition appeared merely as ideal conditions for progress, in his *Szózat*, Wesselényi attributed a more important role to education and erudition, making them necessary for the possession of rights in order to achieve national unity as quickly as possible. The triple criteria of literacy, knowledge of the Hungarian language and basic knowledge of public law are mentioned in the *Szózat* in connection with the reform of municipal and county representation and as a requirement for holding office.

Wesselényi also regarded the triple criteria as a solution to other issues. In the spring of 1843, there were several outbreaks of violence during the election of delegates to the Diet of Pozsony and the drafting of the instructions to delegates. The corrupted, drunken nobles marched to the sessions wearing their swords and invoking their right to exemption from taxation, thus preventing the inclusion in the delegates' instructions of a provision stipulating that the payment of the house tax, a tax levied to cover the expenses of the county, should be extended to the nobility. These events highlighted the need to reform the county forums, which Wesselényi considered crucial. In addition to his proposals to guarantee the security of the assemblies, Wesselényi framed his solution primarily by comparing the rights associated with the county assemblies – that is, participation in the public life of the county – to the holding of office, which could therefore be made conditional on meeting certain requirements apart from merely being a noble. The attachment of conditions to the right to participate in the county assembly was not without precedent as it was an existing practice in Hungary and Transylvania for the holding of certain county offices. The reception of his proposal reflected well Wesselényi's isolation from the political arena and practical politics, as Lajos Kossuth and many other liberal leaders regarded this proposal as tactically dangerous, since it would have opened the door to claims that liberal reforms would diminish the rights of the nobility and undermine their support.[32]

Return to politics and final years

The events of March 1848 gave Wesselényi the opportunity to become, once again, an active participant in politics. At the request of the members of the Transylvanian opposition, he set off for Pozsony, and at the last Diet of the Hungarian estates, he played a significant role in the drafting of the Act of Union between the two historic Hungarian territories. At the end of April 1848, he was appointed lord-lieutenant of Central Szolnok County and government commissioner for the re-annexation of the Partium. The Transylvanian Diet, which convened on 29 May, endorsed the union of Hungary and Transylvania, and on 6 June, the Diet unanimously approved the bill on the emancipation of the serfs drafted by Wesselényi.[33]

In spite of his political successes in Hungary and Transylvania, the fear of ethnic division was constantly present in Wesselényi's mind. In particular, the Croatian threat and the demands of the Romanian nationalist movement influenced his position on the nationality issue. In August 1848, he submitted a bill to the Upper House of the Hungarian Parliament to satisfy Romanian demands but it was not passed. On the one hand, this proposal – more lenient than the views contained in his *Szózat* – granted Orthodox believers and Greek Catholics equal rights with other denominations, thus remedying the religious grievances of the Romanians. In addition, the proposal would have given Romanians concessions on the use of languages in church registers, municipal records and primary education, as well as obliging all authorities to accept Romanian-language applications, petitions and private documents. While Wesselényi's aim in public-political forums remained a search for reconciliation with the ethnic minorities, in his correspondence he expressed a more pessimistic view. Although only two letters from this period deal with this topic, the seriousness of it is shown by the fact that both letters were written to members of the Hungarian government. In his letter of 20 April 1848 to Prime Minister Lajos Batthyány – based on the threat posed by the Croatian Ban Josip Jelačić – he expressed his fears, which he had expressed in his *Szózat*, that in the event of a military conflict with the Croats, the Russians might intervene. He saw the Croats as a lost cause and proposed fulfilling the Croatian demands for independence as they could not be assimilated. In a letter to Gábor Klauzál, the minister of agriculture, industry and trade, in June 1848, he considered the loss of territorial integrity to be a possibility in regard to the Romanians. One can conclude from his proposals that, even if only for a short time, he was uncertain that liberal solutions, the extension of rights and the reconciliation of interests could create unity between Hungarians and nationalities.[34]

Seeing that no agreement with the Croats was possible and that an armed conflict was inevitable, he travelled with his family to Gräfenberg on 29 September 1848. Motivated by the success of the Spring Campaign, by May 1849 he had completed his last work, an anonymously published pamphlet entitled *Die Ursache und die Zweck des Kampfes in Ungarn* (The Origin and Purpose of the Fight in Hungary). The work, written to enlighten foreign public opinion, not only described the grievances of the 1840s and the 1848 April Laws but also defended the April Laws by invoking the ancient constitution, presenting them as the result of the organic development of Hungarian constitutionality. In addition, the pamphlet also included a sharp criticism of the new, centralizing constitution of 4 March 1849 and of the new emperor Francis Joseph.[35]

It was in his isolation at Gräfenberg that the former leader of the liberal opposition saw the fulfilment of his fears, the Russian intervention and the crushing of the War of Independence. In the spring of 1850, he decided to return home to Transylvania. However, he never reached his home in Zsibó, as he caught pneumonia on the way and died on 21 April 1850.

Notes

1. In detail, see James Wilde, "'The Boatman of the Deluge": Miklós Wesselényi and 1838 Flooding of Pest', *Hungarian Studies* 19, no. 1 (2005): 27–50.
2. Fónagy Zoltán, *Wesselényi Miklós* (Budapest: Új Mandátum, 1998), 161.
3. Wesselényi Miklós, *Könyörgés* [A Plea], 1808, Collection of Manuscripts, Ms. 2605, 'Lucian Blaga' Central University Library of Cluj-Napoca.
4. In a surviving educational guide from 1809, we read this about Wesselényi: 'If he sees a poor man, he will give all he has, without any measure.' Between 1813 and 1817 there was a famine in Transylvania, and to help the poor, a group of young aristocrats led by Wesselényi set up a soup kitchen in Kolozsvár to feed the hungry. See Kárpáti Attila István, '"Akit szeret, szive szerint szereti": Id. Teleki László Cserei Helénának írt nevelési tanácsai' ['He Who Loves, Loves According to His Heart': Educational Advice Written by László Teleki Senior to Helena Cserei], *Fons* 23, no. 3 (2016), 325; Kárpáti Attila István, 'Küzdelem az éhínség ellen: Ínségkonyhák Kolozsváron 1817-ben' [Fighting Hunger: Soup Kitchens in Kolozsvár in 1817], *Orvostörténeti Közlemények* 69, no. 1-4 (2018): 86–9.
5. The issue was finally settled in June 1848 with the declaration of serf emancipation.
6. *History of Transylvania*, ed. Béla Köpeczi (New York: Columbia University Press, 2002), 2:698–700, 780–2.
7. Trócsányi Zsolt, *Wesselényi Miklós* (Budapest: Akadémiai, 1965), 61–74, 118–21.
8. Diary of Miklós Wesselényi, January 2, 1836, Fond nr. 928, crt. nr. 657, Romanian National Archives in Județul Cluj. The term 'out of doors' was taken from William

Gerard Hamilton's work titled *Parliamentary Logic*. The influence of Hamilton's book can be seen in Wesselényi's activities, both in terms of preparation and community building. William Gerard Hamilton, *Parliamentary Logick: To which are Subjoined Two Speeches, Delivered in the House of Commons of Ireland, and Other Pieces* (London, 1808), 3, 21-2, 26, 37, 63.

9 Velkey Ferenc, 'Erénygyakorlatok a perfekció társas útján (1825-28): A Széchenyi-Wesselényi-Eszterházy „erényszövetség' működése. [Virtue Exercises on the Social Path of Perfection (1825-28): The Functioning of the Széchenyi-Wesselényi-Eszterházy 'Virtue Alliance'], in *Ludovika Szabadegyetem: Széchenyi 225*, ed. Auer Ádám (Budapest: Dialog Campus, 2018), 197-202.

10 Trócsányi, *Wesselényi Miklós*, 150-3; Dávid Gábor Csaba, *'Célunk tökéletekesédünk': A nemzetnevelő Wesselényi Miklós* ['Our goal is our perfection': The National Educator Miklós Wesselényi] (Budapest: Argumentum, 2013) 9-16; Csorba László, 'Wesselényi és Széchenyi: Balítéletekről-egy barátság dokumentuma' [Wesselényi and Széchenyi: *Balítéletekről*-Document of a Friendship], in *Előadások és tanulmányok Wesselényi Miklósról*, ed. Takács Péter (Debrecen: Erdélytörténeti Alapítvány, 1997), 100-3.

11 Váczy János, ed., *Kazinczy Ferencz összes művei. Harmadik osztály. Levelezés* [Ferenc Kazinczy's Collected Works. Third Class. Correspondence], 21 vols. (Budapest: MTA, 1890-1911), 12:249.

12 Miru György, 'A *Balítéletekről* és a politikai nyelvek' [*Balítéletekről* and Political Languages], in *Natio est semper reformanda: Tanulmányok Gergely András tiszteletére* [Studies in Honor of András Gergely], ed. Anka László et al., (Budapest: L'Harmattan, 2016), 106-7. Miklós Wesselényi, *Balítéletekről* [On False Prejudices] (Bucharest [Leipzig]: 1833), 9-12, 22-4.

13 On his liberal view of history, see Schlett István, *A politikai gondolkodás története Magyarországon* [The History of Political Thought in Hungary] (Budapest: Századvég, 2018), 408-10.

14 Wesselényi, *Balítéletekről*, 13-14; Wesselényi Miklós, *Szózat a magyar és szláv nemzetiség ügyében* [Speech on the Hungarian and Slavic Nationalities] (Budapest: Európa, 1992), 19-27.

15 Kulin Ferenc, *Hódíthatatlan szellem: Dózsa György és a parasztháború reformkori értékeléséről* [An Invincible Spirit: György Dózsa and the Reformist Assessment of the Peasant Revolt] (Budapest: Akadémiai, 1982), 28-34.

16 Miru, 'A *Balítéletekről* és a politikai nyelvek', 108-9.

17 Wesselényi, *Balítéletekről*, 108.

18 Wesselényi, *Balítéletekről*, 120.

19 Wesselényi, *Balítéletekről*, 117-24.

20 Gergely András, *Egy nemzetet az emberiségnek: Tanulmányok a reformkorról és 1848-ról* [A Nation for Mankind: Studies on the Reform Era and 1848] (Budapest: Magvető, 1987), 48-50.

21 Miru, 'A *Balítéletekről* és a politikai nyelvek', 112-13. The tactical role of argumentation was first recognized by Zsolt Trócsányi, see Trócsányi, *Wesselényi Miklós*, 134-7.

22 Takáts József, *Modern magyar politikai eszmetörténet* [Modern Hungarian Political History of Ideas] (Budapest: Osiris, 2007), 16-17; Dobszay Tamás, '"Szokjon gyapjas fülök ezután már gyakrabban hallható igazság szavához": A politikai élet verbális átrendeződése a reformkorban' ['Let Their Woolly Ears Get Used to the Word of Truth That Will Be Heard More Often': The Verbal Reorganization of Political Life in the Reform Era], *Századvég* 13, no. 47 (2008): 116-18.

23 Pál Judit, *Unió vagy 'unificáltatás'? Erdély uniója és a királyi biztos működése (1867–72)* [Union or 'Unification'? The Union of Transylvania and the Work of the Royal Commissioner (1867-1872)] (Kolozsvár: Erdélyi Múzeum Egyesület, 2010), 30–40.
24 Trócsányi Zsolt, *Wesselényi Miklós és világa* [Miklós Wesselényi and His World] (Budapest: Gondolat, 1970), 91–5, 110–14.
25 Trócsányi, *Wesselényi Miklós*, 449–53.
26 'Wesselényi Miklós nyílt levele Udvarhelyszék rendjeinek' [Miklós Wesselényi's Open Letter to the Estates of Udvarhelyszék], *Erdélyi Híradó*, August 9, 1842.
27 Schlett, *A politikai gondolkodás története Magyarországon*, 396–407, 421–2.
28 Trócsányi, *Wesselényi Miklós*, 452–3.
29 János Varga, *A Hungarian Quo Vadis: Political Trends and Theories of the Early 1840s* (Budapest: Akadémiai, 1993), 110–14.
30 Ágnes Deák, 'Miklós Wesselényi on the Future of the Habsburg Empire and Hungary', in *Geopolitics in the Danube Region: Hungarian Reconciliation Efforts 1848–1998*, ed. Ignác Romsics and Béla L. Király. (Budapest: Central European University Press, 1999), 22–4, 32–4.
31 Trócsányi, *Wesselényi Miklós*, 460–5; Schlett, *A politikai gondolkodás története Magyarországon*, 426–33. Wesselényi also established two kindergartens on his own estates in the 1840s, one of which operated in Szilágysomlyó (today Șimleu Silvaniei, Romania); see Kárpáti Attila István, 'Wesselényi Miklós kisdedóvó-alapításai' [The Foundations of Miklós Wesselényi's Nurseries] *Aetas* 35, no. 1 (2020): 5–17.
32 Trócsányi, *Wesselényi Miklós*, 487–91.
33 Egyed Ákos, 'Wesselényi küzdelme az unióért és a jobbágyfelszabadításért 1848-ban' [Wesselényi's Struggle for Union and Serf Emancipation in 1848], *Erdélyi Múzeum* 58, no. 3-4 (1996): 219–28.
34 James Wilde, 'Miklós Wesselényi and the Nationality Issues in 1830–49', *Hungarian Studies* 15, no. 1 (2001): 28–30.
35 Kárpáti Attila István, 'Wesselényi Miklós és az augsburgi Allgemeine Zeitung' [Miklós Wesselényi and the Augsburg Allgemeine Zeitung], *Századok* 153, no. 3 (2019): 578–82.

10

Count Lajos Batthyány (1807–49)

Gábor Erdődy

Legacy and youth

Hungary's first independent prime minister, Lajos Batthyány, whose execution turned him into a martyr, was born on 10 February 1807 in Pozsony (today Bratislava, Slovakia) to an aristocratic family that traced its origins back to the time of the conquest of Hungary. The prestige of the Hungarian ruling class was based on their considerable wealth, and their reputation was enhanced by the historical role of their members. Batthyány's behaviour and decisions were guided by his aristocratic self-confidence and patriotic commitment, nurtured by a family tradition of service to their country. His father, who died in 1812, left his fortune to his son, which permanently alienated him from his mother (Borbála Skerlecz) who thought she should have received the inheritance. He grew up in an emotional desert, bereft of love, as a result of his mother's behaviour and suffered from anxiety. Between 1824 and 1826, his education was entrusted to Nikolas Möller, a Doctor of Philosophy, who introduced him to the world of modern ideas. In addition to German, he also learned English, French and Italian to a level that enabled him to read the founding works of the Enlightenment and Liberalism in the original languages of its authors.

In 1826, he joined the Imperial and Royal Army and also completed his law studies in Zagreb. In 1827, he was transferred to Treviso, where, after four years in the army, he rose to the rank of lieutenant. He then threw himself into social life with feverish enthusiasm. In 1828, during a carnival revelry, he accumulated a huge debt, which his mother denounced him for. He was reprimanded and his promotion was cancelled for behaviour considered unworthy of the Imperial Army. As a result of the legal proceedings that ended the battle between mother and child, his paternal inheritance was made available to him from 10 February 1831, the day he came of age.

Following his return to civilian life, he took over his estates as an educated, ambitious young aristocrat, and by the early 1840s he had established a modern factory there. At the same time as the foundations of modern farming were being laid, his eighteenth-century castle of Ikervár became the centre of a lively social scene. His library, modest by the standards of the aristocratic collections of the time, contained mainly the classics of German and French literature, and the basic works of political, social and national sciences, history and economics. Batthyány, who spent only two of the first twenty-four years of his life in Hungary, had little attachment to his homeland, speaking only in German, his mother tongue.

In the 1830s, following the example of his aristocratic contemporaries, he travelled through most of Europe, becoming acquainted with the political regimes of the most advanced countries on the continent. The body of experience he accumulated on his travels, and earlier, played an indispensable role in the process of his becoming a politician. On 4 December 1834, he married Countess Antonia Zichy, who consciously helped him prepare for this career by helping to organize nationally renowned events (horse races, hunts, balls, etc.). He also benefitted from the support of his father-in-law, Count Károly Zichy, who ensured his financial independence. His career and way of life followed the peculiar path of aristocratic national embourgeoisement, combining aristocratic traditions with an openness to social modernity and public service.

Batthyány's first political appearance was connected with the Polish War of Independence, which broke out in 1830. However, he was not keen on the atmosphere of the county assemblies, appearing in person only three times between 1831 and 1839. A diary entry of 18 September 1831 by István Széchenyi, whom he met in the autumn of 1831, also indicates his lack of public ambitions. The first impressions of Count Széchenyi were that Batthyány was 'not worth much for our goals'. He visited Pozsony several times from 1834 to 1836 but did not attend the meetings of the Diet.[1] However, his activity during the 1839-40 session of the Diet suggests that he must have been consciously preparing for the role of opposition leader, and the experiences of 1831-9 brought him to a decisive stage in his process of becoming Hungarian.

Organizer of the aristocratic liberal opposition and founder of its programme

Batthyány arrived at the Pozsony Diet on 2 June 1839 as a politician with a well-developed plan to establish a magnate casino to be his primary task. This key institution for the organization of the aristocratic opposition was established on 10 June. At his lodgings, gatherings became a daily occurrence, and his receptions became some of the most important public events. His efforts were aimed at working with the liberal grouping in the Lower House to strengthen the popularity of the opposition. His presence, dangerous from the perspective of the court in Vienna (as the absolutist Habsburg court considered national and constitutional aspirations a threat), also attracted the attention of the secret police who noted his cooperation with Baron József Eötvös and identified the essence of their endeavour as the establishment of 'monarchical democracy'.

Batthyány left open the possibility for Széchenyi to join the opposition cooperation. Both men, however, were in sharp disagreement over the details of how to organize the dietal opposition. Batthyány described Széchenyi as a reformer who had reversed his liberal views and turned towards the conservatives, while Széchenyi called him, in response an agitator without a plan. Nevertheless, on 18 November 1839, the opposition in the Upper House of the Diet to Habsburg centralization was officially unified in a single faction by Batthyány with the help of László Teleki, József Eötvös and György Károlyi. They all agreed on the unity of Austria and Hungary, on the need to establish a constitutional monarchy and urged the establishment of equality before the law. In his speeches in the Upper House, Batthyány also spoke out in favour of freedom of expression. In his speeches, he went beyond the usual practice of listing a series of grievances, and instead combined a defence of existing rights and laws with proposals to enact new legislation.[2]

Batthyány set out the principles of his political aspirations in his memorandum, *Emlékirat*,[3] submitted to the Small Casino (also founded in Pozsony by Batthyány, similarly to the Magnate Casino, to organize the aristocratic opposition), which laid out the theoretical basis for the programme of the emerging liberal party which would become a powerful opposition to the Vienna Court in the Diet. In the introduction to this document, he called for 'a predominance of the aristocracy, both parliamentary and extra-parliamentary', defining public service as their social and ethical duty. Batthyány was one of the first to point out the importance of party organization in which the magnates should support a programme of social modernization. Sharing the ideas of classical liberalism, he also indicated that he favoured a path leading to the abolition of privileges and that he wanted to achieve the inclusion of the non-noble classes in the exercise of political rights gradually, on the basis of certain criteria that would be included on the census.

As regards economic relations between Austria and Hungary, Batthyány followed the philosophy of free and competitive capitalism. In outlining the steps to be taken to create a modern Hungary, he called, above all, for the abolition of the ancestral state, the implementation of public taxation and the abolition of serfdom, as he regarded the introduction of these reforms as the basic condition for unifying the opposition. With the inspiring example of his wife and sister-in-law in mind, the draft programme advocated the promotion of patriotism by aristocratic women. The *Emlékirat* memorandum reveals that at the end of 1839, Batthyány had a mature liberal vision of how the feudal social order and absolutist rule should be transformed. The memorandum also highlighted the interconnections between national and sociopolitical aspirations when it linked improving Hungary's international competitiveness and the promotion of tolerance in both politics and religion.

The most important source materials for understanding Batthyány's political ideas are his speeches in the House of Magnates. As he did not speak Hungarian well at the time, he did not make lengthy addresses. Nevertheless, he was clearly most active when defending freedom of expression, freedom of the press, freedom of religion and the autonomy of the county assemblies. Despite wanting to maintain the leading role of the aristocracy on the basis of wealth and meritocracy, sovereignty of the people was a basic strategic element of his concept. Pointing out the differences between free and slave nations, he stressed that 'the fountain of all sovereignty is the nation, and the government is entitled to only as much of it as the nation has entrusted to it'.[4] On 9 September, he explained that the duties of the nation and the ruler are reciprocal, and that the king can only expect obedience from his people if he himself has fulfilled his obligations: 'The principle of reciprocity is established in all constitutional countries, because it distinguishes between absolute and non-absolute rule.'[5] As the leader of the aristocratic opposition, he insisted on the primacy of the legislature over the Habsburg court, and, giving democratic content to his conception of popular sovereignty, he proclaimed the primacy of the Lower House of the Diet when he stated that 'there is in the soul of every two-tier monarchical constitution a duty on the part of the House of Magnates, even in spite of its convictions, to join the House of Representatives the moment it becomes clear to it that it [i.e. the House of Magnates] does not enjoy the sympathy of the greater part of the nation'.[6]

In all this he followed the principles of Ferenc Deák, who had a decisive influence on the formation of his political ideology and was respected by Batthyány as the greatest legal authority. Both men protested against the unconstitutional lawsuits and imprisonments that followed the Diet of 1832-6. However, contrary to Deák, Batthyány was against the king granting amnesty instead of acquitting the unjustly imprisoned, because he believed that law and order should be restored 'not by mercy but by justice'. He reacted furiously to the news of the 1840 pardon, which many hailed as a reconciliation between the nation and the monarch, never accepting its benefits.

Batthyány acted as leader of the liberal opposition grouping at the Diet of 1839-40. Although, unlike Széchenyi, he was not a theoretician, the positions he adopted reveal a portrait of a politician committed to liberal principles and ready to fight for them with fanatical determination. At the centre of his programme, which proclaimed the synthesis of national self-determination and civic constitutionality, was the demand for Hungary to be given complete self-government within the Habsburg Empire. To this end, he called for a policy that unified the various interest groups: granting representation to the burghers and the peasantry, the introduction of peasant property rights and the establishment of equality before the law. He vigorously participated in the successful struggle to pass at least some reforms, and the legal enshrinement of the emancipation of the serfs, of the free founding of factories and the rights of the Jews to trade freely can be considered a success of the aristocratic opposition, which was often more united than the nobles in the Lower House of the Diet.

Organizing the aristocratic opposition, shaping the liberal agenda

After the Diet, Batthyány turned his attention to the counties, and, in close cooperation with Deák, he led the efforts to defend the ancient constitution which was under continuous attack by the Vienna Court. He initially reacted cautiously to the launch of the *Pesti Hirlap* (Pest Gazette), by Lajos Kossuth on 2 January 1841. In the debate that followed the publication of Széchenyi's *A kelet népe* (People of the East) on 23 June 1841, however, the opposition, fearing a split, believed Széchenyi had made a mistake in shattering their unity. A decisive moment for Batthyány's future was his meeting with Lajos Kossuth at the end of 1841. His period of temporary uncertainty was finally brought to an end by Széchenyi's speech at the Academy on 27 November 1842. The lecture, which primarily blamed the opposition for the rise of nationalist movements among the ethnic minorities in Hungary, angered Batthyány, who rightly recognized the Vienna Court's machinations behind these movements. In the confrontation between moderate and democratic liberalism, Batthyány, in the company of all the leading opposition politicians, clearly took a stand in favour of Kossuth. (The moderate liberals wanted to proceed with moderate reforms and keeping the petty nobility out of politics. The democratic liberals urged more radical reforms by mobilizing a larger mass base.)

Following the unsuccessful Diet of 1839–40, many hoped that the development of a social organization that appealed not only to the nobility would afford them greater room for manoeuvre. Batthyány's involvement in the reform movement led to a deepening of his working relationship with Kossuth and was the start of a long-term cooperation between them.[7]

On 18 May 1843, the Diet re-convened and the liberal opposition began to hold its meetings in the newly reorganized Small Casino. A core group of nineteen people played a leading role in its deliberations, along with a wider circle of around forty occasional attendees. In the course of his organizational work, Batthyány's views were marked by the way he distanced himself from extreme proposals. 'I want as little to do with Perczel [i.e. the spokesman of the radicals] as with György Apponyi [i.e. the representative of the governing party]', he announced on 15 December.[8] Maintaining strict discipline in his group, he took particular care to choreograph their interventions in the Diet, personally allocating the roles they would play. At this Diet, as he grew more confident speaking Hungarian, he gave more than 200 speeches, making him one of the opposition's leading speakers. Batthyány again fought steadfastly for the freedom of the press and advocated the reform of the representation of towns and cities in the Diet while staunchly defending the counties' rights of self-government against the centralizing policies of the court in Vienna.

On the issue of nationality, he rejected the compulsory use of Hungarian in education, public administration and the legislature. In his speech to the Diet, he declared:

> I am also of the opinion of those who wish to respect in all nations that which is most worthy of respect among us Hungarians, namely, the national spirit; therefore I do not wish to make the Croats Hungarian by law, but only wish that the chain and link should be Hungarian, which brings the two countries into contact.[9]

In the debate on religious issues, he called for a ban on the unlawful baptisms of children in mixed marriages by Catholic priests. (According to Article XXVI of 1790/1 the sons of Protestant fathers could follow their father's religion.) He also took a strong stand against the policies of the clergy and the court when he declared that the Catholic Church's practice of openly violating the law on religious toleration of 1790 was occurring at the instigation of Vienna, declaring that 'the Hungarian high priests do not seek justification in their spiritual independence, but in the criminal aid of a government', knowing that 'the apostolic kingdom will carry more weight in Vienna than the constitutional',[10] which was a more radical position than the radical speeches made in the Lower House of the Diet. It was in no small part thanks to Batthyány that the opposition's efforts on religious issues were crowned with success, when Article III of 1844 confirmed the validity of mixed marriages performed by Protestant clergymen and permitted the freedom of religious choice. Despite these partial successes, Batthyány was not satisfied, as he considered that no substantial progress had been made on the most important reforms.[11]

By putting forward a programme calling for the abolition of the feudal social order and absolutism, Batthyány, recognizing the interdependence of Hungarian and universal progress, stressed that the country's international reputation depended on the extent to which it transformed itself to overcome its backwardness. He argued that conformity to the universal norms of contemporary progress was both in the country's domestic political self-interest and furthered its aims internationally. He recognized that the cause of the transformation of Hungary could not be separated from the modernization of the Habsburg Empire as a whole and that Hungarian reforms could only be realized if changes were also brought about in Austria: with regard to Hungary, 'the barometer is the government's attitude towards the Hereditary Provinces of Austria. While the current system of things continues there [. . .] it seems impossible' for the Vienna government to support reform in Hungary,[12] he emphasized. Leading those calling for the further development of the reform programme, he proposed the creation of a pure personal union, an independent Hungarian government and an independent system of foreign representation. At a meeting on 16 July 1844, he explained that 'only a wise use of the forces that are awakening can calm the storm that is already gathering on Europe's political horizon, and which must sooner or later break out'.[13] Even at this stage, he envisaged the possibility that the constitutional transformation of Hungary and the empire could be promoted by revolutionary changes in Europe.

Creating a unified opposition and promoting regime change

After his departure from the Diet, Batthyány tried to take advantage of the popular enthusiasm for associations that had emerged in Hungary. He believed that this was the only hope left to advance the cause of 'social reform'. Working with Kossuth, he played a key role in the organization of the *Iparegyesület* (Industrial Association), the *Magyar Kereskedelmi Társaság* (Hungarian Trade Society) and the *Gyáralapító Társaság* (Factory Founding Society). By developing from scratch a series of associations that could lobby for economic and social reform, he sought to counterbalance the administrative system aimed at breaking the autonomy of the counties and to create suitable conditions for a policy that could unify all the interests in the country. In January 1845, he joined the *Védegylet* (League of Protection, an association for the protection of domestic industry, whose members committed themselves to buying only domestic products when available) in order to protest against the existence of the customs frontier between Austria and Hungary, which was damaging to Hungarian economic interests. He also promoted domestic industries and, together with his wife, was at the forefront of upgrading his clothing with Hungarian products.[14]

In addition to his organizational work, Batthyány played a key role in bridging the divisions between the centralists, who were committed to a centralized system of government based on the French model, and the municipalists (the entire opposition leadership including Kossuth), who argued for a reformed county system based on popular representation. As a result of his negotiations with József Eötvös, the centralists gave up their attack on the county system and jointly opposed Vienna's attempt to introduce the administrators' system, which was aimed at drastically limiting the self-government powers of the counties.

From 1845 onwards, Batthyány made the unification of the opposition movement in both houses of the Diet his main goal. He resolutely proclaimed the need for radical social reform, seeking the establishment of a constitutional monarchy based on popular representation, a government accountable to the Diet and the abolition of serfdom, while vigorously promoting the development of a programme that inspired all of the opposition. The lessons learned from the Galician uprising of February 1846 played a decisive role in his radicalization: the Vienna Court mobilized the disaffected serfs to exterminate the Polish nobility. He also endorsed Kossuth's view that the socage system (*urbarium*) could only be reformed if the state also provided compensation for landowners (the amount of which would be determined later).[15]

On 15 March 1847, under the leadership of Batthyány, an opposition meeting was held to counter the programme of the Conservative Party, which had been formed at the end of 1846, and it was his guidance that ensured that the Opposition Statement (*Ellenzéki Nyilatkozat*) was issued on 6-7 June. Batthyány mobilized liberals throughout the country to support this statement with a circular letter, and was actively involved in drafting the final text, edited by Deák and Kossuth. The document – in contrast to the vaguely worded text of the Conservative Party – clearly stated the goal and task of the opposition: it defined Hungary's position on the basis of full self-determination within the Habsburg Empire and pushed for the enactment of similar constitutions in all of the Hereditary Provinces. In addition, the reformers also demanded equality before the law, the abolition of the *ius aviticum* (i.e. the medieval law that did not allow the selling of noble land) and, above all, universal and compulsory emancipation of the serfs with the nobility to be compensated by the Hungarian state.

Batthyány played a decisive role in ensuring that the opposition went into the 1847 elections as an organizationally united group with a broadly consensual programme. Sparing no financial resources, he managed to have Kossuth delegated to the Diet by the leading county (Pest County), together with Móric Szentkirályi. The establishment of a trusting relationship between the two was hindered, above all, by Batthyány's extremely reserved nature and the social differences between the two. Széchenyi viewed their collaboration with jealous dislike and called his rival 'the most arrogant and repellent Hungarian aristocrat'. His distrust was also fuelled by the fact that in a debate on 8 July 1847 Batthyány stated: 'Kings have bayonets and peoples have revolutions to win concessions.'[16] This indicated that although he was working for the peaceful introduction of social reforms, he also regarded revolutionary means as a potentially valid way of forcing through reforms, something Széchenyi never accepted.

The young magnate, who had set out to fight for the abolition of feudal society, absolutist government and Hungary's dependence on Vienna, saw as the historic task of his generation the creation of a Hungary which could enter liberal Europe as an equal partner of the other countries that had replaced their feudal systems. His behaviour was characterized by a sense of mission based on an ethical stance mixed with a naivety that took political morality for granted, a belief in inexorable progress and sometimes utopian optimism. His 'monarchical democratic' concept took a dual approach, its implementation presupposing both the abolition of absolutism and the abolition of Hungary's subordinate role within the empire. Describing his function in the opposition movement, Kossuth wrote in a letter to Wesselényi of 28 October 1847:

> My friend, we take our hats off to this man, for in the most unexpected circumstances he is as sharp as a lynx in his vision, as swift as lightning in his resolve, and then as firm and unyielding as if all his nerves were of iron.[17]

At the forefront of the revolutionary breakthrough

The last Diet opened on 12 November 1847. The debates in the Upper House suggested that Batthyány was throwing himself into the struggle with a special passion and that he was fighting for his goals even though he continued to play by the constitutional rules of the game. He interpreted the prospects of Hungary's rebirth in an imperial and international context and focused on criticizing the policies of the court.

Convinced that the continent was on the brink of decisive changes, he stated in a speech of 7 December 1847:

> When it can be guessed without prophecy that the next war will be a war of principles, and that the two slogans which for some time divided jurists and orators into two hostile camps will be read on banners which just about all the armies of Europe will line up behind – will the Hungarians then, too, be indifferent to the foreign policy of Austria?

His train of thought reveals his concern that Hungary would not be able to assert its national interests in the impending conflict, and therefore required a comprehensive constitutional transformation of the empire to avert the danger. 'For me, it is an axiom that an unrestricted system of government and a restricted system of government cannot fit under the same scepter without this incompatibility having a corrosive effect', he asserted, continuing:

> I think that it is not all the same whether the constitutional movements taking place in the Hereditary Provinces will succeed in making one province a constitutional guarantor for the other; or that they may continue to be oppressed, while envy on the one hand, and contempt on the other, may continue to let the sword of Damocles hang over our lives.[18]

Batthyány's sometimes impatient, peremptory style, while working in a heightened state of anxiety, provoked resentment among many of his fellow reformers. According to Széchenyi's diary entry of 5 February, 'there are many people who would passionately insult Lajos Batthyány and shoot him, including myself'.[19] Menyhért Lónyay, who rejected Kossuth's radicalism, considered that 'Lajos Batthyány is behind everything', and that Kossuth must be 'freed from Batthyány's net'.[20] While the opposition concentrated its agitation on the problem of the administrative system, the government counter-attacked on the basis of Széchenyi's proposal. The attempt to isolate Batthyány and Kossuth and to create a 'moderate centre party' promised success. Batthyány, however, strongly opposed the initiative. According to Széchenyi's diary entry of 5 February, 'Kossuth as hammer, Batthyány as bellows',[21] worked together to thwart the 'conspiracy', and even brought the radical opposition leaders even closer together.

Batthyány went on to play a very active part in the debates on the key issues of the transformation of the country. In his radical motion on the abolition of serfdom, he opposed the draft of the memorandum voted by the Lower House and spoke out against the full compensation of landlords in accordance with Kossuth's earlier defeated attempt to produce a 'just' settlement. He was convinced that 'sooner or later we shall have to give up perfect compensation if we want to achieve this whole thing, and instead of perfect compensation we shall have to be content with just compensation, because by perfect we are close to getting absolutely nothing, and then there will never be any emancipation of the serfs whatsoever'.[22]

On the question of the Hungarian language and nationalities, he proposed, to the indignation of many, that the Croats should be able to use their mother tongue in addition to Latin in their so-called 'internal affairs'. His initiative demonstrated the need to tackle the problem without extremism. In his opinion, 'neither justice nor sound politics can be reconciled with the fact that we, who have given up hopes of imposing our own language on the connected parts [i.e. the Croats with a large self-government], want to condemn them to the use of a dead language in their internal relations and public life'. In order to win the goodwill of the ethnic minorities in Hungary and the neighbouring peoples, he urged the creation of constitutional institutions that would attract them to the Hungarian crown 'like a magnet', proving 'before the whole world that we are not cowards to the stronger, and not tyrants against the weaker; that we [. . .] wish to and can respect the separate nationalities and their adherence to their own language'.[23]

At the turn of 1847-8, Hungary's leading politicians sought to ensure that the country could undergo transformation while setting priorities according to its interests by accurately assessing the international situation. The news of the Paris Revolution at the end of February was greeted with enthusiasm by Batthyány: 'I am not saddened by this news [. . .]. With the deserved downfall of Louis Philippe, freedom has triumphed throughout Europe.'[24] He identified the cause of the violence as the narrow-mindedness of the French royal court and its government, and blamed official policy for the breakdown of the constitutional processes. By interpreting the developments in France in a new way, he contributed to softening the resistance of Hungarian politicians, who had hitherto categorically rejected the possibility of revolutionary transformation.

In line with Kossuth's speech of 3 March, outlining his own demand for the immediate abolition of serfdom, nine days later Batthyány threatened his fellow magnates that he would stand himself at the head of the peasants and the small nobility if the demand was rejected.[25] In the wake of the Vienna Revolution of 13 March, he stepped up his activities. Seeking allies to strengthen the position of the liberal nobility, he was ready to resort to exerting radical pressure for a bloodless revolutionary transformation but rejected the use of violence.[26]

In March 1848, Batthyány was a popular politician in both Vienna and Pozsony. In the wake of the developments in Vienna and the revolution of 15 March, and as the only person capable of uniting and leading the various reformers, with his unquestionable authority, general recognition and enormous influence, Count Batthyány was appointed the first independent prime minister of Hungary by Archduke Stephen of Austria, palatine of Hungary, in Pest, on 17 March. He then worked closely with Kossuth, pushed for radical reform and played a decisive role in the adoption of the April Laws.[27]

March 23 proved to be a particularly significant day in the life of Batthyány, who had only been in office for a few days. In his prime minister's circular, he informed the authorities of the Diet's abolition of tax exemptions for the nobility and the abolition of serfdom while also urging the immediate establishment of the *Nemzetőrség* (National Guard). All this was not unconstitutional but it was an unusual move, which had not been resorted to for hundreds of years as it had not yet been sanctioned by the ruler. Anticipating a further escalation of tension, Batthyány sought to pre-empt the peasants' impatience from turning into an uprising, deprived the conservative representatives of the possibility of sabotaging the bill, and denied Vienna the opportunity to play the role of liberator of the serfs in an attempt to detach the peasantry from the opposition. He took a similarly courageous decision when he announced his proposed cabinet without prior royal approval. He set up the *Miniszteri Országos Ideiglenes Bizottmány* (National Provisional Committee of Ministers) and sent its members to Pest to work on behalf of the executive to maintain order.

By going on the offensive, Batthyány assumed personal responsibility in extraordinary situations. His actions succeeded in neutralizing the machinations of the Vienna Court and placating the radicals who threatened civil war. Meanwhile, in the midst of accelerating processes, he avoided the trap of overreaction: in a display of tactical maturity, he withdrew the parliamentary proposal 'On the Hungarian Army' in order to avoid provoking Vienna. Having settled the most urgent issues, the next day he travelled to Vienna accompanied by Deák to fight for the adoption of the bills, together with Kossuth and the Palatine Stephen. As the main protagonist in the negotiations to obtain their ratification, he was a forceful negotiator, making demands, threatening to back down, but also accepting the inevitable compromises. He knew that for the Hungarian side it was vital to turn the draft reforms into constitutionally irrevocable laws as soon as possible, even at the cost of concessions.[28]

Prime minister of the first independent Hungarian government

The April Laws, signed by Ferdinand V on 11 April, the result of compromises with the court, the nobility, the bourgeoisie and the Catholic Church, in addition to restoring national self-determination, laid the foundations for modern statehood and social transformation, and restored the unity of the kingdom by reuniting Transylvania with Hungary. To preserve a broad social consensus it enacted the most progressive emancipation of the serfs in Central Europe, ordering the general and compulsory abolition of serfdom with the state providing compensation to the nobles. The drafters of these reforms, which meticulously synthesized the preparatory work that had been done throughout the Reform Era, also consciously drew on the European and North American experience. Following the Belgian model of responsible government, the state was subordinated to a representative system.

The Code also had some shortcomings. As a result of concessions it forced, the Vienna Court retained its absolutist rights in the control of the army and the conduct of foreign affairs. Jewish emancipation and the abolition of the guilds were not achieved. County assemblies continued to be dominated by the nobility. There was also a lack of progress in dealing with the ethnic minorities. The Hungarian political elite, following the concept of one political nation, did not acknowledge the existence of other nationalities in the country (with the exception of the Croats who had historical autonomy). The reforms outlined Hungary's future as part of a constitutional Habsburg Empire held together by a personal union.

Batthyány presided over a coalition government, most of whose members had been leading figures in the political struggles of the Reform Era whose autonomy he respected. The organization of the National Guard was concentrated in his hands, independently of any other ministry, and until the arrival of Lázár Mészáros (on 23 May) he also temporarily acted as minister of war. His determination to reintegrate the *Határőrvidék* (military frontier), a part of the kingdom administered by the army from Vienna, and a refusal to take on a share of the imperial debt led, however, to growing tensions with the court.[29]

From the very beginning, the Hungarian government insisted on the independent management of diplomacy, and in its official documents it named Prince Pál Antal Esterházy as foreign minister. Although, according to the law, as minister-beside-the-king, the Prince's role was limited to 'assisting' in the affairs of the court, the Austrian foreign minister anticipated the Hungarian interpretation and adopted the additional term 'Royal Hungarian foreign minister'. Playing a key role in the formulation of a foreign policy, Batthyány focused his policy ideas on the Russian threat. He prioritized resistance to Tsarist expansion in the Lower-Danube region, supported a Polish national revival, and sought close relations with Great Britain to counterbalance St Petersburg. In a briefing note to London, he painted a dramatic picture of the threat to the continent and, warning of consequences that could harm British interests, portrayed the strengthening of Hungary as being in the European interest. In particular, he tried to win over Palmerston by emphasizing the legitimacy of the political transition in April and presented Hungary as the only force capable of ensuring the stability of the Habsburg Empire, but London responded negatively.

After this failure, Hungarian foreign policy then focused on supporting German unification, and at the German Constituent Assembly which convened in Frankfurt am Main on 18 May, Hungary's envoys were welcomed as an ally against pan-Slavism. The Austrian side did not condemn the Hungarian initiative, and the Habsburgs also sent representatives to the Frankfurt Assembly, where the Archduke John acted as imperial governor. The birth of the German unitary state was then seen as a fait accompli even by the counter-revolutionaries. Batthyány and his government looked for a strategic ally in Germany – they saw the freedom of Europe, the unity of Germany and the independence of Hungary as mutually reinforcing developments.[30]

The possibility of a unified Germany, which would include Austria, and the prospect of the disintegration of the Habsburg Empire, which had been (temporarily) driven back from its prized Italian possessions, prompted the Batthyány government to redefine the country's position. The prime minister urged the emperor, who fled to Innsbruck to escape the democratic revolution in Vienna on 15 May, to move to Buda because he was convinced that Hungary could take over Austria's role in Europe's balance of powers. The idea was not alien to some Austrian politicians either. Karl von Hummelauer, the Austrian government's legal expert, explained to an adviser to the Queen of England in London that 'there is a belief in Austria that a new empire must be created [...] and that is why Hungary will be made the nucleus of the new state, and if necessary, even the capital will be located there'.[31]

As well as entertaining such hopes, Batthyány and his colleagues also kept track of the possibility of a Habsburg counter-revolution. However, the prime minister did not openly confront the provocative court, even after being attacked by his radical opposition. In debates with the leading officials of the court, his confidence did not waver, as he considered the nobility of his family to be of the same age as that of the Habsburgs, and, without embarrassment, he lectured Archduchess Sophia – the sister-in-law of the king, who acted as the head of the unofficial, secret circle of imperial officials and aristocrats scheming for power, known as the camarilla – on constitutional customs, telling her to leave the room when he wished to discuss state affairs with his sovereign.[32] He explored the possibility of a peaceful settlement because he was convinced that this was what Hungarian public opinion and the great powers expected. The rebellion of the Croats, supported from Vienna, also convinced him that it was useless to rely on the foundation of the rule of law if he did not have adequate military forces.

The most serious challenge for the government was the ethnic minority problem. By mid-May, movements demanding territorial autonomy were openly opposing Batthyány's government and sought the support of the Habsburg counter-revolution. From the summer of 1848 onwards, the Hungarian political leadership held regular negotiations with the representatives of the ethnic minorities. However, Batthyány blamed the Habsburg counter-revolution, on the one hand, and pan-Slavic agitation, on the other, for exacerbating the situation.[33] Nevertheless, on 28 July 1849, in Szeged, a law was passed, which declared the right of all ethnic groups to develop freely, providing for the use of their own languages at the level of primary education, public administration and the courts, and offering the prospect of political and cultural autonomy.[34]

As tensions increased further, Batthyány's behaviour was determined by the duality of his appointment as prime minister by the emperor, while being responsible at the same time to the parliamentary representatives. He insisted on seizing every opportunity to arrive at a peaceful resolution, while preparing resolutely to defend Hungary's legitimate rights. The news of the Serbian rebellion in the Southern Lands

(*Délvidék*) persuaded him, on 15-16 May, to order the establishment of a mobile National Guard, thus laying the foundations for the Hungarian army. In his appeal of 19 May, he asked for the help of the Szekler border guards to crush the Serbian rebels. Since these troops formed part of the army of the Grand Duchy of Transylvania, which was not yet united with the Kingdom of Hungary, and were subordinate to the Habsburg General Command, the proclamation rightly met with the protest of the Transylvanian governor. Replying on 29 May, Batthyány justified his decision by invoking the paramount right of national self-defence, stating that 'as in the life of individuals, so in the life of countries and nations, there are moments which must be seized and in which it is absolutely necessary to depart from the regular course of action, so as not to run the risk of irreparable damage caused by delay or prolonged deliberation'.[35]

In parallel with the outbreak of the Serbian rebellion, which was supported by the neighbouring Serbian principality, the Croatian crisis continued to deepen. In a memorandum to the Palatine Stephen on 4 July, the Hungarian government provided an overview of the development of the conflict, portraying the negative role of the Croatian Ban Josip Jelačič and the Viennese government, and the attempts of the Hungarian side to prevent the outbreak of violence while preserving the rule of law. In a letter he wrote on the same day, Batthyány pointed out that the government of Austria was not really concerned about the Croatian-Hungarian feud, but 'about the independent governance of the financial and military affairs of our country'.[36] The resolution of the Council of Ministers of 5 July stated that the Hungarian leadership 'is determined not to yield one iota of the independence of the Hungarian nation, sanctioned by His Majesty, at any price, and will respond to allied friendship with similar friendship, and to hostility with lawful retaliation'.[37] With the aim of defusing counter-revolutionary plots, the Batthyány government brought forward the convening of the new Parliament, which was opened by the palatine on 5 July, and focused on taking measures against the counter-revolutionary preparations. Following Kossuth's speech on 11 July, the deputies voted in favour of calling up 200,000 recruits and raising the funds to pay for this new Home Guard (*Honvédség*).

Meanwhile, the international balance of power had taken an unfavourable turn. Following the repression of a demonstration by workers in Paris on 23 June, there was a conservative shift in domestic policy in France. In the German lands, Austria and Prussia's opposition to national unification gained ground. On 25 July, Radetzky scored a victory over the armies of Northern Italy. The successes of the counter-revolution changed the balance of power in Central Europe, enabling the Habsburg court to move against revolutionary Vienna, while Jelačič was mobilized to dismantle the Hungarian constitutional system. 'In the midst of intrigue and treachery, it may even be feared that the restoration of the old order of things may be attempted by force',[38] stated the Council of Ministers in its resolution of 12 August. Batthyány's envoy in Frankfurt, László Szalay, was informed by the prime minister that 'the reaction is now open, no longer hiding its intentions and plans. Hungary has been designated as the first victim.'[39]

Since the majority of the Frankfurt Parliament shared Batthyány's fears, on 26 August Szalay's letter of credentials was handed over in the presence of the imperial governor,

Archduke John, and Hungarian independence was officially recognized. The way seemed to be open for Count László Teleki's diplomatic mission to France. The Paris mission was carefully prepared by Batthyány, who was anticipating the recognition of Frankfurt. French Foreign Minister Jules Bastide had earlier indicated his readiness to officially receive Hungary's ambassador and had even named Pascal Duprat as France's designated representative in Pest.[40] The counteroffensive by the court in the autumn, however, thwarted the completion of the enterprise. The Habsburg diplomats in Paris and Frankfurt protested against the official presence of the Hungarian ambassadors, and the authorities backed away from the Hungarian cause.

At the time of this unfavourable turn of events, Batthyány had gone to Vienna in the company of Deák to try and equalize the Hungarian-Austrian relationship and fend off Jelačič's offensive. In order to improve their negotiating position, the Hungarian government passed a bill on 27 August offering independence to the Croats. Seeking a compromise, the Batthyány government was also determined to make further concessions, even agreeing to assume a share of the imperial debt and to recognize the jurisdiction of the border region by Vienna. However, the *Staatsschrift*, published on the basis of the Austrian government's memorandum of 27 August and approved by the emperor, foreshadowed the conflict provoked by Vienna, when it declared the guarantees of Hungarian self-determination that it had previously agreed to were now null and void and, in particular, demanded the abolition of an independent Hungarian army and Hungary's control over its own financial affairs. Batthyány was not willing to make concessions at the expense of the achievements of the April Laws.

Realizing the impossibility of reaching a peaceful solution, the prime minister and his cabinet resigned on 11 September, but the palatine again asked Batthyány to form a government. Batthyány accepted this mandate on the condition that the emperor recalled Jelačič, who had crossed the Drava River on 11 September , and that the Austrian government helped to replenish the empty Hungarian treasury by paying one million forints, thus enabling the Hungarian government to avoid being forced to issue money without royal approval.

Organizer of the self-defence war as acting prime minister

Batthyány's cabinet had been in a permanent state of crisis since the beginning of August. The premier, torn by the conflict between loyalty to the monarch and the struggle to preserve the April Laws (which the monarch had sanctioned), warned that in the current 'dangerous circumstances, we can expect very few allies [. . .] and this is the path of lawfulness'. 'If we deviate from this [. . .] all our efforts will end in laughable failure', he predicted in his speech on 12 September, and then nuanced his position by adding: 'I will not leave this path [. . .] until I feel within me the power to victoriously fight my enemies.'[41] This explains why he endorsed the principle of popular sovereignty and resolved, in a feat unique in the history of the European revolutions of 1848, to organize a new and powerful national army. Indeed, by the autumn of 1848, Batthyány had reached the point where he had accepted the inevitability and legitimacy of armed resistance against the unconstitutional Habsburgs. The provocative behaviour of the court convinced him of the impossibility of maintaining further loyalty. He explained his change of position in his parliamentary oration of September 16:

> When a nation is forced to defend its life, its existence, and has reached the extreme of no longer having any ray of hope, I am also convinced that loyalty may in some respects become an obstacle. I therefore call upon this House to consider seriously whether the time has not already come when the nation is forced to defend itself to the last and most desperate degree, when it is neither able nor obliged to uphold the rule of law.[42]

However, the Parliament persuaded the politician who had assumed the lion's share in the preparations for the war of self-defence to continue his efforts to ensure the legality of the measures taken to defend the country. In a petition addressed to the Palatine Stephen, he announced the makeup of his planned cabinet, which did not include Kossuth. With this gesture he tried to avoid even the appearance that the Hungarian side had provided the pretext for the emperor's refusal to stop the Croatian rebellion. Then, while he received the negative response of the emperor on 25 September, he personally supervised the resistance to Jelačič, who was advancing unopposed. Batthyány also directed the defence of northwest Upper Hungary against Slovak rebels and mercenaries invading from Moravia, and managed the preparations for the defence of Transylvania, which was now on the verge of civil war.

On 27 September, he was informed that the Palatine Stephen, who had been banned from taking part in the armed struggle by imperial decree, was resigning from his office, and that Count Franz Lamberg, the commander of the imperial army in Pozsony, had been appointed a full royal commissioner. On the basis of the message from the palatine, Batthyány travelled to the Martonvásár camp to meet Lamberg and countersign his appointment. Misled by Latour, the Austrian minister of war, Lamberg went to Pest, where, the day after the parliamentary decision of 27 September declaring his mandate illegal, the outraged people lynched him. Lamberg was deliberately sacrificed by the camarilla to provoke Pest into violent revolutionary outbursts, so that his murder could be used as a justification for the unconstitutional appointment of Jelačič on 3 October.[43]

Feeling that his remaining hopes had been dashed, Batthyány rushed to Jelačič's camp to make a last attempt to dissuade him from attacking Buda. After failing in this attempt, he went to Vienna and on 2 October he handed in his final resignation, at the same time resigning his mandate as a member of parliament.

Volunteer National Guard and the re-elected representative

After his resignation, Batthyány had planned to travel to Switzerland with his wife, but the news of the revolution in Vienna on 6 October changed their minds. He joined the popular uprising in Western Hungary and was injured when he fell from his horse. At the instigation of the radicals in Pest who accused him of treason, he came under political fire from two directions. In his 'apology' published in *Kossuth' Hirlapja*

(Kossuth's Gazette) on 18 October, as a sign of solidarity with the leading politicians, he rejected the unfounded slander:

> If someone outright condemns my policy so far, I will not be offended, but [. . .] no one should suspect me of having used my influence for clandestine activities that threaten the independence of my country [. . .]. I have never done anything without the consent of my fellow ministers, and I would have none of anything that would have mutilated the laws of 1848.[44]

While spending weeks recovering and rethinking the future, on 6 December, Sárvár re-elected him as its representative. According to the recollections of his widow, the former prime minister had by this time decided to confront Lajos Kossuth, his former comrade-in-arms in the struggle for constitutional civic and national transformation. His subsequent actions confirm that he had become convinced that opposing the Habsburg imperial armies should not be attempted. He disagreed with the decision of the Parliament on 7 December, which called Francis Joseph – who had replaced Ferdinand V, deposed in a palace revolution led by Archduchess Sophia, the mother of the new emperor, in violation of the Hungarian constitution – a usurper.

Batthyány was very actively involved in the parliamentary debate of 31 December on the military crisis. He put forward a double proposal against Kossuth, who had initiated the move to Debrecen of the Hungarian Parliament and the National Defence Commission. He considered it necessary, on the one hand, that the Parliament should send a peace commission to the commander-in-chief of the imperial armies, Prince Alfred Windisch-Graetz, which would attempt to promote a negotiated settlement 'on the basis of and with the assurance of the honor, legal freedom and well-being of the nation'. On the other hand, he proposed that the Parliament should not follow the National Defence Commission to Debrecen, but stay in Pest and await the report of the peace delegation, and in the light of the results of the negotiations decide whether to join the legislature or adjourn its sessions. It was clear to the contemporaries that this proposal would have deprived the National Defence Commission – which was now in charge of Hungary's military – of its constitutional basis, and the initiative was rejected. Batthyány was now in the position of having organized the Hungarian army but was not prepared to lead it. Disregarding his personal safety, he accepted a nomination to lead a new peace delegation and set off on his fateful journey. In response to the parliamentarians' proposal, General Windisch-Graetz, who had issued an ultimatum demanding '*unbedingte Unterwerfung*' (unconditional subordination), refused to receive him. In the evening of 8 January he returned to Pest, where he was arrested.

The *Justizmord* was carried out on 6 October 1849, on the anniversary of the Vienna Revolution. Before his execution, Batthyány wrote in his farewell letter to his wife:

> Bless the children and kiss them in my name; let them not be ashamed of their father, for the shame of my death will sooner or later fall back on those who have unjustly and ungratefully murdered me [. . .]. I will die because the law, the King's oath, was my guide, and I would not be taken advantage of, neither from the right

nor from the left. *Viam meam persecutus sum* (I have gone my own way), that's why they're killing me now.[45]

The members of the Habsburg family, motivated by personal resentment, and the representatives of political power, humiliated in their weakness and forced to call on the Tsar to crush the Hungarian War of Independence, were irritated by Batthyány's moral strength, his role in laying the foundations for Hungary's transformation and responsibility for organizing the Hungarian war of self-defence. Absolutism, trampling underfoot the norms of European civilization, could not allow a politician legally appointed as prime minister to disrupt the work of restoration by serving as a living rebuke and the legitimate guardian of the law. The revenge of the victor may have deprived Batthyány of his life, but he became a symbol: a statesman defending the independence and freedom of the Hungarian people against the foreign oppressive power, uncompromisingly enforcing the norms of the constitution against external and internal enemies and sacrificing his life in defence of the rule of law. He insisted to the end on the observance of the April Laws sanctioned by the Habsburg ruler, but the counter-revolution demanded their destruction. In the face of the unlawful attack, he was forced to use radical means to protect the nation. The only alternative to this was completely giving up national self-determination. His life's work, linked to the legacy of the legislators who strove to defend ancient values and forge new ones, forms an outstanding chapter in Hungarian history. His figure embodied the democratic alternative of Hungarian Liberalism. His achievements and heroic stand made him one of the most important Hungarian statesmen.

Notes

1 Molnár András, *Batthyány Lajos a reformkorban* [Lajos Batthyány in the Reform Era] (Zalaegerszeg: Zala Megyei Levéltár, 1996), 29–32.
2 Erdődy Gábor, ed., *Batthyány Lajos,* Magyar Szabadelvűek (Budapest: Új Mandátum Könyvkiadó, 1998), 12–13.
3 Memorandum on the draft programme of the aristocratic opposition on 14 December 1839. Published in Horváth Mihály, *Huszonöt év Magyarország történelméből 1823-tól 1848-ig* [Twenty-five Years from the History of Hungary 1823–48] (Genf: Puky Miklós, 1864), 2:572–5.
4 Batthyány's speech to the Diet of Pozsony, on 26 October 1839. Published in Molnár András, *Viam meam persequor: Batthyány Lajos gróf útja a miniszterelnökségig* [I have gone my own way: Count Lajos Batthyány's Road to the Position of Prime Minister] (Budapest: Osiris Kiadó, 2007), 362–3.
5 Molnár András, *Batthyány Lajos reformkori beszédei, levelei, írásai* [Speeches, Letters and Writings of Lajos Batthyány from the Reform Era] (Zalaegerszeg: Zala Megyei Levéltár, 1998), 28–31.
6 Batthyány's speech to the Diet of Pozsony, on 22 April 1840. Published in Erdődy, ed., *Batthyány Lajos,* 67–9.
7 Molnár, *Viam meam persequor,* 132–41.
8 Cited in Molnár, *Viam meam persequor,* 147.

9 Batthyány's speech to the Diet of Pozsony, on 18 August 1843. Published in Erdődy, ed., *Batthyány Lajos*, 74.
10 Batthyány's speech to the Diet of Pozsony, on 28 September 1843. Published in Erdődy, ed., *Batthyány Lajos*, 75–6.
11 Molnár, *Batthyány Lajos reformkori beszédei, levelei, írásai*, 160–1.
12 Batthyány's speech to the Diet of Pozsony, on 10 November 1844. Published in Molnár, *Batthyány Lajos reformkori beszédei, levelei, írásai*, 161–3.
13 Cited in Molnár, *Batthyány Lajos a reformkorban*, 101.
14 Erdődy Gábor and Hermann Róbert, *Batthyány/Szemere* (Budapest: Pannonica Kiadó, 2002), 51–3.
15 Erdődy and Hermann, *Batthyány/Szemere*, 55–9.
16 Cited in Gergely András, 'Batthyány Lajos a reformellenzék élén' [Lajos Batthyány at the Head of the Reform Opposition], *Századok* 116, no. 6 (1982): 1171.
17 Gergely, 'Batthyány Lajos a reformellenzék élén', 1171.
18 Batthyány's speech to the Diet of Pozsony, on 7 December 1847. Published in Molnár, *Batthyány Lajos reformkori beszédei, levelei, írásai*, 184–8.
19 Széchenyi István, *Napló* [Diary], ed. Oltványi Ambrus (Budapest: Gondolat, 1978), 1192.
20 *Kossuth Lajos Összes Munkái* [Collected Works of Lajos Kossuth], vol. 11, ed. Barta István (Budapest: Akadémiai Kiadó, 1951), 29.
21 Széchenyi, *Napló*, 1192.
22 Batthyány's speech to the Diet of Pozsony on the issue of serf emancipation, on 4 February 1848. Published in Erdődy, *Batthyány Lajos*, 102.
23 Batthyány's speech to the Diet of Pozsony on the issue of language use in Croatia, on 4 February 1848. Published in Erdődy, *Batthyány Lajos*, 103–6.
24 Cited in Molnár, *Batthyány Lajos a reformkorban*, 153.
25 Molnár, *Batthyány Lajos a reformkorban*, 155.
26 Molnár, *Viam meam persequor*, 283–8.
27 Szabad György, *Kossuth politikai pályája: Ismert és ismeretlen megnyilatkozásai tükrében* [The Political Career of Lajos Kossuth: In the Light of His Known and Unknown Utterances] (Budapest: Kossuth Könyvkiadó–Magyar Helikon, 1977), 115–16.
28 Urbán Aladár, *Gróf Batthyány Lajos miniszterelnöksége, fogsága és halála* [Count Lajos Batthyány as Prime Minister, His Captivity and Death] (Budapest: Argumentum Kiadó, 2007), 79–86.
29 Szabad, *Kossuth politikai pályája*, 130–1.
30 Gergely András, *1848-ban hogy is volt? Tanulmányok Magyarország és Közép-Európa 1848–49-es történetéből* [How was it in 1848? Studies from the History of Hungary and Central Europe in 1848–49] (Budapest: Osiris Kiadó, 2001), 319–59.
31 Cited in Erdődy Gábor, *'Én csak fáklyatartó voltam': Kossuth Lajos, a magyar polgári forradalom és szabadságharc irányítója 1848–49* ['I Was Just a Torch Bearer': Lajos Kossuth, the Leader of the Hungarian Civil Revolution and War of Independence] (Budapest: ELTE Eötvös Kiadó, 2006.), 91–2.
32 Urbán Aladár, *Batthyány Lajos miniszterelnöksége* [Lajos Batthyány as Prime Minister], Nemzet és emlékezet (Budapest: Magvető Könyvkiadó, 1986), 733–52.
33 Szabad, *Kossuth politikai pályája*, 132–3.
34 Szabad, *Kossuth politikai pályája*, 162–3.
35 Urbán, *Gróf Batthyány Lajos miniszterelnöksége, fogsága és halála*, 181.
36 Cited in Erdődy, *Batthyány Lajos*, 48.

37 *Kossuth Lajos Összes Munkái*, vol. 12, ed. Sinkovics István (Budapest: Akadémiai Kiadó, 1957), 382-4.
38 *Kossuth Lajos Összes Munkái*, 12:708-9.
39 Urbán Aladár, *Gróf Batthyány Lajos miniszterelnöki, hadügyi és nemzetőri iratai* [Prime Ministerial, Military and Militial Documents of Count Lajos Batthyány] (Budapest: Argumentum Kiadó, 1999), 1:1090.
40 Hajnal István, *A Batthyány-kormány külpolitikája* [The Foreign Policy of the Batthyány Government], Értekezések a történeti tudományok köréből (Budapest: Akadémiai Kiadó, 1957), 100-21.
41 Published in Erdődy, *Batthyány Lajos*, 111-12.
42 Published in Erdődy, *Batthyány Lajos*, 114-16.
43 Urbán, *Gróf Batthyány Lajos miniszterelnöksége, fogsága és halála*, 371-8.
44 Published in Urbán, *Gróf Batthyány Lajos miniszterelnöki, hadügyi és nemzetőri iratai*, 1658-61.
45 Published in Urbán Aladár, *Batthyány Lajos főbenjáró pöre* [The Capital Case of Lajos Batthyány] (Budapest: Európa Könyvkiadó-Batthyány Társaság, 1991), 382-3.

11

Lajos Kossuth (1802–94)

György Miru

The protagonist of this chapter, Lajos Kossuth, belonged to a generation whose activities were a combination of practical politics and political journalism that laid the theoretical groundwork for subsequent generations. Kossuth liked to call politics the science of 'exigencies' and to compare its cultivation to mathematical rationality. He believed that the success of a politician depended on a realistic assessment of the circumstances he found himself in and careful consideration of the factors in play, and rejected empty theories and doctrinarism. Despite his pragmatic (political realist) pronouncements, he was, however, aware that the basic concepts and guidelines of politics had to be spelled out, and that principles had to play a guiding role. He was familiar with the political literature of his time and was also interested in political theory. His sensitivity to theories and ideas also helped him to shape policy in innovative ways, not only in order to be able to evaluate the elements at work but also to be able to inspire new forces and social groups that reshaped Hungarian politics.

Early years

Kossuth came from an old noble Hungarian family that could be traced back to the thirteenth century in Upper Hungary. However, this branch of the family lost its estates, and in the 1780s his father, László Kossuth, moved to his relatives in Zemplén County, where he became a county clerk and later a manorial prosecutor for the Andrássy noble family. His mother, Karolina Weber, came from a German Lutheran family and was the daughter of a postmaster in Olaszliszka, a veteran soldier. The couple's first child, Lajos, was presumably born on 19 September 1802, in Monok, although the exact date of birth is uncertain. He was followed by four daughters.[1]

Despite his noble status, Kossuth came, therefore, from a middle-class background. His parents quickly recognized his talent and took great pains with his education. The son followed his father's example and aspired to become a lawyer. Between September 1816 and 1819, he spent three years at the Lutheran Lycée in Eperjes (today Prešov, Slovakia), where, after completing a course in philosophy, he also studied law. He completed the second year of his legal studies in 1819–20 at the Calvinist College in Sárospatak.

During his education in Eperjes, Kossuth was introduced to the rationalism and perfectionism of the Enlightenment, the contractual, egalitarian criteria of the modern political community and Kantian legal philosophy, primarily during the classes taught by Zsigmond Carlowszky and Mihály Greguss. Greguss, who also took a special interest in the education of this gifted student, was constantly polemicizing against Kant's views, such as his concept of the separation of morality and law. However, while seeking arguments against the Kantian theorems, he basically followed the German philosopher's intentions and espoused the harmony of morality, law and politics, which in turn had a great influence on his student. He was even more critical of Fichte, and especially of Hegel's philosophical system.

It was probably under the inspiration of Greguss that the seventeen-year-old Kossuth set to work translating Volney's *Ruins* (1791), which was banned in his country at the time. From this treatise on the philosophy of history and the history of religion, he learned about the Enlightenment's cult of nature and the mutual conditions of happiness of the individual and the community, and a few years later he even wrote a treatise on the author. Natural law had a strong influence on Kossuth's view of the law and his interpretation of freedom, as he examined political issues in legal categories and always emphasized the moral foundations and limits of politics. He concluded his studies in Eperjes, where his main subjects were natural law, history, rhetoric and philosophy, with a lecture on the immortality of the soul, which, in addition to the influence of Kant and Volney, also revealed the impact Rousseau had made on him.[2] Even Kossuth's early writings testify to his knowledge of the latter author, and later, during the Diet of 1832-6, he translated the works of Rousseau to aid his study of the French language.[3]

Kossuth completed his legal studies in Sárospatak, where he was particularly influenced by Sándor Kövy, a renowned teacher of both private law and Hungarian constitutional law. Kövy instilled the Hungarian patriotism and anti-Habsburg spirit of the school into the young Kossuth. He introduced his students to the functioning of the county's public life, the value of local government and the need to protect the ancient constitution. After finishing school, Kossuth spent a year as an apprentice at the district court in Eperjes (1820-1), and continued his apprenticeship at the royal court in Pest, the high court of the time. This was the period of conflict between the counties and the central government, and the young apprentice lawyer himself attended the Pest County assemblies and sent reports to the leader of the Zemplén County opposition, Baron Pál Vécsey, whose legal affairs were handled by his father. He successfully passed the bar exam and received his diploma on 26 September 1823. He would have preferred to stay in Pest and practise as a lawyer at the royal court, but this plan was thwarted.

He returned home to Zemplén and began to work alongside his father, gradually taking over his father's affairs and representing his clients. He became the lawyer of the Lutheran congregation of Sátoraljaújhely, and then successfully applied for the position of the city prosecutor. In 1827, his county elected him as one of the judges of its county court (*táblabíró*), and as a result he received more and more commissions, quickly distinguishing himself as a good legal draftsman, as well as a talented organizer. The young Kossuth also had literary and scientific ambitions. He attempted to translate and adapt plays, and planned to write a chronicle of world history but only got as far as Ancient Rome. In another early manuscript, he dealt with Greek and Roman history and compiled a collection of aphorisms on issues of power, politics and public morality. He also began a work on the history of the French Revolution, in which he expressed his abhorrence of the horrors of the revolution but welcomed the defeat of absolutism.

Kossuth's interest in public affairs was also demonstrated by his unfinished essay entitled *Értekezés az éhség-mentő intézetekről* (A Treatise on Hunger Relief Institutions, 1828), in which he dealt with a recurring problem of his time, famine. Although at the time he was far from the reformer that he would later become, he was already prepared to criticize the rigidity of the old customs and laws and the obsolescence of the relationship between serf and landlord. He was convinced, for example, that the landlord was not the owner of the serf's plot of land, but only of the annuity that was provided based on that plot. His knowledge of the conditions of the serfs was deepened by the fact that he was the clerk of the committee that reviewed the data from the 1828-9 census of Zemplén County and was directly involved in the verification of the data in 124 settlements as well as drafting the county census. During the cholera epidemic in 1831, he acted as cholera commissioner instead of the county officer staff who had fled, and he organized the defence of Sátoraljaújhely against the threat of peasant rebellion.

As a young lawyer he regularly visited the Sátoraljaújhely Casino, a political club whose statutes he drafted. The intelligentsia was open to new ideas and sensitive to the tensions in Hungarian society. They read both foreign and Hungarian newspapers and the latest works of political literature. Kossuth was elected to the committee that drafted the instructions given to the deputies of the county sent to the Diet of 1830. When the returning deputies gave their reports, the local opposition, including Kossuth, initiated the impeachment of one of the deputies, Baron Miklós Vay, who, in violation of the instructions by the county assembly which sent him to the Diet, voted in favour of increasing the number of recruits, as requested by the king. In connection with the Polish War of Independence of 1830-1, he spoke on behalf of the Poles and translated the Sejm Manifesto and the speech of the Polish minister of foreign affairs.

An important step in Kossuth's public career was his election to the committee tasked with reviewing the late eighteenth-century reform proposals (*operata*). The attention to these earlier proposals led to the formation of new pressure groups and debating societies in many counties, as it renewed hopes of major reform in many important areas. Kossuth, who took part in the work of the subcommittee on public law, stressed the importance of free speech and debate in advancing the cause of reform. He spoke in favour of freedom of the press in the county assembly debates, and drafted a dissenting opinion for the opposition, proposing the exclusion of the lord-lieutenant (*supremus comes*; *főispán*; the leading official in county administration) from the process by which instructions to deputies to the Diet were debated, in order to separate the interests of the legislature and the public administration. In Kossuth's speeches, he took a pro-independence approach[4] based on his admiration for the ancient constitution, but he also advocated the introduction of 'liberal institutions', reflecting his conviction that change and modernization would not be made through social upheaval, but through continuous progress. Although he made some of the usual arguments of the opposition focusing on the protection of the nobles' rights, he also referred to foreign political practices, British parliamentary relations and the role of public opinion, evincing his familiarity with modern political literature.

Entry into national politics

Kossuth supported the opposition to the centralizing measures of the Vienna Court in the early 1830s, but he provoked the disapproval of the county leaders who accused him of financial misconduct. Although he avoided a lawsuit, he lost a significant number of his clients and his position in Zemplén became untenable. His supporters from the peerage decided to entrust him with their representation in the forthcoming Diet, and some reformers even subscribed to his bulletins. Out of this initiative grew the *Országgyűlési Tudósítások* (Reports from the Diet), which he published from 16 December 1832, covering the entire four years of the Diet. Since the opposition had failed to secure the publication of the minutes of the district session (*sessio circularis*; *kerületi ülés*; a forum for substantive discussions at the Diet) or to publish a parliamentary newspaper, this venture was an important source of national publicity for the debates taking place at the Diet. The journal could only be circulated handcopied, because of the strong censorship. Its subscriber base gradually grew to over a hundred, and by the end of the Diet in May 1836, 344 issues and 2 supplements had been published. It was largely edited and written by Kossuth, who diligently attended the meetings and, in a reformist spirit, extracted, summarized and even commented on the speeches and debates. He gained national recognition for his *Reports*, and played a major role in the propagation of reformist ideas. Although he was initially met with distrust in Pozsony (today Bratislava, Slovakia), he gradually won the acceptance of the leaders of the opposition and became a regular participant in private meetings, becoming increasingly close to Baron Miklós Wesselényi, Ferenc Kölcsey and later Ferenc Deák, the leaders of the opposition.

As a result, Kossuth became a formal member of the opposition reform movement organized by Miklós Wesselényi, which sought to resolve the pressing social issues of the time in a manner which increasingly followed the liberal paradigm, by expanding freedoms, extending rights and sharing burdens. He also had ambitious plans to write political works summarizing the debates of the Diet. At the beginning of the Diet, he considered freedom of the press to be the most important issue, and freedom of religion as the foundation of all freedoms, the codification of which had to precede further political reforms. A manuscript he wrote on the question of religion has been lost to us, however. What has survived are parts of a work titled *A magyar főrendek 1833-ban* (The peerage of Hungary in 1833), which recounts the meetings of the Upper House, of which no official minutes were kept. We can infer from these that Kossuth tried to interpret contemporary events through the lens of historical philosophy and political theory. In the light of natural rights and utilitarian anthropology, he stressed the necessity of development, the importance of individual freedom and of ensuring the security of persons and property, and argued for the extension of rights to eliminate privileges and social barriers. By demanding uniform civil liberties that excluded privileges, he clearly broke with the hierarchical view of feudal society.

On the basis of natural law and the Kantian philosophy of law, Kossuth stressed the need for social justice and solidarity. But he was also strongly influenced by the republican concept of liberty and citizenship, which meant that in his political thinking both individual and communal aspects prevailed. He rejected glorifying the past and did not lament the supposed deterioration of the old morals and the passing of the old glory of the nation: its military virtues. He was more interested in expanding the number of people who were permitted to participate in politics, hitherto essentially limited to the nobility, and reconciling private and class interests with the larger public interest. The debates at the Diet also made him understand the importance of the question of serf emancipation and the need to forge a consensus in favour of reform that could win over both the nobility and the serfs.

Kossuth sought the establishment of institutions which would be more in line with the interests of the wider population and social justice through the legislature. In a work he wrote in 1833, he set the legislature a double task: on the one hand, to listen to and identify the real needs of the community and the nation, and on the other hand, to guide and educate public opinion. He attributed an educative, morality-developing role to the laws, which can only be effective if the community itself creates them. As an advocate of a unified legal system, he railed against arguments invoking ancient customs that rejected any change. In addition to the ideas of the Enlightenment and the tradition of natural law, he also used the 'politeness' discourse, which advocated education and erudition and the refinement of social life, that is, the creation of modern social relations, and, influenced by his strong republican attitude, he built his own political imagery based on the primacy of community morals, duty and patriotism.[5]

After the Diet concluded, Kossuth was keen to continue his *Reports*, but now from Pest, particularly as they had also brought him financial benefits. The resulting *Törvényhatósági Tudósítások* (Municipal Reports) which were similarly hand-copied, reported via correspondents on the debates in the county assemblies, in order to continue publicizing the arguments of the reformers and keep himself in the public eye. These efforts were enhanced by the reports he made about his fight to save the paper from closure by the government and about the lawsuit that had been brought against the Dietal Youth (young legal apprentices, who supported the reformist opposition at the Diet), which Kossuth helped defend. The central government, which opposed reform and adopted absolutist methods, had taken steps to close down the paper. Kossuth managed to produce and distribute copies of the reports for nearly a year, until he was arrested on 5 May 1837, despite protests from the counties. His subsequent trial for high treason was protracted, and it was not until 23 February 1839 that he was sentenced to a further three years in prison, which was increased to four years by the seven-member Supreme Court of Justice (*tabula septemviralis; hétszemélyes tábla*). The long imprisonment did not break him: he used the time for self-education, reading literature and travelogues and learning languages. He was also able to obtain and read foreign and Hungarian papers, important works on economics and the volumes of the *Staatslexikon* edited by Rotteck and Welcker.[6]

At the Diet of 1839-40, the deputies succeeded in forcing the government to release all political prisoners, so on 10 May 1840 Kossuth was also allowed to leave prison. He did not accept his friend Miklós Wesselényi's offer of a job as estate manager, as he preferred to stay in the centre of politics, in Pest. Based on some of the reform laws passed at the previous Diet, the liberal opposition expected that the government would not block further reforms. Kossuth decided to start a political newspaper to better prepare the ground for the issues to be discussed in the next Diet but was refused permission. It thus proved fortuitous when a private company, under close government control of course, asked Kossuth to edit a newspaper it was in the process of founding. The newspaper *Pesti Hirlap* (Pest Gazette), launched on 2 January 1841, completely transformed Hungarian political journalism, introducing the genre of the editorial and achieving unprecedented levels of effectiveness and political persuasion. Thanks to Kossuth's vision, and his tireless work-rate, the *Pesti Hirlap* rapidly became very popular and its sales soon exceeded five thousand copies.[7]

Through its network of correspondents, the *Pesti Hirlap* reported on the public life of the counties and free royal cities, promoting the newly adopted reform laws, especially the emancipation of serfs, as well as discussing further reform issues in preparation for the next Diet. Kossuth's emphasis was on the process of social modernization, advocating a civil society based on the principles of freedom and equality, and which was integrated as a national society by the fusion of its various components. Instead of fostering division, Kossuth sought the possibility of fusion, and he reformulated the programme of assimilation based on the extension of rights, which had been developed by the Hungarian liberals.[8]

Kossuth sought to give impetus to the reforms by demanding that they be immediately implemented with the support of the state. He believed that, in the interest of the common good, especially to promote the emancipation of the serfs, the state could intervene in private relations, that is, oblige the parties to do so, and also help to raise the sums necessary for the redemption of the serfs that would compensate landowners and persuade them to support the reform. He was aware of the importance of financial, commercial and industrial interests, and that a strong middle class was essential for the healthy organization of a nation-state. Friedrich List's views also led him to reassess his former economic policies. He called for the creation and growth of an independent national economy – continuing to accept the dominant role of the agricultural sector – as well as for customs protection, industrial development and the expansion of transport infrastructure, financial institutions and trade. He considered the protective duty system to be only a temporary solution which, once it had nurtured domestic industry, could give way to free trade. From a national economic point of view, he saw great potential in the development of the port of Fiume (today Rijeka, Croatia) and the construction of a transport route to the port of Fiume, partly by rail.[9]

Kossuth reinterpreted the concept of the people, not as taxpaying serfs, but as the whole of society, including all 'classes' of the nation, hence also including the privileged. By granting the entire population constitutional protections, he meant not only to guarantee the civil rights of individuals but also to extend their political rights. His republican approach, which placed the public interest above individual interests and the duties of the individual above the rights of the individual, is most evident in his view of the role of local government. Kossuth felt that it was the role of local governments to ensure every citizen's civic activity and protect their freedom, not merely to serve the interests of the nobility.

Kossuth also valued the autonomy of the counties, considering it a peculiarly Hungarian institution and the most important guarantee of constitutional freedom, which had preserved the existence of the nation, protected it against despotism and unrest and promoted the development of freedom. Kossuth wished to reform the local government of the free royal cities on the model of the counties. He wrote extensively about who should be given the vote in the cities and how to democratize the local government there. He did not expect the growing settlements and towns to become independent municipalities and thus separate from the counties, but he wanted to give them political rights within the framework of the counties.

Another objective of Lajos Kossuth was to remedy the irregularities and electoral abuses that afflicted governance in the counties, which were regularly reported in the *Pesti Hirlap*, by introducing the representation of the people, and thereby modernizing the institution. In addition to the introduction of jury trials – the *Pesti Hirlap* supported the liberal proposals of the Criminal Law Reform Committee – he was particularly enthusiastic about granting the vote to urban citizens and a larger share of the inhabitants of each county. Convinced that local government had to be harmonized with the Parliament, he supported retaining their right to have a say in national matters. In the longer term he would have transformed all institutions, even the legislature, into a form which was representative of the entire population, because he saw in the representative system the possibility of incorporating the people into the constitution. In editorials published in the *Pesti Hirlap* in the summer of 1843, and in a speech he made at the Pest County Assembly on 27 August 1844, he outlined the concept of an expanded constitutional and institutional system that, he believed, would also address the lack of responsibility displayed by the imperial government and its officials.

Kossuth also called for the establishment of religious freedom and denominational equality, so that there would be no further legal discrimination on religious grounds. He saw that social modernization was only effective if it was national in character and that a strong nation could not do without the achievements of civilization. He accepted the primary role and self-awareness of the linguistic-ethnic community, and favoured the capacity for self-development over rival visions of universal development. In the 1840s, it was precisely because of such a focus on the nation that he attached greater importance to tradition, history and the constitution. He considered the constitution to be the result of organic development, as was the Hungarian 'nationality', that is, the other factors that determine the national character. In the interests of achieving national goals, he combined the historical and the natural law arguments when, for example, he mobilized both arguments to support Hungarian becoming the official language of the kingdom.

Precisely because of the extension of political rights, it was important how the ethnic minorities related to the Hungarian political community. Therefore, the *Pesti Hirlap* promoted the use of the Hungarian language and urged the assimilation of the ethnic minorities. It not only fought for official status to be granted to the Hungarian language, but also advocated making public life more Hungarian. In the midst of the fierce language debates, the *Pesti Hirlap* was subjected to much criticism, which led Kossuth to strengthen the historical aspect in his interpretation of the nation and to emphasize the community-building role of political-legal elements rather than linguistic-cultural factors. He regarded as a nation only those communities that had a historical tradition, as he saw it, in particular a tradition of the separation of politics and public law, or autonomy. He refused to identify the nation with the language, often referring to the linguistic-ethnic community only as a 'race'. By classifying national communities differently, he also assessed their claims to collective rights differently, denying, for example, that the Serbs, Romanians, Slovaks and Ruthenes deserved any distinct community rights. Essentially, he retained this interpretation of the nation in 1848-9, in the midst of serious conflicts with the minorities, and also during his exile, when he systematically sought a way of resolving these ethnic conflicts.[10]

Kossuth was not doctrinaire, he drew his principles from various traditions and as a practical and professional politician he adapted his ideological tools to the needs of the time and the interests of society. He called for a faster pace of change and the avoidance of half-measures, which led to conflicts with his fellow reformers and others. Count Aurél Dessewffy, the most prominent representative of the neo-conservative group, which had been organized to counterbalance the liberals and to maintain the hierarchical order of society, and who advocated cautious reforms, took up the fight against Kossuth's journalistic efforts, and the newspaper he founded, *Világ* (Light, 1841-4), constantly polemicized against Kossuth.[11] He was also attacked by Count István Széchenyi, who accused him of not following a specific programme, of revolutionary incitement and especially of inciting the resistance of the imperial government and the ethnic minorities. Széchenyi was distrustful of the wider population, who lacked education and political sense, whereas Kossuth had a broader understanding of public opinion and believed that most people could contribute to public life. Kossuth's active dissemination of public opinion also served as a 'school in public life', which he tried to turn into a political factor, and which seriously disrupted Széchenyi's reform strategy. Kossuth also responded to the criticisms in Széchenyi's book with his own work, entitled *Felelet gróf Széchenyi Istvánnak Kossuth Lajostól* (Reply to Count István Széchenyi from Lajos Kossuth, 1841). He saw their dispute as a clash between aristocratism and democratism, and he himself described his ambitions, which had triggered the debate, as democratic. Even then, and even more so in hindsight, he began to understand democracy not only as representing the interests of the people but also as involving the people in politics. In response to the failure of the 1843-4 Diet to enact reforms, he openly declared the need to introduce new elements into politics. His approach to liberalism, precisely because of his acceptance of political equality, was open to democracy even before 1848.[12]

Kossuth's concept of a county-oriented local government system also came under fire from the centralists from the mid-1840s onwards. The group led by Baron József Eötvös saw the counties as a nest of backwardness, inefficiency and political corruption resulting from the concentration of power of the nobility who used them as a barrier to social modernization. Nor did they consider the county system as representing real local government. They wanted to make a bolder break with historical traditions and, based on the results of enlightened government and centralization, they called for a centralized political system but with the strengthening of local, city and municipal governments. It is noteworthy that Tocqueville's arguments against centralization which he advanced in his work *Democracy in America* (1841-3) – in the domestic reception of which the *Pesti Hirlap* also played a role – were used by Kossuth to argue in favour of the counties, although the centralists referred to the same author precisely in order to strengthen their own call for a radical reform of local government.[13]

Kossuth was always distrustful of the concentration of power centrally, especially when it did not operate according to constitutional principles. His opposition to tyranny and despotism made him appreciate the constitutional tradition, which limited monarchical power and subordinated rule to legal norms, while at the same time guaranteeing the country's autonomy. In addition to the demand for economic independence, the liberal opposition's aspirations for greater autonomy for Hungary became increasingly assertive, seeking to increase self-determination within the Habsburg Monarchy by asserting their constitutional rights.

The culmination of Kossuth's political career

Kossuth lost his job as editor of the *Pesti Hirlap* in the summer of 1844 and failed to find a new journal. While he continued to attend the Pest County assembly meetings, his activities increasingly focused on organizing associations and promoting social initiatives, in particular those of the *Védegylet* (League of Protection, whose members pledged to only buy domestic industrial products when available), of which he became director. Seeing the failures of the 1843-4 Diet, he stressed the importance of the 'social way', by which he meant that if a general law failed, its underlying aims should be achieved through grassroots organizations and movements. Alongside the press, these associations also mobilized groups which had previously been excluded from politics. Kossuth was never afraid to use associations to put pressure on the existing institutions. He also used his organizational skills to transform the reform movement into a political party. Building on the national network of associations and working closely with Count Lajos Batthyány, he succeeded in partially unifying the opposition behind a clear programme of reforms (*Ellenzéki Nyilatkozat*, Opposition Statement, 1847). In the pages of the weekly newspaper of the *Iparegyesület* (Industry Association), the *Hetilap* (The Weekly), where he published articles on economic topics, he demanded effective steps in the field of the emancipation of the serfs and equal distribution of the burden of taxation (from which the nobility had hitherto been largely exempted), and condemned the constant delays in enacting reforms. Even though his demands were growing more radical he had not become a revolutionary, as he wanted to operate within the existing laws. He knew that revolutions were dangerous because of their unpredictability, and therefore he urged his fellow deputies to the Diet to take the path of change voluntarily, and not under the influence of coercion, unpredictable movements and rebellions.

With the support of the liberals of Pest County, including some aristocrats, Kossuth was elected deputy of the 'leading county' Pest. This was a big step forward in his political career, because in the circumstances of the time, the members of the Diet were invariably either wealthy landed nobility or aristocrats. He was actively involved in the preparation of detailed, progressive instructions to the deputies of the county, which were also intended to guide the other local assemblies. His organizational work, his visibility and his popularity quickly made him a leader in the Diet, where he was extremely active in the debates, contributing to every topic of discussion and making powerful speeches. He made good use of the effects of the European revolutions and achieved a political breakthrough with his speech of 3 March 1848.[14]

In collaboration with Batthyány, Kossuth became the main protagonist of the lawful revolution that transformed Hungary. He was actively involved in the drafting and adoption of the April Laws, in particular in elaborating the institution of responsible government. The new laws accomplished a large part of his programme and even exceeded his earlier expectations. However, in certain regards he was forced to make concessions. He did not, however, consider the transformation to be either complete or an improvisation, and certainly not the result of either a foreign or domestic revolution, but the outcome of a long-maturing reform process, the roots of which went back to the end of the eighteenth century. He also argued that the reform of the constitution, in particular the establishment of a majority government accountable to Parliament, had not created new rights, but only enforced existing ones. In reality, the new laws reduced the powers of the monarchy and strengthened the position of the Parliament and the constitutional powers. At the same time, the restriction of the rights of the monarchy also loosened imperial ties, and increasingly serious political and jurisdictional disputes arose over the interpretation of common issues arising from the constitutional changes, both with the monarch and the new Austrian government.[15]

Kossuth became a member of Lajos Batthyány's government, and although he presumably wanted the position of minister of the interior, he was given the finance portfolio, which was an almost hopeless task due to the empty treasury. Even so, he still succeeded in stabilizing the country's finances, eventually creating an independent currency and drawing up the country's first budget. He agreed with his fellow ministers that disputes and problems in military, economic and foreign affairs should be resolved by extending the country's right to self-government to more policy areas. In the first popular-sovereignty-based National Assembly, the government had a stable majority and its members often reached a unanimous position. Batthyány expected his ministers to act independently, but he did not like the fact that Kossuth started his own newspaper, *Kossuth Hírlapja* (Kossuth's Newspaper), even if it was under the editorship of József Bajza, indicating that he wished to remain an independent political factor. The minister of finance was the government's keynote speaker in the Parliament and made several major speeches, mainly to organize the country's self-defence in the midst of civil war.

In the increasingly acute conflicts with the emperor, the Austrian government and the ethnic minorities of Hungary, Kossuth declared that the country was willing to defend its civil achievements and constitutional self-determination even at the cost of an armed struggle. Disputes between ministers also deepened, with the finance minister distancing himself from the cabinet, which by early August had reached a crisis point, leading him to repeatedly consider resigning. Nevertheless, the government was held together by the fear that, if he left, the monarch would not appoint a new ministry or would take away certain portfolios. Finally, in a letter dated 31 August, the king conveyed the Austrian government's intention to amend the April Laws and to make military, financial and trade matters common. Among the members of the ministry, Kossuth and Bertalan Szemere showed the strongest determination to continue the struggle to preserve what had already been achieved. Kossuth did not shy away from taking part in the power shift encouraged by the radicals, and took steps to create a more concentrated executive body. In the end, the Parliament found a way to remain legal and not submit to a radical transformation, while at the same time establishing an executive power appropriate to the civil war conditions, in the form of the *Országos Honvédelmi Bizottmány* (National Defence Commission), of which Kossuth was elected president.[16]

At the head of the National Defence Commission, Kossuth enjoyed expanded, but not unrestricted political freedom of movement, and he firmly rejected the offers of both radicals and others to impose a dictatorship. Once again, he demonstrated his ability to cope with a tremendous workload. Hardly ever resting, he carried out an extraordinary organizing effort to ensure the conditions for the struggle for freedom. He never sought to remove control or responsibility from his government. The preservation of the functioning of the Parliament was also important for the legitimacy of the government as he had always stressed, because he repeatedly claimed that the Hungarians had remained within the bounds of the rule of law, which had been violated by the monarch and Austria. He insisted on this lawfulness even in wartime and, despite his increased political influence, he did not become the ruler of the Parliament, let alone a dictator.[17] He used both the techniques of indirect and direct democracy. He was the first Hungarian politician who directly spoke to the people. His speeches and statements during the struggle for freedom were full of appeals to patriotism, national commitment, duty and sacrifice. He often used biblical language and imagery, invoking divine providence and justice, and argued that the Hungarians' struggle for freedom from tyranny was in the interests of the whole civilized world.

European public opinion was late to understand this, and the great powers were either powerless or fearful of upsetting the diplomatic balance of power, and therefore insisted on the integrity of the Habsburg Empire. There was little willingness to negotiate with the Hungarians among either the old or new elites of the empire, and the commander-in-chief of the imperial armies, Prince Alfred zu Windisch-Graetz, demanded unconditional surrender in early 1849. The Hungarians did not trust the new imperial constitution issued in Olmütz (today Olomouc, Czech Republic) in March, finding no guarantees in it, and they explicitly rejected its centralizing measures and the division of the Hungarian territory into provinces. Kossuth wished to issue a worthy response to the imperial constitution. He entirely ruled out the possibility of negotiations, and could not break Hungary's diplomatic isolation – although Count László Teleki, together with some of his agents, tried their best to cultivate foreign allies – but he believed that by declaring independence he could prevent a Russian invasion.[18]

As a result of the military successes enjoyed by the Hungarians in the spring, Kossuth managed to persuade the Parliament, which had fled to Debrecen, to declare independence.[19] He drafted the solemn Declaration of Independence almost entirely on his own, which was also voted on by the Parliament. By dethroning the Habsburgs, the Declaration of Independence severed the last link in the monarchical relationship and ended the monarchical union between the Habsburg Empire and Hungary. Furthermore, it declared the lands of the Hungarian crown to be one independent state with territorial integrity and an international legal status.

Despite pressure from radicals and his own convictions, Kossuth did not declare a republic. He sought to adopt a new constitution with a new National Assembly and, in the meantime, to build an American-style presidential government. However, Szemere, who took a leading role in the organizations, only agreed to participate in the government if the powers of the governor-president and the head of government were separated. In the end, Parliament limited the powers of the governor-president, so that Kossuth's political room for manoeuvre was narrower than it had been as president of the National Defence Commission. There was no time to draft the new constitution, and in the final days of the War of Independence, amidst the growing jurisdictional disputes, the unity of government was loosening, and tensions between the military command and the civilian government were increasing.

Years in exile

Kossuth fled the country after the defeat of the War of Independence. Although he avoided extradition, the Turkish government nevertheless interned him in Kütahya in Asia Minor, where he began to organize and activate his diplomatic contacts in the midst of poor conditions and isolation. After a short period of apathy, he reclaimed the title of governor-president, thus claiming the leadership of the émigrés. He also had plans to unite the Hungarian political and military leadership in a new freedom fight, because he felt that it had been the mistakes and lack of loyalty of the generals that caused the defeat. For this reason, he also pursued serious military studies.[20] His intentions did not win the approval of other émigrés, and when he was released in September 1851, under pressure from the American government, and appeared in London, his former colleagues Count Kázmér Batthyány and Bertalan Szemere criticized him sternly.

For Kossuth, the main goal was the independence of Hungary as a state for which he now focused on obtaining international support. His fame, his skills and the popularity of the Hungarian cause enabled him to earn a global reputation.[21] Seeking a new war of independence, and disappointed with the diplomats, he accepted Giuseppe Mazzini's invitation to join the association of European democrats. He was confident that the oppressed peoples of the continent would soon rise up again against their tyrants, and he authorized his agents to prepare another uprising at home. After the conspiracy was crushed and the failure of Mazzini's operation in Milan (1853), he moved away from these methods and returned to conventional diplomacy. Kossuth wished to convince the major powers that Austria could not hold Russia back, and that it was precisely the weakness and national divisions of the empire that were attracting the Russians to the region. He wanted the principle of non-intervention to be accepted, hence he sought support – including during his tour of the United States (from December 1851 to July 1852) – in persuading the great powers to prevent another Russian intervention in the event Hungary launched a war of independence against Austria.[22]

He also realized that in the ethnically divided region, an independent Hungary would not be strong enough to hold back the expansionist powers, and so he also developed plans for a confederation. In the place of the Habsburg Empire, he proposed a defensive and economic alliance of independent states of equal status, to be established by treaty. Such a confederation of states would, in his view, also address the great problem of the region, by bridging ethnic divisions. The fateful series of conflicts of the War of Independence had made the leaders of the emigration aware that without a final settlement of this question, there could be no successful war of independence. The Hungarian émigrés not only discussed the conditions for winning over the ethnic minorities and the scope of the concessions that should be made to them with the representatives of the other nationalist movements, but also debated these issues with each other.

In the summer of 1850, László Teleki advocated that at least the Serbian and Romanian national movements should be granted territorial autonomy at the provincial level. Instead of provincial autonomy, however, Kossuth recommended that the ethnic minorities should form their own national self-governments on the basis of associations, as social organizations. Or, as another option, he would have guaranteed the rights of ethnic minorities within the framework of local governments with broad powers, which he likened to the federal system of the United States. However, he rejected any territorial autonomy above the level of counties, such as at the provincial level. On the one hand, this was because the country was inhabited by a mixture of ethnic groups that could not be easily divided into separate provinces, and on the other hand, he feared that such ethnic provinces would disrupt the unity and sovereignty of the state and eventually break away from it.

Kossuth's understanding of the nation after 1849 was also influenced by the state-based approach. He saw the state as the surest guarantee of national existence, but he felt that not all national communities were suitable for independent nation-state status. He therefore denied even more emphatically the exclusivity of the linguistic-ethnic concept of nationhood, arguing that law, history, institutions and politics can also form a national community, and that the members of a nation can differ in origin, language, religion and custom. As all this applied to the ethnic minorities in Hungary, he tried to reduce the importance of the national principle, subordinating it to the principle of freedom. When it came to the Hungarians, however, he prioritized national goals, elevating the cause of the nation to the cause of European freedom, and thus seeking to strengthen the formation of national communities by extending their freedoms and autonomy.[23]

On a democratic basis, Kossuth made generous offers to the ethnic minorities, although he was still unable to win their trust. He also expressed his democratic principles clearly and firmly in other respects, and repeatedly declared himself to be a democrat. While the majority of his liberal contemporaries – based on the experience of the revolutions – were horrified by the idea of equality, Kossuth did not reject it, seeing it as a condition of freedom, not its opposite. He called democracy the spirit of the age, towards which human history and perfection were moving. By democracy, he meant first and foremost political equality, that is, equal and active participation in political rights, in the legislature, in public administration and in the judiciary by the entire adult male population. But he also wanted to reduce social inequalities by guaranteeing democratic rights, because he recognized that the freedom created by the gradual extension of rights did not fully eliminate hierarchical relations and social differences. In other words, he also developed the liberal programme to extend rights in the field of social policy. He declared himself a republican, yet he did not insist on a republic, declaring that this question could be resolved after independence had been achieved.

Kossuth repeatedly argued that popular sovereignty does not prevail when there is universal suffrage, if citizens can only exercise their political rights in national elections. He called for the active participation of a wide range of local authorities and identified democracy with self-government: government of the people by the people. In his works in exile, especially in the draft constitution of Kütahya, drawn up in 1851, he paid great attention to the institutions of self-government and to political-administrative bodies, in addition to religious, nationality and associative self-organizations. His opposition to tyranny, his republican orientation, his emphasis on the role of self-government and community morality suggest that Kossuth expressed his democratic aims by reinterpreting the republican approach.[24]

After returning from the United States, he settled in London, where he made a living writing articles and giving public readings. He became more active again during the Franco-Austrian War, when he was willing to set aside his earlier claim to one-man leadership and, on 6 May 1859, founded the *Magyar Nemzeti Igazgatóság* (Hungarian National Directorate) with László Teleki and General György Klapka, who was also popular abroad. Although their military and diplomatic actions did not bring the expected success, Kossuth became extremely cautious about starting a domestic uprising, but because of the unfinished project of Italian unity he kept an alliance with the Italians on the agenda, and therefore he moved his headquarters to Turin.[25]

The waning resistance at home and the increasing willingness to compromise were strongly criticized by Kossuth, and his new confederation plan (Danube Confederation, 1862) was likewise received with great reservations by the Hungarian public. To criticize the emerging concept of a new settlement with Vienna, he launched a newspaper called *Negyvenkilencz* (Forty-Nine), in which he wrote several major analyses of the Settlement then in preparation. In an open letter to his former friend, Ferenc Deák, and in letters to constituents who had nominated or elected him after the general amnesty, he criticized the Settlement. Because of the establishment of common institutions, he interpreted the new relationship being developed as a true union, and demanded, instead, the programme of 1848, a pure personal union. In fact, he held the negotiators to account for the conditions of state independence, while exaggerating the limited capacity for self-rule that Hungary would now possess. However, he did have the good sense to notice the ways in which the construct distorted constitutionality, setting in motion centralizing tendencies that reduced autonomy and infringed political rights.

After the Settlement of 1867, Kossuth ceased to be an active political campaigner, but he kept abreast of changes in his country and expressed his opinion on almost every issue. He did not return home and did not even fully identify with the political direction of his national supporters, stylizing himself as a symbol of independence, representing a future programme. He did not respond to personal attacks; his colleagues took part in these debates in his place. By staying out of the day-to-day political battles, he was able to maintain his authority and popularity, and over time a kind of cult developed around him. He was visited by an increasing number of people, and on the occasion of his eightieth birthday he was greeted by a large number of private individuals, associations, public bodies, counties and cities. He corresponded extensively with private individuals, scholars, his supporters and other politicians until his death on 20 March 1894. His burial became the subject of political controversy. Just as Kossuth did not want to be an Austro-Hungarian subject of Francis Joseph, and therefore lost his Hungarian citizenship as a result of the 1879 citizenship law, so too Francis Joseph preferred to ignore him, and refused to give him an official funeral. But of course, the nation for which he had spoken out so many times mourned him as a national hero.[26]

Notes

1 I present the details of Kossuth's career apart from my own research based on the following works: Barta István, *A fiatal Kossuth* [The Young Kossuth] (Budapest: Akadémiai, 1966); Kosáry Domokos, *Kossuth Lajos a reformkorban* [Lajos Kossuth in the Reform Era] (Budapest: Osiris, 2002); Szabad György, *Kossuth irányadása* [Kossuth's Teaching] (Budapest: Válasz, 2002); Hermann Róbert, *Kossuth Lajos élete és kora* [Kossuth's Life and Era] (Budapest: Pannonica, 2002); Dobszay Tamás, 'Kossuth Lajos', in Fónagy Zoltán and Dobszay Tamás, *Széchenyi és Kossuth* (Budapest: Kossuth, 2003), 133–292.

2 Miskolczy Ambrus, *Kossuth Eperjesen: Carlowszky Zsigmond és Greguss Mihály jogbölcselete* [Kossuth in Eperjes: Zsigmond Carlowszky and Mihály Greguss' Legal Philosophy] (Budapest: ELTE, 2007), 5–66.

3 The Kossuth Collection (R 90) of the National Archives of Hungary (MNL OL) contains a huge amount of manuscript material, but the National Széchényi Library, Manuscript Collection (OSZK Kézirattár) also has valuable manuscripts and letters from Kossuth, alongside several public collections. Several compilations and editions of his writings have been published, but this time I will only refer to two major series. It was Kossuth himself who started publishing his own papers: Lajos Kossuth, *Irataim az emigráczióból* [My Writings from Exile], vol. 1–3 (Budapest: Athenaeum, 1880–82), which was continued after his death by Ignác Helfy and his son Ferenc Kossuth, *Kossuth Lajos iratai* [Lajos Kossuth's Writings], vol. 4–13 (Budapest: Athenaeum, 1894–1911). The professional, academic publication of his papers began in the late 1940s, but the work was not completed: *Kossuth Lajos összes munkái* [Complete Works of Lajos Kossuth], vol. 1–7, 11–15 (Budapest: Magyar Történelmi Társulat-Akadémiai, 1948–89).

4   This opposing political orientation considered the country independent, especially its government, even though they did not want to separate from the Habsburg Empire.
5   Miru György, *Szabadság és politikai közösség: Kossuth Lajos politikai alapfogalmai* [Freedom and Political Community: Lajos Kossuth's Political Key Concepts] (Budapest: Argumentum-Bibó István Szellemi Műhely, 2011), 13–54.
6   Gábor Pajkossy, 'Kossuth hűtlenségi pere' [Kossuth's Trial for Treason], in *A magyar polgári átalakulás kérdései: Tanulmányok Szabad György 60. születésnapjára* [Issues Relating to the Hungarian Social Modernization: Studies in Honor of the 60th Birthday of György Szabad], ed. Dénes Iván Zoltán, Gergely András, and Pajkossy Gábor (Budapest: ELTE, 1984), 165–91; Pajkossy Gábor, 'Kossuth és a kormányzati 'terrorizmus' politikája 1835–39' [Kossuth and the Politics of Governmental 'Terrorism'], *Századok* 128, no. 5 (1994): 809–17.
7   Kosáry Domokos, 'Kossuth és a Pesti Hírlap' [Kossuth and Pest Gazette], in *A magyar sajtó története* [History of the Hungarian Press], vol. 1, 1705–1848, ed. Kókay György (Budapest: Akadémiai, 1979), 660–713; Varga János, *Kereszttűzben a Pesti Hírlap (Az ellenzéki és a középutas liberalizmus elválása 1841–42-ben)* [The Pest Gazette in Crossfire: Divergence of Oppositionist and Moderate Liberalism in 1841–42] (Budapest: Akadémiai, 1983).
8   Iván Zoltán Dénes, 'Political Vocabularies of the Hungarian Liberals and Conservatives before 1848', in *Liberty and the Search for Identity: Liberal Nationalisms and the Legacy of Empires*, ed. Iván Zoltán Dénes (Budapest–New York: CEU Press, 2006), 155–96.
9   Veliky János, *A változások kora: Polgári szerepkörök és változáskoncepciók a reformkor második évtizedében.* [An Age of Changes: Civil Roles and Concepts of Change in the Second Decade of the Reform Era] (Budapest: Új Mandátum, 2009), 138–59.
10 János Varga, *A Hungarian Quo Vadis: Political Trends and Theories of the Early 1840s* (Budapest: Akadémiai, 1993); Dénes Iván Zoltán, 'A közösség ügye és a szabadság ügye: Kossuth nemzet- és szabadság-értelmezése' [The Issue of Community and Liberty: Kossuth's Understanding of the Nation and Liberty], *Tiszatáj* 36, no. 9 (September 2002): 54–77; András Gergely, 'Kossuth's Nationality Policy, 1847–53', in *Lajos Kossuth Sent Word. . .: Papers Delivered on the Occasion of the Bicentenary of Kossuth's Birth*, ed. László Péter, Martyn Rady and Peter Sherwood (London: School of Slavonic and East European Studies, University College London, 2003), 95–104; Katus László, 'Kossuth és a nemzetiségi kérdés' [Kossuth and the Nationality Question], in *Kossuth Lajos, 'a magyarok Mózese'* [Lajos Kossuth, 'a Moses of Hungarians'], ed. Hermann Róbert (Budapest: Osiris, 2006), 45–74; Tevesz László, 'A magyar liberális-nacionalizmus nemzetfogalma a 'Kelet népe-vita' időszakában, 1841–43' [The Concept of Nation in Hungarian Liberal-Nationalistic Thought, in the Period of the 'People of the East' Debate, 1841–43], *Századvég* 12, no. 44 (2007): 31–72.
11 Iván Zoltán Dénes, *Conservative Ideology in the Making* (Budapest–New York: CEU Press, 2009).
12 Kosáry, 'Kossuth és a Pesti Hírlap', 714–30; Varga, *Kereszttűzben a Pesti Hírlap*, 24–108; János Veliky, 'Pozíciókijelölő politikai-ideológiai szempontok a Széchenyi-Kossuth-vita második szakaszában' [Position-Marking Political-Ideological Points of View in the Second Phase of the Széchenyi–Kossuth Debate], *Századok* 150, no. 3 (2016): 585–629; Schlett István, *A politikai gondolkodás története Magyarországon* [The History of Political Thought in Hungary] (Budapest: Századvég, 2018), 1:477–90.
13 Vikol Katalin, 'Tocqueville és hatása Magyarországon: Centralisták és liberálisok vitái a reformkorban' [Tocqueville and His Influence in Hungary: Debates Between

Centralizers and Liberals in the Reform Era], *Világosság* 22, no. 2 (February 1981): 73–9; Horkay Hörcher Ferenc, 'Az *Amerikai demokrácia* Magyarországon: A magyar Tocqueville, 1834–43' [*Democracy in America* in Hungary: The Hungarian Tocqueville, 1834–43], *Holmi* 6, no. 11 (November 1994): 1608–15; Fenyő István, *A centralisták: Egy liberális csoport a reformkori Magyarországon* [The Centralists: A Liberal Group in the Hungary of the Reform Era] (Budapest: Argumentum, 1997); Schlett, *A politikai gondolkodás története Magyarországon*, 1:490–536.

14 On Kossuth's activities in 1848–49 (written with much bias), see István Deák, *The Lawful Revolution: Louis Kossuth and the Hungarians 1848–49* (London: Phoenix, 2001); Erdődy Gábor, *'Én csak fáklyatartó voltam': Kossuth Lajos, a magyar polgári forradalom és szabadságharc irányítója (1848–49)* ['I Was Just a Candle Holder': Lajos Kossuth, Leader of the Hungarian Bourgeois Revolution and the War of Independence (1848–49)] (Budapest: ELTE Eötvös Kiadó, 2006); Gergely András, *1848-ban hogy is volt? Tanulmányok Magyarország és Közép-Európa 1848–49-es történetéből* [How was it in 1848? Studies in the History of Hungary and Central Europe in 1848–49] (Budapest: Osiris, 2001).

15 László Péter, 'Lajos Kossuth and the Conversion of the Constitution', in *Lajos Kossuth Sent Word...*, 81–93; Ferenc Hörcher, 'Reforming or Replacing the Historical Constitution? Lajos Kossuth and the April Laws of 1848', in *A History of the Hungarian Constitution: Law, Government and Political Culture in Central Europe*, ed. Ferenc Hörcher, and Thomas Lorman (New York–London: I. B. Tauris, 2018), 92–121.

16 Aladár Urbán, 'Lajos Kossuth in the Batthyány Cabinet', in *Lajos Kossuth Sent Word...*, 15–40.

17 Róbert Hermann, 'Kossuth, Parliamentary Dictator', in *Lajos Kossuth Sent Word...*, 41–69.

18 Erdődy Gábor, *A magyar kormányzat európai látóköre 1848-ban* [The European Horizon of the Hungarian Government in 1848] (Budapest: Akadémiai, 1988); Erdődy Gábor, *Kényszerpályán: A magyar külpolitikai gondolkodás 1849-ben* [On a Forced Course: Hungarian Foreign Policy Thought in 1849] (Budapest: Argumentum, 1998); Kosáry Domokos, *Magyarország és a nemzetközi politika 1848–49-ben* [Hungary and International Politics in 1848–49] (Budapest: MTA, 1999).

19 *The Hungarian Revolution and War of Independence, 1848–49: A Military History*, ed. Gábor Bona (Boulder: Social Science Monographs, 1999).

20 *A Kossuth-emigráció Törökországban* [The Kossuth Emigration in Turkey], vol. 1, ed. István Hajnal (Budapest: Magyar Történelmi Társulat, 1927).

21 Schlett, *A politikai gondolkodás története Magyarországon*, 2:128–85.

22 *Select Speeches of Kossuth*, ed. Francis W. Newman (London: Trübner, 1853); Dénes Jánossy, 'Great Britain and Kossuth', *Archivum Europae Centro-Orientalis* 3, no. 1–3 (1937): 53–190; John H. Komlos, *Louis Kossuth in America, 1851–52* (Buffalo: East European Institute, 1973).

23 Miru György, 'A szabadság elve és a nemzet elve: Kossuth Lajos és Teleki László vitája a közösségi autonómiák értelmezéséről' [The Principle of Liberty and the Principle of Nation: The Debate of Lajos Kossuth and László Teleki upon the Interpretation of Communal Autonomies], *Századok* 143, no. 3 (2009): 703–24.

24 *Kossuth és alkotmányterve* [Kossuth and his Draft Constitution], ed. György Spira (Debrecen: Csokonai, 1989); Pajkossy Gábor, 'Az 1862. évi Duna-konföderációs tervezet dokumentumai' [Documents of the Danube Confederation Plan of 1862], *Századok* 136, no. 4 (2002): 937–57.

25 Koltay-Kastner Jenő, *A Kossuth-emigráció Olaszországban* [The Kossuth Emigration in Italy] (Budapest: Akadémiai, 1960).
26 Szekfű Gyula, 'Az öreg Kossuth 1867-94' [The Old Kossuth 1867-94], in *Emlékkönyv Kossuth Lajos születésének 150. évfordulójára* [Memorial Volume on the 150th Anniversary of Lajos Kossuth's Birth], vol. 2, ed. I. Tóth Zoltán (Budapest: Magyar Történelmi Társulat-Akadémiai, 1952), 341-433; Csorba László, 'Kritika és kultusz: az öreg Kossuth Turinban' [Critic and Cult: The Old Kossuth in Turin], in Hermann, *Kossuth Lajos, 'a magyarok Mózese'*, 213-51.

12

Baron József Eötvös (1813–71)

Pál Bődy

This chapter will outline the historical and political thought of József Eötvös, a prominent poet, novelist, reformer and political thinker in nineteenth-century Hungary. There is a paradox in the contemporary image and evaluation of Eötvös. While Hungarian commentators and scholars recognize that he made great contributions to Hungarian national policies, his specific role and achievements are typically either unknown or misunderstood. In a recently published biography, the literary historian Balázs Devescovi summarizes this view: 'József Eötvös belongs unquestionably to our classical literary authors and greatest political thinkers. He is a recognized and acknowledged member of our national pantheon. [. . .] But let us be sincere: József Eötvös is today practically unknown even among informed readers.'[1] The prominent British historian Michael Hurst, in a review of my monograph on Eötvös, comments on this issue and provides a convincing explanation:

> The ranks of the statesmen are dwarfed by those of the politicians. But while the triumph of most statesmen, when it comes, be it through birth, striving or the working of circumstances, tends to elevate them in no uncertain way on to fine pedestals, there are those who are denied the greatest acclaim and whose very wisdom was the basic cause of their ultimate and irreversible failure to receive it. One such was Baron Joseph Eötvös, easily the most profound and coherent thinker among the leadership of the Hungarian national movement.[2]

Family, youth, personal commitments

One of the first questions to consider is the complex, even paradoxical process which led to the personal commitment of Eötvös to the Hungarian national revival and the reform of Hungarian traditional society. He was born on 3 September 1813 in Buda, the son of Baron Ignác Eötvös, a member of the higher nobility, a high-ranking official and faithful supporter of the Habsburg imperial government. His father and grandfather implemented the policies of the Vienna Court, which were regarded as violations of traditional Hungarian legal and constitutional principles. His mother, Baroness Anna von der Lilien, was the daughter of Baron Joseph von der Lilien, a cavalry captain from Westphalia, who settled in Hungary and acquired a property near Buda. Anna von der Lilien never learned Hungarian and the native language of her son was also German, the language with which Eötvös continued to speak and correspond with his mother. She was devoted to German classical literature, and he received his early education in German literary culture. He only learned Hungarian at the age of eleven, when he enrolled at the Buda Royal Gymnasium. In view of this family background, it is not surprising that historians have faced substantial difficulties in explaining Eötvös's decision to support the Hungarian national revival and the reform of Hungarian society. It is, however, likely that while the young Eötvös respected his father and mother, he made a personal commitment – based on a gradual process of reflection, nurturing personal friendships, literary activities and his personal experiences in Hungary and contemporary Europe – to devote himself to both of these movements. This hypothesis is supported by a letter he wrote to his son on 28 March 1866: 'The political arena was not especially attractive for me. I loved my father, but his political principles were opposed to my convictions. He was unpopular. I had to work hard to reduce the prejudices of the country against my family in order to attain a position of trust among those who were committed to freedom.'[3]

The first phase of Eötvös's commitment to the reform of Hungarian society is identified with the period of the Reform Era, 1825 to 1848. This is one of the most creative periods of Hungarian history, both from a literary and political point of view. After thirty years of political oppression and stagnation, a revival of literary, political and social reform activity took place following 1825. Eötvös studied philosophy and law at the University of Pest. When he completed his studies at the age of eighteen, he became immersed in an atmosphere of social-political ferment, especially among his fellow students and the leading representatives of his generation. In his memorial address in honour of his lifetime friend and political associate, László Szalay, on 11 December 1865, Eötvös attributed the student enthusiasm of that period to two experiences: the popular lectures by their professor of history István Horvát on Hungarian history, and the July 1830 Revolution in Paris. This is his recollection of that historical transition:

> With the July Revolution and the ideas it represented, the situation had changed. Instead of the memories of our ancient glory, the will to act dominates the nation. The young generation, conscious that it stands on the threshold of a splendid future, accepts the challenge it faces with enthusiasm. [. . .] To lift our country from stagnation, to transform it into one of the first in Europe, that ideal that we believed to be a daydream now seemed to be possible, and our youthful hearts were excited by the thought that we too could grasp with our hands the glory of patriotic accomplishment.[4]

This quotation provides a historical description of the emerging enthusiasm for reform. In contrast, Eötvös's personal commitment to reform and national revival involved a complex, gradual process consisting of three distinct types of youthful experiences in the years from 1831 to 1839: literary efforts seeking to establish his reputation as an author, personal relationships with prominent authors and associates and activities related to his future public role. A review of these experiences is indispensable for an understanding of his commitment to reform politics.

His most important relationship was his lifelong friendship and association with László Szalay (1813–64), his university classmate. Szalay was the son of a prominent civil servant employed by the Locotenential Council (*helytartótanács*) in Buda, who managed to harmonize his loyalty to the Habsburg monarch with Hungarian patriotism. Szalay and Eötvös completed their studies at the same time and their friendship involved a close personal association dedicated to Hungarian patriotism and the reform of Hungarian society. They devoted their initial efforts to the advancement of Hungarian literature, since they believed that their literary activities would clarify both Hungarian and European social-political reform issues. Their literary efforts enabled them to establish close relationships with two of the most prominent senior contemporary Hungarian authors who were dedicated to the renewal of Hungary: Ferenc Kazinczy and Ferenc Kölcsey.

The years following 1832 were a period of literary apprenticeship and a process of intellectual formation which served to clarify his personal commitment. The sources of his intellectual orientation originated from his friendship and correspondence with his classmate Szalay, the personal examples of Kazinczy and Kölcsey and contemporary Western European Romanticism.

The next significant stage in Eötvös's education was his travels to West European countries, including Switzerland, France and Great Britain in 1836-7. We have very limited information concerning his itinerary, experiences and their impact on his views, but it is evident that these journeys contributed significantly to the emergence of his political commitments. Following a brief visit to Geneva, he visited Paris and several provincial cities, including Marseille, Toulon and Bordeaux. He paid a visit to the La Trappe Carthusian monastery in southern France, which inspired a unique literary-personal confession, the novel titled *A karthauzi* (The Carthusian), written after his return to Hungary.

The novel presents the personal memoirs of a French nobleman, who experienced numerous personal disappointments, failures and rejections as well as disillusionment with French society in the period of the July Monarchy. He is profoundly disturbed by the dominance of personal gain, animosities, profiteering and the absence of personal motivation. He makes the decision to enter the La Trappe Carthusian monastery and reflect on the failures of his life. In his memoirs, he comes to the conclusion that his failure was due to his personal selfishness and the refusal to act for the benefit of others. He concludes: 'I wish to be of service, this is our human vocation.' He justifies this conclusion with the following message to posterity:

> Whoever devotes his life to a higher purpose should not expect to see the fruits of his efforts in his lifetime. A long time is required for the fruition of seeds planted in human society. Those whom you have served will not appreciate your services. Instead of gratitude you can expect ridicule, perhaps persecution.[5]

In March 1837, Eötvös travelled to Great Britain, visiting London and the British countryside, where he observed social conditions and collected documents relating to social and national problems in Ireland. The impact of this tour on his subsequent political views can be related to contemporary Western European social progress: he was clearly disappointed with social conditions in France, while contemporary British society and its reformist politicians provided a fruitful source for his subsequent political thought. His European tour can thus be considered a confirmation of his personal commitment to contributing to Hungarian reform politics.

Following his return, he considered his primary task to be the careful review of his experiences during his European tour in relation to his decision to participate in Hungarian public activities. In his letter to Szalay on 19 December 1837, he stated this intention: 'The time has come to define the future course of our nation, this will be the purpose of my activities.'[6]

Political orientation

Eötvös prepared three political statements based on these experiences and his reflections on his European tour. The first was entitled *Szegénység Irlandban* (Poverty in Ireland), the second *A zsidók emancipatiója* (The Emancipation of the Jews) and the third *Kelet népe és Pesti Hirlap* (referring to the debate between Széchenyi and Kossuth). Although the three essays concerned rather divergent issues, there was a common element: the analysis of existing oppression and his own proposals for ending it.

His detailed study of Irish society is a good example of this theme. In this work, the author provides a fact-based overview of the economic exploitation of the Irish peasants by absentee English landowners, as well as a historical summary of Irish-English relationships through the centuries. Social oppression, discrimination due to religious and ethnic identities and economic exploitation are all cited as basic explanations of 'poverty in Ireland'. These issues were also present in contemporary Hungary. But perhaps the most relevant issue related to Hungary was the question of the role of revolution in attaining social reform. While Eötvös recognized the historic role of Daniel O'Connell in the Irish reform initiative, he disapproved of continuous revolutionary agitation as the instrument of social and political reform. He succinctly summarized this position: 'While a revolutionary condition continues, laws cannot exercise their beneficial impact'.[7] Furthermore, the next step should be a mutual acceptance by both parties of a just settlement. This continued to be his firm position up until and following the Revolution of 1848 and represented thereafter a major theme of his political thought.

The essay on Ireland is based on documents of the *Report of the Poor Law Commissioners in Ireland*, as well as on several other sources,[8] and its continuing value has been highlighted by a recent translation of the work into English.[9]

Eötvös's essay on the emancipation of the Jews is equally significant as a reflection of his future political conception. Its basic argument is designed to refute real and invented accusations, prejudices and myths relating to the position of the Jews under the Hungarian Constitution. He is primarily concerned with the public acceptance of legal equality for all inhabitants of Hungary. However, he also had an additional highly important purpose: clarifying the relationships between personal liberty, the constitution and the establishment of a nation of citizens. By protecting the personal liberty of all persons, including the Jews, he was convinced that the Hungarian Constitution could generate patriotism, respect and equality. Eötvös cites the example of two advanced European nations, Great Britain and France, and their constitutions on the principle of legal equality for all citizens. He summarized this principle as follows: 'Every citizen will be loyal to his nation on the basis of the assurance of his equality, his pride as a citizen, and his happiness as a respected citizen. This is the most important condition of our future nation.'[10] This argumentation defined the political position of Eötvös in 1840. It meant the recognition of all the social, religious and ethnic communities of Hungary, and the guarantee of their legal equality, of free scope for their activities and of their development as citizens and members of their communities. This principle was, in fact, the major justification of his essay on Jewish emancipation.

The third principal statement Eötvös made in these years, *Kelet népe és Pesti Hirlap*, was his contribution to a major national controversy relating to the publication of the biweekly *Pesti Hirlap*, which had been edited by Lajos Kossuth since 2 January 1841. This publication served not only to report political events but expressed the political position of Kossuth. Several prominent political leaders published supporting or opposing views of the new publication, but the most dramatic protest was that written by Count István Széchenyi, the leading reformer. Széchenyi criticized the *Pesti Hirlap* primarily for its random approach to reform, by focusing on problems, conflicts and issues rather than on their resolution. While Eötvös agreed with Kossuth that it was important to publicize existing issues, he argued that it was necessary to define the process by which these issues could be resolved. He contended that one basic condition of such a process was the education of the people, in contrast with Széchenyi's view, which emphasized economic and social transformation. He listed two specific impacts of public education: its role in supporting social and economic development and as a prerequisite of reform as the basic process of social transformation. He comments on two other issues raised by Kossuth: ethnic minority rights and the arbitrary actions of the local authorities at the county level. He disagreed with Kossuth on enforcing the assimilation of the minorities by law and expressed the view that 'the principle to be followed is that of mutual agreement and free choice'.[11] With regard to the arbitrary use of authority in the county system, he expressed an essential principle of his subsequent political thought:

> Absolute power without accountability is incompatible with civic freedom, whether exercised by single or several persons, by a county or by a national authority, it will always result in oppression.[12]

In addition to writing these political essays, Eötvös was actively involved in establishing a small circle of associates who all agreed with his approach to Hungarian reform. This group included László Szalay, his closest friend, Ágoston Trefort, who studied and wrote on economic issues, Móric Lukács, Antal Csengery and Zsigmond Kemény. One of their ideas in 1840 was to publish a journal which was to feature articles on social, economic and political issues relevant to Hungarian reform initiatives. This journal, *Budapesti Szemle*, began publication in 1840. Its model was the *Edinburgh Review*, a familiar source of British social thought to Eötvös and his associates. Although the journal existed only for one year, it was an important device in fostering a unified vision among Eötvös's circle of associates,[13] as the circle was to play a significant role in Hungarian political reform after 1840.

Proposals for reform

At the time of the Hungarian Diet of 1843-4, it became evident that both houses of the Diet, dominated by the nobility and controlled by the noble-dominated county system, still refused to consider those reform bills which would transform the social and political structure of Hungary. This reality led Eötvös and Szalay to formulate and publicly announce a comprehensive plan for reform. This conception was outlined by László Szalay in the Lower House of the Diet on 27 September 1843. The reform programme began by extending the right to participate in the Diet to the prosperous inhabitants of the towns. This was considered the first step towards the transformation of the Hungarian Diet into a national legislature representing all classes of Hungarian society and towards the establishment of a comprehensive constitutional system, based on the legal equality of all citizens. The detailed conception was presented in the *Pesti Hirlap* between July 1844 and December 1845, under the editorship of László Szalay and with contributions from the wider Eötvös circle.[14]

The proposed reform programme also consisted of the following major elements: first, to transform the existing noble Diet into an assembly based on the principle of popular representation. Its members would be elected by direct elections, based on specific property or professional qualifications. Noble status would not automatically qualify people to vote or be members of parliament. Second, the Parliament would have the exclusive right to verify all elected members. The right of county assemblies to impose instructions would be abolished. All public policies with a national impact, such as taxation, recruitment, economic policies, justice and public education, would be transferred to the jurisdiction of the Parliament. Third, a national executive, namely a 'ministry' (i.e. government) would be established. This executive would be responsible to the Parliament. It would be a unified government with responsibility for all national policies. Fourth, counties, cities and townships would be organized on the basis of self-government by citizens who were qualified to vote or hold public office.

Eötvös summarized the principles of his programme:

> In order to have a genuine constitution, it is necessary first to establish an independent legislature, and second, to establish an executive which is subject to the legislature in such a way, that the intentions of the legislature will not be frustrated either by actions or neglect.[15]

The presentation of Eötvös's conception in the *Pesti Hirlap* provoked general disapproval and even outright rejection by practically all the prominent leaders of the reform movement and opposition. The conception was correctly perceived as a direct repudiation of the county system, which was considered a national institution with a key historic role in opposing Habsburg absolutist rule. Although Eötvös and his associates were deeply discouraged and disappointed, a compromise solution was adopted: another member of the Eötvös circle, Antal Csengery, took over as editor of the *Pesti Hirlap* and agreed to provide equal access to all reform proposals in the paper. Csengery edited the *Pesti Hirlap* until September 1848. At the same time, the Eötvös circle continued to justify and advocate their original programme of reform in the press, in independent publications and through public statements.

The events and circumstances of the years 1846-7 contributed substantially to the increasing likelihood that the Eötvös programme would prevail. One such event was a major peasant uprising in Galicia, a province of the Habsburg Empire. The uprising was accompanied by atrocities and violence, while the imperial authorities intentionally delayed intervening. This event had a major impact on Hungarian public opinion and contributed to the likelihood of similar events taking place in Hungary. A related event was the public statement of Kossuth, in July 1846, in support of the emancipation of the serfs in Hungary. Concurrently, a comprehensive setting-out of Eötvös's proposals was published both in Hungarian and German, entitled *Reform* and *Reform in Ungarn*. Furthermore, another publication by Eötvös appeared at the same time, the novel *A falu jegyzője* (The Village Notary), a literary portrayal of the county system and the social and personal injustices of Hungarian society. It was a highly effective social critique and justification of Eötvös's own vision of reform.

The Revolution of 1848

The Revolution of 1848 created a completely unexpected and unique situation. The Diet of 1847-8 was in session, but it was preoccupied with debating legislative statements critical of Habsburg government policies towards Hungary. At the same time, revolutions and constitutional movements emerged in the Italian territories of the empire in February, followed by the Revolution in Paris in the same month. Eötvös realized that these movements would spread to Hungary, and he proposed, in a letter to László Teleki on 11 February 1848, that the Hungarian Diet should formulate specific agreements 'which would assure the independence of the Hungarian government and its separation from the other governments of the Empire. I think this is the most important issue to be resolved. I admit this is a difficult proposal, since it involves a constitutional reform, a new or rather a new approach to a constitutional charter.'[16]

In another letter addressed to István Széchenyi on 28 February, four days after the Revolution in Paris, Eötvös expressed his views on the relationship between Hungary and the empire:

> In the first place our proximity to Russia, in the second place our situation and the divergent tendencies of our nationalities have convinced me that while the

stability of the Empire is not a condition of our existence, its future development is definitely in our interest. Therefore, it is the obligation of all Hungarians to support the future integrity of the Empire of which we are a part.[17]

Lajos Kossuth, the leading spokesman of the Hungarian Diet, recognized the threat of a revolutionary upheaval and on 3 March 1848 presented a comprehensive constitutional proposal for Hungary and the Habsburg Empire. He proposed that the dynasty establish a constitutional governmental system for the empire. Most importantly, he called on the Hungarian Diet to approve comprehensive principles of reform, including taxation for all citizens, emancipation of the serfs, a Parliament elected by citizens based on property and professional qualifications, a constitutional agreement between Hungary and the Austrian provinces on their future relationships and the establishment of a Hungarian government responsible to the Hungarian Parliament. These bills were then submitted to the imperial government for review and approval. As expected, this proved to be a highly difficult political procedure but eventually agreement was reached with the enaction of what became known as the April Laws.

Eötvös served as minister of education from April to August 1848 in the Batthyány government, established as a result of the April Laws. He supported efforts to reach an agreement with the Imperial government. In addition, he drafted plans for primary, secondary and university education in the Kingdom of Hungary. He resigned his office the day after the lynching of Count Lamberg, left Hungary with his family and spent the next two years in Munich. He realized that the Imperial government was determined to impose an absolutist system on Hungary. His decision to resign his office and to leave Hungary was an important step that had an impact on his future political position. He left the scene of his political aspirations because he could not visualize his participation in the civil and military struggle he had foreseen. In a letter to his closest friend László Szalay on 20 October 1848, he wrote: 'You will easily understand my reasons for coming here if you will consider my personality and the events now occurring in Pest, which I had foreseen and predicted for months. Hungarian affairs have come to the point where all discussion is impossible.'[18] During his exile in Munich he drafted several manuscripts about the revolution and prepared recommendations for the post-revolutionary reconstruction of the Austrian Empire.

Post-revolutionary ideas and proposals

Two of his manuscripts attempted to formulate a new approach to post-revolutionary policies based on European perspectives. The first was a sketch of the 1848 revolutions in Austria. In this manuscript he attempted to analyse two issues: the relationship between the Hungarian government and the empire, and the nationality issue, as the following comment indicates:

> Those in Austria and Hungary who desired the unity of the Empire were certainly correct. Even the most radical separatists were aware of the consequences of their

support of separatism. The demands for self-governing territories and nationalities could not conceal the fact that self-government and freedom were dependent on the existence of an internationally strong Austrian Empire. Following the transformation of the structure of the Empire, the unity of the Emperor, based on the Pragmatic Sanction, was an inadequate guarantee of the unity and power of the Empire. It was therefore necessary to consider a new charter which was based on constitutional principles.[19]

The second manuscript, known as the *Munich Draft* (Müncheni Vázlat), was significantly different in purpose and content. It outlines the author's proposed principles for the post-revolutionary reconstruction of the empire:

The Revolution had a major consequence. The Monarchy cannot exist according to its pre-revolutionary principles. Our primary task is to construct a new Monarchy. This will be extremely difficult, since the pre-revolutionary conceptions, including those of the Monarchy, have been substantially compromised. The conceptions of Europe are currently in a state of anarchy. In the Monarchy, separatism is dominant and the elements of unity have been damaged. The reconstruction of the Empire is the primary condition for the future of its residents. [. . .] In order to formulate the principles of reconstruction for the Empire, it is necessary to clarify existing political principles first in the European context, secondly in the Empire. The restructured Empire will endure only if its establishment is based on contemporary European political principles and the principles of a reconstructed Empire.[20]

His first post-revolutionary publication, entitled *Ueber die Gleichberechtigung der Nationalitäten in Oesterreich* (On the Equal Rights of Nationalities in Austria), published in 1850, is an analysis and critique of the controversies relating to nationality in the revolutions of 1848.

Nationality as a political theory emerged in pre-revolutionary political literature and borrowed the French revolutionary catchwords: freedom, equality, fraternity. Czech authors, such as František Palacký, Jan Swoboda and others proposed the argument that nationality derived from natural law, and was based on ancient laws and unchanging moral principles. During the Revolution, this theory was proclaimed by a variety of national forums: the Slav Congress of Prague, the Romanian Congress of 1848 and the Slovak Petitioners.

Eötvös attempted to clarify the theory of nationality in the context of political objectives. He observed that: 'Everywhere we hear the same word: "nationality", but everyone has a different conception of it. Every nationality demands its rights, but there is no agreement what those rights are.'[21] He presented the following analysis, based on his personal experience and thinking: 'The common origin of all nationalities is the conviction that it is an advantage to belong to a nationality, based on the premise that its qualities are superior to all others. [. . .] The objective is to develop the potential resources of a people in order to obtain for that people a dominant position over all other peoples. Thus, the primary aim of national aspirations is domination.'[22]

He then presented his views on the concept of the 'equality of nationalities', as it was propagated during the Revolution. He noted that in constitutional states it was not customary to enforce the public role of languages. The political demand for 'the equality of languages', as had been proposed in the Austrian Parliament at Kremsier in January 1849, required that the equal status of all languages should be enforced by law and the appointment of civil servants was to take into account the proportion of ethnic groups in the population. Eötvös considered these proposals incompatible with a constitutional government and the practice of democratic states. Each nationality would attempt to expand its territory, which in turn would preclude a harmonious relationship between the various nationalities.

He concluded therefore that the theory of the equality of nationalities was incompatible with the constitutional system of the Austrian Empire. Consequently, he proposed a conception of nationality rights which would be compatible with the unity and constitutional structure of the empire, as he saw it, which consisted of three elements:

1. Establishment of a unified and stabilized state.
2. Accord between the national identities of territories constituting the Monarchy, based on historic rights and the requirements of a unified state.
3. Mediation between the utilization of several languages, territories based on historic rights and the unified state.[23]

Another purpose of the author was to argue that a constitutional structure was compatible with the stability and unity of the Austrian Empire. He outlined a proposal providing for a unified constitutional system, an accord between the central government and territories based on historic rights and the recognition of nationality rights at the territorial and local levels of government.

The proposal consisted of three conceptional levels of government. The highest level was the unified state authority responsible for the common affairs of the empire: expenses of the emperor and his family, military command, commerce, foreign affairs. A representative parliament of the empire and a ministry were responsible for the administration of the common affairs. The second level of government provided for the historic territories of the empire based on the principle of self-government. Each territory was to be organized according to traditional or newly established constitutions. The third level of government was a network of cities, townships and jurisdictions. One of their responsibilities was to protect linguistic-national rights at the local level.

The proposal was severely criticized in Hungary and did not persuade the Austrian absolutist government, either. Nevertheless, it raised and attempted to clarify the essential issues of how Hungary should be reconstructed following the failure of the revolution and War of Independence in 1848–9.

A comprehensive treatise of political theory

In his *Munich Draft*, prepared in December 1848, Eötvös argued that the restructuring of the empire should be based on an analysis of contemporary European political thought. This manuscript can be considered an initial version of his principal treatise, *A XIX. század uralkodó eszméinek befolyása az álladalomra* (The Influence of the Ruling Ideas of the 19th Century on the State), published in German and Hungarian in 1851-4.[24]

Eötvös studied European history throughout his life and was familiar with its major original sources and interpretations. His historical conception was based on the theory that after the collapse of the Roman Empire and the establishment of the Frankish Empire under Charlemagne, political authority in Europe became gradually centralized by emerging kingdoms. As a consequence, absolutist political systems were established, and individual liberties were gradually but continuously suppressed. The French Revolution continued this process by harnessing the theory of popular sovereignty as an instrument of centralization and through the denial of individual liberties. In his treatise he summarizes this historical theory as follows:

> As a new political system was shaped after the chaos of the migrations, individual freedom was subjected more and more to the state. The French Revolution failed to change this pattern, on the contrary it continued royal policies in the name of the people and absolute state authority was expanded. This was a dominant policy of all states in the modern period, leading to the unconditional rule of the state.[25]

His view can be compared to that of Alexis de Tocqueville, presented in his essay *L'Ancien Régime et la Révolution* (The Old Regime and the French Revolution), published in 1856. Eötvös wrote an extensive and complimentary review of Tocqueville's essay in the *Budapesti Szemle* in 1857, expressing his full agreement with the French author. Tocqueville, in turn, read the German version of the *Ruling Ideas* by Eötvös and expressed his appreciation in a letter to him, dated 1 July 1858.[26]

Eötvös devoted the first volume of his treatise to an analysis of the ideas of liberty, equality and nationality as the key political concepts of the European revolutions. He related the emergence and meaning of these ideas to transformations that had taken place in the course of the French Revolution of 1789. While the idea of liberty was the initial starting point of the Revolution, the political conflicts in France and the threat of international intervention resulted in the establishment of a centralized government and the concentration of executive authority. The political justification for this policy was expressed in the principle of popular sovereignty. This principle served as the primary ideological basis of the Revolution, the Napoleonic system and the post-revolutionary governments alike. Consequently, the principle of popular sovereignty was accepted as the ideological basis of revolutionary movements throughout Europe.

Eötvös interpreted the principle of popular sovereignty as the expansion of state authority, the limitation of individual liberties and the utilization of state authority without the influence of individual citizens or by their exclusion.

Rather than supporting the concept of popular sovereignty, he expressed his commitment to the interpretation of liberty and equality which had emerged in the British constitutional system. In his view, the British conception was that there should be no unlimited power in the political system and that all political institutions should be limited in the exercise of their power. This conception also defined the English principle of equality. According to this view each citizen received the protection of individual liberty, the free movement of citizens was secured and all citizens received equal legal protection. Equality meant therefore equality in the exercise of individual liberty.

Eötvös characterized nationality as the organization of states according to the principle of language. A single language was the determining factor of political systems based on popular or national sovereignty. He observed that national movements prior to and during the Revolution of 1848 claimed linguistic relationships, demanded national rights and territories, expressed policies aiming to unite specific national groups and dreamed of establishing new state formations. These all generated conflicts with other nations.

In contrast to the principle of linguistic nationality, Eötvös proposed the principle of territorial nationality and the legitimacy of historic states. These principles recognized the linguistic, cultural, political and organizational rights of nationalities. In his view, these rights would be protected in a state which recognized individual rights and allowed political activities and the formation of associations.

The second volume of his treatise presented his conception of a constitutional state, essentially his recommendations for the reconstruction of the Habsburg Empire, based on his interpretation of liberty, equality and nationality. This conception emphasized the requirements of individual liberty, the purpose of the state, the legitimate limits of centralization and self-government as an instrument to restrict centralization and protect individual and nationality rights.

In his review of the origin and purpose of the state, he expressed his disagreement with the social contract theory as proposed by Hobbes, Locke and Rousseau. His view was that the first small communities had later united into larger territories. He also rejected the theories of divinity and universality when used to justify state power. He instead defined the purpose of the state as the protection of the material and moral goods of individuals as well as of individual liberty. One of the basic conditions of individual liberty in a state is the participation of individual citizens in the formation of public policies.

The two main issues of Eötvös's treatise are the concept of state centralization and self-government. When discussing centralization, he agreed that the primary functions of the state are the rights of representation, legislation, administration, independence and military defence. He also declared that the state has an obligation to provide education. Another important issue for Eötvös was centralized public administration. Centralized administrators lack vital information concerning the needs of local communities, and are thus generally unable to address the concerns of individual citizens. Appointed officials are also frequently instructed to propagate the interests and political influence of the central government.

Eötvös described his conception of self-government as the emergence of communities which are based on the support and participation of the local population and thereby contribute to the social and political involvement of citizens in public policy decisions. He stated his conception in the context of his historical theory of self-government:

> The creation of self-governing communities is the only way to reduce the threat to the state which the popular aspiration to participate in public policymaking

represents. The defense of individual liberty against arbitrary actions of the state in democratic society is derived from the same source which has defended individual liberty for many centuries against the state: strong self-governing communities.[27]

He considered a central court of justice to be one of the essential requirements of a constitutional system, providing for jurisdictions between the state and local governments. He observed that the judicial system performed a decisive role in the preservation of constitutional principles in the United States. He contended that the American courts established legally based limits on the political activity of legislatures and the people. He also noted that proposals for judicial systems can be traced back to the medieval period. In his view, the judicial system represented a moral arbiter, as the only political force which does not seek power for itself. He referred to the 'moral responsibility' of judges and quoted Bentham's principles on judicial organization.[28] In addition to local autonomy, Eötvös discussed another significant element of individual freedom: the right of association. This was a concept that augmented the principle of local autonomy by providing individual citizens with the opportunity to associate with others in the same community and thereby undertake joint activities to protect their interests, aspirations and community involvement. He added that such associations could also pursue activities beyond their communities, serving as the focus of cooperation among several local communities and coordinating the common aspirations of citizens with interests in areas of culture, education or social activities.

In his concluding remarks, Eötvös reflected on the relationship between patriotism and loyalty to the state as a unifying element of citizenship. His conclusion was that the extensive relationships of individual citizens to their families, place of birth and communities also strengthened their sense of unity to their state:

> The legitimate limitation of state authority and therefore the autonomy of territories and townships will produce a sense of loyalty on the part of all citizens which can only be found in states with comparable organization.[29]

Two prominent English reviews commented on Eötvös's treatise. The *Westminster Review* considered the treatise a 'careful investigation' of the prevailing ideas of liberty, equality and nationality and praised its 'earnest and impartial spirit' but did not discuss the author's political thought.[30] It is conceivable that this omission was explained by the sensitivity of the Irish nationality issue in the United Kingdom. *The Rambler*, edited by Lord Acton, in contrast, provided a clear statement of the author's position:

> Denying the sovereignty of the majority, and the omnipotence of the state, he [i.e. Eötvös] establishes authority and liberty on the autonomy of moral individualities. The foremost of these, he argues, is the nation. As liberty is due to every corporation, as well as to every individual, and as the power of the state is limited by private rights, the same respect is due to the rights, liberties, and independence of each nationality.[31]

Eötvös's treatise presented the principles of his political thought, based on his experiences during the Revolution and his reflections in the post-revolutionary period. It is evident that his treatise and the related essays attempted to present and justify political principles which would serve as guidelines for the reconstruction of the post-revolutionary Habsburg Empire. His essential recommendations can be summarized as follows: The Habsburg Empire should be organized on the basis of a constitutional system at the central, territorial and local levels, the demands for the equality of nationalities need to be addressed on the basis of historic and territorial nationality and, based on these two major principles, the unity of the empire, which was the paramount issue of the Revolution, would be strengthened and augmented.

It is clear, however, that after the publication of his treatise, neither the Habsburg government, nor the political leadership in Hungary and the empire responded to his conceptual programme. In fact, the absolutist government, established in 1849, ruled the empire and its peoples without providing opportunities for political discussion, participation and expression. This being the case, in the 1850s, Eötvös and other Hungarian political leaders were denied the opportunity to initiate political discussions. Eötvös did, however, take part in various activities related to academic, cultural, social and international ventures. In 1855, Eötvös was elected vice-president of the Hungarian Academy of Sciences, allowing him the opportunity to confirm the national, unifying and scientific role of this institution at a time of political repression. He expanded his international contacts with recognized scholars, who read and commented on his treatise, including Karl Theodor Welcker of the University of Heidelberg, Charles de Montalembert, Jakob Philipp Fallmerayer of the University of München and Cherbuliez, the Swiss author of political studies.

Eötvös and the Settlement with Austria, 1859-67

The year 1859 created an entirely new situation for the Habsburg Empire and for Hungary. The defeats suffered by the Austrian army in the Austro-Italian War of 1859 at the battles of Magenta and Solferino, followed by the armistice, forced the emperor to dismantle the absolutist system. He appointed a new government and introduced a transformed political system. As a result of the military defeat, a spirit of national protest and opposition emerged in Hungary, directed against the absolutist system. The unifying focus of Hungarian political efforts was the demand for the restoration of the April Laws of 1848. The unquestioned leader of the Hungarian movement was Ferenc Deák. He regarded the April Laws as the exclusive constitutional basis for negotiations with the emperor.

The principal result of the new political course was the initiation of public discussion between the emperor and the Hungarian parliamentary leadership, concerning the principles of a settlement between Hungary and the empire. This process took place in the period between 1859 and 1867. After the passing of the October Diploma in 1860, the emperor convened the Hungarian Parliament, which then affirmed its constitutional position based on the April Laws of 1848 and rejected the emperor's demands. The result was the dismissal of the Parliament in 1861.

These political developments opened up new possibilities for Eötvös in Hungarian politics and he was now able to actively participate in the political negotiations between the Hungarian Parliament and the emperor. As a prominent and highly respected political figure he was expected to contribute to the political discussions and to participate in the negotiations leading to the Settlement with Austria. He was very much aware of his new role and his public statements reflected this awareness. At the same time, he did not renounce the principles he had stated in his previous publications, but adapted them to the prevailing political currents of 1859. His political position of that year involved three basic elements: acceptance by the emperor of the April Laws as the basis of a constitutional settlement, constitutional government for all parts of the Habsburg Empire and agreement on two essential conditions of the settlement: the common pursuit of the affairs of the empire and Hungary, and the resolution of nationality rights.

Following the dissolution of the Hungarian Parliament in 1861, the absolutist government was restored in Hungary. A central governmental administration was appointed. County and city self-government was suspended. The system was directed by the Minister of the Interior, Anton von Schmerling. The adoption of this absolutist system was intended to prepare the foreign policy of the Habsburg Empire to assume political leadership in the German Confederation. This policy was opposed by the newly appointed Prussian Prime Minister Otto von Bismarck, who declared his intention to establish the dominant position of Prussia in a united Germany. In Hungary, three party formations were extant: the conservative aristocrats, the Deák party and a third party opposed to settlement with Austria. Both the conservatives and the Deák party supported settlement with Austria. The leaders of the Deák party were Ferenc Deák, Count Gyula Andrássy and József Eötvös.

While the members of the Deák party were united in their opposition to the Schmerling system, they were divided regarding their approaches to the Settlement with Austria. Deák pursued a policy of postponing a political initiative until he had received a signal from the emperor, while Eötvös, Andrássy and others pressed for a public proposal. The year 1864 was a difficult year of crisis for Eötvös: his closest friend László Szalay died, ending a lifetime of friendship; he felt that his closest associates had left him; and his differences with Deák were another unresolved issue. In his notes of 1 August 1864, he explained the underlying issue: Deák conceived the approaching settlement as a legal agreement between the monarch and the Parliament, as had been customary in previous such historical situations. This meant that these two parties alone were involved in this process. This was how Eötvös explained Deák's reluctance to make a proposal and his aversion to any controversy. Eötvös's conception of the settlement was completely different: it was not merely a legal bargain, but an agreement between constitutional Hungary and the constitutional territories of Austria. To advance his vision of how a settlement could be reached, in June 1865 Eötvös started to edit the weekly paper, *Politikai Hetilap*, in which he and his associates discussed their proposals.

Eötvös's contribution to the Settlement with Austria can be summarized by his recognition that it was a completely new approach to the relationship between two independent states. In his view, it was not a traditional legal agreement, but an interstate association of Austria and Hungary. He attributed the future durability of the relationship to two conditions: the guarantee of nationality rights and the emergence of a modernized economic, social and intellectual system.

Eötvös and the rights of nationalities

Several proposals were made and negotiations took place in Hungary and Austria relating to nationality rights, that is, the rights of Hungary's ethnic minorities, during and following the Revolution, which had a significant impact on Eötvös's ideas. His principal point was that the best guarantee for the protection of nationality rights was the establishment of a free constitutional system, which would be capable of providing both for individual and nationality rights, as formulated in his treatise of 1851-4. This can be considered the basic model of the legislative proposals which produced the Nationalities Act of 1868.[32]

These recommendations emphasized the equal rights of ethnic minorities both in its statement of principles and in the specific points relating to the public use of languages; instruction in native languages; the right to establish educational institutions at the primary, secondary and university levels; participation in advocating political, social, economic policies; and nationality rights. The 1861 parliamentary committee proposal, drafted under Eötvös's chairmanship and with the agreement of minority nationality members, was the basic model for the 1867 and even the 1868 bills.

The principles of the 1861 proposal were:

1. All citizens of Hungary, regardless of their native language, constitute politically one nation, the united and indivisible Hungarian nation, based on the historical conception of the state of Hungary.
2. All peoples living in Hungary, Hungarians, Slavs, Romanians, Germans, Serbs, Russians, are recognized as nationalities with equal rights. They can implement their nationality aspirations freely, based on the political unity of the country, utilizing individual liberties and the right of association, without further constraints.

A comparison of the Nationalities Act with its predecessors, however, indicates that while the two previous bills of 1861 and 1867 were based on the principle of integrating all the ethnic minorities into the existing Hungarian political structure, the Act of 1868 was clearly an affirmation of the legal-historical conception of the Hungarian state and did not provide for full political equality of ethnic minorities. These two concepts were unquestionably the ideas championed by the two prominent political leaders of Hungary: Eötvös and Deák. Eötvös represented the principle of integration, while Deák that of the legal-historical tradition.

Eötvös as minister of education

In February 1867, following the Settlement with Austria, Count Gyula Andrássy, the new Hungarian prime minister, offered the post of minister of education to Eötvös. He had served in that office in the 1848 Hungarian government, but in view of the armed conflict with Austria he was unable to realize his proposals. As a result of the Settlement with Austria in 1867, a constitutional system was established in Hungary which enabled Eötvös to propose and implement policies in public education. He considered his priority to be the preparation of a bill on elementary education and its parliamentary approval.

The bill on elementary education was submitted to Parliament in June 1868.[33] It was prepared with the assistance of a professional staff with substantial experience in the theories and practical elements of education. It required school attendance for all children from the ages of six to twelve years. Parents had the choice of community, religious or private schools. All church organizations, associations, individuals, communities and the state were entitled to establish and maintain schools in accordance with standards specified in the bill. Organizations maintaining schools had the right to choose teachers, textbooks and methods of instruction. The community school was required in communities without an existing school, in case parents did not wish to utilize religious schools or there was no religious school available for more than thirty children. The language of instruction in all state schools was the native language of the pupils. In communities with mixed languages, an assistant teacher would be provided. In community schools, religious instruction was provided by churches. These provisions were substantial guarantees of religious freedom and nationality rights. The Act afforded special attention to the establishment of teacher training institutes. The new system was comparable to other school systems developed in European countries. It constituted the basis of secondary and university education in nineteenth- and twentieth-century Hungary. Although Eötvös's bills on university reform were not discussed by the Parliament, they served as guidelines and examples for university policies following his death in 1871.[34]

Conclusion

In summary, it may be instructive to list the elements of political thought and practice that are of special importance in an interpretation of Eötvös. One of these was the principle of autonomy. This concept is evident both in his theoretical works and in his political practice. It encompasses the advocacy of autonomy related to church organizations, nationalities, political (self-governing) communities and territories, the autonomy of educational systems, especially as it relates to Protestant and Orthodox organizations, and the autonomy of universities and the associations of citizens to pursue their chosen objectives. Another key element of Eötvös's thought was the role of education in enabling citizens to participate in political activities, in the transition from a traditional to a modern society and in supporting gradualist reform initiatives rather than revolutionary actions. A third element was clearly his contribution to the understanding of nationality rights. As this chapter has indicated, Eötvös made a major contribution to the attempt to resolve this issue in the Habsburg Empire. A fourth evident concept of his thought relates to the principle of constitutional federalism. In his political treatises, and in his role in the negotiations leading to the Settlement, the idea of several levels of political authority based on a constitutional structure, and autonomy for self-governing territories, is clearly evident. A fifth aspect of his political thought is his conception of the modern state and his analysis of the French Revolution, suggesting an affinity with the thought of Alexis de Tocqueville, and his critique of nationalism, absolutism and communism.

Notes

1 Devescovi Balázs, *Eötvös József (1813-71)*, Magyarok emlékezete (Pozsony: Kalligram, 2007), 7.
2 Michael Hurst, 'Joseph Eötvös and the Modernisation [sic] of Hungary, 1840-70: A Study of Ideas of Individuality and Social Pluralism in Modern Politics. By Paul Bödy. Transactions of the American Philosophical Society: New Series - vol. LXII, pt. 2, 1972. Pp. 134. $5', *The Historical Journal* 18, no. 3 (1975): 659.
3 Eötvös to his son, Loránd Eötvös, March 28, 1866. Devescovi, *Eötvös József,* 15.
4 Eötvös József, *Arcképek és programok* [Portraits and Programmes], Eötvös József művei (Budapest: Magyar Helikon, 1975), 219.
5 Eötvös József, *A Karthausi* (Budapest: Révai Testvérek, 1901), 508.
6 Eötvös to László Szalay, 19 December 1837. Eötvös József, *Levelek* [Letters], Eötvös József művei (Budapest: Magyar Helikon, Budapest, 1976), 120.
7 Eötvös József, *Tanulmányok* [Essays], Báró Eötvös József összes munkái, vol. 12 (Budapest: Révai Testvérek, 1902), 102.
8 Cf. H.D. Inglis, *A Journey throughout Ireland during the spring, summer and autumn of 1834*; Henry Hallam, *The Constitutional History of England*; John Lingard, *The History of England*; and the works of Edward Clarendon.
9 Baron József Eötvös, *Poverty in Ireland 1837: A Hungarian View* (Dublin: Phaeton, 2014).
10 Eötvös, *Tanulmányok*, 129.
11 Eötvös József, *Reform és hazafiság: publicisztikai írások* [Reform and Patriotism: Publicistic Writings], Eötvös József művei (Budapest: Magyar Helikon, 1978), 1:228.
12 Eötvös, *Reform és hazafiság*, 1:330.
13 Called centralists (*centralisták*) by the majority of Hungarian historians. - Ed.
14 'The criticism of the system of politics and public life based on the county, [...] made the centralists seem a viable force for Metternich to work with, at least in pushing Kossuth aside. In mid-1844 the publisher of *Pesti Hírlap*, a confidant of the government, provoked the resignation of Kossuth, and his post was offered to Szalay'. László Kontler, *A History of Hungary* (Budapest: Atlantisz Publishing House, 2009), 255. - Ed.
15 Eötvös, *Reform és hazafiság*, 1:579-80.
16 Eötvös to Count László Teleki, 11 February 1848. Eötvös, *Levelek,* 189-90.
17 Eötvös to Count István Széchenyi, 28 February 1848. Eötvös, *Levelek,* 205-6.

18 Eötvös József, *Az 1848iki forradalom története—Müncheni vázlat* [History of the Revolution of 1848—Munich Draft], Eötvös József Történeti és Állambölcseleti Művei (Budapest: Argumentum, 1993), 51-2.
19 Eötvös, *Az 1848iki forradalom története—Müncheni vázlat*, 163-4.
20 Eötvös, *Az 1848iki forradalom története—Müncheni vázlat*, 163-4.
21 Baron Joseph Eötvös [N. N., pseud.], *Ueber die Gleichberechtigung der Nationalitäten in Oesterreich* [On the Equal Rights of Nationalities in Austria] (Pest: Hartleben, 1850), 16-17.
22 Eötvös, *Ueber die Gleichberechtigung der Nationalitäten in Oesterreich*, 17.
23 Eötvös, *Ueber die Gleichberechtigung der Nationalitäten in Oesterreich*, 124.
24 It was also published at the same time in German under the title: *Der Einfluß der herrschenden Ideen des 19. Jahrhunderts auf den Staat*.
25 Baron Joseph Eötvös, *Der Einfluss der herrschenden Ideen des 19. Jahrhunderts auf den Staat* [The Influence of the Ruling Ideas of the 19th Century on the State] (Leipzig: Brockhaus, 1854), 1:254.
26 Alexis de Tocqueville, *Correspondance étrangère d'Alexis de Tocqueville* [Foreign Correspondence of Alexis de Toqueville], Œuvres complètes, vol. 7 (Paris: Gallimard, 1986), 364-365.
27 Eötvös, *Der Einfluss der herrschenden Ideen des 19*, 2:332.
28 Eötvös, *Der Einfluss der herrschenden Ideen des 19*, 2:395.
29 Eötvös, *Der Einfluss der herrschenden Ideen des 19*, 2:491-2.
30 *The Westminster Review: January and April 1855*, New Series 7 (London: Chapman, 1855), 230-1.
31 'Foreign Affairs: Austria and Hungary', *The Rambler*, New Series 5, (September 1861), 411-24, 416.
32 Galántai József, *Nemzet és kisebbség Eötvös József életművében* [Nation and Minority in the Oeuvre of József Eötvös] (Budapest: Korona, 1995), 155-7.
33 Paul Bődy, *Joseph Eötvös and the Modernization of Hungary 1840-70* (New York: East European Monographs, 1985), 104-8.
34 Bődy, *Joseph Eötvös and the Modernization of Hungary 1840-70*, 109-10.

13

Baron Zsigmond Kemény (1814-75)

Ferenc Hörcher

Family background and childhood

Zsigmond Kemény was the son of a Transylvanian aristocratic family who lived the life of a nineteenth-century bourgeois as a writer and journalist, and was of a pragmatic, liberal-conservative persuasion, which raised him into the political elite during the turbulent years of reform and revolution in Hungary. He had a major political impact in the period that led up to the Settlement with Austria in 1867, which created the dual Austro-Hungarian monarchy.[1]

Kemény had a markedly Transylvanian self-perception.[2] Having studied the legal, constitutional and cultural traditions of this principality, a quasi-independent province of the Habsburg Empire, in what is today the western and central part of Romania, he had a deep-rooted, somewhat pessimistic, historically informed knowledge of its misfortunes. He never forgot that it had once been a quasi-independent principality in the early modern period, due to the Turkish invasion of the central parts of the Kingdom of Hungary, which divided the remaining part of the country into the Habsburg territories and the Transylvanian Principality. It had enjoyed a comparative autonomy until Kemény's own days, having been largely governed by its own, ethnic Hungarian, aristocratic elite. The name of the aristocratic Kemény family was well known among the Hungarian political elite of Transylvania, who had a traditional political culture which was persistently different from that of the elite of the Hungarian Kingdom.

The branch of the family that Zsigmond belonged to, however, had become relatively impoverished by the time he was born. Biographers usually cite this financial insecurity to explain the fact that as an adult, Baron Kemény had to earn his living as a professional journalist and fiction writer, although it may also have been due to his rather dissolute manner, as he mismanaged his own financial affairs. These circumstances resulted in him leading a characteristic, nineteenth-century gentry-bourgeois lifestyle, which oscillated between an industriousness which was quite rare among Hungarian aristocrats and a somewhat intemperate nightlife which was typical of certain representatives of the social elite. He never married or had children, and from very early on struggled with a propensity to depression.

Politics is highly context-dependent. Politicians, political analysts and political thinkers alike, can only draw on the existing institutional and cultural settings and the material and immaterial resources of the political community they belong to when they form their views or plan their actions. Local circumstances thus need to be considered before making an attempt to understand the thought of a particular political actor.

In Zsigmond Kemény's case, his family's historical pedigree was a crucial matter.[3] One of his ancestors, János Kemény (1607–62), served as the prince of the Transylvanian Principality for one year, before being killed by the Turks in battle. Zsigmond himself was born in 1814 in the village of Alvincz (today Vinţu de Jos, Romania), to the second wife of his father, Sámuel Kemény. After the early death of his father in 1823, when Zsigmond was only nine years old, a long process of litigation started within his family over the remaining family assets. As a result of the protracted legal procedures, he would lose much of his inheritance. From the year of his father's death, 1823, until 1834, Zsigmond studied at the famous college of Nagyenyed, run by the Reformed Church. Nagyenyed was a prestigious school of learning, not far from Gyulafehérvár, the administrative centre of the province, and former seat of the prince. He lived in the famous headquarters of the family in Nagyenyed called the *Burg*, together with other members of the family who were also attending the same school at the same time.

Two of his tutors are typically mentioned by name in his biographies: Sámuel Köteles, a philosopher with Kantian convictions, and Károly Szász, a professor of law, who later became a close friend of his bright disciple. They belonged to two opposite types of college professors of the age. Köteles had an abstract, theoretical style. Szász, on the other hand, was not only a historically minded law professor, but a passionate and active representative of opposition politics in Transylvania which defended the laws and customs of the principality against encroachments by the officials of the Vienna Court. Szász was also a firm believer in the practical use of science and an avid reader of literature, including the leading lights of both the contemporary French and German Romantic movements.

The Transylvanian context

Kemény's real and practical political education, however, was acquired on the battlefield of parliamentary politics. As a young man, he took part in two eventful Transylvanian Diets of the reform age, one of which convened in Kolozsvár in 1834, while the other took place in 1837 in Nagyszeben. Diets were indeed the true preparatory schools for politicians in nineteenth-century Hungary and Transylvania itself, which had its own provincial Diet. Kemény learnt his lessons at the side of the national hero, Miklós Wesselényi, the charismatic and uncompromising leader of the opposition, in the camp including Dénes Kemény, János Bethlen Sr. and Károly Szász, all of them fighting along the lines of the traditional policy of grievances against Habsburg misrule.[4] The national-liberal lessons he learnt there held that the schisms that beset the opposition occurred because the less daring were not ready to follow the radical initiatives of Wesselényi.[5]

One of his own early published writings reveals his vivid interest in the politics of sixteenth-century Hungary, when the battle of Mohács led to the occupation of large parts of the country, together with Buda, the royal seat, by the Ottoman Turks, followed by the division of the remaining territories among the Habsburgs and the newly established Principality of Transylvania. His views on the tragic fall of the Hungarian Kingdom at Mohács were collected under the title *A mohácsi veszedelem okairól* (On the Reasons of the Peril at Mohács, 1838).

This work was only published, however, after Kemény had absorbed a second series of practical lessons in politics. Kemény summarized his impressions of the second Diet he had witnessed in a general overview of the political life of Transylvania between 1791 and 1849. The following quote from that summary is instructive:

> If we compare the spirit of the seven Diets that have been held since 1834 until the outbreak of the revolution, as far as their wit and calculation were concerned, we shall hand the palm to the one in 1837. During its course, no party won unconditionally above the other [. . .] yet by its end all of them had less irritation in their bosom because of the past, and more hope in the future.[6]

As he saw it, the absent Wesselényi made compromise among members of the opposition against the Habsburgs easier to achieve as a result of his efforts at the Transylvanian Diets.

After holding minor positions in public administration in Marosvásárhely and later in Kolozsvár, in 1838 Kemény left for Vienna where he remained for two years, in order to compose himself following a disappointing love affair.[7] In Vienna he studied medicine (especially anatomy and pathology), apparently without enrolling at the university.[8] It was during his stay in Vienna that he first experimented with novel writing, working on his lost first novel, *Izabella királyné és a remete* (Queen Izabella and the Hermit).

At the political crossroads

In the 1840s, Transylvania, just like the Kingdom of Hungary itself, experienced an unprecedented ferment of reform efforts originating from the opposition. Kemény once again joined their ranks after a short visit to Pest-Buda, where also he met with some of the prominent leaders of the opposition.[9] However, the form of political participation he chose this time was very characteristic of him: with a friend, Lajos Kovács, he became the co-editor of Sámuel Méhes's political journal, the *Erdélyi Híradó* (Transylvanian News). This turned out to be an exceptionally powerful position, since the timing of the move was ideal, with political journalism on the rise in the country. As a talented writer, Kemény was involved from the outset, allowing him to build an unparalleled reputation.[10] He played a major role in defining the style of journalism in Transylvania, establishing the genre of the opinionated columnist.

As a journalist, he became an important voice of opposition politics in his homeland. The synthetic reform programme he defended was not so much a new one but one which was embedded in a comprehensive philosophical and historical framework. It included

> the gradual abolition of the *urbarium* in order to liberate serfs from their obligations, the reform of the tax system in order to extend public burdens to the nobility and the aristocracy, the introduction of a modern civil code, an administrative reform with the reorganization of the relationships between the governorate (*gubernium*) and local authorities, freedom of press, Hungarian as the official language of the kingdom, the introduction of a tolerant policy with the nationalities, and the union between Transylvania and Hungary.[11]

The real depth of Kemény's perspective was not yet clear to most of his readers, but his work *Kodifikáció és históriai iskola* (Codification and the Historical School, 1842) proves that by that time he had grown into an original political strategist who was already able to identify the major trends in the legal thinking of his day.[12] As opposed to the then-fashionable radical position demanding codification along Benthamite lines, Kemény backed a view which was closer to the organic concept of constitutional development, based on unwritten customs and acceptance of Roman law, as presented by Savigny and others. His was a brave thesis, running against the spirit of opposition politics, which sought short-term redresses to the serious encroachments Vienna had made against the rights of the nobility, under the pressure of the day. He did not share the somewhat naïve optimism of Benthamite utilitarianism, the nineteenth-century variation of enlightened rationalism. Kemény's starting point was closer to Burke than to Bentham on both the social and the political issues of the day, even at that time, although his pre-1848 position cannot be deemed conservative in the traditional sense of favouring limited reform only in order to avoid more radical changes. In the pre-1848 era his was a consistently reformist agenda, but he never went so far as to require the artificial restructuring of the whole social body or a radical reconstruction of the whole constitutional system. Kemény feared that such a drastic intervention might have unintended economic and financial consequences, which could lead to mass tumult and the outpouring of unbridled political passions, both of which could result in untamed aggression and very probably lead to civil war. In this respect he was a very early believer in the pessimistic vision of István Széchenyi in the 1840s, who berated the radical reformers for opening a pandora's box of problems with their confrontational approach to both the court and the ethnic minorities in Hungary.

Kemény's early scepticism is illustrated by an unfinished series of articles published in two stages in 1843, in which he made a rather sweeping criticism of the way political campaigns were conducted in the Kingdom of Hungary. This unfinished opus is known by the title *Korteskedés és ellenszerei* (Canvassing and its Antidotes).[13]

The portrait of the young Kemény would be incomplete without mentioning his adventures in fiction, including in the pre-1848 period. He was inspired to write by his own emotional life: by his failures in his love affairs (*Élet és ábránd*, Life and fantasia, [unfinished], 1842-4) or as a journal editor (*A hírlapszerkesztő naplója*, The Diary of the Newspaper Editor [unfinished], 1844–5). The book he first finished, however

(*Gyulai Pál*, Pál Gyulai, 1845-7), was a tragic story set in the sixteenth century, in Kemény's favourite era, when Hungarian history itself turned tragic.

Kemény's position in the pre-1848 Hungarian opposition

By the end of 1845, Kemény had gained the impression that his room for manoeuvre was being radically narrowed in Transylvania. He began to consider how to move to the Kingdom of Hungary and continue his journalistic activity there. He had several options to choose from, as his arrival was forestalled by his reputation, which brought with it a certain celebrity status. Clearly, before he made his choice, he also had to consider practical issues – financial and logistical matters. However, his choice was basically a strategic one: he had to ally himself with one of the power centres within or outside the opposition.[14]

He had to consider the invitation from Count Gyula Andrássy to establish a new journal, as well as the temptation to join the circle of the cautious but also very practically oriented aristocratic reformer, Széchenyi, as urged by his friend Lajos Kovács. Further options also existed. Kemény could have joined in with Széchenyi's effort in 1846 to establish a middle-of-the-road party centred on a new journal, with Deák as its leader, whom Kemény had earlier called the most suitable candidate to lead the opposition. A title had already been chosen for the journal, *Független* (Independent). Yet Deák himself decided to follow Kossuth, and both Deák and Wesselényi urged Kemény to join Kossuth's ever widening and ever more radical circle. Kemény even had an offer from the conservative aristocrat, Count Emil Dessewffy, who also suggested establishing a new party, which would also need a new journal to spread its message around the country. Finally, Kemény decided to join the *Pesti Hírlap* (Pest Gazette), the journal edited by Eötvös's circle, who were known as centralists or centralizers, a group of highly educated intellectuals, united by their common effort to mediate between the different groups of the opposition and even between the opposition and the Vienna Court. In 1843, Eötvös famously and repeatedly wrote to Metternich, offering to cooperate with the court to push through certain reform policies which he claimed would be acceptable for Vienna.[15] Although Metternich did not return this favour, the better-informed, well-positioned and nobility-controlled officials across the country kept gossiping that the moderate opposition was permitted to take over the *Pesti Hírlap* as a result of this interaction. Kemény's decision to choose the *Pesti Hírlap* might also have been motivated by his personal sympathies with the members of the Eötvös circle. They offered him a rather satisfactory honorarium (1,000 forints for twenty-four articles a year). This salary was equal to the one received by Eötvös, Szalay and Trefort, and as such it raised him up to the small circle of the best and most highly honoured journalists of the country.[16] Kemény did not fear the risk of joining this circle in 1847, as the different wings of the opposition were joining forces and many of them now agreed on the strategic aims of the *Pesti Hírlap*.[17] Both the municipalists (who defended the county system) and the centralists (in favour of an administrative reform, based on the idea of a centralized state run by a responsible government) decided to coordinate their attacks on the court in the Diet of 1847 and to overlook the differences that had earlier prevented cooperation, and thus the internal conflict around the *Pesti Hirlap* was resolved.

Journalist and MP in 1848-9

The year 1848 saw the birth of the political regime of modern Hungary, with the establishment of a Parliament based on the principle of popular representation and a government which was primarily responsible to the Parliament rather than the court in Vienna. All these institutional innovations led to the transformations of the feudal order, which could only be achieved thanks to the reforming spirit spreading across Europe. This mood climaxed in the revolutions of 1848. A further factor in the success of the reform movement was the activity of the practical political genius of Kossuth. His tactical moves secured the passage of what became known as the April Laws, with the support of Archduke Stephen Francis Victor (the last palatine of Hungary, who convinced the court to pass the bills of the Hungarian Diet) and with the remarkable self-restraint of the nobility, which acceded to the abrupt changes.[18]

Free elections led to the convocation of the Parliament and the formation of a responsible government led by Count Lajos Batthyány, which started to put the spirit of the April Laws into practice. Yet – in spite of the fact that Metternich and with him the hated establishment of the *ancien regime* had been expelled – Habsburg rule was very soon restored in Austria and with the direct attack of the army of the Croatian military leader Count Josip Jelačić and the involvement of the Russian tsar's troops, the 'lawful revolution' of Hungary was overwhelmed. It is not the task of this chapter to give an account of the events of 1848-9. Even so, in order to make sense of the obvious shift in the discourse of Kemény in this period, it might be helpful to recall the three pivotal phases of the Hungarian Revolution of 1848-9:

1. April 1848 saw the peaceful constitutional innovation of the April Laws, setting up a representative national assembly and a government responsible to the assembly, but still preserving the personal union with Austria within the framework of the ancient constitution.
2. The military campaign against the new regime, which began as early as 1848, led to a war of independence and the resignation of Batthyány and his government.
3. Kossuth proclaimed the Declaration of Independence in 1849, separating the two realms of Austria and Hungary.

This background of the political history of the revolution explains some of the apparent inconsistencies, or even antagonistic contrasts, in Kemény's thought before and after the revolution. As a respectable journalist, Kemény, and the organ he wrote for, the *Pesti Hirlap*, of which he became co-editor alongside Antal Csengery in May 1848, both fully supported the changes which were brought about by the April Laws.[19] He wrote his journal articles – both under his name and anonymously – as an advocate of the reforms. Yet he witnessed the constant radicalization of the reformers and had good reasons to fear a parallel shift towards a reactionary position in Vienna. While the most famous members of the government, including Eötvös, Széchenyi, Batthyány and Deák, soon realized that they would be unable to go along with the radicalization of the regime, Kemény persisted in his capacity as a member of the Peace Party.[20]

There are two overall points which need to be stressed about Kemény's participation in the events of the revolution. One is that he never held a major or leading role in the establishment, he was only involved in the struggle as a lower-ranked member of the state administration (he became a councillor of the Ministry of Interior) or as an elected representative. The other is that he always belonged to the circle known as the *Békepárt* (Peace Party), which tried to negotiate between the opposing camps of the court and the new Hungarian government. They were unable to stop Windischgrätz and his army from attacking the capital, but they succeeded in bringing down László Madarász, a radical revolutionary. Kemény was among those who – behind closed doors – raised objections against the imminent declaration of independence in April 1849, but the next day he, too, remained silent, instead of publicly objecting to it.

After the defeat of the revolution, he and his friend hid for some time, but in December 1849, Kemény turned himself in to the police in Pest-Buda. A long investigation was launched to uncover his role in the revolution, which finished with his acquittal two years later.

The great counter-revolutionary pamphlets

It was in his famous post-revolutionary essays (*Forradalom után* [After the Revolution], 1850 and *Még egy szó a forradalom után* [One More Word After the Revolution], 1851) that Kemény gave a detailed account of his own position during the revolutionary period in the context of a critical assessment of the radicalization of the regime itself. Partly under the pressure of the official accusations he was facing from the authorities, he was also somewhat self-critical, but basically represented himself from the very start as a critic of the events, as well as of its radical leader, Kossuth. As his friend and co-editor, Antal Csengery wrote in a letter on 27 July 1850: 'Kemény wrote a work with the title *After the Revolution*. Its direction is: to let the state of siege be finished [. . .] Often he is sharp with those views announced by those close to him and to his own earlier views, to the extent of becoming unjust. I fear [. . .] that it will have the opposite effect than what he expected.'[21] Kemény's scapegoating of Kossuth was also rather exaggerated and as such morally dubious.

In spite of all the shortcomings they reveal about his private morality, these writings are recognized as among the most enduring pieces of nineteenth-century Hungarian theoretical reflections on politics and history. There is a consistency in their author's position, even if it stemmed from unheroic or even selfish motives. The framework of these ambitious, 'big picture'-narratives remained constitutional modernization, illustrated by this quote from 1848: 'Thanks to God's grace, instead of a mass excluded from rights we have, right now, 12 million citizens.'[22] On the other hand, there is nothing surprising in his condemnation of revolutionary changes: what made him wary of radicalism was always the danger of a mass uprising. In May 1848, he wrote:

'What was earlier regarded as a dream, wants to become real, what was proclaimed by fanatics (*rajongók*), is demanded now by the masses, and that utopia which was earlier the extreme liberty of ideas, now becomes the Jesuitism of ideas, and in the hands of a Barbes, a Blanqui gives the sharpest arms against order and public peace.'[23]

Kemény employed very powerful rhetorical devices to convince his readers of the relevance of these reality checks in politics. He returned to the concept of sobriety (*józanság*), as the key virtue of the Hungarian people. '[H]ere I talk only about political tranquility, and about the sober senses (*józan értelem*) of the Hungarian people, and about those elevated moral virtues which hold it back from all the sins covered by the robe of fanaticism and patriotism, from all those atrocities, which are usually committed at other places in similar circumstances.'[24] This reference to sobriety and peacefulness serves to prepare the way for the key statement: 'Hungary's closer relationship with the Monarchy is by now a finished fact.'[25] This is a strong claim to make straight after what was, by then, being called a revolution against the 'lawful king' and which finally led to the Declaration of Independence. Kemény wanted his readers to accept the premise that the people of Hungary are by their nature peaceful and sober. If they fell into such an internal conflict, it was either with good reason or under the incitement of a demagogue.

For him, historical continuity itself had an intrinsic value, one which is hard to neglect. 'I find it the misfortune of a nation if the historical threads are broken in its institutions and its public life.'[26] He also valued the peaceful cohabitation of the different historical groups within society. His views on the nationalities living within the borders of the kingdom were somewhat different from that of the mainstream representatives of national liberalism. As a Transylvanian, he thought that the presence of a wide variety of nationalities was also part of the tradition of the country.[27] As an Anglophile, he was keenly aware of the British efforts at social reform, beginning with the Reform Act of 1832. He thought that the birth of the middle classes could serve as the glue of social cohesion and that it could also help the nobility to accommodate to the new social-economic environment. Kemény succeeded in linking his post-Romantic historicism, which was also rooted in Savigny's historical school of law, with the nineteenth-century British model of moderate modernization based on a middle-class–dominated society and led by a system of parliamentary representation.

As regards the validity of his long-term judgement, Kemény was right to argue in favour of the Settlement. Almost half a century of peaceful development was made possible by it, bringing an unparalleled market boom and the blossoming of a number of economic, social and cultural sectors.

Key concepts of Kemény, the liberal-conservative thinker

Kemény's post-1849 political vision can be outlined with the help of a few key concepts.[28] Of all of the recurring phrases used by Kemény, *súlyegyen* (meaning balance or equilibrium) was one of the most frequent, and its importance is recognized in the secondary literature.[29] The focus on this term is partly explained by the fact that it already had an old-fashioned overtone in Kemény's days. However, there are more substantial reasons why he frequently made use of the term, and why later scholars have focused on this term in order to understand his thinking, aware that he used *súlyegyen* in the context of internal politics just as much as in his repeated analyses of European politics. Kemény's Aristotelian idea was that to achieve peace in both of these fields one had to find that delicate balance which can lead to a socio-political standstill. In other words, he strove to accelerate the shift from a zero-sum game to a game of cooperation and coordination. In his studies on the history of the Transylvanian Principality, he learnt how deals were made with two opposing great powers, the Habsburgs and the Ottoman Empire who threatened the principality. Along the same lines, but in terms of domestic politics, the peaceful coexistence of the institutional self-governments of the different national groups (symbolically expressed in the treaty of the three 'nations', the Hungarian and the Szekler nobility and the privileged Saxon burghertum, entitled *Unio Trium Nationum*, in 1438) was a necessity in Transylvania, and useful parallels might also be drawn with international relations in his own era. Kemény regarded both these internal and external approaches inherited from Transylvania's past as useful ways to achieve balance and compromise.

There was yet another recurring theme in Kemény's characteristic political discourses. As he saw it, fruitful political leadership depended on sobriety, the ability to remain calm in tense situations and to overcome the natural instincts and inclinations which often divert human action, and which especially capture the imagination of the masses, at moments when they need to act or encourage them to act in hopeless situations. Mass psychology is vulnerable to enthusiasm (*rajongás*), a term Kemény seems to have borrowed from post-revolutionary British political thought, and in particular, from the writings of the Earl of Shaftesbury.[30] According to one of his critics, enthusiasm is another keyword in Kemény's vocabulary.[31] It appears as an explanatory tool in his post-revolutionary writings, as well as in his novels, in particular in *Rajongók* (The Enthusiasts, 1859). József Takáts established the connection between his criticism of populist enthusiasm as the main obstacle facing a sober type of politics aiming at achieving balance, and his appreciation of early modern British political thought, including that of Shaftesbury, Hume and Macaulay.[32] I myself have tried to show that his Anglophilia had a strong Scottish dimension.[33] It is essential to grasp, in the present overview, that in Kemény's theoretical language, balance is the aim of political leadership, and the most important obstacle to achieving it is enthusiasm, most apparent in mass psychology, and the subsequent revolt of the masses. The best form of self-defence against the temptations of enthusiasm is sobriety, which may be achieved by the virtue of moderation.[34]

Kemény also mentions yet another of the cardinal virtues, that of prudence or practical wisdom, an invaluable guide in the realm of *Realpolitik*: 'Let us expect and have hope of everything from our vigilance (*éberségünk*), industriousness (*iparkodásaink*) and prudence (*eszélyességünk*).'[35]

Popular leaders with significant public support are usually unable to maintain a certain level of self-control, lacking the guidance in their actions provided by a sense of reality and political balance. This is the cause of Kemény's tragic view of human fate, of the catastrophes in the early modern history of the Hungarian Kingdom, repeated in 1849, and this crushing disappointment led to a mental breakdown at the end of his life.

Novels, journalism and political portraits

Kemény spent the long years of neo-absolutism, spanning the period from the fall of the revolution in 1849 to the hard-won Settlement of 1867, writing in various genres. He published a series of novels and short stories during this time, together with major portraits, among others, of two of his most beloved contemporary statesmen (István Széchenyi and Miklós Wesselényi) while working as one of the most influential political columnists and editors of the period. This variety of literary genres may seem surprising, but it can be explained by Kemény's conviction that one of the key issues in the political culture of the Hungarian Kingdom is a lack of a properly functioning public sphere. This lack was due to a lack of an adequate widespread public erudition and therefore intellectuals had a responsibility to educate a new reading public. Obviously, this is an old humanist and enlightened ideal, but in the second half of the nineteenth century it was also a recognition of the ever more burning social issues of the day. In a country where illiteracy was still prevalent, and where even among the lower strata of the nobility there were some who had problems with written communication, encouraging the emergence of the middle classes was impossible without public education. It was Kemény's friend and fellow statesman, József Eötvös, who somewhat later, shortly after the 1867 Settlement, introduced a state programme of elementary education as minister of culture and education. Kemény never received such a high position in the executive, yet he, too, embarked on his own personal project of educating his readers – by his own writings.

His great, post-romantic novels had no direct political messages, however. Instead, they served as illustrated lessons of the costs of blind enthusiasm and a missing reality check in different historical contexts. The social issues addressed included romantic relationships between women and men (*A szív örvényei* [Swirls of the Heart], 1851, *Férj és nő* [Husband and Wife], 1852), as well as what was called by his monographer 'romantic irony' (*Ködképek a kedély láthatárán* [Blurry Pictures on the Horizon of One's Temperament], 1853) and 'an effort to overcome romanticism' (*Özvegy és leánya* [The Widow and Her Daughter], 1855). As time passed his stories became even gloomier, as he became convinced that tragedy was inevitable, whether it be on the individual level (*A rajongók* [Fanatics], 1858), or the tragedy of 'communal existence' (*Zord idő* [Murky Times], 1862).[36]

Kemény's novels seem to suggest a profound pessimism about the inability of human beings to control the irresistible inclinations of their nature. As a journalist, however, he tried to keep the conclusions of his analyses in balance, without suggesting that the communal trauma of 1849 could never be healed. In his journal articles, such as the series entitled *Élet és irodalom* (Life and Literature), from October 1852, and *Szellemi tér* (Spiritual Space), from August 1853, Kemény worked out a programme for how to cultivate the minds and hearts of readers through the reading of novels.[37] His effort to connect the two faces of his creative writing found its true home at the *Pesti*

Napló, where he worked along the lines of a wide-ranging programme of 'sentimental education'.[38]

It is also true, however, that his actual political journalism did not often address domestic politics directly, particularly not in the 1850s, for obvious tactical reasons. Instead, he provided interesting commentaries on European affairs. All his careful analyses helped him to prepare the public for the actual process of negotiation which led to the Settlement with Austria. The Hungarian public attributed the success of the Settlement fully to Deák. Yet Deák could not have done it if the ground had not been prepared by – among others, but perhaps most influentially – the journalism of Kemény, as has been pointed out by Pál Gyulai, in his eulogy of Kemény.[39]

One way this preparatory work could be accomplished was by publishing his marvellous portraits of two friends, Wesselényi and Széchenyi, who had been reference points for him since his early years. The two of them belonged to an earlier generation, and they were both masters of Kemény in the political life of the two homelands. While he remained a great admirer of them, he felt that he had to reinterpret his view of them in light of the post-1849 political situation. What he did with Wesselényi was to show how far Wesselényi remained a captive of his illusions, a tragic form of daydreaming, and how he fell victim to his own passions, finally being betrayed even by Kossuth. On the other hand, his portrait of Széchenyi, still alive in the days when Kemény wrote about him, did not simply focus on the fall of Széchenyi in his political rivalry with Kossuth, but repositioned him from a political leader to an intellectual innovator, who was able to offer a vision of the possible future of the country and its people, through his commercial, infrastructural and cultural initiatives.

Kemény's rich literary output is linked to the fact that the wider context of his work beyond the *Pesti Napló* was the literary Deák circle. This was a friendly circle of authors of varying ranks, together with critics and journalists, including Kemény, Antal Csengery, Ferenc Salamon, Pál Gyulai, Károly Szász and József Lévay.[40] This was the intellectual environment in which Kemény made his home, and he enjoyed especially good relations with Pál Gyulai, the charismatic literary critic. In a sense, Kemény was the ideological centre of the group, while the circle provided him with ammunition in his ongoing struggle.

Kemény and Deák – Negotiating the 1867 Settlement

A settlement with Austria required the support of both the Hungarian and the Vienna elites and public. This could not, therefore, be a zero-sum game, which is the usual mentality between two long time, seemingly antagonistic opponents. It took some time for both parties to decipher this, but Kemény played a crucial role in this shift in attitudes.

Deák was generally regarded as perhaps the most substantial, and certainly the most influential statesman in contemporary Hungary. Yet he was a rather cautious politician, and he needed the practical support of people like Kemény. The latter, as the editor of the most influential paper of the day, could bring him to the attention of the public, which would have been otherwise cut off from the behind-the-door political debates of the day, in the dynamically changing inner circles of the regime of the young Francis Joseph. In fact, the division of labour between Deák and Kemény worked very well. One can argue that their tandem activity was an exceptional example of cooperation in Hungarian political history. Gusztáv Beksics was right when he claimed that: 'The statesman of the period of the Settlement was Deák, its journalist was Kemény. The common effect of the two was the unfolding of '67, which was not only the work of Deák, but also that of Kemény.'[41]

The reason why this cooperation between a politician and a journalist became crucial was that public opinion in Hungary was for a long time opposed to any kind of compromise with the absolutist ruler. The charisma of Lajos Kossuth was still alive, even though the leader of the War of Independence was forced into exile for the remainder of his life after 1849. On the other hand, the newspaper columns by Kemény on external affairs also had their impact – they helped the Hungarian political elite to realize that the room for manoeuvre of the emperor was becoming constrained in Europe. The German unification process was also certainly followed closely in Hungarian debates, and a further threat was posed by the Italian efforts of unification, due to the progressive successes of Garibaldi's movement. After a futile attempt in 1860 to break the stalemate by Vienna's October Diploma, the February Patent made it obvious in the circles around the emperor, too, that it was necessary to make a deal with the Hungarians. Deák's Easter Article, published by Kemény in his *Pesti Napló*, served as a signal that started a two-year-long negotiation process, which resulted in the Settlement of 1867.

As described in this article, the premises of the negotiations on the Hungarian side were the following: the unity of the empire, based on the Pragmatic Sanction in 1723; the preservation of the principles of the April Laws in an intact form; and finally, an exclusion of the possibility of integrating the kingdom into a unified and centralized empire. Yet the main point was that Hungarian sovereignty required the preservation of the historical constitution of the country.

All these principles, proposed by Deák, were in agreement with the views first presented by Kemény in his pragmatic post-revolutionary writings. And it was Kemény, too, who suggested first that both the external and the internal political conditions (the weakening international position of Austria in the German and Italian unification process, the threat of the nationalities in the kingdom, the waning role of the nobility) made it possible to make the deal. However, a large part of the public found it difficult to come to terms with the fact that there was a need to take one step back from the stance of the April Laws of 1848. This is why both Deák and Kemény experienced hostile gestures, including physical threats, even before the Settlement was signed. In a letter dated February 1867, Kemény complained: 'Generally speaking, I do not find the overall situation reassuring. Among us, Deák has received more than one letter, in which he is threatened to be killed. I, too, have received three messages of intimidation: I gave them to László, my manservant, to let him enjoy it.'[42] However, they did not seem to have changed their minds and did not withdraw. Even after the Settlement, Kemény was ready to enter into a fierce debate with Kossuth over the evaluation of the Settlement. However, neither he nor Deák wanted to take up a position in the new establishment's regime, as if they were the Moses and Aaron of the great Hungarian historical march from the April Laws to the Settlement.

Mental breakdown and legacy

Kemény's personal life was never in balance. He was a man of passions, prone to mental breakdowns. After a very difficult and troubled childhood he had some rather unfortunate love affairs as a youth. Later, too, as a bachelor, he lived a rather unsettled and hectic life, resembling someone who might now be diagnosed as bipolar, with periods of intense activity, enjoying the night life of the capital to the full, while at other times he was in a rather depressive state, unable to work or socialize. The letter from 1867 just quoted finishes with the following sentence: 'I have never lived in a more unsuitable time than this present one.'[43] Despite his activity in 1848-9, his novels and his political journalism, which eventually brought success, leading to the Settlement with Austria, he remained unhappy and spiritually broken. He remained unsatisfied with the result of the Settlement, and in particular with the output of the Hungarian political elite. His nervous breakdown ended his professional career; he lived the last years of his life in lunacy and was taken back by his younger brother to his beloved Transylvania, to the small settlement of Pusztakamarás and spent his final years like one of the tragic heroes of his novels. This fact led one of his interpreters to the conclusion that in fact his analysis of the economy of human passions and his programme of restraint and sobriety turned out to be itself too ideological, and therefore doomed to fail. In this sense, his mental decline ironically proved his own thesis of the power of irrational impulses in human life.[44]

It is not surprising that Kemény is remembered as a counter-revolutionary thinker, given the nature of his post-1849 writings. It was Gábor Halász, who, in his essay on the Hungarian Victorians, claimed that Kemény embodied the Burkeian tradition of conservatism.[45] The post-revolutionary Kemény also figured as an important voice in Gyula Szekfű's grand narrative. During the decades of Communist rule, little was written about him as he was regarded as a public enemy and his post-revolutionary output was denounced as the low point of his career.[46] Kemény's reputation as a political thinker was growing, however, by 1989, slowly approaching the heights of Eötvös, the accepted champion of political philosophy in nineteenth-century Hungary. Authors as diverse as the philosophers Kristóf Nyíri and M. István Fehér, the intellectual historians József Takáts and Gábor Gángó, as well as the senior literary historians G. Béla Németh and Mihály Szegedy-Maszák and the social scientist Tamás Gusztáv Filep, have argued for a reappraisal of the pamphlets *Forradalom után* and *Még egy szó a forradalom után*.[47] It is therefore perhaps fair to state that these texts have claimed their rightful place in the canon of nineteenth-century political thought. Despite the differences in their interpretations, most scholars reading him today seem to agree: Kemény's achievements as an original and influential political thinker are exceptional and worth further scrutiny.

Notes

1 I will not use the title of Baron in my references to Kemény Zsigmond, although during his lifetime and up to the twentieth century, the aristocratic title was still important in social life.
2 The standard monography on Kemény is still the classic one: Papp Ferencz, *Báró Kemény Zsigmond* [Baron Zsigmond Kemény], 2 vols. (Budapest: MTA, 1922-23). A more modern, less detailed account is: Veress Dániel, *Szerettem a sötétet és szélzúgást: Kemény Zsigmond élete és műve* [I liked darkness and the voice of the wind. The life and work of Zsigmond Kemény] (Kolozsvár-Napoca: Dacia, 1977). For a collection of essays on Kemény, see Szegedy-Maszák Mihály, *Kemény Zsigmond* (Pozsony: Kalligram, 2007). For a recent English language sketch of his life, context and a translation of a short part of his famous essay by Dávid Oláh, see Balázs Trencsényi and Michal Kopeček, eds., *National Romanticism: The Formation of National Movements. Discourses of Collective Identity in Central and Southeast Europe 1770-1945* (Budapest: CEU Press, 2007), 2:455-62.
3 See the mainstream account of Kemény's life and achievements, reviewing his literary and political output in a proper balance: Sőtér István, ed., *A magyar irodalom története* [The History of Hungarian Literature], vol. 4, *A magyar irodalom története 1849-től 1905-ig* [The History of Hungarian Literature from 1849 to 1905] (Budapest: Akadémiai Kiadó, 1965), 243-70. Still relevant for a full assessment of his life and oeuvre, is the classic eulogy by Kemény's associate and collaborator: Gyulai Pál, 'Emlékbeszéd Kemény Zsigmond felett' [Eulogy of Zsigmond Kemény], in *Gyulai Pál válogatott művei*, ed. Hermann István (Budapest: Szépirodalmi Könyvkiadó, 1956), 5:7-22.
4 The policy of grievances was a practice of the Hungarian Diet, of sending written complaints to the ruler about the Vienna Court's disrespect or even violation of the Hungarian constitutional traditions, including traditional liberties.
5 Sőtér, *A magyar irodalom története*, 4:243-70.
6 Kemény Zsigmond, 'Erdély közélete 1791-1849' [The Public Life of Transylvania, 1791-1849], in *Báró Kemény Zsigmond Munkáiból* [From the Works of Baron Zsigmond Kemény], ed. Gyulai Pál (Budapest: Franklin-Társulat, n.d.), 186-264, 259. The hard-won harmony of the opposition parties can be the experience behind his later demand of a unified opposition to the Vienna Court after the loss of 1849.
7 For his work as notary: Papp Ferencz, 'Báró Kemény Zsigmond mint királyi táblai s kormányszéki kanczellista' [Baron Zsigmond Kemény as Notary of the King's Bench and of the Royal Council of Governors], *Irodalomtörténeti Közlemények* 24, no. 2 (1914): 129-40.
8 For his studies of medicine in Vienna, see Pais Dezső, 'B. Kemény Zsigmond a Bécsi Egyetemen' [Baron Zsigmond Kemény at the University of Vienna], *Irodalomtörténeti Közlemények* 21, no. 3 (1911): 328-9.
9 As explained earlier, Hungarian politics in the nineteenth century operated within two institutionally differentiated frameworks: one belonged to the actual Hungarian Kingdom, constitutionally ruled by the ethnically non-Hungarian Habsburg family from Vienna, while the Principality of Transylvania was a separate province of the Habsburg territories, in its south-eastern corner.
10 For an overview of the transformation of the public sphere in nineteenth-century Hungary, see Gergely András and Veliky János, 'A politikai közvélemény fogalma

Magyarországon a XIX. század közepén' [The Concept of Political Public Opinion in Hungary in the Middle of the 19th Century], in *Magyar Történeti Tanulmányok VII*, ed. Fehér András (Debrecen: KLTE, 1974), 5–42.

11   Gábori Kovács József, 'Pártküzdelmek a Pesti Hírlap körül és ezek hatása Kemény Zsigmond pályájára' [Party Struggles Around the Pesti Hírlap and Their Effects on the Career of Zsigmond Kemény], in *Határátlépések: A doktoriskolák III nemzetközi konferenciája, Kolozsvár, 2010. augusztus 26–27.*, ed. Dobos István and Bene Sándor (Budapest: Nemzetközi Magyarságtudományi Társaság, 2011), 145–51.

12   Takáts calls this article 'the sharpest and most sarcastic Hungarian criticism of the rationalist-constructivist branch of liberalism'. Takács József, *Modern magyar politikai eszmetörténet* [History of Modern Hungarian Political Ideas] (Budapest: Osiris Kiadó, 2007), 55.

13   Recent edition in: Kemény Zsigmond, *Változatok a történelemre* [Varieties of History] (Budapest: Szépirodalmi Könyvkiadó, 1982), 5–180.

14   In what follows I draw on two of József Gábori Kovács's accounts: Gábori Kovács, 'Pártküzdelmek a Pesti Hírlap körül és ezek hatása Kemény Zsigmond pályájára', and Gábori Kovács József, 'Kemény Zsigmond útja a Pesti Hírlapig: A centralisták, a municipalisták és Széchenyi hívei vonzásában' [Zsigmond Kemény's Way to the Pesti Hírlap: In the Gravitational Field of the Centralizers, the Municipalists and Széchenyi's Followers], *Irodalomtörténeti Közlemények* 119, no. 4 (2015): 501–27.

15   Gábori Kovács József, '"Kinyilatkoztatom előre, hogy a' régi eretnek vagyok ma is": A centralisták önállósága és integrálódása az 1847-es országgyűlésre való készülődéskor' ['I Declare in Advance, that Even Today I Am Still the Old Heretic': The Autonomy of the Centralists and Their Integration in Preparation for the Diet of 1847], *Századok* 147, no. 5 (2013): 1093–136. A more detailed account of the episode with its evaluation can be found in various works by János Varga, András Gergely and István Fenyő. Particularly interesting is: Veliky János, *A változások kora: Polgári szerepkörök és változáskoncepciók a reformkor második évtizedében* [The Era of Changes: Bourgeois Roles and Concepts of Change in the Second Decade of the Reform Age] (Budapest: Új Mandátum Könyvkiadó, 2009) (Habsburg történeti monográfiák 8.), 83–92. Veliky stresses the secretive nature of Eötvös's encounters with the court.

16   For these details, see Szalay Gábor, ed., *Szalay László levelei* [Letters of László Szalay] (Budapest: Franklin-Társulat, 1913), 113–14. It is worth noting, however, that Kossuth, the favourite of the reading public of the opposition, received an even higher honorarium.

17   For the agreement between these opposition camps towards 1847, see Gábori Kovács, '"Kinyilatkoztatom előre, hogy a' régi eretnek vagyok ma is'.

18   See Ferenc Hörcher, 'Reforming or Replacing the Historical Constitution? Lajos Kossuth and the April Laws of 1848', in *A History of the Hungarian Constitution: Law, Government and Political Culture in Central Europe*, ed. Ferenc Hörcher and Thomas Lorman (London–New York: I. B. Tauris, 2019), 92–121.

19   For his activity as an author and editor of the *Pesti Hirlap* before and during the revolution, see Huszti Tímea, 'Kemény Zsigmond és a Pesti Hírlap' [Zsigmond Kemény and the Pesti Hírlap], in *Miskolci Egyetem Doktoranduszok Fóruma: Bölcsészettudományi Kar szekciókiadványa*, ed. Garadnai Erika and Podlovics Éva Lívia (Miskolc: Miskolci Egyetem Tudományszervezési és Nemzetközi Osztály, 2012), 39–46.

20   Barla Gyula, 'Kemény 1848-ban' [Kemény in 1848], *Studia Litteraria* 1 (1963): 83–100, 85.

21 Quoted by Gyula Tóth in: Kemény, *Változatok a történelemre*, 566–7.
22 *Pesti Hirlap*, 9 May 1848.
23 *Pesti Hirlap*, 31 May 1848.
24 Kemény Zsigmond, 'Forradalom után' [After the Revolution], in Kemény, *Változatok a történelemre*, 181–373, 189.
25 Kemény, 'Forradalom után', 185.
26 Kemény Zsigmond, 'Még egy szó a forradalom után' [One More Word after the Revolution], in Kemény, *Változatok a történelemre*, 375–559, 414.
27 For an overview of Kemény's views of the 'nationality question': Filep Tamás Gusztáv, 'Sok zaj egy tojáslepényért: Kemény Zsigmond a nemzetiségi kérdésről' [Much Ado about an Omelette: Zsigmond Kemény on the Nationality Question], in *A sors kísértései: Tanulmányok Kemény Zsigmond munkásságáról születésének 200. évfordulójára*, ed. Szegedy-Maszák Mihály (Budapest: Ráció Kiadó, 2014), 17–31.
28 For an analysis of the political languages on which Kemény could build, see Veliky János, 'Kemény és a politikai nyelvek a reformkor második évtizedében' [Kemény and the Political Languages in the Second Decade of the Reform Era], in Szegedy-Maszák, *A sors kísértései*, 32–52.
29 Eisemann György, 'Történelem, végzet, forradalom: Esztétika és politika Kemény Zsigmond életművében' [History, Destiny, Revolution: Aesthetics and Politics in the Oeuvre of Zsigmond Kemény], in *Kommentár* 15, no. 2 (2020): 42–51, 45–7.
30 More on this topic: Hörcher Ferenc, 'Shaftesbury és a szenvedélyek retorikája' [Shaftesbury and the Rhetoric of Passions], in *Ész és szenvedély: Filozófiai tanulmányok a XVII-XVIII. századról*, ed. Boros Gábor (Budapest: Áron Kiadó, 2002), 269–86.
31 S. Varga Pál, 'Kemény Zsigmond – 200', *Studia Litteraria* 52, no. 3–4 (2014): 3–5, 5.
32 Takáts József, 'Kemény Zsigmond és a rajongás politikai fogalma' [Zsigmond Kemény and the Political Concept of Fanatism], *Holmi* 24, no. 10 (2012), 1212–18.
33 Hörcher Ferenc, 'A politikai rajongás egy kései kritikusa: Kemény Zsigmond' [A Late Critic of Political Fanatism], in *Értelem és érzelem az európai gondolkodásban: Tanulmányok a 60 éves Boros Gábor tiszteletére*, ed. Olay Csaba and Schmal Dániel (Budapest: KRE – L'Harmattan Kiadó, 2019), 253–62. On the concept of moderation in the Scottish Enlightenment, see Hörcher Ferenc, ed., *A skót felvilágosodás: Morálfilozófiai szöveggyűjtemény* [The Scottish Enlightenment: A Chrestomathy of Moral Philosophy] (Budapest: Osiris Kiadó, 1996), 295–396.
34 This claim is not far removed from the idea behind Lord Acton's famous claim: 'Power tends to corrupt, and absolute power corrupts absolutely'. Letter to Bishop Mandell Creighton, 5 April 1887. Transcript published in John Neville Figgis and Reginald Vere Laurence, eds., *Historical Essays and Studies* (London: Macmillan, 1907), 504.
35 Kemény, 'Forradalom után', 369, trans. Dávid Oláh.
36 These labels were coined by Mihály Szegedy-Maszák in Szegedy-Maszák, *Kemény Zsigmond* (see note 2).
37 This interpretation is based on the work of (among others) Dezső Pais, Mihály Szegedy-Maszák, and a recent article of Ágnes Hansági: Hansági Ágnes, 'Kemény Zsigmond, a Pesti Napló, az 'olvasási vágy' és egy drámai költemény' [Zsigmond Kemény, the Pesti Napló, the Desire to Read, and a Dramatic Poem], in *Studia Litteraria* 53, no. 3–4 (2014): 25–50.
38 Compare this effort to Flaubert's *L'Éducation sentimentale*, 1869.
39 Gyulai Pál, *Emlékbeszédek* [Eulogies] (Budapest: Franklin-Társulat, 1879), 157–86.

40 Imre László, *Az irodalomtudomány távlatai* [The Horizons of Literary Theory] (Nap Kiadó, 2014), 153–66. One should also note that there were those, like János Barta, who denied the existence of an actual circle of literary Deák supporters.
41 Beksics Gusztáv, *Kemény Zsigmond, a forradalom s a kiegyezés* [Zsigmond Kemény, the Revolution, and the Settlement] (Budapest: Athenaeum, 1883), 3.
42 Zsigmond Kemény to János Danielik, 7 February 1867, in: Pintér Borbála, ed., *Kemény Zsigmond levelezése* [The Correspondence of Zsigmond Kemény] (Budapest: Balassi Kiadó–ELTE, 2007), 397–400, 397.
43 Pintér, *Kemény Zsigmond levelezése*, 398.
44 'The theorist Zsigmond Kemény can be conceptualised as one of the heroes of his own novels'. Eisemann, 'Történelem, végzet, forradalom', 51.
45 Halász Gábor, 'Magyar viktoriánusok' [Hungarian Victorians], in: Halász Gábor, *Tiltakozó nemzedék: Összegyűjtött írások* (Budapest: Magvető Kiadó, 1981), 92–124, 96. I owe this reference to József Takáts.
46 Eisemann, 'Történelem, végzet, forradalom', 42. For a typical interaction see the exchange between János Barta, who made a revisionist move, and Pál Pándi, the ideologist, who defended the official line. Barta János, 'Kemény Zsigmond mint szépíró' [Zsigmond Kemény as Fiction Writer], *Irodalomtörténet* 49, no. 3 (1961): 236–54; Barta János, 'A politikus Kemény: Válasz Pándi Pálnak' [The Politician Kemény: Response to Pál Pándi], *Irodalomtörténet* 50, no. 2 (1962): 269–74; Pándi Pál, A politikus Kemény: Válasz Barta Jánosnak [The Politician Kemény: Response to János Barta], *Irodalomtörténet* 50, no. 2 (1962): 275–85.
47 There is a third essay from the same period, the text of which, however, is not reliable, and for that reason we shall omit it from the present discussion: *Emlékirat 1849-ből* [Memoir from 1849], published by Pál Gyulai in: Gyulai Pál, ed., *Kemény Zsigmond: Történelmi és irodalmi tanulmányok* [Zsigmond Kemény: Historical and Literary Essays] (Budapest: Franklin-Társulat, 1907), 1:47–142. A manuscript of it is held in the MNL OL (Hungarian National Archive) written by a foreign hand, which merits further investigation.

14

Ferenc Deák (1803-76)

István Schlett

'When Deák dies and they erect a memorial to him, what will they write on his memorial stone? That he was popular? Yes, but what did he do? What did he use his popularity for?' Aurél Kecskeméthy, in *Gr. Széchenyi István utolsó évei és halála* (The final years and death of Count István Széchenyi), published in 1866, attributes these sentences to Széchenyi, who had committed suicide in 1860.[1] If by deeds we mean 'positive works' – to use a popular phrase of the time – such as the founding of the Hungarian Academy of Sciences or the construction of the Chain Bridge, the creation of a successful daily newspaper, leading the constitutional revolution of 1848 or writing philosophical and literary works, influential political essays, pamphlets and newspaper articles, then Deák had few achievements to boast of compared to István Széchenyi, Lajos Kossuth, József Eötvös or Zsigmond Kemény. However, shortly after this statement was made, Deák, the 'sage of the fatherland', was to play a key role in the political process, precisely because of his popularity and, of course, thanks to his personal qualities. He was an authority who could not be ignored by those 'above' (the Viennese government and the political elite with links to the court, the courtly conservative aristocracy), because he could count on solid support from 'below', that is, the Hungarian liberal politicians and their supporters, who dominated public opinion.

Attempts and failures: Deák's political activities between 1833 and 1849

The early years of a career

Ferenc Deák was born on 27 October 1803, in Söjtör, a small village in Zala County, the seventh child of a wealthy noble family. Three of his siblings died before he was born; Ferenc's mother did not survive his birth. After the death of their father in 1808, young Ferenc was raised by his nineteen-year-old brother Antal and fifteen-year-old sister Klára, who performed their educational duties with exemplary dedication. The growing child acquired the pleasant, jovial conversational style that later made Deák so attractive to many.

His older brother's lifestyle was certainly an example to him, and his schooling followed a similar pattern. Like Antal, Ferenc also studied law and his career followed a similar path. Antal also made a direct contribution to Ferenc's entry into politics. In the spring of 1833, citing health reasons, he resigned his mandate as one of Zala County's delegates to the Diet and sent his younger brother, 'who has more in his little finger' than him, in his stead.[2]

Almost nothing is known about Deák's early career ambitions, perhaps partly because, some sources claim, he burnt some of his correspondence during the investigations launched against him in 1850. He was not attracted to a career as a lawyer or as a clerk, and he also found the burden of managing the estate, which fell to him because of his brother's many commitments, to be too great. Nor did he have any literary or scientific ambitions. He was, however, an active participant in the public life of the county, even when the management of the estate fell to him due to his brother's absence.

In 1831, he became a member of the county committee entrusted with the task, in accordance with the decision of the Diet of 1830, of reviewing the 'systematic works' (*operata*) of the 1790s for the renewal of the fatherland. It was also then that the palatine sent out to the counties the nine printed volumes of the *Operata*, which were conceived in the spirit of enlightened feudalism, to allow them to express their views on the changes needed in the country. The draft of the comments for Zala County was prepared by the Deák brothers and they also participated in the deliberations over it that lasted for almost two years.

The county assemblies were an important arena for national as well as regional politics and had a significant influence on the decisions of the Lower House. They were also responsible for local public administration and the administration of justice. At the same time, the counties were able to assert themselves even against the decisions of the Vienna Court, and it had the means, albeit limited, to enforce its will. The resistance of the counties forced Vienna to back down on more than one occasion.

As we have seen in the earlier chapters of this book, in the early 1830s a new way of thinking, one which contrasted with the thinking of the feudal opposition, had already appeared in the history of political thought in Hungary: Liberalism. This doctrine also captivated Ferenc Deák, as well as important circles of his contemporaries, such as young aristocrats, intellectuals, scientists, writers and publicists from noble and occasionally bourgeois backgrounds, as well as a significant number of the county nobility who were involved in politics. What happened with Deák in Zala also happened elsewhere, for example with Ferenc Kölcsey in Szatmár County, with Kálmán Ghyczy from Komárom, Menyhért Lónyay from Zemplén, and István Gorove from Temes, to name but a few of the figures who were to play a significant role in the political movement over the three or four decades that transformed the social and constitutional order of the Kingdom of Hungary. Without the contribution of this social stratum – which often called itself the 'middle class' and later the 'gentry' – the transformation of the country could not have taken place, just as it could not have taken place without the contribution of the other previously mentioned groups.

It seems that Deák was aware of the socio-cultural characteristics of his own milieu, especially the honorary judges (*táblabírák*), who played a significant role in the public life of the counties, and he took the characteristics of this milieu into account when formulating his political programme.

It can be seen that even back then he was aware that, on the one hand, it is not possible to pursue politics in Hungary outside the feudal institutions, that is, without the landed aristocrats who actually ruled the counties, while on the other hand, he realized that the previous practice and style of politics of the feudal opposition – the 'politics of grievances' obsessed only with preventing further encroachment by the Vienna Court onto their ancient rights – would not suffice to break out of the vicious circle of absolutism followed by resistance followed by more absolutism, or could be used to create a viable reform programme able to modernize the country.

Deák was conscientiously preparing for his vocation and, knowingly or unknowingly, he organized his life accordingly. He did not start a family, even leaving the management of the estate to his brother when he could. Following his brother's example, he attended the Diet at his own expense, refusing to accept the per diem from the county. He never held a paid office – except for the justice portfolio of the Batthyány government in 1848 – and accepted no honours. He later even protested against the holding of a torchlight procession in his honour, asking instead that the costs be used to set up a foundation to help the education of poor children (to which he himself also contributed). He thus maintained his 'independent status', as we shall see, for the rest of his life. In every respect, he was what Max Weber calls an 'honorary politician' or a politician who, unlike those who make a living from politics, lives for politics.

It was important to him to live a life of integrity and incorruptibility, and he made sure that he was seen to be doing so. Kölcsey's slogan, 'the Fatherland before all else', was not an empty phrase for this group of politicians from the ranks of the nobility.

The effectiveness of Deák's preparation was evident from the way that he burst into national politics with surprising speed and soon became one of the leading figures of the liberal opposition. All the liberal movements of the 1840s – including those of Széchenyi, Kossuth and the 'centralists' organized around Eötvös and László Szalay – claimed his support. However, he did not take part in party struggles but preserved his independence.

The unfolding of a career: On a rollercoaster of partial successes and partial failures

Ferenc Deák appeared in May 1833 at the deliberations of the Diet which was convened on 16 December 1832 and dissolved in May 1836. His political programme was known beforehand, partly from the delegates' instructions, drawn up jointly with his brother, and partly from his proposals, which had been rejected by the county assembly in 1832: the extension of 'civil rights' to the 'tax-paying people', including the ownership of land, the right to hold office, and access to the 'legislative and executive powers' hitherto reserved for the nobility, in order to 'raise them to the rank of free Hungarian citizens'. His political programme also raised the most sensitive issue, the introduction of taxation of the nobility.[3] It was therefore clear that Ferenc Deák belonged to the liberal opposition of the Diet, and his position was fundamentally different from that of the 'Werbőczyan' wing of the opposition, which adhered to the principles laid down in the *Tripartitum* – the collection of customary law of 1514, which excluded the serfs from the 'Natio Hungarica'.

It was also noticeable, however, that Deák added a new voice to the chorus of opposition, in which, in addition to the references to natural law, the dominant element became a new interpretation of certain passages of the *Corpus Juris*, the collection of Hungary's laws stretching back to the foundation of the state. The difference was also reflected in its political content. Its tone was different from the radicalism of Miklós Wesselényi, but it was also different from that of István Széchenyi, who did not hold the Lower House of the Diet, including the opposition, in high esteem. The three personalities cited as examples shared the same principles, pursued the same goals and respected each other, but they clearly had different ideas about the exact path to success.

The Diets of the Reform Era saw the emergence of a split between feudal conservatism and liberalism, alongside the fault line between the pro-government stance versus that of the opposition, which made relations even more complex. From a liberal point of view, the situation became delicate. Two tasks had to be tackled at the same time: one was to prevent the absolutist government from pursuing its ambitions, the other was to break with the feudal order that was opposed to social reform. The debate within the liberal opposition increasingly began to focus on the question of how and when the Gordian knot could be untied.

The rise

This task fell to Deák who, almost unnoticed, became the leader of the liberal opposition and the most influential figure in the Lower House of the Diet, especially after Kölcsey was forced to leave the Diet in 1835 because his county changed its instructions on the emancipation of the serfs, which exposed the precarious position of the liberal opposition and undermined the goal Kölcsey had set, to serve 'fatherland and progress'. The problem was further complicated by the deterioration of relations between the Upper and the Lower Houses of the Diet, and the hardening of government policy. The government charged Wesselényi first with violating the censorship law – which he was accused of having committed by printing the parliamentary diary at the Transylvanian Diet – and then for disloyalty, for his speech at the Szatmár County Assembly. Serious sentences were handed down in the trials of the leaders of the Dietal youth group (law students of noble origin who supported the liberal opposition at the Diet of 1832-6) and later of Kossuth, the publisher of the *Országgyűlési Tudósítások* (Reports from the Diet).

Following a compromise reached with Deák's personal involvement, the prisoners were released in 1840, but without the ruler's acknowledgement that it had violated the law. For a liberal politician like Deák, for whom not only the pursuit of his goals, but also the way in which they were pursued – that is, avoidance of revolution, gradualism, moderation, the alignment of interests and the maintenance of the rule of law – was an important principle, this was an acceptable price to pay.

For Deák, the issue of the nation was above all an issue of sovereignty. In his interpretation, the relationship between the Diet, which embodies national sovereignty, and the ruler was governed by an 'ancient constitution' composed of contracts, a multitude of laws and customary law. The precedents he cited were historically well founded; the state law of the feudal monarchy was indeed based on the principle of shared power, as also reflected in Werbőczy's *Tripartitum*; the validity of laws and contracts was based on the agreement between two parties, that is, the ruler and the 'nation', understood as a 'body politic', so any change of laws and contracts can only be based on agreement; and the executive, or the judiciary, were in a subordinate position to the legislative power. In this vein, Deák usually referred to treaties and laws that were passed to end conflicts between ruler and nation – such as the 1608 treaties following Bocskai's uprising, the laws that ended Rákóczi's War of Independence, the laws regulating the relationship between Austria and the Kingdom of Hungary, and the laws that ended Joseph II's 'enlightened absolutism' – all of which confirmed the Hungarian Kingdom's separate status within the empire. Furthermore, he regarded as a constitutional violation and a breach of national sovereignty not only the restriction of the use of the Hungarian language and the limitation of the Hungarian Kingdom's integrity – that is, the maintenance of the militarily administered border territories after the expulsion of the Turks, which were directly controlled from Vienna – but also the expropriation of the right to control public education, the army, economic policy, public administration and the judiciary. Deák considered the Diet to be the custodian of national sovereignty, thereby obviously breaking with the state law of the monarchy, and claimed the right to have a say in matters – such as foreign and military affairs – which he himself recognized were among the sovereign's prerogatives. Along with some of his fellow delegates, he almost spoke as if he were in Westminster and not in the Diet of Pozsony (today Bratislava, Slovakia). In a feudal guise, he actually called the ruler to account for the principles of liberal constitutionality. It is also noteworthy that there is not even a hint in his speeches of the possibility of secession from the Habsburg Empire; based on the treaties concluded with the Habsburgs, instead he demanded a reordering and constitutionalization of the relationship between the Kingdom of Hungary and the empire.

Debates were also starting at this time on the law-making process itself and the opposition succeeded in changing the codification practice. Previously, dietal resolutions were formulated into law by the Viennese government that sometimes changed their content. From this time onwards, bills would be submitted for debate in the Lower House, which had the right to initiate legislation, or committees were set up to draft bills, which in both cases, if approved, would constitute the final version of the law. For example, the Diet of 1839–40 established a committee to draft a new penal code. Although it never became a law, this act represented a major step forward in the transformation of the legislature, bringing it closer to the liberal conception of parliamentarianism.

The dismantling of the feudal system also became an important issue at the Diets of 1832–6 and 1839–40. The argumentation at this time presented the problem of the serfs as a matter of human rights, and the dismantling of noble privileges as the main means of nation-building, which obviously did not follow from the values of feudal constitutionality. Religious affairs were also a suitable vehicle for emphasizing the new principle of freedom of conscience, raising the problem of Jewish emancipation, the education of the people and the broader question of progress and civilization: in short, all the issues that were part of the liberal vision of the time.

Deák created a conceptual framework in which he considered it possible to combine the activities of the opposition of the estates and that of the liberal opposition, which would also involve the reordering of the relationship between the Habsburg Empire and the Kingdom of Hungary, and the transformation of the social and political system.

Deák built this programme on the liberal paradigm's view of history and society, creating his own particular version of it, which can be compared to one of the then contemporary interpretations of Liberalism, termed 'governing liberalism', as distinguished from the other type that existed in the period, the grassroots 'movement liberalism'. This division was not a Hungarian peculiarity; both variants also existed in England and France, which Hungary took as its models. Alexis de Tocqueville's *Recollections of the 1848 Revolution* (1893) contains convincing descriptions of the nature of these two conceptions of liberalism. The 'national specificities' that appeared in this programme were therefore not the result of 'distortions' in the reception of ideas. Movement liberalism did, however, also appear in the political life of Hungary in the months following the Revolution of 1848, although it is true that it was most prominent in the poetry of Sándor Petőfi – one of the greatest Hungarian poets – and not in politics.

Of course, the Hungarian version of liberalism was different from the English or French versions. For Hungarian liberal politicians, it was obvious that the situation of the Kingdom of Hungary differed in crucial respects from that of their model countries.

Deák was already aware of these circumstances and the tasks they entailed at the beginning of his political activity, and he adapted to them. But how did this adaptation manifest itself? In part, it was his rejection of both doctrinaire politics and radicalism. Consequently, his guiding policy principle was pragmatism, taking into account what was feasible, while at the same time striving for moderation to reduce risks.

Again, this was not some kind of Hungarian 'peculiarity'. The Hungarian liberals who monitored the situation in Europe were well aware that there were several types of interpretations of liberalism. They knew and studied the work of Constant, Guizot, Tocqueville, Lamartine, Burke, Fox, Bentham, John Stuart Mill and others, noting the similarities that united them as well as the differences that divided them. In other words, they knew the basic assumptions and questions of the liberal paradigm and the basic answers to them, but they were also aware that the alternatives that emerge in decision-making situations are necessarily different. László Szalay's book on English, French and North American liberal politicians, which won the Academy's Grand Prize, is just one example of this awareness.[4]

Deák's modus operandi supports this thesis. Liberalism and revolution are not at all inseparable. It was England's conception of liberalism which prevailed in Hungary, and not that of France, which had been unable to complete its series of revolutions. Furthermore, since there were many arguments in favour of maintaining the Austro-Hungarian 'mixed marriage', a significant number of Hungarian liberal politicians, especially under the influence of the pan-Slavic aspirations, preferred federation to secession, provided, of course, that a form of it could be created in which both national interest and liberal constitutionality, and the need for the country's catching up, could be asserted.

Deák earned the respect not only of his supporters but also of his opponents. In 1840, Deák was presented with an album of honour by his admirers at the adjournment of the Diet. The first of the signatures was that of István Széchenyi, followed by the members of the aristocracy, the delegates to the Lower House and the representatives of the parliamentary youth. Deák's choice of tactics, his patience, rhetorical skills and personal charm certainly played a role in the results achieved by the Diets of the 1830s, and yet the breakthrough continued to elude him.

The downturn

Deák reached the peak of his career in 1840. In 1843, however, he declined to be elected as delegate and did so again in 1847, because he saw no hope of continuing the strategy he had advocated in previous Diets in the changed political situation. He reappeared at the Diet only after the great turning point (the bloodless revolution of 15 March), on 20 March 1848, two days before the General Assembly of Zala County elected him as a delegate by public acclamation, after accepting the resignation of one of the delegates. He accepted Batthyány's invitation and became minister of justice in the Hungarian government now responsible to the Parliament.

By the autumn of 1843, the results of the 1840 Diet and the hopes arising from a slight change in government policy had faded. The political situation had escalated, and there was an unbridgeable gap not only between the Viennese government and the opposition, but also within the opposition – which had been held together by national grievances – between the forces of feudal conservatism and liberalism. The parties used similarly pragmatic means of electoral canvassing, which made the liberals' chances of success doubtful, unless they resorted to the same means, bribery and violence, as their opponents.

Deák did not withdraw from political life, but neither did he create an independent programme. Széchenyi's public suggestion to create a 'centre party', separate from the opposition under Kossuth's leadership, was met with silence. He also resisted Kossuth's request and did not participate in the debates on freedom of the press. He did not oppose Kossuth, however, and even supported some of his initiatives, such as the *Védegylet* (League of Protection, an association for the protection of domestic industry, whose members committed themselves to buying only domestic products when available), albeit with reservations. 'I'd have my doubts', he wrote to Kossuth in November 1844, but 'now that the first step has been taken, I would consider it a crime against the fatherland to discard or diminish it by neglect, coldness, or dissent'.[5] This may have been the reasoning behind his decision, despite his poor health, to take part in Batthyány's government in March 1848, as he explained in another one of his letters.

True, the political situation had changed radically. A moment had arisen for a realistic opportunity to break out of the vicious circle in which Hungarian politicians had been locked for a century, since the centralizing reforms initiated by Maria Theresa. Kossuth, the leader of the liberal opposition in the Diet, seized the moment. Taking advantage of the outbreak of the February Revolution in France, with the rapid spread of the revolutionary wave across Europe and the fears that it stirred, he made a breakthrough in the assembly hall that fundamentally transformed Hungary's political system within weeks. Under the circumstances of the 'lawful revolution', not only were more than two dozen major laws passed and sanctioned in less than three weeks, but the quality of the Diet itself changed. On 15 March 1848, the 'body of delegates' transformed itself into a true National Assembly with a single declaration that changed the process and expanded the franchise by which the legislature would be chosen.

The reordering of the relationship between the Habsburg Empire and the Kingdom of Hungary took place at a similar pace and in a similar manner. The appointment of an independent, Hungarian 'Ministry' (i.e. government) was interpreted by the National Assembly as the restoration of the rule of law, and the transformation of the empire into a confederation of states united by the personal union. According to this interpretation, in addition to dismantling the system of feudalism, Hungarian freedom and autonomy were also secured in the context of the *Pragmatica Sanctio*, which was therefore not equivalent to secession, but to an alliance based on a treaty, in which – as Kossuth put it on 31 March 1848 – the nation's independence, constitutionality, freedom and influence in military affairs were secured. Add to this the fact that the Vienna Revolution had led to a constitutional revolution in the other half of the empire, and their optimism was not unjustified.

The most prominent opinion leaders of the liberal movement were all present in the first government. Naturally, Ferenc Deák had to be among them. Lajos Batthyány, the prime minister, sent a delegation to Kehida on 14 March 1848 to invite Deák to Pozsony. Deák acquiesced, but his correspondence reveals that he did not take up his ministerial post with high hopes.

Yet, true to his commitment, as minister of justice, Deák saw in the work of law-making a chance to reform the relationship between the empire and Hungary and the internal legal order of the Kingdom of Hungary. In his ministerial programme, presented on 30 March 1848, he promised to pass a series of laws.[6] He regarded the framework provided by the April Laws (i.e. the laws sanctioned in April 1848) as a suitable framework for achieving the aims he had in mind.

However, he did not take up a portfolio in the government reconstituted on 17 September 1848. He gave two reasons for this: 'I left the ministry when it was dissolved, because it could not survive under the policy [. . .] pursued by the Court unless it wanted to be part of that policy. This evil policy of the Court against our fatherland has not changed, but has become even more evil.' The second: 'Jelačić is approaching with his army; seditious agitations are breeding among the Slovaks and the Romanians, and this country is beginning a general disintegration. This is what I have been prophesying for months, but they thought me overly pessimistic.'[7]

It was not only Deák who was missing from the new government. Széchenyi was also absent, by then a resident of a mental asylum, nor was Minister of Agriculture, Industry and Trade Gábor Klauzál, who had retired. József Eötvös was still involved, but he left the country with his family on 29 September. Deák did not leave politics completely and did not give up his mandate as a member of parliament, speaking a few times in the Parliament, and finally becoming a member of the peace delegation that attempted to stop the Austrian army against Hungary on 31 December 1848. The response to these efforts, however, was a demand for 'unconditional submission'.

This was Deák's last act in the Revolution and the War of Independence. In June 1849, he returned to Pest, which had been liberated by the Hungarian army, but did not take part in the work of the Parliament – despite the fact that his absence was considered justified – because he rejected the dethronement of the House of Habsburg proclaimed in Debrecen and the Olmütz (today Olomouc, Czech Republic) Constitution, which was based on the principle of a completely unified Hungary and Austria.[8]

After the defeat of the War of Independence, Deák returned to stay in Kehida, from where he wrote a letter rejecting the invitation of the liberal minister of justice of the Austrian government to a conference on Hungarian private law. He gave the following reason for his decision: 'After the mournful events of recent times, in the conditions which still prevail, it is impossible for me to take part in public affairs.'[9] This was the beginning of a period of passive resistance for Deák, from which he only emerged, despite being urged, when he felt that the conditions had been established for creating a solution that met his objectives.

Deák and the Settlement

Passive resistance

Apart from organizing a fundraising campaign to help Vörösmarty's family after his death in 1855, and the controversy that arose in 1858 over the amendment of the statutes of the Academy of Sciences, in which he participated as a member of the Board of Directors, Deák did not speak in public forums, did not make any statements in the press and did not write any press articles during this period.

This passivity was not a sign of fatalism, but because he was waiting for the moment that opens up the possibility of further action. Many politicians, including conservatives, often visited Deák at his Kehida estate, looking to him for guidance. Public opinion also placed its trust in him and expected him to save the fatherland.

Deák sold his property in exchange for an annuity to ensure a respectable living and moved to Pest in the autumn of 1854. He rented a suite at the *Angol Királynő* (Queen of England) hotel, where he took with him some of his furniture, his books – of which the *Corpus Juris* was always at hand – and the tools he needed for his favourite pastime, woodcarving. Nevertheless, he continued to spend his summers in Zala County, on the estate of his sister and brother-in-law. His small hotel suite became a social, intellectual and political centre.

The Deák party, which was organized around him and sought to restore constitutional relations, although it did not engage in any partisan activities or initiate any political actions, was nevertheless present as a political force.

It may seem paradoxical, but the survival and consolidation of Deák's liberalism was facilitated by the defeat of 1849, in part because the absolutist regime overseen by

Alexander Bach used its new-found powers to dismantle feudalism, divide property after the emancipation of the serfs, introduce a new civil code and enforce on the nobility the duty to contribute to public revenues, thus setting in motion the process of modernization. Although this did not happen exactly the way the Hungarian liberals would have imagined it, it was not entirely dissimilar to what Deák and his party wanted. Hence, Hungarian liberals escaped some of the burdens that went hand in hand with the tensions and conflicts that inevitably accompanied the transformation of society and resulted in the continuation of the revolution in some countries in turbulent Europe.

The way in which the political system of the empire attained its shape was also helpful. The constitutional and federalist elements of the Olmütz Constitution were abolished by the imperial edict of late December 1851 and replaced by a system of neo-absolutism in which the rights of the ruler were not limited.

The programme of the New Austria was widely rejected. The alliance between feudal conservatism and the absolutist-modernist state was broken, and the new system of government was rejected by the majority of liberals not only in Hungary but also in other provinces of the empire. Autonomy for the national minorities could not exist in this state structure either, since – as a popular saying went – the minorities would receive as a reward what the Hungarians received as a punishment. In addition, the manner of the Revolution's defeat also served to underpin a belief that liberalism could be resurrected. The empire was able to defeat the Hungarians only with Russian help, and the War of Independence did not fail because of internal difficulties, the inadequacy of the representative system or the outbreak of social tensions, as in the revolutions in France or Germany. The Hungarian political elite had also proved its ability to act in a difficult situation; true, it was defeated, but it had held out for a relatively long time against the armies of two great powers.

These facts may explain why liberalism underwent a revival and found its feet again in Hungary more quickly than in Germany or France. No viable alternative to liberalism emerged within Hungarian society. The in-depth critique of movement liberalism and the redefinition of liberalism, as well as the theoretical foundation of governing liberalism, was quickly carried out, primarily in the political philosophy of József Eötvös, in the pamphlets, essays and novels of Zsigmond Kemény and in the historical works of László Szalay, to mention only the most important names. The majority of Hungarian liberals were not characterized by either the disillusionment which turned some of the adherents of liberalism in Western countries towards socialism and others towards the acceptance of 'Realpolitik' and the 'fait accompli', or the 'dread' which, by his own admission, had already filled Tocqueville after the June Revolution, that the process set in motion by the 'abuse of liberty' was 'inevitable' and that 'we shall have great difficulty in not rolling far beyond the point we had reached before February'.[10] They considered that the process that had begun in the Kingdom of Hungary in 1830 could be continued, after drawing the necessary lessons. Deák's principles, based more on practical experience, contrasted pragmatism with doctrinaire approaches, moderation with radicalism, prudence with recklessness and common sense with emotions, while also adhering to his principles. For him, too, the example was England, not France, which tended to impose political theories and was therefore prone to radicalism and excesses, thus proving to Deák that lack of restraint leads first to anarchy and then to tyranny. The regime of Napoleon III was a powerful proof of this thesis.

At the same time, however, the limitations of Austria's power that had been exposed were also an important factor. It could be hoped that it was only a matter of time before the ruler and the power that relied on the army and the bureaucracy would be forced to change.

Deák's strategy was based on these assumptions. Miksa Falk, one of the leading journalists of the period, later summarized Deák's 'instructions' in a letter received from him in 1858 as follows:

> The primary task is to keep alive in the nation a sense and enthusiasm for constitutional freedom, because then, at a favorable moment, the Hungarian constitution can be restored with the stroke of a pen, and our free, constitutional state can be restored in twenty-four hours.[11]

Deák tied himself to the achievements of 1848. He did not criticize them in public, but it was well known that he rejected both the conservative position of 1847 and Eötvös's proposal in his pamphlet *Die Garantien der Macht und Einheit Oesterreichs*, published in Leipzig in 1859, which saw a revised version of the Olmütz Constitution as the best solution to the crisis.

'Intransigence and opportunity': The creation of the nation-state within a new confederation

Austria's defeat by the Franco-Italian armies in 1859, the threat of national bankruptcy and the isolation of the empire confirmed Deák's suspicions about Austria's weakness. It became clear that the so-called New Austria programme, which asserted that centralization was the best way of preserving the authority of the empire, had failed, and that the monarch would have to find a new solution to the crisis, including a settlement of Austro-Hungarian relations. Hungarian politicians also felt this, and the conservatives reacted swiftly to the new situation. As early as July 1859, Emil Dessewffy submitted a detailed plan to the ruler suggestively titled *Tervezete egy hadjáratnak Ausztria belsejében, hogy az 1859. évi szerencsétlen háború következéseinek eleje vétessék és tartós erőhöz lehessen jutni* (Draft for a campaign in the interior of Austria to remedy the consequences of the unfortunate war of 1859 and to gain lasting power), which, after a scathing critique of the system, concludes that 'the only means of averting trouble' is 'a complete and honest break with the system' based on the 'great lie' that 'Austria is, or can ever be, a German state'. The agreement between the government and the conservatives (the October Diploma of late 1860) was not, however, based on Dessewffy's draft.

Principles and rules: Deák's preparation for the negotiations

During the hot autumn of 1860, in the days following the publication of the October Diploma, everyone was waiting for Deák to make a statement, and his supporters also urged him to speak out. It was clear that the solution offered in the Diploma would not be accepted even as a basis for negotiation by 'the sage of the fatherland', but he did not make his counter-proposal public. He also seems to have had doubts about his own abilities and strength at this point:

> I, whose faith in men and hopes for the future have been shaken by age and the events, could not, if I would, play a decisive part; I'm but a relic of times past, and a new generation and so many new elements are unknown to me, as I'm unknown to them.[12]

In December 1860, at the request of the emperor, he presented his position together with Eötvös. Deák told Francis Joseph that he considered the laws of 1848 'in their entirety' as a starting point. He did not dispute the existence of shared affairs and showed a willingness to renegotiate them, but he was adamant about his insistence on the 1848 April Laws, including the social, national and political demands of the liberal programme of the Reform Era, parliamentary government and the rejection of any form of imperial annexation: in other words he asserted the (somewhat limited) national sovereignty and the integrity of the Kingdom of Hungary.

Deák considered the task to be completed 'almost impossible'. He anticipated difficulties in various areas, including the distribution of the vast state debt of Austria, the military affairs, the management of the claims of the ethnic minorities and the handling of common affairs.

Clearly, then, he knew full well, as the theorists of the liberal 'constitutional party' such as Zsigmond Kemény and József Eötvös had stated before, that the problems listed above could not be solved by adhering closely to the laws of 1848. In fact, it was precisely these issues that remained unresolved. At the same time, he felt that it was no longer possible to maintain a passive stance.

Competing alternatives were also emerging on the political scene, and this too spurred Deák to action, although he had no plan of action at that time. Deák used the public sphere, above all the Parliament, as the main arena of politics, and rational argumentation, or 'lawyering', as a tool. He did not compromise but chose means and procedures that were in line with his goals and values and which were directly consistent with his political philosophy, rejecting instruments which were not. For this political method to work it needed the right partners and opponents. Only in the normal state of politics can rational argumentation be used; in exceptional situations it cannot produce results.

We have seen – and we shall see – that when this condition was not met, Deák retreated, because he was not a man of war, not a man of revolution and certainly not a man of counter-revolution.

In the spring of 1861, it was not yet clear whether suitable conditions had emerged for Deák's policy. It had not yet been decided whether Francis Joseph would choose diktat or compromise, nor whether the majority of the nation would choose Kossuth or Deák.

The process

Deák believed that a 'peace treaty' could be feasible if it passed through two stages: first, the task was to prove that 'the Hungarian constitution legally exists and has not lost its validity [. . .] in a word, that we are right'. In the second phase, from 1865 onwards, it was possible to prove and enshrine in law that 'the Hungarian constitution and the legal independence of Hungary do not conflict with the existence and power of Austria, on the contrary, the two can even coexist well'.[13]

However, a precondition for this was to gain clear support from the Hungarian public. At the opening of Parliament in 1861, the Deák party did not have a majority in the Lower House. There were fierce debates in the Parliament, and Deák's proposal for a memorandum, which was firm in content but moderate in form, was only adopted by a narrow majority, and was, in any case, rejected by Francis Joseph.

Deák, in his reply, made it clear that he would not concede any of the principles he had already expressed, and therefore that he considered the negotiations to be completed, but also indicated his readiness to continue negotiations, provided that the principles proposed in the memorandum were accepted by the ruler. This speech created unity among almost all members of the Lower House. If anyone had feared that Deák's position would lead to submission, then that fear had been allayed. The National Assembly demonstrated the unity of the nation in spectacular fashion.

The winner of the debates with the conservatives and the Kossuth supporters was the 'sage of the fatherland'. Although the former did not stop devising various 'development plans', they could no longer conceive of achieving results without Deák. The strength of the Kossuth Party, on the other hand, dwindled, as the war between the Franco-Italian coalition and Austria ended without the Hungarian question being raised, emigration decreased and its domestic support weakened and began to disintegrate. In 1863, when the album containing the portraits of the participants of the 1861 Diet, a gift to Deák, was completed, the large delegation which went to his home at the Queen of England Hotel included many of his former political opponents.

When negotiations resumed in 1865, 'the sage of the fatherland' was in fact already the leader of the vast majority of the nation. The Hungarian conservatives gave up their independent efforts, and Kálmán Tisza himself, the former leader of the Resolution Party (*Határozati Párt*), expected and even urged Deák to make a decision, saying, 'he who can remain silent when one should remain silent, and speak up when one should speak, should also act when it's time to act'.

In Vienna they also realized that Deák was the critical partner in any negotiations. Deák, however, considered there was only one person to be an acceptable negotiating partner: the one whom he regarded as their common ruler. However, after the negotiations had begun, he sent his 'plenipotentiary envoys', Gyula Andrássy, József Eötvös and Menyhért Lónyay, to the negotiations. Being a comfort-loving man, he was perhaps not in the mood for a train journey of several hours to Vienna. His 'laziness' can also be interpreted as a political gesture. Deák was displaying the dignity of a true 'leader of the nation' towards the negotiations.

The stalemate ended in December 1864, at the initiative of the emperor, when he sent Baron Antal Augusz, the former vice-president of the Lieutenancy Council

(*Helytartóság*), to Deák to assess the Hungarian position. Augusz prepared a report on their conversation, presented it to Deák and incorporated his corrections into the text. Two weeks later, the Baron reported again, and by personal mandate of Francis Joseph, he announced that the emperor had accepted the principles laid down in the report.

Negotiations were resumed, thus beginning the two-year process that led in turn – from Schmerling's downfall to the Battle of Königgrätz (today Sadová, Czech Republic) and the abandonment of the concept of a unified Austria – finally to the establishment of the Austro-Hungarian Dual Monarchy.

As usual, the politician of the 'centre' was forced to reconcile conflicting values. As regards the relationship between the Kingdom of Hungary and the Habsburg Empire, this meant, on the one hand, safeguarding the sovereignty of the nation, which included all of the country's citizens, and, on the other, finding a way to ensure the 'solid existence of the Empire'.

Intransigence and opportunity – these two words sum up Deák's position at the turning point of the negotiations. He showed rigidity as long as principles were at stake, but when it came to legislating the new political system of the federation and of the Kingdom of Hungary into norms and forms, he also took into account the interests of his partner. It was not within the power of either party to achieve the totality of its aims and thus create a state which it could call perfect from its own point of view.

However, it was not an easy task to recognize this or to make the other side recognize it, since the parties to the debate could not be sure exactly what their own options were, nor those of the other side at a moment when the transformation of the European power relations had reached a critical point: it was unclear how the future of Central Europe would develop, what the consequences of the creation of a 'small German unity' (*kleindeutsche Einheit*) would be or what direction the solution of the 'Eastern question' would take, to mention only a few of the open questions. Moreover, it was not clear how the Austrian and Hungarian public would react to the reform of the federation and the political system. Another warning sign was that the Austrian defeat in the war with Prussia had revived hopes of independence in Hungary, and as a result the centre-left had become radicalized again. Intransigence could not, therefore, be entirely replaced by opportunity.

At the end of 1866, negotiations stalled, especially after the ruler tried to break the Hungarian Parliament's resistance to forced recruitment to the imperial army by issuing an imperial edict. Deák reacted strongly to this measure, which was radically at odds with the principles on which the concept of the Settlement could be based.

The crisis was finally resolved by a new turn in Austrian government policy. Friedrich Ferdinand von Beust, the newly appointed minister of state, made reconciliation with the Hungarians one of his first tasks. He did what Schmerling had previously failed to do; in December 1866 he travelled to Pest to visit Deák.

Deák set as a basic condition the reorganization of the empire on the basis of the principles of dualism and liberal constitutionality, and limited the subject of further negotiations to the 'settlement of common relations'.

The negotiations resumed in the first days of January, without Deák's personal participation, but all those present – including the ruler – knew that an agreement that did not meet with Deák's agreement was pointless. After a few attempts, the ruler even gave up trying to put pressure on Deák through delegates who were perceived to be more lenient (Andrássy, Eötvös, Lónyay). After the ruler was persuaded to accept Deák's conditions, the negotiations were completed in two days. They also reached agreement on the timetable that had been debated by that point: if the all-party committee of the Parliament voted in favour of the prepared draft, the ruler agreed to immediately appoint a new Hungarian government, and as soon as the Parliament accepted the committee's proposal, the coronation would take place, thus ending the absolutist interregnum and restoring constitutionality.

The reshaping of the constitutional structure included two elements. This meant, on the one hand, the transformation of the empire into a confederation of states, based on the parity of the two parties – Austria, which included the Hereditary Provinces, and the Kingdom of Hungary in its integrity – while recognizing the existence of common affairs, and on the other hand, the establishment in both states of a constitutional structure in which sovereignty was not only formally but also de facto shared between the sovereign and the Parliament of each state. In both states, the laws that codified some elements of the agreement into legislation established a political system that conformed to the prevailing interpretations of liberalism at the time. In both states, we can speak of a representative system in which the Parliament, elected by the citizens and thus expressing the national will, has a decisive role, although clearly – to avoid any misunderstanding – not quite in the same way as in their English model. In the Austro-Hungarian Monarchy, largely as a result of the dual structure, the common monarch had more extensive powers and responsibilities than in contemporary Britain (e.g. the right of preliminary royal assent to every bill). The state structure was also different. Great Britain had a common Parliament and government, while the Austro-Hungarian Monarchy did not, aside from three common ministers and an occasional oversight body comprised of delegates from the two Parliaments who focused on changes to the tax system. The role of the monarch was also different from that in Britain: he not only ruled, but also governed. For the Hungarian side, this structure was more acceptable than a joint Parliament, which could have provided greater scope for efforts to limit or destroy the nation's sovereignty, if only because the population of the Hereditary Provinces far exceeded that of the Kingdom of Hungary, and the Hungarians would have been in a minority.

This solution also suited the other side. The small German unity created by the German 'Iron Chancellor' Bismarck pushed Austria eastwards, so that dualism became the most favourable option for the German-Austrian political elite of the Habsburg Emperor and Monarchy. With the fall of Schmerling, the Austro-German liberals became the dominant group in the extremely divided Austrian Parliament.

All this created the constellation in which Deák's master plan could be fulfilled. On 14 February 1867, the monarch presided over the Council of Ministers of the Hungarian government responsible to the Parliament, on 17 February he 'restored the Constitution' by decree and on 8 June the coronation took place.

Achieving agreement

Surprisingly, in January 1867, Deák was ambivalent about the outcome of the Vienna conference, even though he had achieved his goal. Lónyay's diary records Deák's sharp mood swings in the days following the agreement. On 12 January he expressed his satisfaction, but a few days later he voiced doubts and spooked his colleagues by announcing that he would publicly express his reservations about some elements of the agreement.

Even so, Deák himself knew that he could not shirk his responsibility, so he had to give up his independence, which he had guarded closely even from his own party. In the negotiations of the Committee of '67, which began a few days later, Deák confronted the opponents of the Settlement with all his authority and intellect. Even if he had reservations about the results, he did not express them. Whereas a month earlier he had shown himself to be intransigent against Beust, he now took up the fight against the policy of 'no compromise' demanded by the remaining followers of Kossuth and advocated seizing the opportunity. As a result, new features emerged in his argumentation. On more than one occasion, he explained to his debating partners that the system for managing common affairs must be examined pragmatically, not only in terms of law and justice but also in terms of the interests of the country and its overall utility.

It was essential for the new government to win the support it needed to function properly, to prove that it could build the institutions necessary to govern and to create and enforce new norms under the circumstances and conditions. Deák knew that the results that had been negotiated, and the conditions accepted in exchange for them, had to be accepted not only by the Parliament but also by the 'people', that is, the wider public, the electorate. Before the final vote on the proposal, Deák himself announced that he was speaking to the fatherland, rather than trying to change the views of the members of parliament. The addressee of this speech was the nation as a 'corpus politicum', and Deák's arguments were directed above all against Kossuth, whose name symbolized the alternative to the Settlement. At this point, Deák could not avoid a debate with the 'Great Exile'. He knew that 1849, that is, the dethronement of the Habsburg dynasty, was a popular idea, especially among the Hungarian population of the country, and that the prestige of 'our father Kossuth' endured in popular culture.

Deák used the following arguments against Kossuth, whose goal was nothing short of complete separation from the Habsburgs:

> Arms and revolution, even with the hope of success, are tools that one should only reach for on the threshold of despair. [. . .] To expect a dubious future from uncertain events, while letting the nation's strength, prosperity, confidence and hope dwindle more and more each day, would have been a wrong and even harmful calculation, because it could easily have happened that the expected event would not occur, or would occur when it was too late to help our weakened nation. [. . .] [T]he people would not thank us if, having thwarted the success of peaceful reconciliation, we were to fall back with it into the whirlpool of uncertainty, of confusion and disorder, from which it is so difficult to escape;

and for the sufferings which it has endured and ought still to endure, we could offer them nothing but the doubtful consolation that an accidental turn of events in Europe might yet bring us a better fate than we can at present obtain by this peaceful settlement.[14]

In the days before the parliamentary vote, an open letter from Kossuth to Deák – known as the Cassandra Letter – was published in the 'extreme leftist' *Magyar Újság* (Hungarian Newspaper). This very personal and emotional letter, written in a friendly, familiar tone, foresaw in the Settlement the death of the nation. It warned Deák for his faulty 'political arithmetic' and begged him to change his standpoint in the interest of the nation. In Kossuth's view, there was no justification for the fatal consequences of the deal.[15]

Deák's reaction was again restrained: in his response he reiterated in a few words the position he had expressed in his speeches.

This debate died down relatively quickly. It is therefore fair to say that the Cassandra Letter did not play as significant a role in the debate about the Settlement as public opinion after the collapse of the Monarchy in 1918 believed. This later assessment, and renewed admiration for Kossuth's predictions, was the result of the collapse of the Monarchy, and within it the Kingdom of Hungary, in 1918, which retrospectively increased the significance of the 'prophecy'.

This is not the place to take sides in this debate, but it is interesting to note that the two positions were in opposition to each other down to the very last detail. For it was not only a question of Deák's expectation that the future and security of Hungary and the assertion of Hungarian interests would depend on an alliance with Austria – as opposed to Kossuth's expectation that the Habsburg Empire would be destroyed – but also of the very nature of the socio-political system that was produced by the 1867 Settlement.

Fatigue or withdrawal?

As it transpired, Deák's concerns following the Settlement were not allayed. Despite all his efforts, he did not succeed in creating reconciliation in the subsequent years, either in the rivalries between the different ethnicities in Hungary or the conflicts around the issue of the separation of church and state, due not only to individual biases and passions but perhaps also because there was simply no 'middle ground' between beliefs and convictions where their proponents could meet. The question of 'who's to blame' has no answer. Even the historian's 'miracle weapon', that is, hindsight, cannot help us to reach a verdict. It is enough to recall how the 'Irish question' developed in England, the '*Kulturkampf*' in Germany or the African American issue in the United States. It is also worth reflecting on the extent to which relations between the great European powers, which finally put an end to the Austro-Hungarian Empire, conformed to the rules of 'sober politics'. It seems, therefore, that political will is not shaped by the principles and rules of 'common sense' alone.

It can be argued, however, that Hungary, having found its place within the dual monarchy, partly lived up to the expectations of its founders in the half-century it existed in this form. They succeeded in creating a socio-political system which was more or less in line with their political creed and embarked on a path which they believed would lead to the prosperity of the country, the expansion of its liberty, the creation of equal rights, the eradication of underdevelopment, the creation of a unified nation, in short, the realization of a liberal vision of the future. At the same time, however, it is clear that many of their hopes were not fulfilled. Metaphorically speaking, the Kossuth-Deák debate was not over, and it defined party membership until the dissolution of the Monarchy. The fundamental fault line remained the 'public law issue', that is, the question of how to evaluate the Settlement.

At the same time, however, many of Deák's hopes were not fulfilled. This was partly because the world had changed. The process of the loss of illusions, which is the subject of many literary works of the nineteenth century all over Europe, also began in Hungary. Doubts arose as to whether development based on the principles of liberalism was really building a 'temple of perfection'. Instead of the expected harmony, new fault lines were emerging in societies, faith in parliamentarism was shaken and the centre of political life was shifting increasingly to parties and interest groups, and sometimes, as in Paris in 1871, to the streets. The early 1870s saw the beginning of a new era in Europe and the impact of the Great Depression of 1873 led to a prolonged political crisis in Hungary. These unwelcome developments also occurred partly because the political reconciliation Deák had hoped for did not take place in Hungary. His decisive role had effectively come to an end. The force of wisdom, as so often happens, broke on the reef of constraints, interests and passions.

His last speech, which can be considered his last political testament, was delivered in Parliament in 1873, although he retained his mandate until his death on 28 January 1876. While his withdrawal from political life may be explained by his illness, the possibility that he too knew that he had lost his place in a changed world cannot be ruled out.

Notes

1 Áldor Imre, *Deák Ferencz élete: Emlékkönyv* [The Life of Ferenc Deák: Memorial Book] (Budapest: Franklin-Társulat, [1879?]), 191.
2 Molnár András, *A fiatal Deák Ferenc* [The Young Ferenc Deák] (Budapest: Osiris Kiadó, 2003), 272.
3 Deák Ferenc, *Válogatott politikai írások és beszédek* [Selected Political Writings and Speeches], ed. Molnár András and Deák Ágnes (Budapest: Osiris, 2001), 2:620–1.
4 Szalay László, *Státusférfiak és szónokok könyve* [Book of Statesmen and Orators] (Pest: Heckenast, 1846).
5 Deák, *Válogatott politikai írások és beszédek*, 1:430.
6 Deák, *Válogatott politikai írások és beszédek*, 1: 495–6.
7 Deák, *Válogatott politikai írások és beszédek*, 1: 581–2.
8 Deák, *Válogatott politikai írások és beszédek*, 2:643.
9 Deák, *Válogatott politikai írások és beszédek*, 2:13.

10 *The Recollections of Alexis de Tocqueville*, trans. Alexander Teixeira de Mattos (New York: The MacMillan Co. 1896), 231.
11 *Deák Ferencz beszédei* [Speeches of Ferenc Deák], ed. Kónyi Manó (Budapest: Franklin-Társulat, 1903), 2:396.
12 Deák, *Válogatott politikai írások és beszédek*, 2:26–7.
13 Deák, *Válogatott politikai írások és beszédek*, 2:429.
14 Deák, *Válogatott politikai írások és beszédek*, 2:443–63.
15 *Deák Ferencz beszédei*, 5:1–8.

Index of Names

Acton, John Emerich Edward (Lord)   196
Alexander Leopold (Archduke)   67-8, 91
Alfieri, Vittorio   118
Andrássy Gyula (Count)   10, 198, 200, 207, 232, 234
Andrássy József   15
Apponyi Albert (Count)   31
Apponyi György (Count)   151
Aranka György   90
Arany János   129
Armbruster, Johann Michael   93, 101, 102 n.11
Arnstein, Nathan (Baron)   120
Augusz Antal (Baron)   232-3

Bach, Alexander   9-10, 229
Bajza József   175
Balásházy János   110
Balogh Péter (ócsai)   70-1
Barcsay Ábrahám   95
Bariț, George   50
Bărnuțiu, Simion   51
Báróczy Sándor   89, 95
Barta István   108
Bastide, Jules   160
Batsányi János   6, 74, 78-9, 80
Batthyány Alajos (Count)   74
Batthyány József (Count)   72
Batthyány Kázmér (Count)   177
Batthyány Lajos (Count)   8, 10, 17, 22-3, 112, 129, 143, 147-163, 175, 191, 208-9, 222, 226-7
Beksics Gusztáv   214
Bentham, Jeremy   118, 196, 206, 225
Beöthy Zsigmond   27-8
Berzeviczy Gergely   6, 13, 78-80, 91, 94
Bessenyei György   88-9, 95, 101
Beust, Friedrich Ferdinand von   233, 235
Bezerédy István   15
Bismarck, Otto von   198, 234
Burke, Edmund   206, 225

Buteanu, Ioan   51
Byron, George Gordon (Lord)   118

Carlowszky Zsigmond   167
Charles III (VI as Holy Roman Emperor)   4
Charles X (of Bourbon)   109
Cherbuliez, Antoine-Elisée   197
Cipariu, Timotei   50-1
Constant, Benjamin   225
Csengery Antal   22, 188, 190, 208-9, 213
Csillag Gyula   31-2

Danton, Georges Jacques   126
Deák Antal   220-1
Deák Ferenc   9-11, 16-17, 22-3, 26, 31, 33, 40, 54, 129, 133, 150, 153, 156, 160, 169, 179, 197-9, 207, 209, 213-14, 220-37
De La Motte Károly   15
Desmoulins, Camille   126
Dessewffy Aurél (Count)   14, 17, 21-2, 173
Dessewffy Emil (Count)   207, 230
Dessewffy József (Count)   96-7, 109, 123
Devescovi Balázs   184
Döbrentei Gábor   93, 100
Dobriansky, Adolf   55-6
Drašković, Janko (Count)   48
Dümmerth Dezső   96
Duprat, Pascal   160

Egyed István   32
Emmer Kornél   32
Enfantin, Barthélemy-Prosper   126
Eötvös Ignác (Baron)   184
Eötvös József (Baron)   8-9, 11, 13, 17, 19-23, 35, 54, 122, 129, 148-9, 153, 173, 184-201, 209, 212, 220, 222, 227, 229-32, 234
Esterházy Pál Antal (Prince)   157
Eszterházy Károly (Count)   135

Falk Miksa 230
Fallmerayer, Jakob Philipp 197
Fehér M. István 215
Ferdinand I 3-5, 96-7
Ferdinand V 8-9, 156, 162
Festetics Julianna (Countess) 117
Fichte, Johann Gottlieb 167
Filep Tamás Gusztáv 215
Fogarasi János 40
Fouqué, Friedrich de la Motte 118
Francis I 7, 68, 77, 91-2, 101, 134
Francis Joseph I 9-10, 26, 38, 54-5, 144, 162, 180, 214, 231-3
Frank Ignác 34
Franklin, Benjamin 118

Gaj, Ljudevit 48
Gángó Gábor 215
Gergely András 120, 124
Gerő András 112
Ghyczy Kálmán 221
Girtanner, Christoph 109, 111
Goethe, Johann Wolfgang 118
Gorove István 221
Greguss Mihály 167
Grotius, Hugo 34, 121
Guizot, François Pierre Guillaume 225
Gunst Péter 40
Gustermann, Anton Wilhelm 80-1, 97
Gvadányi József (Count) 72
Gyulai Pál 213

Hajnik Imre 33, 41
Hajnóczy József 13, 27, 31, 76-8, 90-1, 100
Halász Gábor 215
Hegel, Georg Wilhelm Friedrich 113, 167
Herder, Johann Gottfried 118, 141
Hites Sándor 122
Hobbes, Thomas 34, 121, 195
Hoffmann, Ernst Theodor Amadeus 118
Hoffmann Pál 35
Hoič, Samuel 53
Hont István 121
Hörcher Ferenc (Horkay Hörcher Ferenc) 121, 123
Horvát István 97, 185
Huber, Ulrich 34

Hume, David 118, 211
Hummelauer, Karl von 158
Hurst, Michael 184

Jelačić, Josip 49, 52, 143, 159-61, 208, 227
John (Archduke) 73, 157, 160
Joseph (Archduke) 17, 68, 73, 75
Joseph II 5-7, 26, 65-6, 69-70, 74-6, 80, 88-91, 117, 134, 224

Kállay Ferenc 109
Kant, Immanuel 34, 105, 113, 167
Karadžić, Vuk Štefanović 52
Károlyi György (Count) 149
Kazinczy Ferenc 11, 13, 87-102, 106, 111, 133, 136, 186
Kecskeméthy Aurél 220
Kelsen, Hans 37
Kemény János (Prince) 204
Kemény Zsigmond (Baron) 102, 129, 188, 203-215, 220, 229, 231
Kisfaludy Sándor 73, 79, 98-9
Klapka György 179
Klauzál Gábor 17, 144, 227
Kölcsey Ferenc 11, 15, 23, 98-9, 105-14, 128, 169, 186, 221-3
Kollár, Ján 53
Kollár Ádám Ferenc (Adam František Kollár) 80
Koppi Károly 76
Koselleck, Reinhart 13, 23 n.1
Kossics József 56
Kossuth, Juraj 54
Kossuth Lajos 9, 11, 13-14, 16-22, 30, 38, 54-5, 100, 108, 111, 124-9, 133, 143, 150-6, 159, 161-2, 166-80, 187-8, 190-1, 207-9, 213-14, 220, 222-3, 226-7, 231-2, 235-7
Kossuth László 166
Köteles Sámuel 204
Kovachich Márton György 69, 81, 90, 97
Kövy Sándor 167
Kvaternik, Eugen 49

Laczkovics János 91
Lakits Zsigmond György 80-1
Lamartine, Alphonse de 225

Lamberg, Franz Philipp von (Count)   161, 191
Lamennais, Felicité de   126
Latour, Theodor Baillet von (Count)   161
Leibniz, Gottfried Wilhelm   34
Leopold I   50, 70
Leopold II   7, 65-8, 70, 77, 90-1, 97
Lessing, Gotthold Ephraim   72
Lévay József   213
Lilien, Anna von der (Baroness)   184-5
Lilien, Joseph von der (Baron)   185
List, Friedrich   171
Locke, John   34, 118, 195
Lolme, Jean-Louis de   118
Lónyay Menyhért   154, 221, 232, 234-5
Louis Philippe I   155
Lukacs, John   113
Lukács Móric   188

Macaulay, Thomas Babington   211
Madarász László   209
Maine, Henry   35
Maior, Petru   50
Majláth György   97
Majthényi László   15
Malthus, Thomas   118
Marat, Jean-Paul   126
Marczali Henrik   26
Maria Theresa   4-5, 29, 32, 34, 57, 67, 77, 80, 88, 134, 227
Marquard, Odo   113
Martini, Karl Anton   32, 34, 80
Martinovics Ignác   77-8, 89, 91, 100-1
Márton József   6
Mazzini, Giuseppe   177
Méhes Sámuel   205
Mészáros Lázár   157
Metternich, Klemens Wenzel Lothar von   9, 17, 123, 201 n.14, 207-8
Micaş, Florian   51
Micu-Klein, Samuil   50
Mill, John Stuart   118, 225
Mirabeau, Honoré-Gabriel Riqueti de   126
Möller, Nikolas   147
Montaigne, Michel de   118
Montalembert, Charles de (Count)   197
Montesquieu, Charles-Louis de Secondat   69, 74, 81, 118
Moór Gyula   35

Müllner, Adolf   118
Mušicki, Lukijan   100
Nagy Ernő   29-30
Napoleon I   6, 48, 72, 78-80, 92, 118
Napoleon III   230
Németh G. Béla   215
Nicholas I (Russian tsar)   9
Nyíri Kristóf   215

O'Connell, Daniel   187
Őz Pál   91

Palacký, František   192
Palmerston, Henry John Temple (Lord)   157
Pauler Tivadar   28-9, 33-5, 39
Péchy Imre   97
Perczel Mór   151
Petőfi Sándor   225
Pikler Gyula   36-7
Piringer, Michael   80-1, 97
Pocock, John Greville Agard   121
Prónay László (Baron)   88
Puchta, Georg Friedrich   35
Pufendorf, Samuel   34, 80, 121
Pulszky Ágost   34-5, 37
Pulszky Ferenc   17

Radbruch, Gustav   37
Radetzky, Joseph Wenzel   159
Rajačić, Josip   52
Rauch, Levin (Baron)   49
Révai Miklós   93, 96
Ribiny János   88
Ricardo, David   118, 121
Richardson, Samuel   118
Robespierre, Maximilien de   126
Rousseau, Jean-Jacques   72, 74, 76, 90, 118, 167, 195
Ruszek József   99

Šafárik, Pavel Jozef   53
Saint-Just, Louis Antoine de   126
Salamon Ferenc   213
Savigny, Friedrich Carl von   35, 206, 210
Schiller, Friedrich   113, 118
Schmerling, Anton (Ritter von)   10, 198, 233-4
Schvarcz Gyula   29

Schwarzenberg, Felix (Prince)   9
Scott, Walter   118
Shaftesbury, Anthony Ashley-Cooper, 3rd Earl of   211
Șincai, Gheorghe   50
Smith, Adam   14, 110, 118, 121
Smith, Anthony D.   71
Somló Bódog   36-8
Somogyi Gedeon   98
Sonnenfels, Joseph von   80
Sophia (Archduchess)   9, 158, 162
Spencer, Herbert   35, 37
Staël, Germaine de   118
Stammler, Rudolf   37
Starčević, Ante   49
Stephen (Archduke)   22, 156, 159, 161, 208
Stephen I (Saint)   6, 27, 49, 81
Strossmayer, Josip Juraj   49
Štúr, Ľudovít   53-4
Suciu, Ioan   51
Suhayda János   29
Sumerau, Joseph Thaddäus Freiherr von   102 n.11
Süssmilch, Johann Peter   108
Swoboda, Jan   192
Szabadfalvi József   34
Szabó László, Z.   92
Szalay László   22, 159, 185-9, 191, 198, 207, 222, 225, 229
Szász Károly, Jr.   213
Szász Károly, Sr.   204
Szauder József   105
Széchényi Ferenc (Count)   75-6, 100, 117
Széchenyi István (Count)   9, 11, 13-14, 16-22, 38, 100-2, 107-10, 117-130, 133-5, 137, 148, 150, 153-5, 173, 187-8, 190, 206-7, 209, 212-13, 220, 222-3, 226-7
Szegedy-Maszák Mihály   215
Szekfű Gyula   215
Szemere Bertalan   176-7
Szemere Pál   98
Szentkirályi Móric   153
Szentmarjay Ferenc   91
Szijártó M. István   83 n.2
Szolártsik Sándor   91

Takáts József   122, 127, 211, 215
Tasso, Torquato   118
Taxner-Tóth Ernő   106
Teleki László (Count)   10, 129, 149, 160, 176, 178-9, 190
Thomasius, Christian   34
Tisza Kálmán   30, 35, 232
Tocqueville, Alexis de   174, 194, 201, 225, 229
Toldy Ferenc   28-30
Török János   29
Török Lajos (Count)   90
Trefort Ágoston   188, 207
Trócsányi Zsolt   133

Ürményi József   97

Vay Miklós (Baron)   168
Vécsey Pál (Baron)   167
Verdross, Alfred   37
Verseghy Ferenc   92
Virozsil Antal   33-5, 40
Vitkovits Mihály   100
Volney (Constantin-François Chasseboeuf de La Giraudais)   167
Voltaire   72, 74, 118
Vörösmarty Mihály   228

Weber, Max   222
Weber Karolina   166
Welcker, Karl Theodor   197
Wenzel Gusztáv   34, 37, 41
Werbőczy István   5, 33, 37, 39, 69, 82 n.1, 95, 224
Wesselényi Miklós (Baron)   13, 15, 18, 110, 119-20, 128, 133-44, 154, 169, 171, 204-5, 207, 212-13, 223
Wiegand, Otto   136
Winckelmann, Johann Joachim   112
Windisch-Graetz (Windischgrätz), Alfred zu (Prince)   162, 176, 209
Wirkner, Ludwig von   17
Wolff, Christian   34, 80

Zichy Antonia (Countess)   148
Zichy Károly (Count)   148
Zsigray Jakab (Count)   91

Index of Subjects

abolition of noble privileges   7, 9, 23, 91, 94, 100, 149, 156, 169-70, 224, 229
abolition of serfdom (emancipation of the serfs)   7, 9, 14-16, 18-19, 23, 33, 48, 51, 74, 77-8, 107, 128, 137, 139, 140-1, 143, 149-50, 153, 155-6, 170-1, 174, 190-1, 206, 223, 229
  compulsory   23, 137, 153, 157
  self-redemption   15-16, 18, 137
absolutism   14, 26, 70-1, 87, 95, 99, 101, 138-9, 149, 152-4, 157, 163, 170, 190-1, 194, 201, 222-3
  enlightened absolutism   5, 77, 80, 90, 224
  neo-absolutism   9, 23, 197, 212, 229, 234
Address Party   10
ancient constitution (historical constitution)   5-6, 11, 27, 31-2, 35, 38, 69-73, 77, 80-2, 88, 100-1, 134, 138, 150, 168, 214, 224
April Laws of 1848   8-11, 23, 28, 31-2, 51, 144, 156, 160, 163, 175-6, 191, 197-8, 208, 214-15, 227, 231
Armenians   45-6, 57-8

Banat   49, 52
bene possessionatus (prosperous landowning gentry)   65-6, 70-1, 88

camarilla   158
cardinal (cornerstone) law   29, 30
Cassandra Letter   236
centralizers (centralists, Eötvös circle)   22, 152-3, 173, 188-90, 207, 222
classical liberalism   7-8, 18, 36, 78, 100-2, 107, 112, 127, 135-6, 138, 139-43, 147-51, 163, 168-9, 171, 173-4, 179, 221-6, 229, 234, 237
  governing liberalism   225, 229
  movement liberalism   225, 229

Code Napoléon   79
common good   5, 78, 80, 88, 94, 117, 133, 171
Conservative Party   22, 153
contributio   66, 68, 75
Corpus Juris Hungarici   69, 223
Croatian-Hungarian Settlement of 1868   49
Croats   45-6, 48-9, 52, 57, 127, 142-3, 151, 155, 157-61
customary law   26-7, 33, 37-8, 69, 224

Daco-Roman theory   50
Danube Confederation   178-9
Declaration of Independence of 1849   9, 129, 177, 208-10, 228
deputatio regnicolaris   67
Deutsch-Ungarischer Landes Bauerbund   57
Dietal Youth   170, 223
diploma inaugurale (coronation charter)   67, 70
doctrine of the Holy Crown   27, 33. *See also* Holy Crown

enlightenment   21, 35, 74, 76, 82, 87-8, 90, 92-5, 112, 117, 119, 121, 147, 167, 170, 212
  Hungarian Enlightenment   88, 90, 101
equality before the law (legal equality)   16, 21, 137, 140, 149-50, 153, 187-9, 195, 237

February Patent of 1861   10, 214
freedom of speech   30, 33, 124, 138, 149
freedom of the press   23, 30, 90, 149, 151, 168-9
freemasonry   74, 90, 117
free royal towns   19, 57, 65, 70, 117, 171-2
fundamental laws   27-30, 32

Gazeta de Transilvania 50
Germans 45-7, 56-7, 87, 141, 199
Golden Bull of 1222 27, 28
gravamina (grievance petitions) 5-6, 65, 97
grievance-politics 7, 67, 69, 144, 149, 204, 222

Habsburg dynasty (House of Habsburg-Lorraine) 3-6, 8-9, 26, 82, 88-9, 94, 97, 99, 139, 163, 177, 228, 235
Hereditary Provinces (Hereditary Lands) 4, 71, 76, 80, 88, 123, 141, 152-4, 234
historia litteraria 94
Holy Crown 66-7, 70. See also doctrine of the Holy Crown
Hungarian Academy of Sciences (Hungarian Learned Society) 15, 22, 100-1, 107, 119, 150, 220, 228
Hungarian Diet 5-8, 11, 29, 31, 52, 55, 66, 68, 70-1, 79, 81-2, 138, 168, 191
  1790-1 7, 32, 65-7, 71, 88, 90, 97
  1796 72
  1807 93, 107
  1808 73
  1811-12 82, 96-8
  1825-7 100-1, 107, 119, 135
  1830 135, 168, 221
  1832-6 15, 107, 109, 112-13, 135-6, 139, 150, 167, 169-70, 221-4
  1839-40 16, 18-20, 148, 150-1, 171, 224, 226
  1843-4 16, 142, 151, 173, 189
  1847-8 19, 23, 143, 154, 190, 207, 226-7
Hungarian estates 4-7, 21, 29, 31, 65-82, 112, 117
Hungarian Jacobin movement 6, 67-8, 77, 82, 90-1, 94, 100
Hungarian National Assembly 175, 177, 227
Hungarian War of Independence of 1848-9 9, 11, 23, 57, 129, 163, 177-8, 193, 208-9, 212, 214, 228-9
Hungarus patriotism 46, 53, 78

Illyrianism 48
insurrectio (noble levy) 6, 66, 68, 72-3, 75

ius ad bellum 68
ius aviticum (aviticitas) 17-8, 23, 153
ius resistendi 27, 30, 70

Jelenkor 22
Josephinism 5, 76, 100

Kelet Népe debate 14, 16-22, 124, 150, 187-8

Liberal Party (Opposition Party) 22, 149, 153, 174

March Revolution of 1848 (lawful revolution) 8, 22, 27-9, 31, 51, 57, 129, 143, 156, 187, 190, 227
market towns 19
Matica Srpska 52
Military Frontier 52
misera plebs contribuens 65, 78
municipalists 152, 207
municipal system (county system) 20, 30, 66, 172-4, 189-90

Natio Hungarica (Hungarian noble nation) 6, 50, 70, 79, 90, 223
National Casino 14, 17, 120
National Defence Commission (*Országos Honvédelmi Bizottmány*) 9, 162, 176, 177
natural law 32-7, 70, 170, 172, 192

October Diploma 197, 214, 230
official language 5, 7-8, 88-9, 93-4, 96-7, 101, 142, 172
operata systematica (systematic reform works) 67-8, 107-8, 168, 221
Opposition Statement (*Ellenzéki Nyilatkozat*) 22, 153, 174
Országgyűlési Tudósítások (Reports from the Diet) 169, 223

Partium 23, 49, 105-6
personal union 3, 9, 26, 152, 157, 179, 227
Pesti Hirlap 13-4, 17-8, 20, 22, 124, 126-7, 150, 171-4, 188-90, 207-8
popular sovereignty (sovereignty of the people) 70, 149-50, 160, 175, 179, 194-5

Pragmatic Sanction   4, 10, 214, 227
principle of non-intervention   178
public law   26-7, 29, 31, 33, 39-41, 107, 142, 168, 173

Resolution Party   10
Romanians   45-7, 49-51, 127, 141-3, 173, 178, 199, 227
Roman law   33-5, 206
Rusyns (Ruthenes)   45-7, 55-6, 173

Sabor   48-9
Serbs   45-7, 51-3, 57, 127, 158-9, 173, 178, 199
Settlement of 1867   8, 10-11, 32, 34-5, 38, 40, 48-9, 179-80, 198, 200-1, 203, 210, 212-15, 233-7
Slovaks   45-7, 52-5, 127, 161, 173, 227
Slovenes   45-7, 56
sovereignty   5, 70, 79, 99, 178, 214, 224, 231, 233-4
subsidium   66, 68
Supplex Libellus Valachorum   50, 51

Törvényhatósági Tudósítások (Municipal Reports)   170
Transylvania (Principality of Transylvania)   4-5, 15, 23, 27, 45, 49-52, 56-7, 75, 87, 90, 105-6, 119, 133-4, 136, 138-40, 142-4, 157, 159, 161, 203-5, 207, 211, 215
Transylvanian Diet   50, 57, 138, 205, 223
   1790-1   134, 139
   1810-11   134
   1834-5   139, 204
   1837-8   204
   1848   143
Tripartitum   5, 28, 33, 39, 69, 82 n.1, 223-4
Triune Kingdom   49

Ungarlandische Deutsche Volkspartei   57
urbarium   134, 139, 153, 206
utilitarianism   14

Védegylet (League of Protection)   152, 174, 226
Vienna Court   7, 34, 67-8, 80, 88, 92-3, 95, 97-8, 101, 124, 134, 138, 148-51, 153, 156-7, 169, 204, 221-2, 227

www.ingramcontent.com/pod-product-compliance
Lightning Source LLC
Chambersburg PA
CBHW071822300426
44116CB00009B/1404